Cross-Cultural Aspects of Tourism and Hospitality

Cross-Cultural Aspects of Tourism and Hospitality is the first textbook to offer students, lecturers, researchers and practitioners a comprehensive guide to the influence of culture on service providers as well as on customers, affecting both the supply and the demand sides of the industry – organisational behaviour, and human resource management, and marketing and consumer behaviour.

Given the need for delivering superior customer value, understanding different cultures from both demand and supply sides of tourism and hospitality and the impact of culture on these international industries is an essential part of all students' and practitioners' learning and development. This book takes a research-based approach critically reviewing seminal cultural theories and evaluating how these influence employee and customer behaviour in service encounters, marketing, and management processes and activities. Individual chapters cover a diverse range of cultural aspects including intercultural competence and intercultural sensitivity, uncertainty and risk avoidance, context in communication, power distance, indulgence and restraint, time orientation, gender, assertiveness, individualism and collectivism, performance orientation, and humane orientation.

This book integrates international case studies throughout to show the application of theory, includes self-test questions, activities, further reading, and a set of PowerPoint slides to accompany each chapter. This will be essential reading for all students, lecturers, researchers and practitioners and future managers in the fields of Tourism and Hospitality.

Erdogan Koc is Professor of Services Marketing and Management at Bahçeşehir University. He received his BA in Communication Studies from the University of Istanbul, MBA from the Cardiff Business School, and Ph.D. from Oxford Brookes University in Business and Management. He has extensively published in top-tier journals such as *Tourism Management, International Journal of Human Resource Management, Journal of Travel and Tourism Marketing, International Journal of Intercultural Relations, Journal of Hospitality Marketing and Management*, among others, and serves on the editorial boards of several high-ranking journals and acts as a referee for top-tier journals. He has published two international books in the area of tourism and hospitality. As well as his research and academic experience, he provides training to a wide range of businesses and has management experience of reputable brands.

Cross-Cultural Aspects of Tourism and Hospitality

A Services Marketing and Management Perspective

Erdogan Koc

LONDON AND NEW YORK

First published 2021
by Routledge
2 Park Square, Milton Park, Abingdon, Oxon OX14 4RN

and by Routledge
52 Vanderbilt Avenue, New York, NY 10017

Routledge is an imprint of the Taylor and Francis Group, an informa business

British Library Cataloguing-in-Publication Data
A catalogue record for this book is available from the British Library

Library of Congress Cataloging-in-Publication Data
Names: Koc, Erdogan, author.
Title: Cross-cultural aspects of tourism and hospitality: a services marketing and management perspective / Erdogan Koc.
Description: Abingdon, Oxon; New York, NY: Routledge, 2021. | Includes bibliographical references and index.
Identifiers: LCCN 2020014255 (print) | LCCN 2020014256 (ebook) | ISBN 9780367862893 (hardback) | ISBN 9780367860745 (paperback) | ISBN 9781003018193 (ebook)
Subjects: LCSH: Tourism–Cross-cultural studies. | Tourism–Marketing–Cross-cultural studies. | Tourism–Management–Cross-cultural studies.
Classification: LCC G155.A1 K595 2021 (print) | LCC G155.A1 (ebook) | DDC 910.68–dc23
LC record available at https://lccn.loc.gov/2020014255
LC ebook record available at https://lccn.loc.gov/2020014256

ISBN: 978-0-367-86289-3 (hbk)
ISBN: 978-0-367-86074-5 (pbk)
ISBN: 978-1-003-01819-3 (ebk)

Typeset in Frutiger and Sabon
by Newgen Publishing UK

Visit the eResources: www.routledge.com/9780367860745

Contents

Figures

Tables

Preface

The rationale for this book

As stated by Peter Drucker "Culture eats strategy for breakfast", culture has an overriding influence on human behaviour as it shapes both the perceptions and the attitudes of people. Hence, the way in which systems, processes, and businesses are established and managed, and the interactions that take place among the stakeholders of this system (e.g., customers, employees, managers, suppliers) are very much culture-bound.

Owing to the general service characteristics of intangibility, inseparability, heterogeneity, and perishability, and given the fact that interactions and communication which take place between customers, employees, managers, and processes are frequent and intense, tourism and hospitality is probably the most relevant industry for the study of culture. As explained in Chapter 1, tourism is the largest industry in the world in terms of revenues generated, directly and indirectly, and the employment created. Moreover, with the participation of more and more people from different countries and cultures in tourism and hospitality, there is an increasing need to better understand intercultural interactions between people (customers, employees and managers) and processes, and systems.

The perspective of this book

The book has a dyadic perspective in that it explains cross-cultural aspects of tourism and the implications of culture based on the following disciplines:

1. *Customer/Marketing perspective:* marketing, consumer behaviour, services marketing and management, and international marketing.
2. *Service provider/management perspective:* organisational behaviour, human resource management, international management, and management.

As explained in Chapter 1, the reason for the dyadic perspective of this book is due to the highly interactive nature of processes in services in general and in tourism and hospitality in particular. Compared with manufacturing and marketing tangible products, in service businesses, especially in tourism and hospitality, business functions such as marketing and human resource management are highly interlinked and intertwined and require a more integrated approach. Hence, any human resource manager needs to understand marketing, consumer behaviour, and the service's marketing implications of her/his policies, strategies, and activities. Conversely, any marketing manager needs to understand human resource management, organisational behaviour, and the management implications of her/his policies, strategies, and activities.

Topics and concepts explained in this book from a marketing perspective

The marketing topics, concepts, and theories explained and discussed in this book comprise the following:

marketing mix elements (product, price, place, promotion, physical evidence, people, and process)	customer satisfaction	customers' repurchase and word-of-mouth (WOM) intentions	customer complaints
customer loyalty	variety-seeking behaviour	service quality and service quality dimensions	service failures
customer involvement, and participation	service orientation	customer switching behaviour	service recovery, service recovery paradox attribution and justice

Topics and concepts explained in the book from the management perspective

The management topics, concepts, and theories explained and discussed in the book comprise the following:

employee empowerment, skill development, organisational training and development, accountability	bureaucracy, hierarchy and organisational structure, systems	organisational communication, subordinate-superior communication, relationships	organisational citizenship behaviour, organisational commitment
entrepreneurship, intrapreneurship	leadership, organisational culture	change management, motivation	teamwork, groupthink, emotional labour, emotional contagion
employee job satisfaction, performance orientation	employee turnover, absenteeism, stress, burnout syndrome	ethics, legitimacy, nepotism, ethnocentrism	recruitment, selection, performance appraisal, reward systems, staff training, promotion

Features of this book

Each chapter in this book explains and discusses cross-cultural theories and dimensions and their characteristics. Based on the relevant research findings published in top tourism and hospitality and in other relevant journals and books, the implications of these cross-cultural theories, dimensions, and characteristics are explained and discussed. As the book is aimed at understanding people, where relevant, findings from the fields of psychology, sociology, anthropology, biology, and neurology are provided.

The book has the following features to enhance the teaching and learning experiences:

- presentation slides for each chapter for in-class use by lecturers;
- case studies;
- exercises;
- activity boxes;
- recommendations for further reading;
- end-of-chapter questions;
- research questions/ideas to pursue for researchers.

The above features aim to develop knowledge as well as skills and abilities. Hence, many of the activity boxes contain scales (such as intercultural sensitivity, ethnocentrism, intercultural competence) for readers to get to know themselves and oversee their development as a result of the learning experience offered by the book. It is recommended that these scales/tests should also be filled in after completing of the book in order to see personal development in terms of knowledge, skills, and abilities.

Each chapter (except Chapter 1) presents at least one original research question or idea to pursue and carry out as a study by researchers. These research ideas may be instrumental for researchers to publish original research in leading international tourism and hospitality journals.

The cases presented in the chapters are in various forms. While some of the cases are company cases, others provide cultural anecdotes or interesting experiments on relevant topics.

This book presents many exercises for self-learning and development. The exercises are aimed at involving the reader, and they require her/him to explore a specific aspect of culture in order to develop knowledge, skills, and abilities pertaining to a specific aspect of a cross-cultural characteristic.

Contents of the book

Chapter 1

This chapter provides an introduction and an overview to tourism and hospitality. The chapter particularly explains and emphasises the importance of the tourism and hospitality industry, and demonstrates the growing importance of the international and global nature of tourism and hospitality. As tourism and hospitality activities are becoming increasingly international and global, from both the demand and suppply sides, there is a growing need to understand the multicultural aspects of these activities. The chapter also provides an outline of the types and categories of tourism and hospitality businesses to draw the framework for the book.

Chapter 2

This chapter explains the basic concepts and components of culture and provides a rationale for the dyadic perspective of the book: a) marketing and consumer behaviour, and b) human resource management, organisational behaviour, and management. The importance of studying cross-cultural aspects of tourism and hospitality from the perspectives of both service providers and customers are explained and discussed with the support of relevant research findings.

Chapter 3

This chapter explains the concepts of intercultural competence, intercultural sensitivity, and intercultural intelligence and their relevance for tourism and hospitality. The chapter also provides a number of scales/tests that will enable readers to get to know themselves better, and to measure their tendency in a specific field relating to cross-cultural aspects of tourism and hospitality.

Chapter 4

This chapter explains the characteristics of high- and low-context cultures, and the implications of contextual orientations of service providers and customers for the effective and efficient marketing and management of various tourism and hospitality operations. Based on relevant research, the chapter demonstrates that the contextual orientation of people (both as service providers and as customers) can significantly influence their perceptions, attitudes, and behaviours as well as the way in which they communicate, form, and maintain relationships.

Chapter 5

This chapter explains the indulgence and restraint paradigm, and the implications of this paradigm for tourism and hospitality. Indulgence and restraint orientations of people determine their involvement with tourism and hospitality activities, how they view leisure, pleasure, and fun. Moreover, indulgence and restraint orientation of people influences the experiences (positive or negative) they tend to remember. As tourism and hospitality services are mainly hedonistic experiences, the concept of indulgence and restraint are highly relevant for tourism and hospitality, from both the supply and the demand perspectives. However, a review of the literature shows that this dimension seems to have been largely overlooked by researchers in the field.

Chapter 6

This chapter presents the power distance paradigm and explains its influence on relationships, how people communicate, establish, and sustain systems. Power distance orientation of people, both as service providers and as customers, appears to influence a wide range of issues. For instance, power distance influences the approach taken by customers towards various elements of the marketing mix (7Ps), and the way in which service providers design and implement marketing mix elements. Moreover, power distance tends to determine how customers evaluate overall service quality and the individual service quality dimensions. As power distance significantly affects relationships and communications among people, it shapes the approaches of people to management and organisational issues such as empowerment, and the upward and downward communication that takes place between subordinates and superiors in an organisation.

Chapter 7

This chapter explains uncertainty avoidance or risk aversion paradigm as a cultural orientation. Tourism and hospitality experiences are mainly intangible, that is, they cannot be tested beforehand, and involve encounters with the unknown in terms of destinations, the concept of uncertainty avoidance is particularly relevant for the design and management of tourism and hospitality activities. For instance, the type of tourism and hospitality products customers purchase and the informational channels they use are all influenced by whether they are highly risk aversive or not. The chapter focuses on concepts and the types of risks associated with tourism and hospitality and the theory of control as a risk reduction strategy. The chapter also shows how uncertainty avoidance may influence employees' and managers' approaches to change, innovation, and development.

Chapter 8

This chapter explains the masculinity and femininity dimension and the concepts of assertiveness and egalitarianism. The chapter demonstrates how masculine and feminine characteristics may influence customers' and employees' perceptions, attitudes, and behaviours in tourism and hospitality contexts. Gender orientation of customers influences not only how they collect information in making their purchase decisions, but also how they perceive various marketing mix elements and how they evaluate overall service quality and particular service quality dimensions. In addition, gender orientation influences various aspects of service providers in terms of service orientation and the provision of efficient and effective services.

Chapter 9

This chapter presents the individualism and collectivism paradigm as one of the oldest and pervasive cultural paradigms. The chapter explains how individualism and collectivism orientations of customers may influence customers' choice of holiday or hospitality products, how they make their purchase decisions, and how they evaluate their tourism and hospitality experiences. From a management perspective, the chapter explains how individualism and collectivism may influence people's relationships and communication patterns within a business establishment, and the degree of comfort they may have with employee empowerment.

Chapter 10

This chapter explains the performance and humane orientations based on the GLOBE project/framework and how these dimensions relate to other dimensions explained throughout the book. These dimensions significantly influence the efficient and effective provision of services in tourism and hospitality businesses. The chapter explains and discusses the concepts of performance and humane orientation in relation to other cultural dimensions explained in other chapters of the book.

Chapter 11

This chapter presents the concept time orientation and its potential influence on service providers and customers in tourism and hospitality. The chapter shows that long- and short-term orientation, past/present/future orientation, or polychronism and monochronism orientations of customers influence the type of tourism and hospitality services they prefer, the characteristics of tourism and hospitality services, and how they evaluate these services. Moreover, time orientation influences customers' approach towards marketing mix elements. For instance, while past-oriented customers tend to avoid advertisements, present-and future oriented customers tend to be interested in advertisements, though with different motivations. Also, time orientations of employees and managers tend to influence how they perceive other people, work, processes, and systems.

Chapter 12

This chapter explains the cultural dimensions proposed by Trompenaars and Hampden-Turner, namely, universalism vs particularism, individualism vs collectivism (communitarianism), neutral vs emotional, specific vs diffuse, achievement vs ascription, sequential vs synchronic, and internal vs external control. The dimensions offered by Trompenaars and Hampden-Turner are highly interlinked with the other dimensions explained throughout the book. The chapter explains Trompenaars and Hampden-Turner's dimensions in relation with the other dimensions since there appears to be a dearth of research publications which specifically focus on them.

Chapter 13

This final chapter provides an overview and summary of the book together with the concepts and theories explained. The chapter demonstrates the concepts and theories explained from a dyadic perspective, that is, from the perspective of both customers and service providers. It can be seen that cross-cultural aspects influence a wide range of marketing, consumer behaviour, human resource management, organisational behaviour, and management issues in tourism and hospitality.

Acknowledgements

Writing a textbook aimed at developing new knowledge in an area in which no comprehensive book has been published previously requires years of research and really hard work. I would like to thank my past and present students from various universities and various countries, whose curiosity motivated me to relentlessly search, explore, learn, and make connections. I also would like to thank employees and managers in several companies I have provided training for. I have learned immensely from them.

My teachers, lecturers, and professors have been extremely instrumental in my professional and academic development, and career, spreading over 25 years. I particularly would like to acknowledge the influential role of my Ph.D. supervisor at Oxford Brookes University, UK, who supervised me many years ago. Her guidance still illuminates my path during my journey. May her soul rest in peace.

I also thank all researchers and authors whose publications I have read and used, and the ones who have given consent to use their scales and cultural dimension tables. I particularly thank my colleague Jim (Professor James William Neuliep, the author of the book *Intercultural Communication: A Contextual Approach*) from St Norbert College, for his kind and timely support, and his consent for the use of his scales. My special thanks go to the late Professor Geert Hofstede for granting permission to use country scores data for preparing cultural dimensions and the scales. I also would like to thank Professor Stella Ting-Toomey (California State University, Fullerton) for granting permission to use their scale.

Last but by no means the least, I would like to thank the editorial and production team at Routledge, Emma Travis (editor), Lydia Kessell (editorial assistant) and Claudia Austin (production editor) for their hard work, assistance, and encouragement throughout this book project.

Erdogan Koc
Professor of Services Marketing and Management
Bahçeşehir University

Chapter 1

Introduction: international and global nature of tourism and hospitality

Learning Objectives

After reading this chapter, you should be able to:

- understand the international nature of tourism and hospitality operations;
- explain the intertwined and dyadic perspective of management (human resource management and organisational behaviour) and marketing (consumer behaviour and services marketing);
- explain service characteristics in relation to tourism and hospitality;
- understand the influence of culture on the design and implementation of marketing mix elements and service quality dimensions;
- develop a service blueprint for a tourism or hospitality service by taking dyadic cross-cultural aspects of tourism and hospitality services into account.

Introduction

This introductory chapter sets the scene for the whole of the book by explaining the importance and potential of international tourism and hospitality activities and the influence of culture on customers, employees, managers, and systems. As increasingly more and more international customers, employees, and managers with different cultural backgrounds participate in tourism and hospitality activities, a cross-cultural study of the dyadic aspects of their interactions is of paramount importance in a dynamic and fast-growth market. As the setting up and maintenance of tourism and hospitality businesses require a significant amount of financial resources, the stakes are high and complexities often result in business failures.

Disneyland Paris (Euro Disney), which was the second-largest construction project at the time of its opening in 1992 (Hartley, 2006), can be given as an example. Euro Disney (see the Euro Disney case study in Chapter 2) made a total loss of two billion dollars at end of its third year (Matusitz, 2010), as result of several business and management mistakes, and the inability to understand the cultural environment, customers, employees, managers, and systems. Primarily, the Euro Disney management ignored the basic quote "When in Rome do as the Romans do", and had an ethnocentric approach in its operations in France. This was partly due to the overconfidence emanating from the success of the company's previous project, Tokyo Disneyland, opened up in Tokyo, Japan in 1982.

Activity

GENE (Generalised ethnocentrism) scale

You can measure whether you are ethnocentric or not by doing the following test.

Important Note: Throughout the book there are several self-report scales/tests like the one below. Please save your personal test score records (especially the ones relating to cultural awareness, cultural competence, ethnocentrism, cultural intelligence, etc.) in order to make comparisons later. After studying the whole book, you are advised to go back and redo all these tests once more. By doing this you can compare these scores with your earlier ones. This is expected to help you to see the changes that have taken place as a result of the learning experience.

The Intercultural Communication Competence Scale Instructions

Please read the statements below and indicate how much each statement describes you by assigning a value, in the blank section on the left of each statement, from 1 to 5 as follows:

(5) strongly agree (4) agree (3) neutral (2) disagree (1) strongly disagree

Please keep in mind that there is no right or wrong response for each statement. In order to avoid biased responses, you are recommended to record your initial response without elaborating too much on the statements.

______ **1.** Most other cultures are backward compared to my culture.
______ **2.** My culture should be the role model for other cultures.
______ **3.** People from other cultures act strange when they come into my culture.
______ **4.** Lifestyles in other cultures are just as valid as those in my culture.
______ **5.** Other cultures should try to be more like my culture.
______ **6.** I'm not interested in the values and customs of other cultures.
______ **7.** People in my culture could learn a lot from people of other cultures.
______ **8.** Most people from other cultures just don't know what's good for them.

_____ **9.** I respect the values and customs of other cultures.
_____ **10.** Other cultures are smart to look up to our culture.
_____ **11.** Most people would be happier if they lived like people in my culture.
_____ **12.** I have many friends from other cultures.
_____ **13.** People in my culture have just about the best lifestyles of anywhere.
_____ **14.** Lifestyles in other cultures are not as valid as those in my culture.
_____ **15.** I'm very interested in the values and customs of other cultures.
_____ **16.** I apply my values when judging people who are different.
_____ **17.** I see people who are similar to me as virtuous.
_____ **18.** I do not cooperate with people who are different.
_____ **19.** Most people in my culture just don't know what is good for them.
_____ 20. I do not trust people who are different.
_____ 21. I dislike interacting with people from different cultures.
_____ 22. I have little respect for the values and customs of other cultures.
_____ YOUR TOTAL SCORE (Please calculate your score as follows).

Scoring:

Step 1: Please add your scores for items 4, 7, and 9.
Step 2: Add your scores for 1, 2, 5, 8, 10, 11, 13, 14, 18, 20, 21, and 22 (note that not all items are used in scoring).
Step 3: Subtract the sum from Step 1 from 18 (i.e., 18 minus Step 1 sum)
Step 4: Add the results of Step 2 and Step 3. This sum is your generalised ethnocentrism score.
Higher scores (e.g., scores above 55) indicate a higher level of ethnocentrism.

Source: Neely (2002).

Used with permission given by the author (James W. Neuliep).

However, unlike the French, the Japanese did not ask or expect anything to be Japanese, that is, adjusted to their culture and habits. Disneyland did not have to make significant cultural considerations in Disneyland Tokyo as the Japanese wanted to have a truly American experience.

The case of the Mardan Place Hotel, Antalya, Turkey can also be related here as a major failure in tourism and hospitality. The failure of this hotel is also primarily due to ignoring the cross-cultural aspects of tourism and hospitality. The Mardan Palace Hotel, which was described as Europe's most ostentatious resort hotel at the time of its opening in 2009, could not pay its debts and went bankrupt in 2015. The total investment made for the project at the time was 1.5 billion dollars. The cases of Disneyland Paris and the Mardan Palace Hotel demonstrate how failure to understand customers, employees, managers, and systems can produce disastrous results for tourism and hospitality businesses. Research shows that the failure rate in tourism and hospitality is quite high. For instance, in the hospitality industry, almost 30% of new restaurants go out of business in their first year of operation (Parsa et al., 2005; Fields, 2014).

Given the frequency and intensity of interaction (both between customers and staff, and among the staff themselves), and the tangibility, inseparability, heterogeneity, and perishability nature of tourism and hospitality services, the need to understand the influence of culture in the design and management of tourism and hospitality businesses is extremely evident. Based on this background, this chapter explains the international and multicultural nature of tourism and hospitality operations, and how culture may influence the efficient and effective management of these operations.

International and global nature of tourism and hospitality

Tourism is the largest industry in the world, in terms not only of revenues generated but also of employment created in this industry (WTTC, 2019). In 2019 the tourism and hospitality industry generated total revenue of $1.7 trillion (WTTC, 2019). The direct contribution of travel and tourism to gross domestic product (GDP) is expected to grow by 3.6% annually to $4,065 billion, representing 3.5% of the world's total GDP by 2029. With its relatively high multiplier effect, the tourism and hospitality industry enables the creation of revenues and employment not only in tourism and hospitality directly, but also in and other tertiary (i.e., services), secondary (i.e., manufacturing), and primary (e.g., agriculture) sectors indirectly.

Activity

The multiplier refers to the total addition to income resulting from initial expenditure within a sector. It measures the impact of additional expenditure introduced into an economy (Fletcher, 1995). In tourism, the multiplier effect shows the additional volume of income earned by the expenditures of tourists that will contribute to the economy in general. Basically, the tourism multiplier value of a country shows how many times the money spent by a tourist circulates through a country's economy.

Look at the following countries' tourism multiplier values and discuss the likely role and potential of the tourism industry in these countries from both the perspective of revenues generated and the employment created. What could be the main reason behind the difference between countries such as Turkey and Barbados? Please discuss.

Country – Region	*Multiplier Value*	*Country – Region*	*Multiplier Value*
Turkey	1.96	Hong Kong	0.87
United Kingdom	1.73	Philippines	0.82
Jamaica	1.27	Bahamas	0.73
Egypt	1.23	Malta	0.68
Dominican Republic	1.20	Iceland	0.64
Seychelles	1.03	Barbados	0.60

Adapted from Fletcher (1995) and Cooper et al. (2008).

In other words, the importance of the tourism and hospitality industry is much more significant than the tourism revenue and employment figures may singly suggest. As travel and tourism are interlinked with a variety of other industries, as many as 30, ranging from food, furniture, transportation, construction, to durable goods (Koc and Altinay, 2007), its total contribution to the world economy is estimated to be about $9,000 billion (WTTC, 2019). Additionally, as a labour-intensive industry, with about 320 million people working in travel and tourism, employment in this industry represents about 10.5% of total employment in the world (WTTC, 2019). The tourism and hospitality industry may be instrumental, especially in creating jobs for developing countries where unemployment rates are high (Noja and Cristea, 2018; Marcu et al., 2018).

Moreover, it must be kept in mind that the percentage of people participating in tourism and hospitality activities in the world is on the rise. A report by the United Nations World Tourism Organisation (UNWTO, 1998) estimated that 7% of the world's population would be travelling internationally[1] by the year 2020. Considering that, currently, a rather small proportion of the world population engage in international travel and tourism activities, there is a significant potential for growth in the international tourism and travel industry when larger proportions of the world population engage in travel and tourism activities.

Information zone

Three of the main factors contributing to the growth of services which influence the demand for tourism and hospitality services are provided in the following table (Koc, 2018).

Factor	*Explanation/Example*
Increase in leisure time and disposable income	With the decrease in working hours and an increase in the annual paid holidays, the demand for tourism and hospitality services has gradually risen. More and more people tend to have more time and money for going on holiday and eating out in restaurants more frequently.
Changing demographics and life styles	People in large towns and cities are more likely to frequently use services. Urbanisation is one of the important drivers of holidays, eating out, etc. Households are increasingly getting smaller with fewer children in the family. This results in families being more able to afford tourism and hospitality services such as holidays, or eating out in restaurants, in addition to being able to afford other services such as insurance, private education, and private healthcare.
The advent of innovative products and developments in technology	The word travel comes from the Old French word *travail* (or *travailler*), which means to work, to labour; a suffering or painful effort. With the development of large passenger planes, travelling has become relatively easier. International air travel accounts for a significant proportion of transportation relating to tourism and hospitality activities.

Factor	*Explanation/Example*
	With the developments in media and communications and easier access to various media, people are becoming more knowledgeable about other countries and regions. Being more knowledgeable about foreigners reduces xenophobia, fear or hatred towards anything foreign or strange and increases interest in foreign people, lands, foods, etc. Knowledge reduces risks and increases liking.

As stated above, tourism and hospitality activities are increasingly becoming international in nature, with the participation of people from different countries and cultures (Mihalič and Fennell, 2015). This means that there is a need for a better understanding of culture and cultural issues relating to tourism and hospitality. In the highly internationalised environment of tourism and hospitality, there is a need for a dyadic perspective, understanding both the demand and the supply side. The demand side represents customers, for example, tourists/guests. The supply side represents the service providers, for example, employees, managers, systems, and businesses that offer tourism and hospitality services. Considering that over one-third of Fortune Top 500 companies disappear after a decade (ICS-UNIDO, 2000), there is an apparent need for organisational development and a need for adapting to the changes and differences that take place in the market.

The dyadic influence of culture on tourism and hospitality services

The dyadic perspective

This book has a dyadic perspective, that is, it explains and discusses the implications of cross-cultural matters for tourism and hospitality based on the following framework:

1. *Customer/Marketing perspective:* marketing, consumer behaviour, services marketing and management, and international marketing.
2. *Service provider/management perspective:* organisational behaviour, human resource management, international management, and management.

The rationale for the dyadic perspective

With the worldwide growth in the tourism and hospitality sector, the number of establishments in this sector is increasing steadily together in parallel with the increase in the number of international tourists/customers participating in tourism and hospitality activities. In line with this growth, tourism and hospitality establishments need to understand their international customers better, and to be able to manage effectively their diverse workforce whose attitudes and behaviours may be significantly influenced by their diverse cultural backgrounds (Koc et al., 2017; Koc, 2019).

Tourism and hospitality services take place in a social servicescape (Tombs and McColl-Kennedy, 2003; Koc and Boz, 2020) within which intense and frequent social interactions take place involving both customers and employees. The social servicescape can be defined as customer and employee elements that exist in the consumption setting (Rosenbaum and Montoya, 2007; Kim and Baker, 2017). Owing to this intense social contact and interaction, tourism and hospitality industry businesses are often referred to as *people* businesses (Kim et al., 2010). This frequent and intense social contact and interaction between the service personnel and customers often forms the basis of service quality evaluations of customers in tourism and hospitality (Prayag and Ryan, 2012; Rauch et al., 2015).

This is probably why a significant number of service quality elements in service quality models such as SERVQUAL (Parasuraman et al., 1988) (e.g., service quality dimensions) are to do with service encounters and social interactions which take place between the service personnel and the customer. Research shows that customers' perceptions of service interactions have a significant influence on their overall service quality evaluations and satisfaction (Wang and Mattila, 2010; Koc and Bozkurt, 2017). Services marketing mix (7Ps) comprises the *people* element, together with process and physical evidence, in addition to the traditional marketing mix (4Ps) designed for the marketing of tangible products. People may be considered as the most important marketing mix element in the marketing and managment of any service or experience.

As social interactions are significantly influenced by the culture of people, the cultures customers and employees come from may have important implications for the effective management of service encounters, customer satisfaction, service quality, and, eventually, business success (Lai et al., 2018; Koc, 2019). The greater the cultural distance, which is the extent to which national cultures differ from the culture of the host, the greater the influence of cultural dimensions on tourism and hospitality operations (Shenkar, 2001; Litvin et al., 2004).

The abilities of tourism and hospitality staff in terms of understanding customers' and other employees' cultures and behaving accordingly is often referred to as the *intercultural sensitivity* of staff. Intercultural sensitivity can be a major strength of a tourism and hospitality business catering for international customers, and employing staff with diverse cultural backgrounds (Irimias and Franch, 2019; Yurur et al., 2020). In addition to the interactions of staff with customers, the interactions among staff (both front and backstage) are also important and may be significantly culture-bound in today's multicultural work environments. In services, it is accepted that the quality of the service received by internal customers (i.e., by employees) cannot be higher than the quality of service received by external customers (i.e., actual customers). This means that not only customers but also employees and managers need to be approached by all staff members in an interculturally sensitive and highly professional manner. This is why this book takes a dyadic perspective to explain culture's influence on the social servicescape in tourism and hospitality, as well as the physical servicescape. In other words, the book explains and explores cross-cultural aspects of tourism and hospitality from the perspectives of both the customer (consumer behaviour and marketing) and staff (human resource management, organisational behaviour, and management) (see Figure 1.1).

It should be kept in mind that the human resource management and marketing functions in services, especially in tourism and hospitality services, are very much intertwined as shown in Table 1.1. The design and implementation of the marketing mix (7Ps) when carrying out the marketing function requires considerations relating to

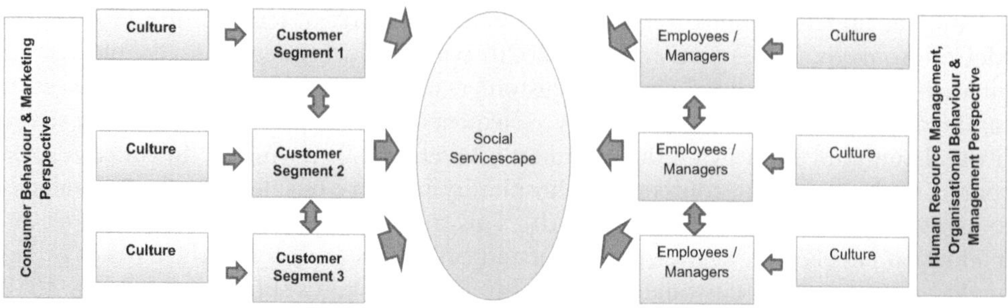

Figure 1.1 Dyadic influence of cross-cultural characteristics on tourism and hospitality social servicescape

people and processes (i.e., human resource management, organisational behaviour, and management) and vice versa.

Owing to the high level of customer and employee interaction and communication and the general service characteristics of, especially, inseparability, heterogeneity, and perishability, tourism and hospitality services are highly prone to service failures (Koc, 2017, 2019).

Information zone

General service characteristics

Service Characteristic	*Explanation*	*Implications for Tourism and Hospitality Businesses*
Inseparability	Consumption and production or hospitality services often take place simultaneously. The influence of other customers (e.g., in terms of their attitudes and behaviours) may also be an important determinant of customer satisfaction (Cakici and Guler, 2017).	The service needs to meet the demands of the customer at the right time. Both the provision and the consumption of the service often require the participation of the customer. The customer may need to be present and may be needed to participate in the service, in terms not only of consumption but also of production of the service.
Heterogeneity	The difficulty of standardising service performance elements. The heterogeneity of a service is largely due to	The high degree of social interaction and communication means that the product and service experience consistency depends very much on the

Service Characteristic	*Explanation*	*Implications for Tourism and Hospitality Businesses*
	the vagaries of human interaction between and among service contact employees and consumers (Koc, 2006). No two services would be exactly alike as the person who delivers the service may have different attitudes or be in a different mood during the delivery of two consecutive services. Services are highly variable and heterogeneous as they depend on who provides them, and when, where, and for whom they are provided (Koc, 2006).	tourism and hospitality service provider's skills and various characteristics (including culture) and performance at the time of the encounter. Organisational systems and processes in the tourism and hospitality business need to be designed in such a way that the service is consistently produced. The processes and systems in the business need to ensure that: • each customer has a high-quality experience that meets her/his expectations; • the service is nearly equal to that experienced by every other customer (except for differences supplied by servers in response to each customer's unique needs and coproduction capabilities).
Intangibility	The inability to see or touch the "product" of service.	Tourism and hospitality services may involve many uncertainties and unknowns. Customers' risk perceptions tend to be high. Employees are expected to behave and communicate in a manner to close the information gap and reduce customers' risk perceptions.
Perishability	The difficulty in synchronising supply and demand	The demand is usually seasonal (e.g., throughout the year or depending the day of the week for a resort hotel or an airline) or during the hours of the day or the day of the week (e.g., for a restaurant). This has implications for revenues, process, and service quality management. Perishability may place additional demands on managers' abilities.

Adapted from Koc (2017).

The dyadic influence of culture's influence on tourism and hospitality activities can also be seen through the marketing mix elements (7Ps) (Table 1.1).

Table 1.1 Marketing mix elements in tourism and hospitality

Marketing Mix Element	*Explanation and Examples*
Product	Comprises all tourism and hospitality products and services – for example, a package holiday, menus, all food items, and beverages served in a restaurant. According to Conell (2013), compared with overall tourism activity, people who engage in medical tourism take cultural differences more into account when they make their purchase decisions. Tourists from masculine and high-power distance cultures tend to allocate more monetary resources to shopping when they are on a holiday (Su et al., 2018). Cultural differences in tourism may increase the likelihood of purchasing souvenirs which can reflect local uniqueness (Su et al., 2018). For instance, while tourists from culturally different destinations tend to shop for souvenirs or gifts (Ozdemir and Yolal, 2017), people from similar cultures (like Canadian tourists visiting the United States) tend to shop for more for daily use items such as groceries, foods, and clothes (Timothy and Butler, 1995).
Price	Pricing refers to all the activities regarding how the business sets up its prices and their influence on customers. Pricing requires an analysis of monetary and non-monetary prices, competitors' prices, packages, price-related discounts, etc. Pricing is significantly more important in services, and particularly in tourism and hospitality, due to the intangibility and perishability nature of these services (Boz et al., 2017). Dynamic pricing (also referred to as surge pricing, demand pricing, time-based pricing, or yield management) is commonly used in tourism and hospitality both to manage demand and capacity effectively and to increase revenues and profits. Koc's (2013) study shows that more risk-averse customers are more likely to require more cognitive control and often tend to purchase all-inclusive holidays.[2] An all-inclusive package holiday is defined as a trip planned and paid for as a single price in advance which covers commercial transportation and accommodation, meals, and sightseeing, and sometimes with an escort or guide. All-inclusive holidays attract risk-aversive tourists and/or tourists with a pre-determined spending budget who do not wish to make additional expenditures when they are on holiday.
Place	In tourism and hospitality marketing and management, the place element is interlinked with almost all other elements of the marketing mix where customers are exposed to all aspects of the tourism and hospitality business including tangible features (location of a hotel or a restaurant), personnel (how they look, and the way they communicate with customers), web pages (the nature, type of information provided on the web pages of a hotel or a restaurant, or the cues used in the messages). The design and the management of a distribution system (i.e., the system

Table 1.1 continued

Marketing Mix Element	*Explanation and Examples*
	comprising intermediaries such as tour operators, online and brick-and-mortar travel agencies, airlines) to reach the customers are among the issues which relate to place decisions. Lee et al.'s (2012) research showed that travel agencies had a significant influence on Japanese people's medical tourism decisions. Money and Crotts's (2003) and Litvin et al.'s (2004) studies showed that people from cultures with a high level of risk avoidance are more likely to depend on personal information sources like travel agencies, tour operators, friends, and relatives.
Promotion	Promotion comprises all marketing communication mediums and messages customers are exposed to, ranging from advertisements to public relations, sales promotions, and all communication with tourism and hospitality staff. In addition to all planned messages in the form of advertising, public relations, sales promotions and personal selling, tourism, and hospitality products (i.e., the tangible aspects, such as the freshness and the variety of food served at a hotel) and services (e.g., the social skills and the capabilities of service staff) convey a significant amount of information to customers as well. According to Correia et al.'s (2011) study, tourists from cultures with long-term orientation are more likely to depend on multiple information sources when making their decisions.[3]
People	People as a marketing mix element comprise all the human resources (e.g., front stage employees, such as stewards and stewardesses, receptionists, and waiters who interact with customers; backstage employees, such as cooks, housekeeping employees, and technical staff working for an airline) whose work outcomes influence customers' satisfaction and perception of the business establishment People's decisions comprise all human resource management (HRM) activities (ranging from human resource planning; recruitment and selection; orientation, training and development; performance appraisal; benefits – pay and rewards; to health, safety, and security of all employees). According to Koc (2003) staff in tourism businesses act as a major tool in conveying marketing communications messages to customers. As stated above, the inability to see and manage the cultural differences of human resources and HRM practices resulted in substantial losses for Disney, when they set up Euro Disney in France in 1992.
Process	The process element of the marketing mix is about the way and which sub-services that make up a whole service (e.g., a service product) are designed and implemented. Booking and reservations at a hotel, check-in for an airline, taking orders of customers in a restaurant, cooking and serving of food in a restaurant are examples of such sub-services. The service blueprint[4] shows all of the sub-services that make up a service and the staff employed at each phase. Given the inseparability and heterogeneity nature of tourism and hospitality services, the smooth, efficient and effective running of all activities in a timely manner is highly important for tourism and hospitality businesses. The fact that while product quality (goods/service

Table 1.1 continued

Marketing Mix Element	*Explanation and Examples*
	products) may account for 14% of all switching behaviours, and the dissatisfaction, the quality of social exchange may account for as much as 67% of all switching behaviours (Doyle, 2008) shows the interconnected nature of sub-services that make-up an overall service product or experience, and the need for the smooth running of processes and operations.
Physical Evidence	Physical evidence decisions cover a wide range of aspects of tourism and hospitality ranging from buildings, furniture, decoration, equipment to the appearance of service personnel. Hsieh and Tsai's (2009) research showed that Taiwanese tourists (people from a highly risk-averse culture) are more likely to place a higher degree of importance on the tangible elements of the service than American tourists (a low-risk-averse culture) when making their quality judgements.

The influence of culture on the customer is not limited to its influence on the design and implementation of marketing mix elements. Apart from the customer's perception of marketing mix elements (7Ps), the customer's perceptions of himself/herself, service employees, and managers, other customers, systems, and processes may have a significant influence on the success or failure of tourism and hospitality businesses (Figure 1.2). This is because, coupled with the perceptions of marketing mix elements, these factors can result in important emotional states and behaviours (pre-purchase, consumption and post-purchase phases) which collectively determine the eventual success or failure of the tourism and hospitality business. These emotional states and behaviours comprise approach-avoidance behaviours (i.e., whether to stay or not in the service environment of the tourism and hospitality business), satisfaction, dissatisfaction, making evaluations (i.e., whether to make a complaint or a praise), repurchase intentions, loyalty, switching, and engaging in positive or negative word-of-mouth (WOM) communication (Figure 1.2).

On the other hand, from a supply-side, the cultural background of employees or managers may have a significant influence on their perceptions of themselves, their roles, tasks, jobs, and careers, together with how they perceive customers, subordinates, peers, managers, systems, and processes (Figure 1.3). These perceptions result in important emotional states, attitudes, and outward behaviours that may have a significant influence in determining the success or failure of a tourism and hospitality business. These emotional states, attitudes, and outward behaviours, determine attitudes and behaviours towards teamwork, job satisfaction, commitment, organisational citizenship, stress, absenteeism, staff turnover, and productivity and performance.

In addition to the general influences explained in Figures 1.1, 1.2, and 1.3, cross-cultural factors have a major influence (actual and perceived) on service quality dimensions (see Table 1.2 and the explanations below).

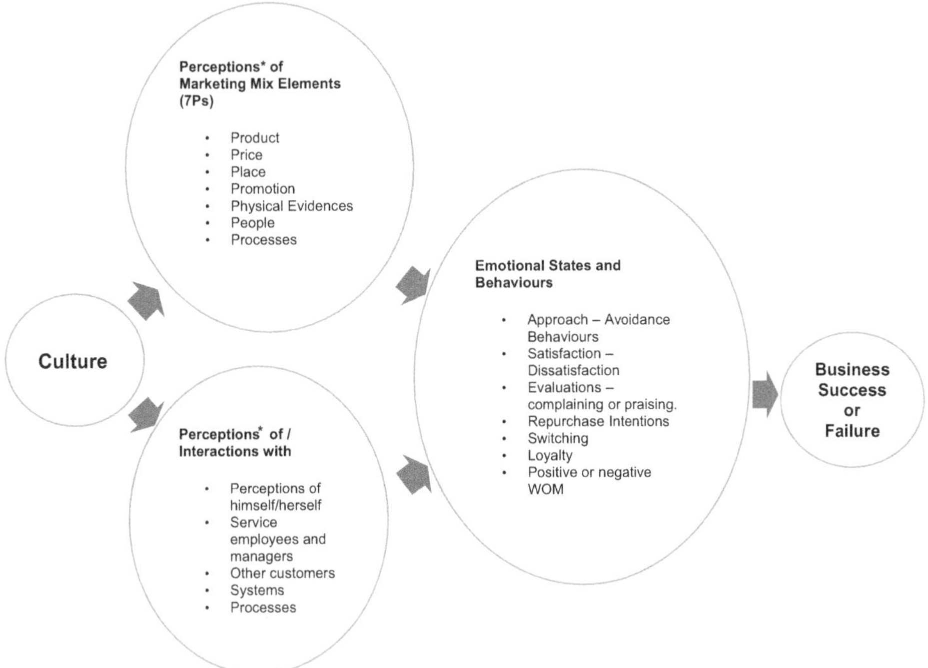

Figure 1.2 Customer/marketing perspective: the influence of culture on customers (marketing management, consumer behaviour, services marketing, and international marketing aspects)

* Pre-purchase and consumption, purchase and consumption, post-purchase and consumption phases.

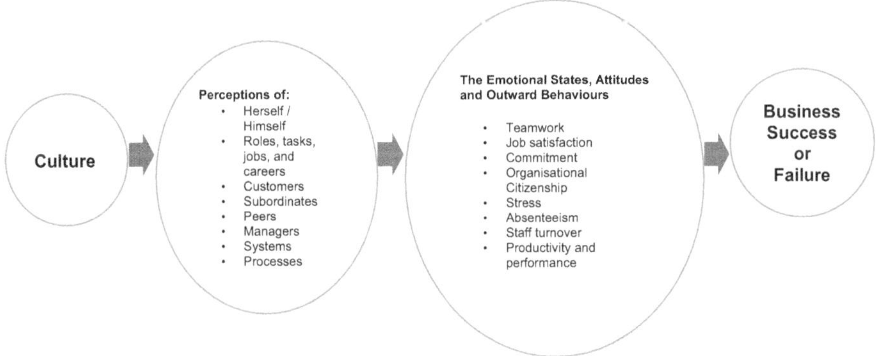

Figure 1.3 Service provider/management perspective: influence of culture on employees and managers (organisational behaviour, human resource management and management, and international management aspects)

Table 1.2 Service quality dimensions and marketing mix elements

SERVQUAL Dimensions	*Explanation and Examples*	*Association with Marketing Mix Elements (7Ps)*	*Cross-Cultural Examples*
Tangibles	Physical facilities, equipment, furniture, decoration and appearance of personnel	Physical evidence Place Product Promotion People	Suppliers of medical tourism packages are expected to pay more attention to designing and modifying their product offers to suit people from different cultures. Kim and Lee (2000) found that tourists from individualistic cultures[5] were more likely to seek novelty compared with tourists from collectivistic cultures. According to Huang and Teng (2009), feng shui is an important element of Chinese superstition and influences people's service quality judgements.[6]
Reliability	The ability to perform the promised service dependably and accurately; for example, a correct and accurate payment transaction	People Process Physical evidence Price Place	Due to the high level and intense contact with customers, the quality of tourism and hospitality services are mainly judged by customers based on their evaluations of human resources alone (Maxwell, 1994; Villi and Koc, 2018). According to Correia et al.'s (2011) study, tourists from collectivistic cultures tend to be more price and brand conscious.
Responsiveness	The willingness and the ability to help customers and provide prompt service; for example, providing timely service, not keeping customers waiting	People Process Product Physical evidence	Bilgili et al.'s (2020) study in Turkey showed that the red colour of lighting in restaurants increased customers' perception of the duration of waiting time. Koc's (2013) study showed that hospitality employees from a high-power distance culture (e.g., Turkey) were less empowered compared with a low-power distance culture (e.g., the UK) causing a delay in responding to and recovering service failures.

Table 1.2 continued

SERVQUAL Dimensions	*Explanation and Examples*	*Association with Marketing Mix Elements (7Ps)*	*Cross-Cultural Examples*
Assurance	The knowledge and courtesy of employees and their ability to convey trust and confidence; for example, greeting and thanking customers, the level of expertise (e.g., the expertise of a chef in a restaurant)	People Process Product Place	Koc's (2006) research showed that in Turkey tourists' expectations regarding the skills and abilities of staff on all-inclusive holidays were relatively lower. However, as all-inclusive establishments employed largely unskilled staff and expected them to overwork, the level of satisfaction with the employees in all-inclusive establishments was much lower.
Empathy	The provision of care and individualised attention to customers.	People Process	Tourists with relatively high intercultural competence and intercultural sensitivity tend to be more empathetic with the service provider (Ye et al., 2013).

Exercise

Watch a few sessions of the TV shows *Restaurant Express* and *Restaurant: Impossible* (presented by Robert Irvine) on YouTube. Take down notes and explain how the 7Ps (marketing mix elements) and service quality dimensions influence customer satisfaction and service business success.

Additionally, as service quality gaps/problems and service failures occur due to misunderstandings, misperceptions, and unexpected behaviours, culture may significantly influence the emergence of service quality gaps. Service quality problems or service failures in service businesses occur due to the service quality gaps shown in Table 1.3 (Parasuraman et al., 1991). The SERVQUAL model focuses on the service quality elements of reliability, assurance, tangibles, empathy, and responsiveness (Parasuraman et al., 1988).

The previous explanations regarding the marketing mix elements, service quality dimensions, and service quality gaps demonstrate the intertwined dyadic nature of tourism and hospitality services, and how they may be influenced by cross-cultural characteristics. Managers are recommended to develop a service blueprint (see the following exercise) for each service product/element that they have so they themselves and their employees better understand the dyadic nature of culture and its implications for the services they provide.

Table 1.3 Gap model of service quality

Gap	*Explanation*
The Knowledge or Perception Gap	Difference between what customers expect and what managers think customers expect from the service business
The Standards Gap	Difference between service managers' perceptions of customer expectations and the service procedures, standards, and specifications established
The Delivery Gap	Difference between service quality specifications and the actual service delivered to the customers
The Communications Gap	Difference between what is communicated to the customer and the actual service delivered
The Customer Gap	Difference between customer expectations and customer perceptions; customers may not always understand what the service has done for them or they may misinterpret the service quality

Exercise

A service blueprint is an operational planning tool that shows how a service will be provided, specifying the physical evidence, staff actions, and support systems/infrastructure needed to deliver the service through its various phases. The service blueprint diagram enables the visualisation of the relationship between various service components of people, physical to evidence, and processes that are directly tied to touch points in the pre-, during and post-service encounter stages in the delivery of a service.

The key elements of a service blueprint are as follows:

- **Customer actions:** comprise the steps, activities, and interactions that a customer performs in relation to the use or consumption of a service.
- **Front stage actions:** the activities that occur directly in the view of the service consumer and include all human-to-human and non-human-to human actions.
- **Backstage actions:** the steps and activities behind the scenes supporting on-stage activities.
- **Processes:** the internal steps and all the interactions that support the employees during the delivery of a service.

The above key elements of a service blueprint are organised around the following zones:

- **The Line of Interaction:** shows the direct interaction between the customers with any element of the service offer.

- **The Line of Visibility:** separates the front stage (all service activities that are visible to the customer) and backstage activities (all service activities that are not visible to the customer).
- **The Line of Internal Interaction:** separates the customer contact employees and activities from those who employees and activities that indirectly support the customer and users.

Study the blueprint for a restaurant shown in Figure 1.4.

Tasks

1. Understand the interconnected dyadic nature (i.e., both the marketing and the management perspectives) and how each perspective may interact with one another.
2. Identify and discuss the likely fall points (problem areas) which may take place due to cross-cultural differences of customers and service providers.
3. Try to find specific cultural characteristics (examples) which may be the likely causes of these fall points.
4. Discuss how these fall points may be avoided.

Physical evidence (tangibles) ➡	Parking lot Exterior and interior of the restaurant Furniture Decor Signs	Welcoming staff or the waiter (appearance, grooming, etc.). waiting area in the restaurant Seating arrangements	Waiter (appearance, grooming, etc.). Air conditioning Lighting and colour Music	Waiter Menu Table cloth Plates Serviettes Serviette holders Cutlery Pans	Waiter Menu Food delivery Tray Food and drinks	Food and drinks	The bill.=	The bill POS machine
Customer actions ➡	Arrives at the restaurant	Waits to be assigned to a table	Receives the menu Selects food and drinks to order Waits for the waiter	Gives the order to the waiter	Receives the food and drinks	Eats and drinks	Asks for the bill	Pays the bill and leaves
Line of Interaction	- - - - - - - -							
On-stage employee contact (e.g., welcoming staff, waiter, runner) ➡	Greets the customers	Directs the customers to the waiting area until the customers are shown to their tables	Directs the customers to their tables Gives the customers the menu. Tells them s/he will be with the customers when they are ready to order	Takes the order and gives it to the kitchen staff	Brings the food to the table	Asks customers whether they were happy with the food Asks for more orders	Prepares the bill Brings the bill	Processes the bill paid
Line of Visibility	————————							
Back-stage employee contact (e.g., receptionist) ➡	Checks the customers in			Processes the order – prepares the food and drinks				Checks the customers out
Line of Internal Interaction	- - - - - - - -							
Support processes ➡	Registration process		Prepares food					Registration process

Figure 1.4 Service blueprint for a restaurant

Several examples have been provided to show how motivations of tourism and hospitality customers may be influenced by their culture. Pine and Gilmore (2011) have identified four service experience motivations alongside the dimensions of Passive–Active and Immerse–Absorb (see Figure 1.5). The degree of activity is about the extent to which a customer prefers to remain a passive observer or the extent to which s/he becomes an active participant. For instance, as explained in Chapter 7, depending on whether a customer is from a high-uncertainty avoidance culture or low-uncertainty avoidance culture, s/he may participate in tourism and hospitality experiences in an active or passive manner.

As explained in Chapter 7, a customer with a high level of uncertainty avoidance (risk aversive) may prefer to participate in passive tourism and hospitality experiences (e.g., taking part in package holidays with a group of people). Again, as explained in Chapter 9, customers' individualistic or collectivistic orientation may influence the types of services in which they want to participate actively or passively. When customers passively participate in a tourism and hospitality experience, they may have no influence on the course of the experience. However, when they participate actively in a tourism and hospitality service they may have a significant influence on the service experience. When a customer participates passively with entertainment motivation, this activity is associated with absorption. The aim of participation in this type of experience is to have fun, which does not require too much activity and commitment on the part of the customer (Kacprzak et al., 2015). However, an experience with aesthetic motivation allows customers to immerse themselves in sensations, but do not require participation from them, for example, a tourist admiring the view of Lake Como in Italy.

The third type of experience is based on educational motivation, which requires active participation, but the individual customer does not have a major impact on their role in the experience (Pine and Gilmore, 2011; Kacprzak et al., 2015). For example, a tourist from an indulgence culture (see Chapter 5) can take golf lessons in Antalya, Turkey during their holidays with an educational motivation. As explained in Chapter 10, tourists who are past-oriented are more likely to have holidays motivated by the intention of sensation seeking (hedonistic, indulgent) (e.g., 3S – sun, sand, and sea holidays), while tourists who are future-oriented are more likely to have holidays motivated by the intention of self-fulfilment and knowledge enhancement (Miao et al., 2011; Lu et al., 2016).

Finally, the escapist motivation requires the individual customer to both immerse herself/himself in the experience and actively influence the experience (Pine and Gilmore, 2011; Kacprzak et al., 2015). For example, a customer from an individualistic and low-uncertainty avoidance culture may take part in a mountain climbing holiday in Tibet.

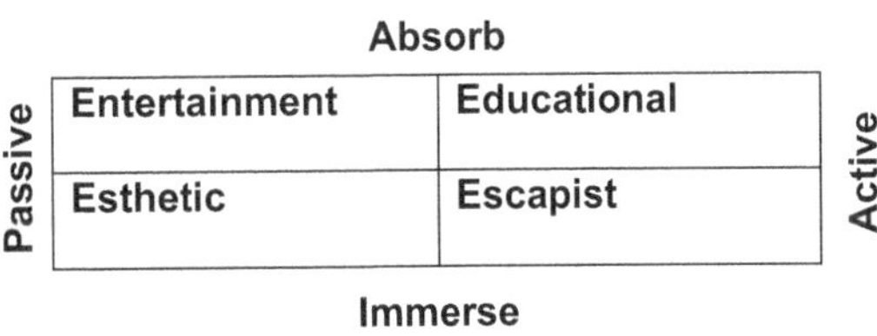

Figure 1.5 Service experiences

The dyadic perspective and approach to business management

Today much of the knowledge developed in marketing and management rests on the knowledge developed in relation to businesses and organisations involved in the production and marketing of tangible products. However, today, with the growth of the service sector, a significant proportion of gross domestic product (GDP) in many countries is produced in the services sector. For instance, in the United States, the UK, France, the Netherlands, Japan, Germany, and Russia the contribution of the services sector to the country's GDP is about 80%, 79.2%, 78.8%, 70.2%, 68.7%, 68.6%, and 62.3%, respectively (The World Fact Book, 2016). Likewise, the total employment in services in these countries constitute between 50% and 80% of total employment. Moreover, the contribution of the service sector to GDP and employment shows significant growth every decade. As mentioned previously, as the world's largest industry, tourism is a service sector industry, and more than 70% of the largest 100 companies in the world are service businesses (FORTUNE, 2020).

Hence, publications presenting knowledge about businesses and the business environment need to reflect this transition or transformation. For instance, marketing and consumer books are expected to present knowledge reflecting the dominant influence of services, and hence they should be written overwhelmingly from the perspective of services. Owing to the nature of service characteristics (such as intangibility, inseparability, heterogeneity, and perishability), as explained previously, production, marketing, and human resource management functions are significantly more interconnected in services than in manufacturing businesses that produce and market tangible products. Therefore marketing managers in services need to be more knowledgeable about the human resource management function, while human resources or operations managers need to be more knowledgeable about the marketing function. As explained previously, this is why this cross-cultural book has been written with this dyadic perspective in mind, reflecting aspects relating to customers, employees, and managers. In addition to general service characteristics, the following characteristics of services necessitate an intertwined approach to the development of knowledge (Koc, 2018):

- Services comprise performances, and unlike tangible products, they are not manufactured.
- Although the relative importance of technology in services is growing significantly, services are more human-based (labour intensive) rather than technology-based.
- The supply of services cannot be easily changed to match fluctuations in demand.
- The demand for services can be more seasonal and flexible.
- Services involve unique service quality and service delivery problems.
- Overall service quality depends on the quality of intertwined sub-services and process.

Barabba (2004) argues that "make and sell" and "sense and respond" orientations prevalent in the manufacturing businesses (producing tangible products) in the past are not suitable for today's service businesses. Service businesses need to have an "anticipate and lead" orientation to survive and prosper in today's competitive markets. According to Barabba (2004) establishing and sustaining an "anticipate and lead" orientation requires a high level of interaction and dependence between the marketing, operations management, and human resource management functions in service businesses. Ruekert and Walker (1987) also argued that providing a high-quality service, creating unique value propositions, development of skills and abilities, and increasing productivity requires strong cooperation and interaction among human resource management, marketing, and operations management functions.

Therefore, it could be argued that as service industry businesses, tourism, and hospitality establishments require a more combined, interlinked, and intertwined approach in the design and implementation of human resource management, marketing and operations management (production and operations management of services) functions.

CASE STUDY

Business functions in hospitality

Assume that you work as the human resource manager of a resort hotel in Alicante in Spain. The hotel has been recently purchased by a young entrepreneur. The new owner of the hotel wishes to change the concept of the hotel to an all-inclusive pricing concept in order to increase the hotel's occupancy rate.

The owner and the general manager arranged an urgent meeting with the managers and supervisors to take place on Monday the following week. All managers, including yourself, have been invited to the meeting, except for managers who had to be away for previously scheduled meetings and commitments. You have a valid excuse for not attending the meeting. Although you can rearrange your other commitment and attend this meeting, you do not wish to do so because you believe that all-inclusive pricing would mainly involve marketing, accounting, and finance managers and their departments, not your human resource management department.

Whether they attend the meeting or not all managers and supervisors have been asked to prepare a short report and send it to the general manager in two days. The report asks the following:

1. Write down the advantages and disadvantages of the all-inclusive pricing system for the hotel.
2. Write down specific courses of action to reduce costs in the all-inclusive system. First, try to be as creative as possible, without thinking about the quality implications of the courses of action you suggest to reduce the costs.
3. Then, write down the potential negative implications of some of the courses of action you have recommended.

Tasks

1. As the human resource manager, who will not be attending the meeting, write a report addressing the above three items.
2. Now re-consider your role as the human resource manager of the hotel. Do you still think that all-inclusive pricing involves only the marketing, accounting, and finance managers and their departments? Or do you feel that marketing and human resource management activities are not separate; that is, they are significantly interlinked in a tourism and hospitality establishment?

The context: tourism and hospitality businesses and the stakeholders

This section provides an overview of the context, that is, the tourism and hospitality businesses, and the stakeholders, who are influenced by cross-cultural differences. The explanations provided throughout the book refer to the tourism and hospitality businesses, and stakeholders stated below.

Tourism and hospitality businesses

The tourism and hospitality businesses referred to in this book comprise the following four categories of businesses:

- lodging and accommodation
- food and beverage
- recreation
- travel and tourism.

Lodging and accommodation businesses

Lodging and accommodation businesses comprise hotels, motels, B&Bs, inns, resorts, apartments, villas, chalets, time-shares that provide accommodation services to their customers who stay away from their homes for leisure and business purposes. Accommodation establishments may be classified according to their a) size (number of rooms, for example, under 50 rooms, over 500 rooms), b) location (e.g., city hotels, airports, resort hotels), c) level of service (e.g., economy – limited service, luxury), d) ownership and affiliation (e.g., individual or chain hotels), e) market served (e.g., bed-and-breakfast, all-inclusive, boutique, casino, conference, resort), and f) level/standard (e.g., 5-star hotels, AAA rated hotels). People may stay in these hotels to engage in business and leisure related tourism activities (Table 1.4).

Food and beverage businesses

Although people participating in the tourism activities listed in Table 1.4 may consume food and beverages provided at the premises of the listed types of accommodation establishments, there is a large hospitality market providing food and beverages to its guests/customers. Hospitality businesses such as restaurants, cafes, pubs, bars, wine houses, tea, and coffee houses provide food and beverages to their guests/customers, whether they are tourists or not. As one of the largest group of food and beverage providers, restaurants may be categorised as bistros, fine-dining restaurants, take-aways, ethnic restaurants, taverns, trattorias, pizzerias, fast-food restaurants, drive-in or drive-through restaurants, pop-up restaurants, cafes, pubs, luncheonettes, steakhouses, a la carte restaurants, etc.

Recreation businesses

Recreation businesses may comprise parks, zoos, theatres, concert halls, cinemas, sports, fitness and hobby centres, spas, skiing centres, night clubs, and sporting events organisers (competitions, cups, and tournaments), etc.

Table 1.4 Types of tourism

3S tourism (sun, sand, and sea)	Adventure tourism, mountain tourism, hunting, fishing tourism,	Agri/Agro tourism, farm tourism, rural tourism, ecotourism	Cultural tourism	Heritage tourism	Event tourism (conferences, corporate meetings, incentives, weddings, etc.)
Dark tourism (thanatourism) disaster tourism, war tourism	Individual business tourism (company representatives travelling for business purposes)	Nature tourism, wildlife tourism, botanical tourism, safari tourism, bird watching tourism	Sex tourism	Gastro and culinary tourism, wine tourism	LGBT tourism
Religious and faith tourism	Slum/Ghetto tourism	Sports tourism, skiing tourism, water sports tourism, rafting, paragliding, golf tourism, etc.	Medical tourism, health and wellness tourism	Educational tourism	Shopping tourism, festival tourism
Civic tourism	Space tourism	Exhibitions, trade shows, trade fairs	Urban tourism	Cruising and yacht tourism	Gambling tourism

Travel and tourism businesses

Travel and tourism businesses may comprise tour operators, travel agencies, airports, airlines, railways, coach businesses, cruise businesses and car rental businesses, etc.

The stakeholders

A stakeholder can be defined as "any group of people organised, who share a common interest or stake in a particular issue or system" (Grimble and Wellard, 1997: 175), and who can influence or be influenced directly or indirectly by using a system (Freeman 1984). Culture influences the attitudes, behaviours, and systems developed by the stakeholders. The following tourism and hospitality stakeholders may be influenced by cultural differences.

Customers of tourism and hospitality businesses

Customers of tourism and hospitality businesses may comprise, but are not limited to, guests at hotels, hostels, guest houses, time-shares, restaurants, cruise chips; passengers in transportation businesses, for example, airlines, railways, coaches; participants in any tourism and hospitality-related events. As shown previously in Figure 1.2, cultural characteristics may influence customers in a variety of ways.

Staff at tourism and hospitality businesses

Staff or employees at tourism and hospitality businesses include all back and front stage employees, and managers. They may also include people such as entrepreneurs, managers (e.g., general managers, marketing managers, human resource managers), employees (e.g., waiters, cooks, cleaners, ticketing officers).

As shown in Figure 1.3, cultural characteristics may shape perceptions, emotional states, attitudes, and outward behaviours of tourism and hospitality employees which impinge on the success and failure of the business.

Suppliers and intermediaries

Suppliers and intermediaries in tourism and hospitality may be tour operators, travel agencies, airlines, convention and event organisers, food and beverage providers to hotels and restaurants, etc. Tourism and hospitality businesses may be affected by how suppliers and intermediaries operate or interact with them. For instance, service quality problems in suppliers and intermediaries (e.g., a lack of responsiveness) arising as a result of cultural characteristics (e.g., polychronism – see Chapter 10) may prevent a tourism and hospitality business from providing a high-quality service to its final customers.

Tourism authorities

Tourism authorities may comprise tourism ministries, government officials, tourism offices and bureaus, destination marketing management officials, etc. As it can be seen in the Travel and Tourism Competitiveness Report (World Economic Forum, 2019) several of the measurements in the competitiveness index relate to the performance of tourism authorities in a country. The cultural characteristics of officials in tourism authorities may influence the laws, regulations, systems, incentives, and processes they develop. Consequently, the laws, regulations, systems, incentives, and processes developed by the authorities influence the way and which tourism and hospitality businesses operate.

Related industries and businesses and the general public

As mentioned previously, there are as many as 30 industries that may be interlinked with tourism and hospitality, ranging from food, furniture, transportation, construction, to durable goods (Koc and Altinay, 2007). Additionally, the cultural characteristics of a country may influence the attitudes and behaviours of the general public, or the society as a whole, towards tourism and hospitality in general, and towards customers, in particular. For instance, ethnocentricism or xenophobia in a society may influence people's attitudes towards international visitors.

Conclusion

This introductory chapter explains the importance of tourism and hospitality and the potential influences of culture on tourism and hospitality activities. Owing to the intense and frequent social contact between customers and service staff in tourism, there is a significant need to understand cross-cultural aspects of tourism and hospitality. This understanding would help managers design and implement marketing mix elements and service quality dimensions, which in turn are believed to determine a business's success or failure.

The dyadic influence of culture, that is, from the perspectives of both management (human resource management and organisational behaviour) and marketing (consumer behaviour) in tourism and hospitality are explained in Figures 1.1, 1.2, and 1.3. The rest of the book will explore, explain, and discuss the dyadic perspectives of tourism and hospitality presented in Figures 1.1, 1.2, and 1.3.

Questions

1. Explain the three groups of factors that have been influential for the growth of tourism and hospitality services. What other factors may have contributed to the growth of tourism and hospitality services? Discuss.
2. What is meant by the dyadic perspective of culture? What does this dyadic perspective suggest for a marketing and human resources manager in a tourism or hospitality business?
3. What are the key emotional states, attitudes, and behaviours culture that may influence customers, employees, and managers? What are the antecedents of these emotional states, attitudes, and behaviours?
4. Explain the marketing mix and the dimensions of service quality for a tourism or hospitality business having a cultural perspective in mind.
5. Explain the components of a service blueprint and discuss how cross-cultural factors may pose potential problems for a tourism or hospitality business.
6. Explain and discuss Michel de Montaigne's (1533–1592) quote "There is as much difference between us and ourselves as there is between us and others" from the perspective of analysing cultures from an intercultural perspective.

Notes

1 In 1996 this figure was estimated to be 3.5%.
2 Risk aversion may be due to cultural and personal factors. Certain cultures are more risk averse than other cultures as explained in Chapter 7.
3 Time orientation as a cultural variable is explained in Chapter 11.
4 See Figure 1.1 for an example of a service blueprint.
5 Individualism-collectivism as a cultural variable is explained in Chapter 9.
6 Feng shui is ancient Chinese wisdom relating to architecture and the built environment. The basis of feng shui is to achieve a level of harmony between heaven, earth, and human by providing an equilibrium between nature, building, and people.

Recommended further reading

Barker, S., and Härtel, C. E. (2004). Intercultural service encounters: An exploratory study of customer experiences. *Cross Cultural Management: An International Journal*, 11(1), 3–14.

Koc. E. (2017). Cross-cultural aspects of service failures and recovery. In E. Koc (Ed.), *Service failures and recovery in tourism and hospitality: A practical manual* (pp. 197–213). Wallingford, Oxford: CABI.

Matusitz, J. (2010). Disneyland Paris: A case analysis demonstrating how glocalization works. *Journal of Strategic Marketing*, 18(3), 223–237.

Sharma, P., Tam, J. L. M., and Kim, N. (2012). Intercultural service encounters (ICSE): An extended framework and empirical validation. *Journal of Services Marketing*, 26, 521–534.

Sharma, P., Tam, J. L., and Kim, N. (2015). Service role and outcome as moderators in intercultural service encounters. *Journal of Service Management*, 26(1), 137–155.

Sizoo, S. (2008) Analysis of employee performance during cross-cultural service encounters at luxury hotels in Hawaii, London and Florida. *Asia Pacific Journal of Tourism Research*, 13(2), 113–128.

Yurur, S., Koc, E., Taskin, C., and Boz, H. (2020). Factors influencing intercultural sensitivity of hospitality employees. International *Journal of Hospitality and Tourism Administration*. Article in Press.

References

Barabba, V. P. (2004). *Surviving transformation: lessons from GM's surprising turnaround*. Oxford; New York: Oxford University Press.

Bilgili, B., Ozkul, E., and Koc, E. (2020). The influence of colour of lighting on customers' waiting time perceptions. *Total Quality Management and Business Excellence*. Article in Press.

Boz, H., Arslan, A., and Koc, E. (2017). Neuromarketing aspect of tourism pricing psychology. *Tourism Management Perspectives*, 23, 119–128.

Cakici, C., and Guler, O. (2017). Emotional contagion and the influence of groups on service failures and recovery. In E. Koc (Ed.), *Service failures and recovery in tourism and hospitality* (pp. 135–159). Wallingford, Oxford: CABI.

Connell, J. (2013). Contemporary medical tourism: Conceptualisation, culture and commodification. *Tourism Management*, 34, 1–13.

Cooper, C. P. Fletcher, J., Gilbert, D., Shephard, R., and Wanhill, S. (2008). *Tourism: Principles and Practice* (4th ed.). New York: Longman.

Correia, A., Kozak, M., and Ferradeira, J. (2011). Impact of culture on tourist decision-making styles. *International Journal of Tourism Research*, 13(5), 433–446.

Doyle, P. (2008), *Value-based marketing: Marketing strategies for corporate growth and shareholder value* (2nd ed.), West Sussex: John Wiley and Sons.

Fields, R. (2014). Restaurant success by the numbers: A money guy's guide to operating the next new hot spot (2nd ed.). New York: Ten Speed Press.

Fletcher, J. 1995. Economics and forecasting—economic impact. In S. F. Witt, and L. Moutinho (Eds.), *Tourism marketing management handbook* (455–467). Englewood Cliffs, NJ: Prentice Hall.

FORTUNE (2020). Fortune top 500 companies. https://fortune.com/fortune500/search/ (accessed 1 February 2020).

Freeman, R. E. (1984). *Strategic management: A stakeholder approach*. Boston, MA: Pitman.

Grimble, R., and Wellard, K. (1997). Stakeholder methodologies in natural resource management: A review of concepts, contexts, experiences and opportunities. *Agricultural Systems*, 55(2), 173–193.

Hartley, R. H. (2006). *Marketing mistakes and successes*. Hoboken, NJ: John Wiley and Sons.

Hsieh, A. T., and Tsai, C. W. (2009). Does national culture really matter? Hotel service perceptions by Taiwan and American tourists. *International Journal of Culture, Tourism and Hospitality Research*, 3(1), 54–69.

Huang, L. S., and Teng, C. I. (2009). Development of a Chinese superstitious belief scale. *Psychological Reports*, 104(3), 807–819.

ICS (International Centre for Science) (2000). *Signals for change: Training course book on technology management*. Trieste, Italy: International Centre for Science and High Technology (UNIDO, United Nations Industrial Development Organization).

Irimias, A., and Franch, M. (2019). Developing intercultural sensitivity as an emotional ability. In E. Koc (Ed.), *Emotional intelligence in tourism and hospitality: A practical manual* (pp. 95- 107). Wallingford, Oxford: CABI.

Kacprzak, A., Dziewanowska, K., and Skorek, M. (2015). The empirical analysis of consumers' attitudes towards experience realms. In *Proceedings of Annual Paris Business Research Conference*, Crowne Plaza Hotel Republique, 13–14 August.

Kim, C., and Lee, S. (2000). Understanding the cultural differences in tourist motivation between AngloAmerican and Japanese tourists. *Journal of Travel and Tourism Marketing*, 9(1/2), 153–170.

Kim, K., and Baker, M. A. (2017). The influence of other customers in service failure and recovery. In E. Koc (Ed.), *Service failures and recovery in tourism and hospitality: A practical manual* (pp. 122–134). Wallingford, Oxford: CABI.

Kim, M. G., Wang, C., and Mattila, A. S. (2010). The relationship between consumer complaining behavior and service recovery: an integrative review. *International Journal of Contemporary Hospitality Management*, 22(7), 975–991.

Koc, E. (2003). The role and potential of travel agency staff as a marketing communications tool. *Tourism Analysis*, 8(1), 105 111.

Koc, E. (2006). Total quality management and business excellence in services: The implications of all-inclusive pricing system on internal and external customer satisfaction in the Turkish tourism market. *Total Quality Management and Business Excellence*, 17(7), 857–877.

Koc, E. (2013). Power distance and its implications for upward communication and empowerment: Crisis management and recovery in hospitality services. *The International Journal of Human Resource Management*, 24(19), 3681–3696.

Koc, E. (2017). Cross-cultural aspects of service failures and recovery. In E. Koc (Ed.), *Service failures and recovery in tourism and hospitality: A practical manual* (pp. 197–213). Wallingford, Oxford: CABI.

Koc, E. (2018). *Hizmet Pazarlaması ve Yönetimi, Global ve Yerel Yaklaşım, 3*. Ankara: Baskı, Seçkin Yayıncılık.

Koc, E. (2019). Service failures and recovery in hospitality and tourism: A review of literature and recommendations for future research. *Journal of Hospitality Marketing and Management*, 28(5), 513–537.

Koc, E., and Altinay, G. (2007). An analysis of seasonality in monthly per person tourist spending in Turkish inbound tourism from a market segmentation perspective. *Tourism Management*, 28(1), 227–237.

Koc, E., and Boz, H. (2020). Development of hospitality and tourism employees' emotional intelligence through developing their emotion recognition abilities. *Journal of Hospitality Marketing and Management*, 29(2), 121–128.

Koc, E., and Bozkurt, G. A. (2017). Hospitality employees' future expectations: Dissatisfaction, stress, and burnout. *International Journal of Hospitality and Tourism Administration*, 18(4), 459–473.

Koc, E., Ulukoy, M., Kilic, R., Yumusak, S., and Bahar, R. (2017). The influence of customer participation on service failure perceptions. *Total Quality Management and Business Excellence*, 28(3–4), 390–404.

Lai, I. K., Hitchcock, M., Yang, T., and Lu, T. W. (2018). Literature review on service quality in hospitality and tourism (1984–2014): Future directions and trends. *International Journal of Contemporary Hospitality Management*, 30(1), 114–159.

Lee, M., Han, H., and Lockyer, T. (2012). Medical tourism: Attracting Japanese tourists for medical tourism experience. *Journal of Travel and Tourism Marketing*, 29(1), 69–86.

Litvin, S. W., Crotts, J. C., and Hefner, F. L. (2004). Cross-cultural tourist behaviour: A replication and extension involving Hofstede's uncertainty avoidance dimension. *International Journal of Tourism Research*, 6(1), 29–37.

Lu, J., Hung, K., Wang, L., Schuett, M. A., and Hu, L. (2016). Do perceptions of time affect outbound-travel motivations and intention? An investigation among Chinese seniors. *Tourism Management*, 53, 1–12.

Marcu, N., Siminică, M., Noja, G. G., Cristea, M., and Dobrotă, C. E. (2018). Migrants' Integration on the European Labor Market: A Spatial Bootstrap, SEM and Network Approach. *Sustainability*, 10(12), 1–21.

Matusitz, J. (2010). Disneyland Paris: A case analysis demonstrating how glocalization works. *Journal of Strategic Marketing*, 18(3), 223–237.

Maxwell, G. A. (1994). Human resource management and quality in the UK hospitality industry: Where is the strategy?. *Total Quality Management*, 5(3), 45–52.

Miao, L., Lehto, X., and Wei, W. (2011). The hedonic experience of travel-related consumption. International CHRIE conference-referred track. Paper 7. http:// scholarworks.umass.edu/refereed/ICHRIE_2011/Saturday/7.

Mihalič, T. and Fennell, D. (2015). In pursuit of a more just international tourism: The concept of trading tourism rights. *Journal of Sustainable Tourism*, 23(2), 188–206.

Money, R. B., and Crotts, J. C. (2003). The effect of uncertainty avoidance on information search, planning, and purchases of international travel vacations. *Tourism Management*, 24, 191–202.

Neuliep, J. W. (2002). Assessing the reliability and validity of the generalized ethnocentrism scale. *Journal of Intercultural Communication Research*, 31(4), 201–215.

Noja, G. G., and Cristea, M. (2018). Working conditions and flexicurity measures as key drivers of economic growth: Empirical Evidence for Europe. *Ekonomický časopis* (Journal of Economics), 66(7), 719–749.

Ozdemir, C., and Yolal, M. (2017). Cross-cultural tourist behavior: An examination of tourists' behavior in guided tours. *Tourism and Hospitality Research*, 17, 314–324.

Parasuraman, A., Berry, L. L., and Zeithaml, V. A. (1991). Understanding customer expectations of service. *MIT Sloan Management Review*, 32(3), 39.

Parasuraman, A., Zeithaml, V. A., and Berry, L. L. (1988). SERVQUAL: A multiple-item scale for measuring customer perceptions of service quality. *Journal of Retailing*, 64(1), 12–40.

Parsa, H. G., Self, J. T., Njite, D., and King, T. (2005). Why restaurants fail. *Cornell Hotel and Restaurant Administration Quarterly*, 46, 304–322.

Pine, B. J., and Gilmore, J. H. (2011). The experience economy: Work is theatre and every business a stage. Boston: Harvard Business School Press.

Prayag, G., and Ryan, C. (2012). Visitor interactions with hotel employees: The role of nationality. *International Journal of Culture, Tourism and Hospitality Research*, 6(2), 173–185.

Rauch, D. A., Collins, M. D., Nale, R. D., and Barr, P. B. (2015). Measuring service quality in mid-scale hotels. *International Journal of Contemporary Hospitality Management*, 27(1), 87–106.

Rosenbaum, M. S., and Montoya, D. Y. (2007). Am I welcome here? Exploring how ethnic consumers assess their place identity. *Journal of Business Research*, 60(3), 206–214.

Ruekert, R. W., and Walker, O. C. 1987. Interactions between marketing and RandD departments in implementing different business strategies. *Strategic Management Journa*, 8, 233–248.

Shenkar O. 2001. Cultural distance revisited: Towards a more rigorous conceptualization and measurement of cultural differences. *Journal of International Business Studies*, 32(3), 519–535

Su, N., Min, H., Chen, M. H., and Swanger, N. (2018). Cultural characteristics and tourist shopping spending. *Journal of Hospitality and Tourism Research*, 42(8), 1210–1231.

Timothy, D. J., and Butler, R. W. (1995). Cross-border shopping: A North American perspective. *Annals of Tourism Research*, 22, 16–34.

Tombs, A., and McColl-Kennedy, J. R. (2003). Social-servicescape conceptual model. *Marketing Theory*, 3, 447–475.

United Nations World Tourism Organisation (UNWTO). (1998). World Tourism Organisation, Council for Trade in Services. Background note by the Secretariat. https://docs.wto.org/dol2fe/Pages/FE_Search/FE_S_S009-DP.aspx?language=EandCatalogueIdList=69812,74140,72076,50858,9868,54805,29130,28519andCurrentCatalogueIdIndex=6andFullTextHash=andHasEnglishRecord=TrueandHasFrenchRecord=TrueandHasSpanishRecord=True (accessed 11 December 2019).

Villi, B., and Koc, E. (2018). Employee attractiveness and customers' service failure perceptions. *Journal of Hospitality Marketing and Management*, 27(1), 41–60.

Wang, C., and Mattila, A. S. (2010). A grounded theory model of service providers' stress, emotion, and coping during intercultural service encounters. *Managing Service Quality: An International Journal*, 20(4), 328–342.

World Economic Forum. (2019). Travel and Tourism Competitiveness Report https://www.weforum.org/reports/the-travel-tourism-competitiveness-report-2019 (accessed 25 January 2020).

The World Factbook. (2016). Country statistics https://www.cia.gov/library/publications/the-world-factbook/ (accessed 30 January 2020).

World Travel and Tourism Council (WTTC). (2018). Travel and tourism global economic impact and issues 2018. https://www.wttc.org/-/media/files/reports/economic-impactresearch/documents-2018/global-economic-impact-and-issues-2018-eng.pdf (accessed 11 December 2019).

World Travel and Tourism Council (WTTC). (2019). Economic impact 2019. https://www.wttc.org/economic-impact/country-analysis/ (accessed 11 December 2019).

Ye, B. H., Zhang, H. Q., and Yuen, P. P. (2013). Cultural conflicts or cultural cushion?. *Annals of Tourism Research*, 43, 321–349.

Yurur, S., Koc, E., Taskin, C., and Boz, H. (2020). Factors influencing intercultural sensitivity of hospitality employees. *International Journal of Hospitality and Tourism Administration*, Article in Press.

Chapter 2

Culture: a cross-cultural perspective

Learning Objectives

After reading this chapter, you should be able to:

- explain culture and what it encompasses;
- understand the influence of culture in shaping people's attitudes and behaviours;
- understand the contributions of prominent scholars on culture;
- evaluate the potential influence of each cultural dimension on attitudes and behaviours of people;
- explain the influence of culture on the design and implementation of marketing mix elements, service quality dimensions.

Introduction

As explained in Chapter 1 (see especially Figures 1.1, 1.2, and 1.3 and the related explanations) culture has a dyadic influence on tourism and hospitality as it influences both customers and service providers. As culture shapes personal, and psychological factors, and influences how people perceive their environment (people, events, and objects), people's responses are mainly determined by their culture. Learning cross-cultural characteristics resembles learning an international language that one can use in communicating with people from different cultures. As explained in Chapter 1, tourism and hospitality activities are increasingly becoming international with the participation of people from different countries and cultures. Understanding people from these countries and cultures through learning cross-cultural characteristics can be considered a key skill. An excellent service employee, a human resource manager, or a marketing manager in tourism and hospitality business serving the domestic market within a country may prove to be a poor performer when serving the international market unless s/he has an understanding of cross-cultural characteristics. Based on this background, this chapter, following a summary of the influences of culture, provides an introduction to culture and concepts relating to culture, and a brief overview of the cultural theories and dimensions explained throughout the book.

Influence of culture

The influence of culture on tourism and hospitality customers may take place during pre-purchase and consumption, purchase and consumption, and post-purchase and consumption phases. Table 2.1 shows the potential influences of culture on tourism and hospitality customers.

Table 2.1 The influence of culture on customers

Examples of Potential Influences in the Pre-Purchase and Consumption Phase	*Examples of Potential Influences in the Purchase and Consumption Phase*	*Examples of Potential Influences in Post-Purchase and Consumption Phase*
Customers' cultural characteristics may influence: • how they collect information and where they collect information from • their overall approach towards and response to advertisements, and the cues used in advertisements • their evaluations of corporate social responsibility activities of the tourism and hospitality business • the types of tourism and hospitality products, destinations, their various features, how they are designed and delivered • the distribution channels they use • their response to tools and types of sales promotions • their evaluations of location and physical evidence • their evaluations of tourism and hospitality staff • their perceptions of reservation, booking and payment and purchase processes	Customers' cultural characteristics may influence: • how they perceive payment systems • their perceptions of reservation, booking and payment, purchase, and service delivery processes • how they evaluate tourism and hospitality products • how they evaluate their interactions with products, physical evidence, and service staff • how they evaluate other customers • how they evaluate service encounters, their satisfaction, and dissatisfaction • how they evaluate service quality and the service quality dimensions they view as important • their evaluations of service failures (e.g., attribution) and service recovery attempts • whether they make complaints or not, and how they make complaints	Customers' cultural characteristics may influence: • what they remember from their tourism and hospitality experiences • their satisfaction and dissatisfaction regarding the individual elements of tourism and hospitality products and processes • how they evaluate the service and the feedback they provide • their repurchase intentions • their loyalty • whether they engage in WOM and the type of WOM they engage in

The pre-purchase and consumption phase

This stage is critical as it determines whether customers will make a purchase or not. For instance, as it is explained in Chapter 7, tourists from high-uncertainty avoidance cultures are more likely to purchase prepaid tour packages, travel in larger groups, stay for shorter periods, and visit fewer destinations than tourists from low-uncertainty avoidance cultures (Money and Crotts, 2003; Reisinger and Crotts, 2010; Koc, 2013a). Again, research shows that about 99% of customers do not purchase products or services from the website they visited for the first time (WorldPay, 2013). Hence, any failure in the design of web pages, or any element or activity relating to the pre-purchase and consumption phase, may result in an inability to attract sufficient numbers of customers for the tourism and hospitality business.

Purchase and consumption phase

Success in the pre-purchase and consumption phase, that is, attracting sufficient customers in the first place, does not guarantee the eventual success of the business, as dissatisfaction in the purchase and consumption process may result in customer dissatisfaction. Customer dissatisfaction would lead to customer switching and engaging in negative WOM communications (Koc, 2017).

Ringberg et al. (2007) investigated the influence of culture on service quality expectations and proposed three cultural models as relational, oppositional, and utilitarian. The relationship cultural model relates to people who express a strong desire to maintain emotional ties with the service provider even in the case of adverse events such as service failures (Ringberg et al., 2007). They tend to be accommodating and understanding when they encounter a service failure and would like to rectify and correct the emotional attachment. When emotional customers experience a satisfactory recovery, their loyalty tends to increase, which is consistent with the service recovery paradox (Smith and Bolton, 1998).

On the other hand, the utilitarian model embraces the idea of pragmatism, rationality, and subjective utility theory. The success of a service recovery depends on the service provider's ability to be fast and efficient, offer compensation in relation to the effort and time invested (Ringberg et al., 2007). Utilitarian people tend to be less likely to become emotional during a service failure and perceive failures as financial and time-related inconveniences (Baker, 2017).

Finally, the oppositional cultural model represents a consistently aggressive position toward service providers during service failures. Customers with oppositional cultural model orientation wish to have control and do not want to be at the mercy of the service provider. These customers may tend to believe that all providers are cunning, and they may view customer–provider interactions as a temporary armistice in which both parties compete for control (Ringberg et al., 2007; Kim, 2017).

The cultural model developed by Ringberg et al. (2007), which was adapted by Baker (2017), may be related to cultural characteristics as listed in Table 2.2.

The above explanations demonstrate the potential influence of culture on one particular issue, the service recovery process, during the purchase and consumption process. There are several instances where culture may influence customers during the purchase and consumption phase. As mentioned in Table 2.1, the influence of culture during the purchase consumption phase is also multifaceted. Chapters 4 to 13 explain these various cultural influences on customers, as well as service providers.

Table 2.2 Cultural models in service recovery

	Cultural Models		
	Relational	*Oppositional*	*Utilitarian*
Cultural dimensions	High context, collectivistic, femininity, low assertiveness, low performance orientation, high humane orientation, long-term orientation	Masculine, individualistic, short-term orientation, restraint, high power distance, high assertiveness	Masculine, individualistic, short-term oriented, high performance orientation, high assertiveness
Key justice principle	Interactional Justice	Distributive Justice	Procedural Justice
Response to failure	• Emotional • Anxious • Embarrassed • Willing to forgive • Looking for consolation	• Aggressive • Does not forgive easily • Emotional/angry • Sceptical/cynical	• Pragmatic • Shows irritation for the time-related inconvenience • Does not want an excuse, wants the problem solved
How to identify	• Expresses hurt/ vulnerability • Is helpful • May blame self • Shows understanding • Will work with the provider • Understands limitations	• Is antagonistic • Blames provider • Is aggressive • Is overly demanding • Suggests excessive compensation	• Rational • Not emotional, but firm • Expects recovery for time/inconvenience
Expectations from recovery	• Sincere apology • Show interpersonal respect • Demonstrate genuine care • Provide an explanation of why things went wrong • Assert the importance of the relationship	• Voices a range of recovery options • Desires to maintain control • Demands excessive compensation	• Compensate for time/energy • Offer exchange/ refund • Make procedure easy • Solve the problem quickly

Adapted from Ringberg et al. (2007) and Baker (2017).

Post-purchase and consumption phase

A close monitoring of customers, staff, and all business activities during the pre-purchase and consumption and purchase and consumption phases would not be sufficient. Customers, staff, and all business activities need to be followed up and closely monitored after purchasing or consuming tourism and hospitality products or services.

Studies show that only 4% to 6% of customers make a complaint (Courtney and Hoch, 2006; Tronvoll, 2012; OFCOM, 2019), the remaining switch to other service providers without letting the business know about any dissatisfaction. Hence, many problems encountered by customers may go unnoticed. As explained in Chapter 9, while tourism and hospitality customers from individualistic countries are more likely to complain and engage in negative electronic word-of-mouth communication (eWOM), tourism and hospitality customers from collectivistic countries are less likely to complain and engage in negative eWOM when they encounter service problems (Patterson et al., 2006; Yuksel et al., 2006; Gi Park et al., 2014; Koc, 2019a).

Culture

Culture has been frequently investigated by various science disciplines such as philosophy, sociology, psychology, and anthropology (Hofstede, 2001). Over the past decades, culture has attracted a growing number of researchers to investigate a wide variety of the influences of culture in the areas of communication, business, management, and industry.

Culture teaches individual members of a society how to *think*, conditions them how to *feel*, and guides them on how to *interact* with others, that is, to *communicate*. Therefore, culture and communication are two extremely interconnected activities (Neuliep, 2018), and any communication between people would have verbal or non-verbal cultural cues in it. For instance, as explained in Chapter 6, while employees in hospitality establishments from low power-distance cultures communicate service failures directly to their superiors, employees in hospitality establishments from high power-distance cultures communicate service failures indirectly to their superiors (Koc, 2013b). This, in turn, may have important implications for service quality (and its dimensions, such as responsiveness and reliability) and customer satisfaction.

Exercise

Search the keywords *cultural differences gestures* and *cultural differences facial expressions* on YouTube. You may also wish to visit the Cultural Atlas webpages (https://culturalatlas.sbs.com.au) to find out about different cultures.

Look at various materials available in the these sources, and prepare a table for the various countries you select, and explain how certain gestures or expressions may be offensive, rude, or odd in other cultures or countries.

As culture shapes the perceptions, thoughts, feelings, and behaviour of people (Mosquera et al., 2011), social interactions and exchanges taking place between service personnel and customers can be strongly influenced by the culture of service personnel and customers. Moreover, customers' evaluations of service encounters in international service settings are influenced by their perceptions of the service failure and recovery, which are strongly influenced by their cultural orientations (Wong, 2004; Baker, 2017).

Among the factors influencing consumer behaviour, culture takes precedence over all the others. The model developed by Kotler and Armstrong (2018) (Figure 2.1) shows that culture

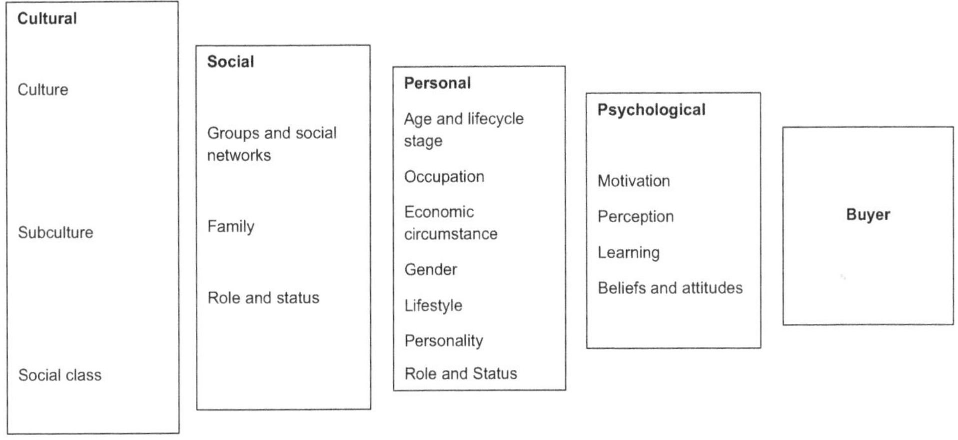

Figure 2.1 Factors influencing consumer behaviour

has the primary or overriding influence on other factors and consumer behaviour. Though the model has been developed to explain consumer behaviour and decision making, it could also be used to understand organisational or employee behaviour and decision making.

Crotts and Erdmann (2000) argue that culture significantly influences tourism activities, and that tourism customers generally think and act in accordance with their cultural "mental programme." Moutinho (1987) emphasises how social influence and personal traits are the fundamental factors influencing tourism and hospitality behaviours. Koc (2017) argues that culture significantly influences service encounters due to its influence on both customer and employee attitudes and behaviours.

While, social factors (culture, subculture, social class, and other people) influence the individual at a social level, personal factors influence a person at an individual level and in terms of her/his their relation to their environment. Personal factors may include individual characteristics such as age, income, level, and type of education, language skills, past overseas experiences, beliefs, attitudes, and motivation. For instance, past exposure of tourism and hospitality employees to other cultures (e.g., spending time abroad through educational exchange programmes at universities through ERASMUS exchange programs) has a significant influence on their level of intercultural sensitivity, which results in positive outcomes across almost all service quality dimensions (Yurur et al., 2020).

Litvin et al. (2004) argue that tourists engage in tourism activities (e.g., the choice of a destination) that are congruent with their self-image, which is very much shaped by their cultural orientations.

Information Zone

Psychoneurobiochemistry of behaviour in tourism and hospitality

Koc and Boz (2014) developed a multidisciplinary approach called psychoneurobiochemistry to understand behaviour (both customer and employee) in tourism. By using this approach the researchers investigated consumer and employee behaviour in tourism and hospitality. Their studies analysed and synthesised findings relating to psychology, neurology, biology, and chemistry by using neuromarketing tools such as electroencephalography (EEG), eye tracker, galvanic skin response (GSR), heart rate (HR), and facial recognition. This approach and the use of these methods in understanding behaviour are important as in many instances data collected through the accounts and evaluations of the participants (through traditional data collection methods such as surveys and interviews) may not reflect the actual truth. This may be due to a) the participants in research studies having hidden motives, which even they themselves may not be aware of, or b) in many instances participants engaging in impression management, that is, a type of goal-directed conscious or unconscious behaviour where people try to influence the perceptions of others through regulating and controlling information in social interaction (Koc and Boz, 2014).

Koc and Boz (2014) argue that jet lag, caused by melatonin deficiency due to the change in circadian rhythm, can have a number of negative consequences for the tourists and customers.

Jet lag, medically referred to as desynchronosis, is a physiological condition which results from alterations to the body of the individual's circadian rhythm from rapid long-distance transmeridian (east–west or west–east) travel by (typically jet) aircraft (Waterhouse et al., 2004). Jet lag tends to be worse for people when they move from west to east. In the instance of this travel, the individual's body finds it harder to adapt to a shorter day than a longer one. As most of the tourism flow in the world is from the west to the east (WTO, 2018), jet lag may be considered an important phenomenon in tourism from the perspective of tourist satisfaction. The physical and emotional symptoms of jet lag may comprise anxiety, constipation, diarrhoea, confusion, dehydration, headache, irritability, nausea, indigestion, difficulty concentrating, sweating, coordination problems, dizziness, daytime sleepiness, malaise (a general feeling of being unwell), and even memory loss (Ruscitto and Ogden, 2017). Some individuals report additional symptoms, such as heartbeat irregularities and increased susceptibility to illness. Hence, when investigating the general dissatisfaction of tourists arriving at a particular destination, considerations other than culture also need be taken into account. This is why, from time to time, this book refers to findings and experiments relating to psychology, biology, anthropology, etc.

A basic Google Scholar search of the keywords *tourism*, *hospitality*, and *culture* returns about 500,000 hits, and the number of researchers carrying out research to explore the influence of culture on a wide variety aspects of tourism and hospitality is on the rise. Culture and strategies in relation to tourism and hospitality businesses are mutually interdependent. Culture shapes strategies and strategies shape culture.

Defining the term *culture* can be a complex task as many researchers have taken different perspectives to explain the phenomenon of culture (Yeniyurt and Townsend, 2003; Schwartz, 2007; Socha, 2012) (Table 2.3).

Table 2.3 Perspectives of the definitions of culture

Culture	*Authors/Researchers*
Entails a pattern in the ways of thinking	Berkman and Gilson (1986); Singh, (2006)
Comprises common meanings shared by a society or is a system of meanings	Peter and Olson (2009); Geertz (1973)
Shared by a group	Hofstede, (2001); Yeniyurt and Townsend (2003); Mooij (2004, 2010); House and Javidan (2004); Schwartz (2007); Dinnie (2008)
Differentiates groups from each other	Hofstede (2001); Triandis (2004)
Transmissible through symbols (acts and items) and language	Dorfman (2004); Triandis (2004)
Influences the way individuals see the world and the way they react to this world	Berkman and Gilson (1986); Mooij (2004, 2011)

Adapted from Socha (2012).

Trompenaars and Hampden-Turner (2004: 21) consider Schein's (1985) following definition as "probably the best definition of culture":

> A pattern of assumptions, invented, discovered, or developed by a given group, as it learns to cope with the problem of external adaptation and internal integration that has worked well enough to be considered valid, and be taught to new members, as the correct way to perceive, think, and feel in relation to these problems.

According to Helman (1990: 2–3), culture can be defined as "a set of guidelines (both explicit and implicit) which individuals inherit as members of a particular society, and which conditions them how to view the world, how to experience it emotionally, and how to behave in relation to other people, to supernatural forces or gods, and the natural environment". Hence, culture comprises a set of meanings, memes (elements of culture passed from one individual to another by non-genetic means, especially imitation), norms, beliefs, and values shared by a society (Matsumoto, 1996) and can shape all the patterns of perceptions, thinking, feeling, and behaviours of individuals within a society (Schwartz, 1997). Hall (1977) likens culture to an iceberg where traditions and customers constitute the part above the water, and values, beliefs, and thoughts constitute the unseen below the water part.

Hofstede (1995) views culture as patterns of mental programmes, that is, a "software of the mind", partially influencing a person's behaviour. The social environment to which the individual belongs is the primary source of these mental programmes. People who belong to the same social environment share the same collective mental software formed by this social environment. According to Zein (2015) (see Figure 2.2), at the heart of every culture there are values that represent what the society believes to be absolute, in terms of good or bad. Values are the concepts and beliefs about desirable end states or behaviours that transcend specific situations, guide the selection or evaluation of behaviour and events, and are ordered by their relative importance (Schwartz and Bilsky,

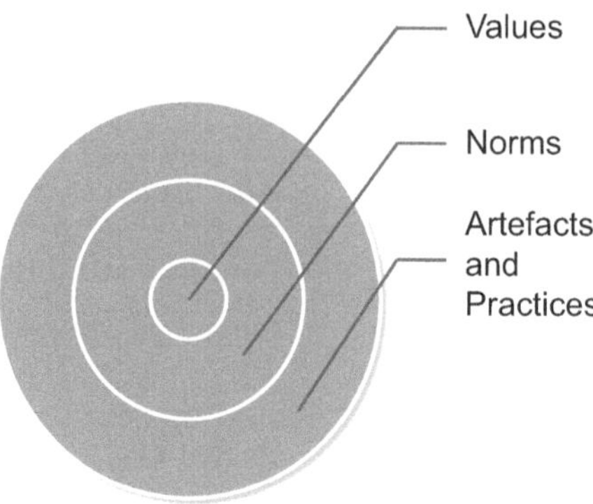

Figure 2.2 Values, norms, and artefacts and practices
Source: Zein (2015).

1987). In other words, societal dictations such as "you should rather be ...... than ......" and "you should rather do ...... than ......" show the values of a specific society.

For instance, a culture that has changed to respond to invaders is expected to emphasise values that favour strength and bravery in men over older values of being in harmony with the environment. Again, a society that experienced poverty for a prolonged period of time in its history may emphasise values that favour wealth and accomplishment rather than other values (Zein, 2015).

CASE STUDY

The influence of plagues on physical contact and touch

As explained in Chapter 9 (and mentioned in Chapters 3, 4, 10, and 12), physical contact and touch show caring and have a number of positive implications for relationships among people.

The disastrous mortal disease known as the Black Death spread across Europe in 1346–1353, and killed about 50 million, 60% of Europe's entire population.

Later, the Great Plague epidemic (Bubonic plague), also referred to as the Black Death, started in London in 1665. It resulted in over 100,000 deaths, about 15% of London's population. Between July and August 1665 more than 7,000 people a week died in London.

Koc (2019b) argues that such great plagues may have influenced culture in Europe. As a result of these plagues, people may have started avoiding physical contact with others and maintaining a larger personal/physical distance that eventually may have turned into a cultural meme. The coronavirus pandemic that started in Wuhan, China at the end of 2019 and the beginning of 2020 resulted in about 400,000 deaths and about 7 million infected people (as of June 2020). It has also resulted in the avoidance of physical contact in countries worldwide with people increasing their personal/physical distance when interacting with each other. Moreover, the prevalence of working from home and online education has gained momentum following the outbreak of this pandemic. As tourism and hospitality services involve constant and close interaction with customers, the coronavirus pandemic will have serious implications in terms of marketing, consumer behaviour, human resource management, organisational behaviour and management.

Task

Think about the major events and catastrophes in history such as those mentioned here and explain how these events may have influenced the culture of people.

Values are formed as an outcome of life experiences and passed from generation to generation through education so that newer generations are fit for survival. Members of a society develop norms to ensure the preservation of the values. Social norms such as the favouring of the national language (e.g., in France and Germany) are expected to preserve values relating to national identity (Zein, 2015). On the other hand, norms are reflected in the artefacts (material culture elements) and cultural practices (traditional and customary practices) within a culture.

Activity

Identify five countries whose culture you are interested in exploring. Then, visit Hofstede's webpage (https://www.hofstede-insights.com/product/compare-countries/) and compare countries' cultural dimension scores.

CASE STUDY

The influence of climate, geography, and anthropology on behaviour and culture

Apart from the catastrophic events explained in the previous case study, climate, geography, topography, and anthropology may also influence the culture of people, how people interact with each other, and the systems they establish.

Geography

The eating of spicy and hot food in warmer countries, such as Mexico and India, is traditionally based on the motivation to preserve the food. Preservation of food was more difficult in hot climates before the advent of refrigerators.

Topography

In Japan, mountains cover over 75% of the land surface. Flatter areas of land are usually allocated for agriculture, mainly rice. Coupled with a dense population, this means there is very limited land for housing in Japan, which makes land and house prices extremely high. As a result, Japanese houses and flats tend to be extremely small compared with most houses in other countries. This is also why there are several capsule hotels, or pad hotels, in Japan, providing cheap, basic overnight accommodation for guests who do not require or who cannot afford larger, more expensive rooms offered by more conventional hotels. Traditionally, the "small is beautiful" philosophy has become a part of the Japanese culture, and influenced people in terms of art, the way in which cities were established, the systems they set up, as well as how people shop and how they interact with each other. Bonsai is a Japanese art form using miniature trees grown in containers. The idea of bonsai is based on the notion of limited space availability in Japan. Owing to the density of population and people having to live in crowded and small spaces, maintaining privacy is an important issue in Japan. Because of this, maintaining eye contact with people is often considered disrespectful. Additionally, most toilets in Japan are more modern and elaborate than toilets commonly found in other developed countries. This is because toilets are a few of the places allowing privacy for people. Also, many Japanese women wear masks (even before the Covid-19 pandemic), not only for health reasons but also to cover up their faces due to their social anxiety.

Anthropology

The reason why men are traditionally involved with barbecues can be explained through anthropology. As explained in Chapters 7 and 8, before the start of the agrarian (agricultural) society, circa 8000 BCE in Mesopotamia, people used to be hunters and gatherers. Men were hunters and women were gatherers. When men succeeded in hunting an animal, they used to bring it to the cave to feed the family. With the pride of saving the whole family from starvation, the men used to cut, carve and cook the game meat themselves. Of course, as hunters, the men knew how to cut and carve the meat better than others in the family. But more importantly, they most probably did not want to share the pride of saving the family from starvation (Koc, 2019b).

People tend to eat larger amounts of food and enjoy their eating more when they are in groups than when they are by themselves. De Castro (1994) attributes this overeating to "social facilitation". However, it must be kept in mind that when anthropological ancestors ate with a crowd of people, this usually created anxiety as there may not be sufficient food for everyone. Hence, some of the overeating may be attributable to anthropological habits and feelings.

Table 2.4 Main features of culture

- Culture is learned.
- Culture refers to a system of meanings.
- Culture acts as a shaping template.
- Culture is taught and reproduced.
- Culture exists in a constant state of change.
- Culture includes patterns of both subjective and objective components of human behaviour.

Source: Adapted from Gaw (2011).

According to Gaw (2001), there are six essential features of culture (see Table 2.4).

CASE STUDY

Euro Disney (Paris): a dyadic perspective of culture

In April 1992, in the middle of a European economic slump, Disney officially opened Euro Disney in Marne-la-Vallée (Paris), France. Euro Disney or Disneyland Paris was a $4.4 billion investment on 4,400 acres of land, and it made a total loss of $1.03 billion in its first two years of operation. At the time it was forecast that the company was to lose approximately $1 million a day for the foreseeable future (Matusitz, 2010). Later total losses surpassed $2 billion. Disney failed to take into account the huge differences between themselves and the Europeans, especially the French. The entire theme park was designed along the same guidelines as the original Disneyland in Orlando, Florida in the United States and the one in Tokyo, Japan. A significant part of this strategic reasoning was based on the success of Tokyo Disneyland. However, in the Japanese market people stated "We came here for America. Don't give us Japan, we know Japan." Disney believed that the French and Europeans would want the same as the Japanese, that is, an American experience. Hence, Disney management did not make any significant adjustments in the Euro Disney project.

On the opening day of Euro Disney, company management estimated that 500,000 visitors would visit the theme park. However, at the close of the day, the visitor numbers barely reached 50,000. This may have been partly due to protests from French locals who felt that their culture would be damaged by Euro Disney.

In addition to various business- and economics-related mistakes, many cultural mistakes played a major role in the losses the company made. Some of the mistakes Disneymade, from a dyadic perspective, that is, mistakes regarding aspects of both customers and employees were as follows:

- based financial projections on American vacationing habits;
- expected one-month family vacations as Americans did;
- served American foods rather than local foods;
- refused to sell cigarettes/alcohol;
- required employees to behave in ways that conflicted with their social customs in France;
- marketing communications messages focused on the size of the park and glamour behind it and failed to explain what the theme park was and what attractions it had to offer.

Task

Read the following article (you may collect data from other sources as well) and study all the blunders made by Disney management from a dyadic perspective, that is, from the perspectives of both customers and employees, and discuss how they may have been avoided.

Source: Matusitz, J. (2010). Disneyland Paris: A case analysis demonstrating how glocalization works. *Journal of Strategic Marketing*, 18(3), 223–237.
NB: In Chapter 13, you will be asked to re-evaluate this case study based on the theories and examples you have learned throughout the book.

Culture is learned and, hence, can be taught and reproduced within a society (Gaw, 2001; Ton and Lim, 2015). Culture shapes how individuals make sense of social and natural environments through a system of meanings formed by words, behaviours, and symbols, and the meanings attached to them (Ton and Lim, 2015). However, Keesing (1974: 89) suggests that culture is not a just collection of symbols fitted together, but rather a system of knowledge, shaped and constrained by the way the human brain acquires, organses, and processes information and creates internal modes of reality. In basic terms culture shapes the delivery and interpretation of both verbal and non-verbal messages

Culture can also be said to encompass a set of attitudes, values, goals, and learned behaviours that serve as a template (a system or method that can be copied and used) to shape, guide, and adapt future attitudes and behaviours from one generation to another, and as new situations emerge (Gaw, 2001). Culture also comprises both the subjective components of behaviour (in the form of shared meanings and ideas in the individuals' minds) and the objective components (in the form of shared observable behaviours and interactions of individuals (Ton and Lim, 2015). Culture's components can be summarised as follows (Bamossy and Solomon, 2016):

Norms	Rules dictating what is right or wrong, acceptable or unacceptable.
Myths	Stories containing symbolic elements that represent the shared emotions and ideals of a culture.
Rituals	Sets of multiple, symbolic behaviours that occur in a fixed sequence, and that tend to be repeated regularly.
Ritual Artefacts	Items needed to perform rituals, such as wedding rice, birthday candles, ikebana flowers in the Japanese tea ceremonies, diplomas, specialised food and beverages, trophies and plaques, band uniforms, greeting cards, and retirement watches.

Table 2.5 Meanings shared by a society

Common Meanings	*Explanations and Examples*
Typical cognitions	Common beliefs and attitudes people in a society may have (e.g., food taboos, superstitions). The design of the exterior or interior of a hotel or a restaurant may make a Chinese person believe that it will bring either good or bad fortune. Hence, Chinese people's decisions regarding tourism and hospitality may be significantly influenced by their beliefs regarding feng shui. In Taiwan, people do not eat mangoes at work, because when pronounced in Chinese, mango sounds like "busy". They believe that if someone eats mangoes that person is lazy and laid back. French people usually consider being positive as a bad thing. They associate ignoring the negative side of things as being naïve. They also believe that seeing the defects is a sign of competence and intelligence. So for French people, it may be more common to criticise than to praise a person. Eating fish is largely a taboo in Somalia. Although Somalia has 3,300 kilometres of coastline, except for people who live on the coast, in general, people in Somalia tend to refrain from eating fish.
Affective reactions	Common likes and dislikes; expected and actual emotions people may have. Spitting is not considered as a negative act in China. In general, Brazilian people tend to be patient. They do not tend to be angry when they are kept waiting for a certain amount of time. Indonesians hate loud voices even when it is used to attract attention or call someone at a distance.
Characteristic patterns of behaviour	Common behavioural patterns that may exist in society. While in many countries children eat plenty of burgers, hotdogs, chicken fingers, and chips (fries), in France it is more common to see children eating "adult" food. In the UK raising a hand to call a waiter in a restaurant is considered inappropriate. The customer waits for the waiter to come. In Finland, water and milk are the most popular drinks with meals. Finnish people may drink milk with their lunch and dinner.

Culture can also be defined as common meanings for members of a society share. In a general sense, the meanings shared by a society may include a) typical cognitions (beliefs), b) common affective reactions, and c) characteristic patterns of behaviour (Peter and Olson, 2009) (see Table 2.5).

Exercise

Visit the Cultural Atlas webpages (https://culturalatlas.sbs.com.au) and prepare a table comprising typical cognitions, affective reactions and characteristic patterns of behaviour from countries you wish to include. Compare what you have found with your own country culture and discuss how strange they may seem in your own culture.

Cross-cultural theories and dimensions

This section provides a brief overview of the cross-cultural theories and dimensions explained and discussed throughout the book. A review of the literature cultural theories, dimensions and values shows that the following paradigms have been proposed by scholars (see Table 2.6).

Table 2.6 Cultural theories, dimensions proposed by scholars

Scholars	*Dimensions*
Parsons (1952)	• Affective/Affective Neutrality • Ascription/Achievement • Universalism/Particularism • Instrumental/Expressive) Diffuseness/Specificity • Self-oriented/Collective-oriented
Kluckhohn and Strodtbeck (1961)	• Good/A mixture of good and evil/Evil • Individualistic/Collateral (Collectivistic) • Changeable/Unchangeable • Linear (Hierarchical) • Subjugate/Harmony/Mastery • Past/Present/Future-oriented • Doing/Being/Being-in-becoming • Public/Private/Mixed
Stewart (1971)	• Changeable/Unchangeable • Egalitarian/Hierarchical • Subjugation/Harmony/Control • Direct/Indirect) Doing/Being/Becoming • Self-oriented/Group-oriented • Formal/Informal • Present/Future oriented

Table 2.6 continued

Scholars	*Dimensions*
Hall (1983); Hall and Hall (1987)	• Agreement • Authority • Monochronic/Polychronic • Amount of space/Low/High context • Possessions • Public/Private/Intimate/Personal/Social • In-group/Out-group • Covert/Overt messages • Friendship
Hofstede (1980, 2010); Minkov (2009); Hofstede et al. (2010)	i) Low/High Power Distance, ii) Individualism/Collectivism, iii) Low/High-uncertainty avoidance, iv) Masculinity/Femininity, v) Long/Short-Term Orientation, vi) Indulgence/Restraint
Argyle (1986)	• Formal/Informal • Contact/Non-contact
Schein (1992)	• Individualism/Groupism • Control/Harmony/Subjugation • Participation and involvement • Past/Present/Near (or far future) Role relationships • Monochronic/Polychronic • Doing/Being/Being-in-becoming • Planning/Development • Work/Family/Personal • Discretionary time horizons (Function/Occupation/Rank) • Evil/Good/Mixed • Temporal symmetry/Pacing
Trompenaars (1993); Trompenaars and Hampden-Turner (1998, 2014)	• Universalism/Particularism • Control/Harmony/Subjugation • Participation and involvement • Individualism/Communitarianism (Collectivism) • Internal/External • Affective/Neutral • Inner/Outer directed • Sequential/Synchronic • Achievement/Ascription, • Sequential/Synchronic • Analysing/Integrating • Past/Present/Future Orientation • Equality/Hierarchy

Table 2.6 continued

Scholars	*Dimensions*
Schwartz (1992, 1994)	Schwartz's (1992) Value Inventory • Power • Achievement • Hedonism • Stimulation • Self-direction • Universalism • Benevolence • Tradition • Conformity • Security • Super-grouping Schwartz's (1994) Cultural Values • Embeddedness/Autonomy • Mastery /Harmony • Hierarchy vs. Egalitarianism
Maznevski (1994)	• Good/Evil • Containing/Controlling • Changeable • Individual/Collective • Subjugation/Harmony/Mastery • Hierarchical • Doing/Being
Triandis (1995)	Vertical/Horizontal Individualism/Collectivism

Some of these proposed dimensions have been extensively applied in business, management, marketing, and communication, while some others have not attracted much attention by scholars. The commonly used and cited dimensions (in business and management, including tourism and hospitality management) have been selected to be explained in this book. The commonly used dimensions and the ones explained in Chapters 4 to 13 of are shown in Table 2.7. As they will be explained and discussed in detail in the assigned chapters they are explained only briefly in the table.

Table 2.7 Cross-cultural dimensions

Dimension	*Brief Explanation*	*Chapter*
Power Distance	The degree of tolerance for class discrepancies in a society	6
Individualism/ Collectivism	The degree to which the welfare of the individual is valued more or less than the group	9
Uncertainty Avoidance	The degree of tolerance for uncertainty, ambiguity, and risk	7
Masculinity/Femininity	Masculinity represents a preference for achievement, heroism, assertiveness, and material rewards for success in society. Femininity represents a preference for cooperation, modesty, caring for the weak and quality of life.	8
Long-/Short-Term Orientation	Long-term orientation represents a focus on the future, willingness to delay short-term material or social success or even short-term emotional gratification in order to prepare for the future	11
Indulgence/Restraint	Indulgence-oriented cultures allow relatively free gratification of basic and natural human drives related to enjoying life and having fun. Restraint-oriented cultures suppress the gratification of needs and regulate it by means of strict social norms.	5
High/Low Context	High-context cultures communicate in ways that are implicit and rely heavily on context. Low-context cultures rely on explicit verbal communication.	4
Past Orientation	Past-oriented cultures focus on traditional values and ways of doing things. They tend to be conservative in management and slow to change those things that are tied to the past.	11
Present Orientation	Present-oriented societies see the past as passed, and the future as uncertain. They prefer short-term benefits.	11
Future Orientation	Cultures that value the sacrifice of short-term pleasures and satisfactions in favour of long-term success and prosperity	11
Assertiveness	Cultural assertiveness is the extent to which whether people in a society are or should be encouraged to be assertive, aggressive, and tough or non-assertive, non-aggressive, and tender in social relationships.	8

Table 2.7 continued

Dimension	*Brief Explanation*	*Chapter*
Egalitarianism	Egalitarianism represents an open display of justice, freedom, and the associated responsibilities accompanying these values. Gender egalitarianism shows the extent to which a society minimises gender role differences while promoting gender equality.	8
Performance Orientation	Performance orientation is the extent to which a society encourages and rewards group members for performance improvement and excellence.	10
Humane Orientation	Humane orientation is the extent to which members of a society are fair, altruistic, friendly, generous, caring and kind to others	10
Monochronism/ Polychronism	Preference to perform many activities/tasks (i.e., multitasking) at the same time or carrying out tasks one at a time (i.e., sequentially)	11

Conclusion

This introductory chapter explains the concept of culture, cultural theories, and dimensions, together with concepts relating to culture. It is seen that culture has an overriding influence on people's attitudes and behaviours. As tourism and hospitality operations involve continuous and intense interaction between customers, most of the attitudes and behaviours of people involved in service encounters may be culture-bound. On the part of the service provider, understanding cultural characteristics, and making the necessary adjustments are expected to produce positive outcomes such as customer satisfaction, purchase, repurchase, loyalty, and positive WOM. These positive outcomes are expected to come about if the tourism and hospitality staff have a high level of intercultural sensitivity and intercultural competency. The development of intercultural sensitivity and intercultural competency begins with understanding cross-cultural characteristics. Hence, managers in tourism and hospitality businesses are recommended to make plans and programmes to train their employees continually, as well as themselves, on cross-cultural knowledge, abilities, and skills.

Questions

1. Explain the quote "Culture eats strategy for breakfast" (Peter Drucker) from the perspective of the influence of national culture on organisational culture.
2. Explain the three groups of factors which have been influential for the growth of tourism and hospitality.
3. Explain the concept of culture, its essentials, and its main components.

4. Explain the influence of culture on customers during the pre-purchase and consumption, purchase and consumption, and post-purchase and consumption phases.
5. "Culture can also be defined as common meanings members of a society share." Explain the three groups of meanings with examples relating to tourism and hospitality operations.

Research questions/ideas to pursue for researchers

Ringberg et al.'s (2007) cultural model on service recovery perceptions of customers was explained previously. It was suggested that there may be a relationship between each cultural model and the cultural characteristics of people. A research study may be carried out to investigate tourism and hospitality customers' cultural model orientations, as specified by Ringberg et al. (2007) in relation to their cultural characteristics, such as indulgence and restraint, or individualism and collectivism. The study may produce important research outcomes for the practitioners in terms of designing and implementing service recovery processes.

Recommended further reading

Hall, E. T. (1977). *Beyond culture*. Garden City, NY: Anchor Press.

Hofstede, G. H. (2001). *Culture's consequences: Comparing values, behaviors, institutions, and organizations across nations*. Thousand Oaks, CA: Sage.

Hofstede, G. (2010). Cultures and organizations: Software of the mind (3rd ed.). New York: McGraw-Hill.

House, R. J., and Javidan, M. (2004) Overview of the GLOBE. In R. J. House, P. J. Hanges, M. Javidan, P. W, Dorfman, and V. Gupta (Eds), *Culture, leadership, and organizations: The GLOBE study of 62 societies* (pp. 9–26). Thousand Oaks, CA: Sage.

Neuliep, J. W. (2018). *Intercultural communication: A contextual approach* (7th ed.). Thousand Oaks, CA: Sage.

Trompenaars, A., and Hampden-Turner, C. (1998). *Riding the waves of cultural diversity in global business*. Boston, MA: Nicholas Brealey Publishing.

References

Argyle, M. (1986). Rules for social relationships in four cultures. *Australian Journal of Psychology*, 38, 309–318.

Baker, M. (2017). Service failures and recovery: Theories and models. In E. Koc (Ed.), *Service failures and recovery in tourism and hospitality* (pp. 27–41). Wallingford, Oxford: CABI.

Bamossy, G. J., and Solomon, M. R. (2016). *Consumer behaviour: A European perspective*. Harlow: Pearson Education.

Berkman, H. W., and Gilson C. C., (1986). *Consumer behavior: Concepts and strategies*. Boston, MA.: Kent Publishing.

Crotts, J. C., and Erdmann, R. (2000). Does national culture influence consumers' evaluation of travel services? A test of Hofstede's model of cross-cultural differences. *Managing Service Quality*, 10, 5, p410–419.

Courtney, P., and Hoch, S. J. (2006). One negative experience can keep many customers away. *Souvenirs, Gifts and Novelties*, May, 118–119.

De Castro, J. M. (1994). Family and friends produce greater social facilitation of food intake than other companions. *Physiology and Behavior*, 56(3), 445–455.

Dinnie, K. (2008). *Nation branding: Concepts, issues, practice*. Burlington, MA: Butterworth-Heinemann.

Dorfman, P. W. (2004). Prior literature. In R. J. House, P. J. Hanges, M. Javidan, P. W. Dorfman, and V. Gupta (Eds), *Culture, leadership, and organizations: The GLOBE study of 62 societies* (pp. 51–67). Thousand Oaks, CA: Sage.

Gaw, A. (2001). *Concise guide to cross-cultural psychiatry*. Washington, DC: American Psychiatric Pub.

Geertz, C., 1973. *The interpretation of cultures*. New York: Basic Books.

Gi Park, S., Kim, K., and O'Neill, M. (2014). Complaint behavior intentions and expectation of service recovery in individualistic and collectivistic cultures. *International Journal of Culture, Tourism and Hospitality Research*, 8(3), 255–271.

Hall, E. T. (1977). *Beyond culture*. Garden City, NY: Anchor Press.

Hall, E. T. (1983). *The dance of life: The other dimensions of time*. New York: Doubleday.

Hall, E.T., and Hall, M.R. (1987). *Hidden differences: Doing business with the Japanese*. New York: Anchor Press/Doubleday.

Helman, C. G., 1990. *Culture, health and illness*. Oxford: Butterworth-Heinemann.

Hofstede, G. (1980). *Culture's consequences: International differences in work-related values*. Beverly Hills: Sage.

Hofstede, G. (1995). Motivation, leadership and organizations: Do American theories apply abroad? In D. A. Kolb, D. A. Osland, and J. Rubin (Eds) *The Organizational Behavior Reader* (6th ed., pp. 375–394). London: Prentice-Hall International.

Hofstede, G. H. (2001). *Culture's consequences: Comparing values, behaviors, institutions, and organizations across nations*. Thousand Oaks, CA: Sage.

Hofstede, G. Hofstede, G. J., and Minkov, M. (2010). *Cultures and organizations: Software of the mind* (3rd ed.). New York: McGraw-Hill.

House, R. J., and Javidan, M. (2004). Overview of the GLOBE. In R. J. House, P. J. Hanges, M. Javidan, P. W. Dorfman, and V. Gupta (Eds) *Culture, leadership, and organizations: The GLOBE study of 62 societies* (pp. 9–26). Thousand Oaks, CA: Sage.

Keesing, R. (1974). Theories of culture. *Annual Review of Anthropology*, 3, 73–97.

Kim, J. H. (2017). Memorable service experiences: A service failure and recovery perspective. In E. Koc (Ed.), *Service failures and recovery in tourism and hospitality: A practical manual* (pp. 56–69). Wallingford, Oxford: CABI.

Kluckhohn, F. R., and Strodtbeck, F. L. (1961). *Variations in value orientations*. New York: Harper and Row.

Koc, E. (2013a). Inversionary and liminoidal consumption: Gluttony on holidays and obesity. *Journal of Travel and Tourism Marketing*, 30(8), 825–838.

Koc, E. (2013b). Power distance and its implications for upward communication and empowerment: Crisis management and recovery in hospitality services. *The International Journal of Human Resource Management*, 24(19), 3681–3696.

Koc, E. (2017). *Service failures and recovery in tourism and hospitality*. Wallingford, Oxford: CABI.

Koc, E. (2019a). Service failures and recovery in hospitality and tourism: a review of literature and recommendations for future research. *Journal of Hospitality Marketing and Management*, 28(5), 513–537.

Koc, E. (2019b). *Tüketici Davranışı ve Pazarlama Stratehileri, 8*. Ankara: Baskı, Seçkin Yayıncılık.

Koc, E., and Boz, H. (2014). Psychoneurobiochemistry of tourism marketing. *Tourism Management*, 44, 140–148.

Kotler, P. and Amstrong, G. (2018). *Principles of marketing* (global ed.). Harlow: Pearson.

Litvin, S. W., Crotts, J. C., and Hefner, F. L. (2004). Cross-cultural tourist behaviour: A replication and extension involving Hofstede's uncertainty avoidance dimension. *International Journal of Tourism Research*, 6(1), 29–37.

Matsumoto, D. (1996). *Culture and psychology*. Pacific Grove, CA: Brooks/Cole.

Matusitz, J. (2010). Disneyland Paris: A case analysis demonstrating how glocalization works. *Journal of Strategic Marketing*, 18(3), 223–237.

Maznevski, M. L. (1994). *Synergy and performance in multi-cultural teams* (Unpublished doctoral dissertation). University of Western Ontario, London, Canada.

Minkov, M. (2009). Predictors of differences in subjective wellbeing across 97 nations. *Cross-Cultural Research*, 43, 152–179.

Money, B., and Crotts, J. (2003). The effect of uncertainty avoidance on information search, planning and purchases of international travel vacations. *Tourism Management*, 24(2), 191–202.

Mooij, M. K. d. (2010). *Global marketing and advertising: Understanding cultural paradoxes*. Los Angeles: Sage.

Mosquera, R. P. M., Uskul, A.K., and Cross, S.E. (2011) The centrality of social image in social psychology. *European Journal of Social Psychology*, 41(4), 403–410.

Moutinho, L. (1987), Consumer behavior in tourism. *European Journal of Marketing*, 21(10), 1–44.

Neuliep, J. W. (2018). *Intercultural communication: A contextual approach* (7th ed.). Thousand Oaks, CA: Sage.

OFCOM (2019). Communications Market Report 2018 Ofcom. https://www.ofcom.org.uk/__data/assets/pdf_file/0016/113632/research-reason-complain-2018.pdf (accessed 30 December 2019).

Parsons, T. (1952). *The Social System*. New York: Free Press.

Patterson, P., Cowley, K., and Prasongsukarn, K. (2006). Service failure recovery: The moderating impact of individual-level cultural value orientation on perceptions of justice. *International Journal of Research in Marketing*, 23(3), 263–277.

Peter, J. P. and Olson, J. (2009), *Consumer Behaviour*. New York: McGraw-Hill.

Reisinger, Y., and Crotts. J. (2010). Applying Hofstede's national culture measures in tourism research: illuminating issues of divergence and convergence. *Journal of Travel Research*, 49(2), 153–164.

Ringberg, T., Odekerken-Schroder, G., and Christensen, G. L. (2007). A cultural models approach to service recovery. *Journal of Marketing*, 71(3), 194–214.

Ruscitto, C., and Ogden, J. (2017). The impact of an implementation intention to improve mealtimes and reduce jet lag in long-haul cabin crew. *Psychology and Health*, 32(1), 61–77.

Schein, E. H. (1985). *Organization, culture, and leadership*. San Francisco: Jossey-Bass.

Schein, E. H. (1992). *Organisational culture and leadership* (2nd ed.). San Francisco: Jossey-Bass.

Schwartz, S. H. (1992). Universals in the content and structure of values: Theoretical advances and empirical tests in 20 countries. In M. Zanna (Ed.), *Advances in experimental social psychology* (Vol. 25, pp. 1–65). Orlando, FL: Academic.

Schwartz, S. H. (1994). Beyond individualism-collectivism: New cultural dimensions of values. In U. Kim, H. C. Triandis, C. Kagitcibasi, S.-C. Choi, and G. Yoon (Eds.), *Individualism and collectivism: Theory, method, and application* (pp. 77–119). Newbury Park, CA: Sage.

Schwartz, S. (1997). Values and culture. In M. S. Munro et al. (Eds), *Motivation and culture*. New York: Routledge.

Schwartz, S. H. (2007). A theory of cultural value orientations: Explications and applications. In Y. R. Esmer, and T. Pettersson (Eds) *Measuring and mapping cultures: 25 years of comparative value surveys* (pp. 137–182). Boston: Brill.

Schwartz, S. H., and Bilsky, W. (1987). Toward a psychological structure of human values. *Journal of Personality and Social Psychology*, 53, 550–562.

Singh, S. (2006). Cultural differences in, and influences on, consumers' propensity to adopt innovations. *International Marketing Review*, 23(2), 173–191.

Smith, A. K., and Bolton, R. N. (1998). An experimental investigation of customer reactions to service failure and recovery encounters paradox or peril? *Journal of Service Research*, 1(1), 65–81.

Socha, A. C. (2012). *The influence of the culture dimension "power distance" on product choice: A cross cultural exploration of effects of country of origin on the choice of branded products* (Unpublished doctoral dissertation). University of Guelph.

Stewart, R. A. (1971), Cross-cultural personality research and basic cultural dimensions through factor analysis. *Personality*, 2, 45–72.

Ton, H., and Lim, R. (2015). Assessment of culturally diverse individuals: Introduction and foundations. In R. F. Lim (ed.) *Clinical manual of cultural psychiatry* (2nd ed., pp. 1–41). Washington, DC: American Psychiatric Publishing.

Triandis, H. C. (1995). *Individualism and collectivism*. Boulder, CO: Westview Press.

Triandis, H. C. (2004). Dimensions of culture beyond Hofstede. In H. Vinken, J. Soeters, and P. Ester (Eds) *Comparing cultures: Dimensions of culture in a comparative perspective* (pp. 28–42). Boston: Brill.

Trompenaars F. (1993). *Riding the waves of culture: Understanding cultural diversity in business*. London: Brealey.

Trompenaars, F., and Hampden-Turner, C. (1998). Riding the waves of cultural diversity in global business. Boston, MA: Nicholas Brealey Publishing

Trompenaars, F. and Hampden-Turner, C. (2014). *Riding the waves of culture: Understanding cultural diversity in business* (3rd ed.). London: Nicholas Brealey Publishing.

Tronvoll, B. (2012). A dynamic model of customer complaining behaviour from the perspective of service-dominant logic. *European Journal of Marketing*, 46(1), 284–305.

Waterhouse, J., Reilly, T., and Edwards, B., (2004), The Stress of Travel, *Journal of Sport Sciences*, 22(10), 946–966.

Wong, N. Y. (2004). The role of culture in the perception of service recovery. *Journal of Business Research*, 57(9), 957–963.

WorldPay. (2013). Online Trading Report. www.worldpay.com: www.worldpay.com/onlinetrading/index.php?page=explainandsub=howandei=dRlmU4aYA4amrQe N9YCYA gandusg=AFQjCNGo5Houn3OKl7kkke30mXj2lCGE4Qandsig2=8aHNTzU9l6ykWZyo JrYzWwand bvm=bv.65788261,d.bmk (accessed 30 January 2020).

WTO (World Tourism Organisation) (2018). Compendium of Tourism Statistics. http://statistics.unwto.org/content/compendium-tourism-statistics (accessed 5 February 2020).

Yeniyurt, S., and Townsend, J. D. (2003). Does culture explain acceptance of new products in a country? An empirical investigation. *International Marketing Review*, 20(4), 377–396.

Yuksel, A., Kilinc, U. K. and Yuksel, F. (2006), Cross-national analysis of hotel customers' attitudes toward complaining and their complaining behaviors. *Tourism Management*, 27(1), 11–24.

Yurur, S., Koc, E., Taskin, C., and Boz, H. (2020). Factors influencing intercultural sensitivity of hospitality employees. International journal of hospitality and tourism administration, Article in Press.

Zein, O. (2015). *Culture and project management: Managing diversity in multicultural projects*. Farnham, UK: Gower.

Chapter 3

Intercultural competence, intercultural sensitivity, and cultural intelligence

Learning Objectives

After reading this chapter, you should be able to:

- understand the concept of intercultural sensitivity and its influence on tourism and hospitality service encounters;
- explain the role of familiarity, mimicking and mirroring in developing rapport and positive emotions when interacting with people from other cultures;
- understand the components of intercultural competence;
- understand how intercultural competence can be developed;
- explain the relevancy of the dimensions of intercultural sensitivity to various service encounter situations.

Introduction

The quote "When in Rome, do as the Romans do" is a famous axiom attributed to St Ambrose, a well-known bishop who lived in Milan in the fourth century. St Ambrose added, "When I go to Rome, I fast on a Saturday, but here in Milan, I do not." In a broad sense, the axiom suggests that when one is in Rome one should act like the Romans, that is, should respect other people's way of life by following the traditions and customs of people living there.

From the viewpoint of tourism and hospitality service encounters, this axiom may be looked at from the other side. The tourism and hospitality business should allow the customers "to make themselves feel at home" by adjusting various aspects of their services (including their communication and behaviour) to suit their customers. As explained in Chapter 2, when Disney opened up Euro Disney, Paris, the company took an ethnocentric approach and ignored the culture and the local conditions. This ethnocentric approach caused the company to incur major financial losses in this investment.

As tourism and hospitality services necessitate intense and continuous interactions with customers, and also intense and continuous interactions among employees, the intercultural competencies of service employees and managers are of paramount importance for the efficient and effective management of operations. Additionally, as explained in Chapter 1, tourism and hospitality services have increasingly become international in nature, in terms of both the international backgrounds of customers receiving service from these businesses and the diversity of the workforce working in these businesses. When an individual meets with a person from a different culture, s/he may feel uncertain, apprehensive, and anxious (Neuliep, 2018). Though these feelings can be stressful, they are natural responses and can be felt in most intercultural communication contexts during tourism and hospitality service encounters. It is believed that this chapter, by enabling the acquisition of knowledge and skills, is expected to reduce anxiety and stress and increase confidence and enjoyment in intercultural communication contexts.

Based on the above, this chapter explores and explains the role and potential of intercultural competencies and intercultural sensitivity of service employees from the viewpoint of their interactions both with customers and with colleagues. Intercultural competencies and intercultural sensitivity can play a significant role in terms of the adjustment and adaptation of intercultural communication abilities of staff and hence, enable the establishment of competitive advantage for tourism and hospitality businesses.

The adjustment and adaptation of interaction and communication, mimicking and mirroring

Whenever people interact with people from different cultures, they tend to base their interaction and exchange on assumptions and impressions (i.e., stereotypes) (Neuliep, 2018). The specific verbal and non-verbal messages people exchange are based on those stereotypes often framed by their own culture, race, age, sex, and occupation. People's cultures, races, ages, sexes, occupations, etc. influence how they perceive their environment. Perception can be defined as making meaning out of the sensory cues (sight, hearing, smell, taste, and touch) they select, organise, and interpret (Wolfe et al., 2006). However, the perceptions and stereotypes people make can be false. As put by forward by the maxim of Alexander Dumas "All generalisations are dangerous, including this one", stereotypes may be incorrect.

Information zone

Common perceptual mistakes people make

Perceptions people make can be wronq as how they select, organise, and interpret perceptual cues may be influenced by their culture, race, age, sex, occupation, etc. Hence, their perceptions of people, objects, and events may be biased.

The common perceptual mistakes/errors people are as follows.

Perceptual Mistake	*Explanation*	*Examples*
Stereotyping	Making positive or negative generalisations about a group or category of people, objects, or events usually based on inaccurate assumptions and beliefs and applying these generalisations to an individual object, person, or event.	Ethnocentrism, xenophobia, and xenophilia are based on stereotypes. For example, French people are ……; Chinese are ……; Germans are ……; Young people are …… .
Halo effect	Drawing a general impression of the individual based on a single characteristic.	For example, the attractiveness of a person can make people attach more credibility to her/him. As explained by Villi and Koc (2018), physically attractive people tend to receive better grades in school, are more likely to be hired as a result of job interviews, tend to be paid more when they get the job, and are much more likely to win political elections compared with their less attractive counterparts. Villi and Koc's (2018) research showed that tourism and hospitality customers gave milder responses to service failures when the service provider was attractive.
Similarity – contrast effect	People tend to favour/like or give favourable judgements to those who are similar to them. In contrast, they do not tend to favour/like or give favourable judgements to those who are different from them.	Sometimes it may work other way round. For instance, Turkish service providers tend to be more hospitable towards international tourists, especially the ones from western countries (Koc, 2006).
Projection	Projection is the tendency to attribute one's own beliefs, feelings, tendencies, motives, or needs to other people.	For instance, a supervisor who prefers taking on new responsibilities may project this tendency onto her/his employees by assigning them additional job duties without first consulting them. A manager from an individualistic and masculine

Perceptual Mistake	*Explanation*	*Examples*
		culture may find it difficult to understand why her/his employees (from collectivistic and feminine cultures) do not take imitative easily and are not so comfortable with empowerment (Magnini et al., 2013).

It should also be noted that developing intercultural competence does not mean that people surrender their culture's values, beliefs, and behaviours (Neuliep, 2018). In other words, cultures can be criticised when something is wrong. For instance, any form of discrimination people (e.g., women and race) should not be accepted. To some extent everyone is ethnocentric. Ethnocentrism[1] can be defined as the act of judging people, objects, and events based on their own cultural values and standards, especially with regards to language, behaviour, customs, and religion. Developing intercultural competence begins by recognising (becoming aware) that the individual does stereotype, and then managing it (Neuliep, 2018) by adjusting and adapting her/his various behaviours, including verbal and non-verbal communication.

CASE STUDY

Intercultural sensitivity, masculinity, and femininity in bonobo monkeys

Tan et al.'s (2017) research showed that bonobo monkeys (*Pan paniscus*) showed prosocial and xenophilic responses towards unfamiliar (non-group member) monkeys. Xenophily or xenophilia means affection towards unknown/foreign objects or people. It is the opposite of xenophobia, which is the dislike of or prejudice against people unknown/foreign objects or people. Bonobo monkeys behave in a hospitable manner and share their food with strangers. The bonobo monkeys' behaviours contrast with that of the chimpanzees, their more aggressive counterparts. Due to their female-clan bonding, bonobo monkeys allow strange bonobos to wander into their camp freely, instead of killing them and eating them, as the male-dominant-ranking baboons would do.

In Tan et al.'s (2017) research, bonobo monkeys voluntarily helped an unfamiliar, non-group member (with different cultural characteristics and behaviour) in obtaining food even when he/she did not make overt requests for help. Additionally, bonobo monkeys involuntarily yawned in response to videos of yawning monkeys who were complete strangers.

While male-dominant-ranking "pecking orders" (bullying) are maintained in other monkey groups and in humans, female-clan bonding social networks (or matrifocal societies) are maintained by pleasure sharing and nurturing in bonobo clans. Bonobos engage in mutual grooming, sharing and affection, food gifts or "food-offerings", and petting-soothing and consensual sex (de Waal, 1995).

Adjustment and adaptation

Human beings are not objective processors of information (Neuliep, 2018). They tend to be biased in processing the information they receive through their five senses. Hence, in most situations, depending on their interactional abilities, people need to adjust and adapt their communication according to the context and various characteristics of people with whom they interact. A lack of adjustment and adaptation may lead to failures and even crises in communication with others. For instance, when people interact with their spouse, children, subordinates, superiors, people they know and do not know, they use different verbal and non-verbal communication elements and patterns. People need to adjust and adapt their verbal and non-verbal communication even when they interact with people from the same culture, a culture that they may be fairly accustomed with. This is because the adjustment and adapting of verbal and non-verbal communication increases the feeling of resemblance, similarity, commonness and mutuality, and hence, familiarity.

The establishment of a feeling of familiarity increases trust and liking (Westerman et al., 2015) by reducing the risk and threat unfamiliar people and contexts may present. Faraji-Rad et al. (2015), who studied the influence of stereotyping on persuasion in consumption, found that similarity (as opposed to contrast) increased liking and persuasion. In another interesting piece of research in the United States, Jones et al. (2004) showed that people were significantly more likely to marry people whose first or last names resembled their own. Pelham et al. (2003) observed similar findings in a dozen systematic studies that investigated the above relationship in terms of names, initials, birthday numbers, towns of birth, etc. Research studies such as Pelham et al. (2003), Jones et al. (2004) and Westerman et al. (2015) show the importance of resemblance and familiarity, as a bias or anchor, in increasing liking and trust by reducing risk and threat, driven by the survival motive. According to Navarrete et al. (2007) women tend to be uncomfortable with strangers and avoid encountering strangers in the first twelve weeks of their pregnancy, that is, when the probability of fetus catching a disease is higher. People are more likely to develop rapport and social relationships with people with whom they are familiar and have something in common. The concept of the mere exposure effect is also in parallel with the previous explanations regarding the increase in positive affect that results from repeated exposure (i.e., thorough becoming familiar) to previously novel stimuli (Inoue et al., 2018).

From an anthropological perspective, people form social relationships with other people with the instinct to survive and prosper (Harari, 2016; Erber and Erber, 2017). Even, primitive human beings knew by instinct that they cannot survive on their own and needed to establish relationships with others. Holt-Lunstad et al.'s (2015) work showed that loneliness and social isolation as important risk factors for mortality even in today's modern world. Moreover, due to the survival need, risky and threatening situations increase people's liking and romantic attraction for the opposite sex and attenuate reproductive behaviours (Dutton and Aron, 1974; Finke et al., 2018).

Mimicry and mirroring

Mimicry, as a form of establishing similarity and familiarity, can be defined as "doing what others are doing", a conscious or unconscious tendency to imitate behaviours, speech patterns, words, gestures, facial expressions, etc. (Stel et al., 2008). Mimicry, also referred to as the "Chameleon effect" (Chartrand and Bargh 1999), facilitates bonding, trust, and positive emotions between people (Lakin et al., 2003; Van Baaren et al., 2003; Stel et al., 2008). Other research studies also show that mimicry relates to rapport, liking, interpersonal closeness, felt similarity towards others, and smoothness of the interaction (e.g., Bernieri and Rosenthal, 1991; Bailenson and Yee, 2005; Stel et al., 2008). Mimicking tends to fulfil people's need to form and maintain stable relationships with other people (Baumeister and Leary, 1995; Stel et al., 2008; Ashton-James and Chartrand, 2009; MacKenzie and Baumeister, 2019).

Additionally, mimicry appears to play an important role in emotional contagion. Emotional contagion refers to the idea that people are likely to personally experience the various perceived emotions of others (Hatfield et al., 1992). According to Cakici and Guler (2017), emotional contagion influences both customers and employees in tourism and hospitality settings. Mimicry can be seen as an important facilitator of emotional contagion (Stel et al., 2008). Thus, emotional contagion can be thought of as an affective form of empathy (Hoffman, 1984; Olszanowski et al., 2019).

Being mimicked on the part of the mimickee establishes feelings of rapport, affiliation, and closeness towards the mimicker (i.e., prosocial emotions; (Lakin et al. 2003; Tanner et al., 2007) and has been shown to create feelings of helpfulness towards others; in other words, prosocial behavior (van Baaren et al. 2003; Stel et al., 2008). Empathy, reliability, responsiveness, and assurance, as the four service quality dimensions, relate to helpfulness and helping behaviour. Likewise, empathy has been shown as the key enabler of helping behaviour (Oswald, 2002; Stel et al., 2008).

As a similar concept in interpersonal communication *mirroring* can be defined as a reflection of one's behaviour, thinking, and traits according to the context and people (Friedman, 2016). Mirroring results in the obtaining of individual recognition, appreciation, esteem, and admiration from the people with whom the individual interacts (Friedman, 2016). However, as in the case of surface acting in emotional labour (Koc, 2017), any fake attempts of mimicry and mirroring may result in the development of negative attitudes in communication.

Information zone

Emotional labour

Koc (2017) emphasised the importance of emotional labour in tourism and hospitality service encounters. In service encounters, employees try to use the words, mimics, and body language to exude the positive emotions expected from them. According to Hochschild (1983), jobs which involve emotional labour are the jobs that*:

- require face-to-face or voice-to-voice contact with the customers;
- require the employee to produce an emotional state in another person (e.g., the customer);
- allow the service managers, through training and supervision, to exercise a degree of control over the emotional activities of employees.

The dimensions of emotional labour are deep acting and surface acting (Hochschild, 1983; Diefendorff et al., 2005). When service employees engage in deep acting, they try to feel the emotions, reflected by their verbal and non-verbal communication, that they are expected to feel and internalise the emotions due to the role expectations. On the other hand, surface acting is the act of service employees hiding their real feelings and showing different emotional exhibitions towards others in the business. On the part of the employees, this dissonance, not only results in emotional exhaustion and a decrease in job satisfaction, but also eventually leads to employee burnout (Wiens, 2016), while causing negative feelings on the part of the customers (Koc, 2017).

* Tourism and hospitality jobs significantly fit the above criteria.

Emotions developed during tourism and hospitality service encounters

The emotions people develop during service encounters can be explained with reference to the Similarity-Attraction Theory (Byrne, 1971), the Social Identity Theory (Tajfel, 1974), and the Role Theory (Biddle, 1986; Yurur et al., 2020).

Similarity-Attraction Theory

According to the Similarity-Attraction Theory, people tend to be more attracted to other people who are similar to themselves (Byrne, 1971; Sharma et al., 2009). As explained above, as people, in general, tend to perceive people who are similar to themselves positively (Koc, 2016), they are more likely to be attracted to other people who are similar to themselves. Interpersonal interactions such as marriages, friendships, etc. more often tend to occur among people who are similar demographically, culturally, and attitudinally (Yurur et al., 2020).

Social Identity Theory

The Social Identity Theory is based on the psychological concept of intergroup discrimination (Yurur et al., 2020). People who are members of a group (i.e., people from a specific culture) may be biased (see the concept of ethnocentrism mentioned previously) to discriminate in favour of the in-group (e.g., people from their own culture) with which they associate themselves and against another out-group (e.g., people from other cultures). People may be in a position to base their in-group/out-group categorisation on cues relating to cultural differences (Brickson, 2000; Hopkins et al., 2005). Service personnel and customers may use identity cues such as physical characteristics, accent, verbal, and non-verbal behaviours to understand whether the person they interact with are from the same cultural group or not (Hopkins et al., 2005; Kim et al., 2010; Yurur et al., 2020). The categorisation of people into an in-group may intensify the perceived differences, and result in the favouring of in-group members, and disfavouring outgroup members (Sharma et al., 2009; Tajfel et al., 1971; Yurur et al., 2020). For instance, Yurur et al. (2020) proposed that despite its various disadvantages, all-inclusive holidays may result in fewer conflicts in intercultural interactions, as these types of holidays may reduce the number and intensity of social interactions with locals (Koc, 2006). For instance, all-inclusive holidays may reduce the frequency of unpleasant incidences such as the cheating and swindling of tourism and hospitality customers by local service providers such as taxi drivers or local restaurants (Koc, 2007).

Role Theory

According to the role theory, people tend to behave in ways that are often different and predictable depending on their specific social identities and the nature of the context they are in (Biddle, 1986; Yurur et al., 2020).

The role theory has been applied to explore and explain the dyadic interaction between service employees and customers in service encounters (Solomon et al., 1985). The specific cultural orientations of customers and service personnel intensify the complexity of service encounters and service interactions. Service personnel and customers with different cultural backgrounds tend to have different expectations (Koc, 2016). As explained in various chapters of this book, tourism and hospitality customers from different cultures may evaluate the same service differently (Koc, 2013).

Differences in cultural backgrounds may cause a variety of misunderstandings, dissatisfactions, and frustrations on the part of both customers and service personnel (Koc, 2013; Kim et al., 2010; Yurur et al., 2020). When people interact during a service interaction, they may not be aware of the modelled roles and expectations. Hence, service encounters may cause tension, frustration, and dissatisfaction for both parties (Stauss, 2016). However, when people interact in a service encounter and are aware of their roles (e.g., service personnel being aware of their roles), and the expectations of the others (e.g., service personnel being aware of the expectations of customers), then service encounters will more likely produce the desired outcomes (Khan et al., 2016; Stauss, 2016). This means that cultural sensitivity relates significantly to all services marketing mix elements, service quality dimensions and most behaviours (e.g., employees' service orientations), and the attitudes of service personnel (Yurur et al., 2020).

Intercultural competency, intercultural sensitivity and cultural intelligence

Activity

Intercultural Communication Competence Scale

Before you read this section on intercultural competence, first you are recommended to test your current level of intercultural communication abilities. Please complete the Intercultural Communication Competence Scale in this Activity box.

Important Note: Throughout the book, there are a number of self-report scales/tests like the following one. Please save your personal test score records (especially the ones relating to cultural awareness, cultural competence, ethnocentrism, cultural intelligence, etc.) to make comparisons later. After studying the whole book, you are advised to go back and redo all these tests once more. By doing this you can compare your scores with the ones you had earlier on. This should enable you to see the changes taking place as a result of the learning experience.

The Intercultural Communication Competence Scale Instructions

Please read the statements below and indicate how much each statement describes you when you interact with people from other cultures by assigning a value, in the blank section on the left of each statement, from 1 to 5 as follows:

(5) strongly agree (4) agree (3) neutral (2) disagree (1) strongly disagree

Please keep in mind that there is no right or wrong response for each statement. In order to avoid biased responses, you are recommended to record your initial response without elaborating too much on the statements.

______ **1.** I often find it difficult to differentiate between similar cultures (e.g., Europeans, Asians, Asians, Africans).

______ **2.** I feel a sense of belonging to a group of people based on relationships (i.e., family, friends) instead of cultural identity (i.e., people from my own culture, people from other cultures).

______ **3.** I often find it easier to categorise people based on their cultural identity than their personality.

______ **4.** I often notice similarities in personality between people who belong to completely different cultures.

______ **5.** If I were to put people in groups, I would group them by their culture rather than by their personality.

______ **6.** I feel that people from other cultures have many valuable things to learn from them.

_____ **7.** I feel more comfortable with people from my own culture than with people from other cultures.
_____ **8.** I feel closer to people with whom I have a good relationship, regardless of whether they belong to my culture or not.
_____ **9.** I usually feel closer to people who are from my own culture because I can relate to them better.
_____ **10.** I feel more comfortable with people who are open to people from other cultures than with people who are not.
_____ **11.** Most of my close friends are from other cultures.
_____ **12.** I usually change the way I communicate depending on whom I am communicating with.
_____ **13.** When I interact with someone from a different culture, I usually try to adopt some of her or his ways.
_____ **14.** Most of my friends are from my own culture.
_____ **15.** I usually look for opportunities to interact with people from other cultures.
_____ **YOUR TOTAL SCORE (Please adjust your initial scores as follows).**

Scoring: Please reverse your responses for items 1, 2, 7, 8, 9, and 14. For these six items, if your original response was a 5, reverse it to a 1; if your original score was a 4, reverse it to a 2; if your original score was a 3, leave it a 3; if your original score was a 2, reverse it to a 4; and if your original score was a 1, reverse it to a 5. After reversing your scores for these items, sum all 15 items. The total score should be between the range of 15 and 75.

Higher scores (above 55) mean a higher intercultural communication competence. Lower scores (below 35) indicate lower intercultural communication competence.

Source: Arasaratnam (2009).

Intercultural competency

Based on the previous explanations, it may be stated that intercultural competency and sensitivity, as important skills in intercultural communication, require mimicry and mirroring to form rapport, affiliation, and closeness (in other words, prosocial emotions; Lakin et al., 2003; Tanner et al., 2007), and has been shown to engender helping towards others (in other words, prosocial behaviour; van Baaren et al., 2003). Helpful or prosocial behaviours may form the basis of customers' expectations relating to service quality dimensions of empathy, reliability, responsiveness, and assurance. Mimicry, mirroring, and intercultural sensitivity can be thought to have positive implications not only for service employees' relationships with customers but also for employee-to-employee communications and employee-to-manager communications.

As explained in Chapter 1, due to the inseparable nature of tourism and hospitality services, and the fact that frequency and intensity of social exchange and interaction are high, the quality of social exchange and interaction is very influential on service quality perceptions of customers (Koc, 2017). In intercultural tourism and hospitality service encounters, that is, with customers, service employees and managers from different cultural backgrounds, there may be incongruencies and incompatibilities, causing conflicts in customer-to-service personnel interactions, as well as in service personnel-to-service personnel interactions (Koc, 2010; Cushner and Chang, 2015; Weber et al., 2016).

Therefore, the service employees and managers with intercultural competencies may form rapport and trust in their dealings by adjusting their behaviours. This, in turn, may increase customer satisfaction and help establish competitive advantage for the tourism and hospitality business. Noja et al. (2018) emphasise the role of intercultural abilities in cross-cultural adjustment and employability in today's multicultural work environments.

Intercultural competence can be defined as the ability of an individual to communicate effectively in cross-cultural situations and to relate appropriately in a variety of cultural contexts (Bennett and Bennett, 2004). Intercultural competence increases customer satisfaction and reliability (Baum and Deviine, 2008; Sharma et al., 2009). Sharma et al.'s (2018) findings show that while perceived cultural distance has a strong negative influence on inter-role congruence and interaction comfort, intercultural competence moderates the influence of perceived cultural distance on interaction comfort and inter-role congruence, and increases service quality perceptions.

The Intercultural Competence Model developed by Neuliep (2018) (see Figure 3.1) shows the four components of intercultural competence as knowledge, affective features, contextual/situational characteristics, and psychomotor features.

Knowledge component

The knowledge component (Figure 3.1) comprises *the knowledge of cultural norms, values, beliefs and behaviours, verbal and non-verbal scripts, cognitive simplicity-rigidity,* and *ethnocentrism*. The *knowledge* component of intercultural competence is about the extent to which a person knows about the culture of the person with whom s/he interacts (Neuliep, 2018). Although it is not fully guaranteed, if an individual has knowledge of other cultures, s/he can be considered as culturally competent to the extent to which s/he has knowledge of other cultures. Cultural awareness can be tested through thc Cross-Cultural Self-Awareness Test (see following Activity box) developed by Goodman (1994) (loosely adapted by Neuliep, 2018).

Activity

Cross-cultural awareness test

Instructions: The scale consists of 15 items relating to what you know or do not know about other cultures.

For each statement please indicate your response by assigning a value from 1 to 5; 1 = definitely no, 2 = not likely, 3 = not sure, 4 = likely, and 5 = definitely yes. Try to be as objective and truthful possible as and possible.

_____ **1.** I can accurately list three countries that are considered collectivistic.

_____ **2.** I can accurately identify three countries that have large power distance.
_____ **3.** I can conduct business in a language other than my own.
_____ **4.** I know the appropriate distance at which to stand when interacting with people in at least two other cultures.
_____ **5.** I know the appropriate touch rules in at least two other cultures.
_____ **6.** I know in what countries I can use first names when conducting business.
_____ **7.** I can name the (political/governmental) leaders of four other countries.
_____ **8.** I understand and can practice appropriate gift-giving in three other countries.
_____ **9.** I can identify some gestures appropriate in my culture that are considered obscene in other countries.
_____ **10.** I understand sex-role differences in at least two other countries.
_____ **11.** I can name three countries that are considered polychronic.
_____ **12.** I understand the proper protocol for exchanging business cards in at least two other countries.
_____ **13.** I understand the business philosophies of at least two other countries.
_____ **14.** I can name my country's top three trading partners.
_____ **15.** I can name the currencies in four other countries.
_____ **YOUR TOTAL SCORE**

Scoring: Your scores which should range between 15 and 75 to show the extent to which you are aware of other cultures. Scores 50 and above show a relatively good degree of cultural awareness.

Source: This scale is a loosely adapted version of the scale loosely adapted by Neuliep (2008) of the original scale developed by Goodman (1994).

For someone to be considered as having *knowledge of cultural norms, values, beliefs*, and *behaviours*, s/he is expected to have a certain degree of comprehension of other person's distinct cultural values and beliefs (Neuliep, 2018). Additionally, the individual is expected to know whether the other person is from an individualistic or collectivistic, high- or low-context, high- or low-power distance, and high- or low-uncertainty avoidance culture, that is, the cultural dimensions explained throughout this book.

In terms of the *verbal and non-verbal scripts* (see Figure 3.1) it could be stated that interculturally knowledgeable communicators tend to develop and maintain a repertoire of scripts that enable them to interact efficiently in intercultural communications, as both senders and receivers of messages (Berger and Jordan, 1992; Neuliep, 2018). Verbal and non-verbal scripts (plans or patterns of thoughts) guide individuals when they communicate (Berger, 1992). When people interact with someone from a different culture, they tend to search their long-term memory for similar experiences and the

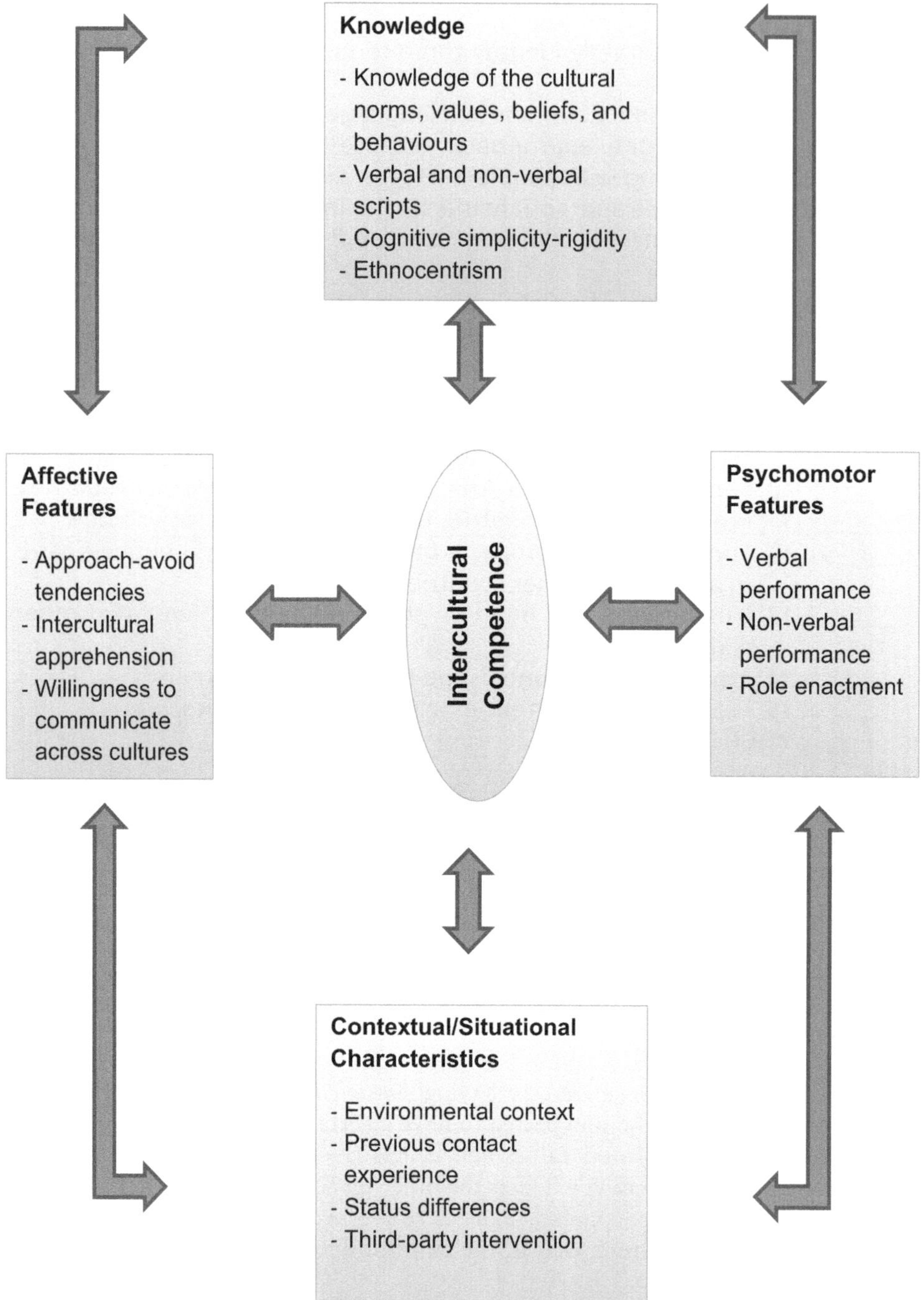

Figure 3.1 Model of intercultural competence. Loosely adapted from Neuliep (2018)

patterns of behaviour and communication they had in the past (Berger and Jordan, 1992; Neuliep, 2018).

Cognitive simplicity and rigidity (see Figure 3.1) refer to the extent to which a person would process information relating to other cultures in a more simplistic and rigid manner (Neuliep, 2018). According to Kim (1990), people with simplistic and rigid cognitive systems tend to develop more narrowly defined and inflexible categories, and be more dogmatic (i.e., narrow-minded), make more negative judgements, and are more likely to make more confident judgements about other people and engage in gross stereotyping (Kim, 1990; Neuliep, 2018). People with simple and rigid cognitive systems are more likely to have poor intercultural competence skills. Interculturally competent communicators are expected to possess an open and flexible cognitive system.

As classification and categorisation systems such as stereotyping are often resorted to by people to be used as uncertainty and ambiguity reduction strategies (Kramer, 1999; Allen et al., 2001), people from high-uncertainty avoidance cultures (see Chapter 7) may be more likely to engage in stereotyping, that is, may be more likely to have a simplistic and rigid cognitive systems. Hence, further research may investigate whether people from high-uncertainty avoidance cultures would have less intercultural competence.

As explained in Chapter 2, *ethnocentrism* is about the degree to which an individual perceives her/his own group (e.g., her/his culture) as the centre of everything and judges other groups (e.g., other cultures) with reference to it (Neuliep, 2018). Ethnocentric people are likely to establish and reinforce negative attitudes and behaviours towards people from other groups (i.e., cultures). Ethnocentric people view themselves as righteous and exceptional and tend to perceive their own standards as universal and moral. Ethnocentric people view people from other groups (i.e., cultures) as immoral, subordinate, and impotent (Neuliep, 2018). As ethnocentrics have narrow categories and simple and rigid cognitive systems, they are more likely to lack intercultural competence. Hewstone and Ward (1985) and Wiseman et al. (1989) see the level of ethnocentrism as one of the most significant predictors of the level of cultural understanding (i.e., intercultural competence and intercultural sensitivity).

The affective component

The affective component (Figure 3.1) comprises the approach-avoid tendencies, intercultural apprehension and cognitive simplicity-rigidity, and willingness to communicate. The affective component of intercultural communication is about the extent to which an individual *approaches* or *avoids* intercultural communication, that is, her/his level of motivation to engage in intercultural communication (Neuliep, 2018).

An important determinant of intercultural communication is intercultural apprehension, which is the fear or anxiety which may be associated with either real or potential interactions with people from other cultures (Neuliep, 2018). People with a high level of intercultural apprehension may avoid interacting with people from other cultures (Neuliep, 2018). The Intercultural Communication Apprehension scale developed by Neuliep and McCroskey (1997) can be used as an effective tool to assess the extent to which an individual has an apprehension of intercultural communication.

Activity

Intercultural communication apprehension test

Instructions: This scale comprises 14 statements relating to your feelings about communicating with people from other cultures. Please read the statements below and indicate how much each statement describes you when you interact with people from other cultures by assigning a value, in the blank section on the left of each statement, from 1 to 5 as follows:

(5) strongly agree (4) agree (3) neutral (2) disagree (1) strongly disagree

Please keep in mind that there is no right or wrong response for each statement. In order to avoid biased responses, you are recommended to record your initial response without elaborating too much on the statements.

______ **1.** Generally, I am comfortable interacting with a group of people from different cultures.

______ **2.** I am tense and nervous while interacting in group discussions with people from different cultures.

______ **3.** I like to get involved in discussions with other people from different cultures.

______ 4. Engaging in a discussion with people from different cultures makes me tense and nervous.

______ **5.** I am calm and relaxed when interacting with a group of people who are from different cultures.

______ **6.** While participating in a conversation with a person from a different culture, I feel very nervous.

______ **7.** I have no fear of speaking up in a conversation with a person from a different culture.

______ **8.** Usually, I am very tense and nervous in conversations with a person from a different culture.

______ **9.** Usually, I am very calm and relaxed in conversations with a person from a different culture.

______ **10.** While conversing with a person from a different culture, I feel very relaxed.

______ **11.** I am afraid to speak up in conversations with a person from a different culture.

______ **12.** I view the anticipated interaction with people from different cultures with confidence.

______ **13.** My thoughts become confused and tangled when interacting with people from different cultures.

______ **14.** Communicating with people from different cultures makes me feel uncomfortable.

______ **YOUR TOTAL SCORE**

Scoring: Please reverse your responses for Items 2, 4, 6, 8, 11, 13, and 14. For these questions items, if your original response was a 5, reverse it to a 1; if your original score was a 4, reverse it to a 2; if your original score was a 3, leave it a 3; if your original score was a 2, reverse it to a 4; and if your original score was a 1, reverse it to a 5. After reversing your scores for these items, sum all 14 items. The total score should be between the range of 14 and 77.

Higher scores (e.g., between 50 and 70) mean a higher intercultural communication apprehension. Lower scores (e.g., between 14 and 28) indicate lower intercultural communication apprehension.

SOURCE: Loosely adapted from Neuliep and McCroskey (1997). Used with permission given by the author (James W. Neuliep).

Apart from intercultural communication apprehension, people may have social anxiety and avoidance which can cause them to refrain not only from intercultural communication in particular but also from any type of social interaction.

Social anxiety, sometimes referred to as social phobia, is the discomfort or fear of being judged or evaluated negatively by others (Liebowitz et al., 1985). People who have a high level of social anxiety tend to have an intense fear (fear of embarrassment or humiliation, criticism, or rejection) of what others think about them (Liebowitz et al., 1985; Kashdan et al., 2013; Koc, 2018). People with a social anxiety disorder are likely to demonstrate social avoidance behaviour by avoiding people, places, and unfamiliar situations, in fact, almost all social interactions (Cisler et al., 2010). By using Liebowitz et al.'s (1985) social anxiety and social avoidance scales, Koc (2018) found that significant proportion of students studying tourism and hospitality at Turkish universities had social anxiety and social avoidance. This means that tourism and hospitality programme managers at Turkish universities need to evaluate their syllabi to reduce social anxiety and social avoidance among their students and increase their social and interpersonal skills. Moreover, they need to recruit students without social anxiety and avoidance. To develop intercultural competence, people first need to have basic interpersonal and interactional skills.

Exercise

To test your level of social anxiety (fear) and avoidance please do Liebowitz et al.'s (1985) test provided in the following URL.
https://nationalsocialanxietycenter.com/liebowitz-sa-scale/

Some people may be more positively disposed, that is, willing to initiate and engage in, intercultural communication, while some others may not be positively disposed, that is, unwilling to initiate and engage in intercultural communication with others. On the other hand, some people may be positively predisposed to initiate intercultural interactions even when they are completely free to choose whether or not to communicate. This predisposition, labelled by Jeffrey Kassing, is called intercultural willingness to communicate (Kassing, 1997).

Exercise

To test your willingness to engage in intercultural communication, first, find the paper by Kassing (1997; details provided below) through a basic Google Scholar search and complete the Intercultural Willingness to Communicate Test published in this paper. Also, ask your colleagues from different cultures to fill in the test and compare your scores. Discuss whether the differences may be attributed largely to cultural factors or whether other factors such as personality, education, and upbringing may be influential.

Kassing, J. W. (1997). Development of the Intercultural Willingness to Communicate Scale. *Communication Research Reports*, 14, 399–407.

Psychomotor features

The psychomotor features component comprises (Figure 3.1) the *verbal* and *non-verbal performance* and the *role enactment*. *Verbal performance* is about how people use language based on their linguistic knowledge and abilities (Neuliep, 2018). Non-verbal performance is the extent to which a person has the ability and willingness to pay close attention to nuances of the kinesic (gestures, body position, head, posture, hand, and arm movements) paralinguistic (vocalics – pitch, tone, rate, volume, intensity, and accent pattern in verbal communication), haptic (touch), olfactic (smell), and proxemic (use of space) codes of the other cultures (Neuliep, 2018). While touching, in general, can be perceived as a positive thing when communicating in certain countries such as France (Guéguen, 2007), it may not be the case in certain other cultures.

Koc's (2020) study showed that women tend to have higher levels of emotional intelligence and may have a higher level of intercultural competence when given the opportunity. Irimias and Franch (2019), Rivera (2019), Wilson-Wünsch and Decosta (2019), and Koc and Boz (2020) proposed that there may be a strong relationship between emotional intelligence and cultural sensitivity. Koc's (2020) study which related service quality dimensions and customer satisfaction to gender characteristics, proposed that female employees, managers, and entrepreneurs may perform better than men in tourism and hospitality businesses.

Exercise

Visit the Cultural Atlas Webpages (https://culturalatlas.sbs.com.au/) as you did when you read Chapter 1. This time find out about the kinesic, paralinguistic, haptic, olfactic, and proxemic codes present in other cultures (by determining three different countries). Explain how some of these codes may be perceived as strange or even rude in your country.

Role enactment is to do with the extent to which individuals can execute verbal and non-verbal messages according to their gender, position and role when interacting with people from other cultures (Gudykunst and Kim, 1991; Neuliep, 2018).

Contextual/Situational characteristics

The contextual/situational characteristics component comprises (Figure 3.1) *environmental context*, *previous contact experience*, *status differences*, and *third-party intervention*. It should be kept in mind that while one person may be considered as interculturally competent in one context/situation, in another s/he may not be considered as such. Previous contact experience increases cultural competence abilities and may help an individual to develop skills (Neuliep, 2018). Yurur et al.'s (2020) study found that there was a significant relationship between the level of Turkish hospitality employees' intercultural sensitivity and a) spending time abroad through study abroad or student exchange programs (e.g., ERASMUS and work and travel programmes) when they were students, b) spending long periods of time on business vacations, and c) previous experience of serving international customers. Yurur et al.'s (2020) study also showed that tourism and hospitality education at Turkish universities had no influence on tourism and hospitality employees' level of intercultural sensitivity as tourism and hospitality employees who graduated from tourism and hospitality programmes at Turkish universities performed poorly in intercultural sensitivity. This means that, in addition to the recommendations mentioned previously regarding social anxiety and social avoidance, Turkish tourism and hospitality programme managers need to re-design their syllabi and student recruitment processes to make sure that their graduates have a higher level of intercultural sensitivity.

The ability to adjust and adapt verbal and non-verbal communication according to the status of the other person with whom an individual interacts from a different culture is an important skill in intercultural communication. The third-party intervention in the form of someone of different status or gender may require individuals to make adaptations and adjustments in their interaction with people from different cultures (Neuliep, 2018).

Intercultural sensitivity

As a prerequisite of intercultural competence (Chen and Starosta, 2000), intercultural sensitivity can be defined as the ability of an individual to notice and experience cultural differences and the sensitivity to the importance of cultural differences, and to the points of view of people in other cultures (Wang and Zhou, 2016). Research shows that the performance of interculturally sensitive employees is higher than those who are not interculturally sensitive (Sizoo et al., 2003; Sizoo, 2008). There is plenty of research supporting the idea that interculturally sensitive employees tend to provide better service to customers (Sizoo et al., 2003; Sizoo, 2008; Khan et al., 2016; Sharma et al., 2015; Stauss, 2016). This is attributable to the fact that service employees with higher intercultural sensitivity are able to adapt more rapidly and be more able to deal and cope with customers from different cultures (Peng and Wu, 2016). The importance of the adjustment and adaptation of verbal and non-verbal communication was outlined previous in explanation on the concepts of mimicry and mirroring.

Service quality perceptions of a tourism and hospitality business can be increased by recruiting staff with higher intercultural sensitivity and improving intercultural sensitivity levels of current staff (Yurur et al., 2020). As a skill, intercultural sensitivity can be measured, learned, and developed (Cusher and Chang, 2015). In addition to various positive influences mentioned previously, service staff with high intercultural sensitivity scores also tend to score significantly higher on a number of other service measures such as service attentiveness, revenue contribution, interpersonal skills, job satisfaction, and social satisfaction as they relate to cross-cultural encounters (Sizoo, 2008; Sizoo et al., 2003; Yurur et al., 2020). While attentiveness may relate to responsiveness, empathy, reliability, and assurance, interpersonal skills may relate empathy and reliability in the SERVQUAL model (Yurur et al., 2020). Ihtiyar et al. (2013) showed that intercultural sensitivity had a significant influence on customers' service quality evaluations and their overall satisfaction with the service. Additionally, intercultural sensitivity reduces the level of ethnocentrism and communication apprehension among employees (Chen, 2010). As explained previously, and in Chapter I, the ethnocentricity of Disney management resulted in major losses for the company when they opened up Euro Disney, Paris.

In tourism and hospitality service encounters, although cultural differences may be present in physical environments (tangibles – both as an element of the services marketing mix and as a service quality dimension), service personnel, service systems, and various factors relating to other customers, individual behaviours of service personnel may be significantly more influential in the determination of overall quality evaluations of customers (Reisinger and Turner, 2002; Koc, 2006).

Activity

Intercultural Sensitivity Scale

Instructions: This scale comprises 24 statements relating to your feelings about interacting with people from other cultures. Please read the statements below and indicate how much each statement describes you when you interact with people from other cultures by assigning a value, in the blank section on the left of each statement, from 1 to 5 as follows:

(5) strongly agree (4) agree (3) neutral (2) disagree (1) strongly disagree

Please keep in mind that there is no right or wrong response for each statement. In order to avoid biased responses, you are recommended to record your initial response without elaborating too much on the statements.

______ **1.** I enjoy interacting with people from different cultures.
______ **2.** I think people from other cultures are narrow-minded.
______ **3.** I am pretty sure of myself in interacting with people from different cultures.
______ **4.** I find it very hard to talk in front of people from different cultures.
______ **5.** I always know what to say when interacting with people from different cultures.
______ **6.** I can be as sociable as I want to be when interacting with people from different cultures.
______ **7.** I don't like to be with people from different cultures.
______ **8.** I respect the values of people from different cultures.
______ **9.** I get upset easily when interacting with people from different cultures.
______ **10.** I feel confident when interacting with people from different cultures.

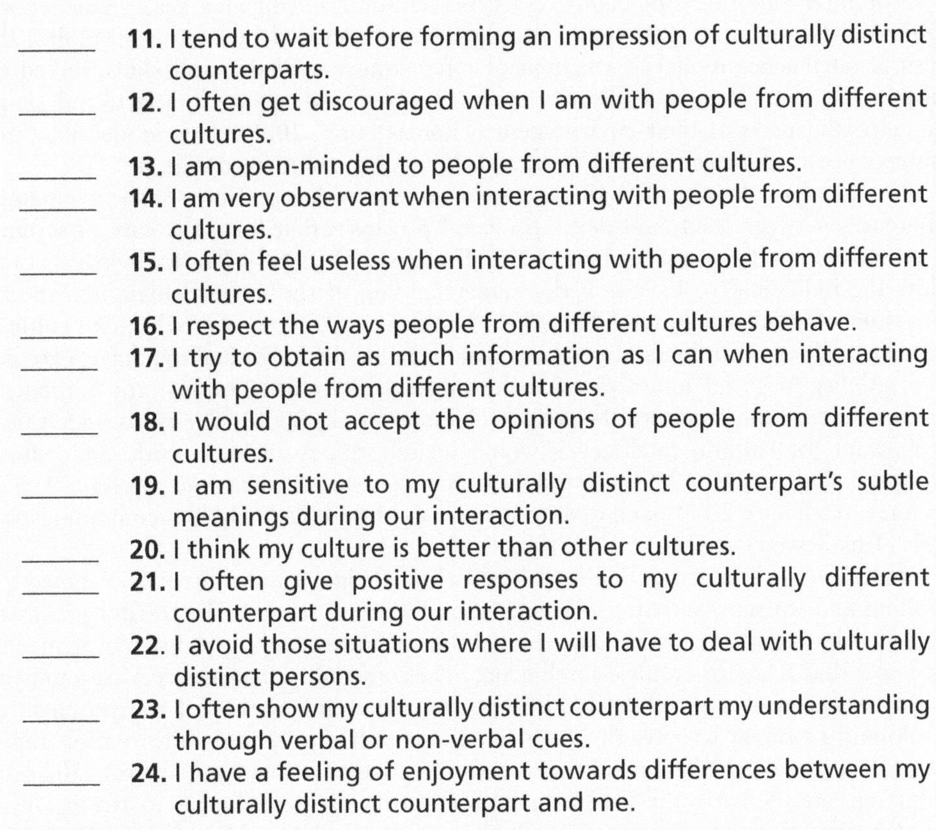

______ **11.** I tend to wait before forming an impression of culturally distinct counterparts.

______ **12.** I often get discouraged when I am with people from different cultures.

______ **13.** I am open-minded to people from different cultures.

______ **14.** I am very observant when interacting with people from different cultures.

______ **15.** I often feel useless when interacting with people from different cultures.

______ **16.** I respect the ways people from different cultures behave.

______ **17.** I try to obtain as much information as I can when interacting with people from different cultures.

______ **18.** I would not accept the opinions of people from different cultures.

______ **19.** I am sensitive to my culturally distinct counterpart's subtle meanings during our interaction.

______ **20.** I think my culture is better than other cultures.

______ **21.** I often give positive responses to my culturally different counterpart during our interaction.

______ **22.** I avoid those situations where I will have to deal with culturally distinct persons.

______ **23.** I often show my culturally distinct counterpart my understanding through verbal or non-verbal cues.

______ **24.** I have a feeling of enjoyment towards differences between my culturally distinct counterpart and me.

Scoring: Please reverse your responses for Items 2, 4, 7, 9, 12, 15, 18, 20, and 22. For these questions items, if your original response was a 5, reverse it to a 1; if your original score was a 4, reverse it to a 2; if your original score was a 3, leave it a 3; if your original score was a 2, reverse it to a 4; and if your original score was a 1, reverse it to a 5. After reversing your scores for these items, sum all 14 items. The total score should be between the range of 24 and 120. Higher scores (e.g., between 90 and120) mean a higher level of intercultural sensitivity, while lower scores (e.g., between 24 and48) indicate a lower level of intercultural sensitivity.

Dimension	*Items*	*Dimension*	*Items*
Interaction Engagement	1, 11, 13, 21, 22, 23, and 24	*Interaction Enjoyment*	9, 12, and 15
Respect for Cultural Differences	2, 7, 8, 16, 18, and 20	*Interaction Attentiveness*	14, 17, and 19
Interaction Confidence	3, 4, 5, 6, and 10		

Source: Chen and Starosta (2000).

As a final cultural competence construct cultural intelligence scale (Ang et al., 2007; Van Dayne et al., 2015) can be explained. Developed by Ang et al. (2007) the cultural intelligence model is a system of interacting knowledge and skills, linked by cultural metacognition, that allows people to adjust and adapt to, select, and shape the cultural aspects of their environment (Thomas et al., 2008). This model has three components (or dimensions) such as knowledge, skills, and metacognition.

Through *knowledge,* individuals can recognise other cultures and distinguish differences between them and develop mental processes that form the core of systems definitions of intelligence (Sternberg, 1997; Thomas et al., 2008). This knowledge would allow the individual to have a better understanding of the internal logic and modal behaviour of another culture (Adler, 1997; Thomas et al., 2008). Knowledge of cultural identities, values, attitudes, and practices would enable the individual to a have a greater predictability of social interactions, make more accurate attributions, and ultimately be more effective intercultural behaviour (Thomas et al., 2008). The *skills* which may be relevant for cultural intelligence would include things such as world-mindedness (Sampson and Smith, 1957), personality characteristics (Costa and McRae, 1992), openness (Caligiuri, 2000), and a wide variety of other skills, including communication skills (Ting-Toomey, 1999).

Finally, *cultural metacognition* is to do with knowledge of and control over someone's thinking and learning activities (Flavel, 1979; Swanson, 1990). The mental processes suggested by Sternberg (1985) may be helpful in understanding the scope of mental processes that relate to cultural intelligence. These mental processes are a) recognising of the existence of a problem, b) defining the scope and nature of the problem, c) developing a strategy to solve the problem, d) mentally representing information about the problem, e) allocating mental resources (e.g., concentrating, comparing, evaluating, deducting, etc.) solving the problem, f) monitoring of the solution to the problem through time, and g) evaluating individual's solution to the problem (Sternberg, 1985; Thomas et al., 2008).

Exercise

To test your level of cultural intelligence, first, find papers by Ang et al. (2007) and Ang and van Dyn (2015) (details given below) through basic Google Scholar search and complete the Cultural Intelligence Test (Ang et al. 2007) as you did other tests above. Later, after studying the book, redo the test, re-calculate your score, and compare it with your earlier score to see the potential influence of the learning experience.

Ang, S., Van Dyne, L., Koh, C., Ng, K. Y., Templer, K. J., Tay, C., and Chandrasekar, N. A. (2007). Cultural intelligence: Its measurement and effects on cultural judgment and decision making, cultural adaptation and task performance. *Management and Organization Review*, 3(3), 335–371.

Ang, S., and Van Dyne, L. (2015). Conceptualization of cultural intelligence: Definition, distinctiveness, and nomological network. In *Handbook of cultural intelligence* (pp. 21–33). Abingdon: Routledge.

Conclusions

This chapter explained the role and potential of intercultural competence on tourism and hospitality services and the main components and factors which may influence intercultural competence. As explained previously in the Intercultural Competence Model (Figure 3.1), various factors influence the level of intercultural competence. Universities offering tourism and hospitality programmes and tourism and hospitality businesses may design courses and training programmes to address each component of intercultural competence such as knowledge, affective features, contextual/situational characteristics, and psychomotor features. Additionally, as found by Yurur et al. (2020) tourism and hospitality students and employees may be encouraged and supported to a) spend time abroad through study abroad or student exchange programs (e.g., ERASMUS and work and travel programmes), b) spend periods of time on business vacations abroad, and c) to have experience of serving international customers. However, all these activities should be seen as learning experiences and should be programmed and monitored in terms of inputs, processes, and outputs. Finally, as mentioned above, as women tend to have a higher level of emotional intelligence and cultural sensitivity, the proportion of female employees and managers may be increased in tourism and hospitality businesses. Also, authorities may establish the necessary support systems to increase the proportion of female entrepreneurs in tourism and hospitality.

Questions

1. What is the relationship between similarity and liking?
2. What is the role of mimicking and mirroring in interpersonal communication?
3. Explain the theories relating to emotions in tourism and hospitality service encounters.
4. What are the components of intercultural competence? Discuss how one may use them to develop intercultural competence.
5. What is the relationship between ethnocentricism, intercultural apprehensions, social anxiety, social avoidance, and cultural competence?
6. What are the components of intercultural sensitivity and cultural intelligence? How can one develop intercultural sensitivity and cultural intelligence? How do intercultural sensitivity and cultural intelligence models relate to the intercultural competence model presented in Figure 3.1?
7. Explain and discuss St Ambrose's quote "When in Rome, do as the Romans do" from the perspective of both customers (demand) and service providers (supply) in tourism and hospitality.

Research questions/ideas to pursue for researchers

As explained above people with simplistic and rigid cognitive systems tend to develop more narrowly defined and inflexible categories, be more dogmatic (i.e., narrow-minded), make more negative judgements, and are more likely to make more confident judgements about other people and engage in gross stereotyping (Kim, 1990; Neuliep, 2018). People with simple and rigid cognitive systems are more likely to have poor intercultural competence skills. This means that interculturally competent communicators would be expected to have an open and flexible cognitive system.

As classification and categorisation systems such as stereotyping are often resorted to as an uncertainty and ambiguity reduction strategy (Kramer, 1999; Allen et al., 2001), people from high-uncertainty avoidance cultures may be expected to engage in stereotyping more often, that is, may be more likely to have a simplistic and rigid cognitive systems. Moreover, ethnocentrics tend to have narrow categories and simple and rigid cognitive systems. Hence, based on this background, a comparative research study may be carried out to investigate whether tourism and hospitality employees (or people in general) from a high-uncertainty culture are more ethnocentric, are more likely to stereotype and perform more poorly in terms of cultural competence and intercultural sensitivity.

Note

1 An ethnocentrism scale is presented in Chapter 1.

Recommended further reading

Daniels, M. A., and Greguras, G. J. (2014). Exploring the nature of power distance implications for micro-and macro-level theories, processes, and outcomes. *Journal of Management*, 40(5), 1202–1229.

Gao, B., Li, X., Liu, S., and Fang, D. (2018). How power distance affects online hotel ratings: The positive moderating roles of hotel chain and reviewers' travel experience. *Tourism Management*, 65, 176–186.

Hofstede, G., (2010). *Cultures and organizations: Software of the mind* (3rd ed.). New York: McGraw-Hill.

Hsieh, A. T., and Tsai, C. W. (2009). Does national culture really matter? Hotel service perceptions by Taiwan and American tourists. *International Journal of Culture, Tourism and Hospitality Research*, 3(1), 54–69.

Koc, E. (2013). Power distance and its implications for upward communication and empowerment: Crisis management and recovery in hospitality services. *The International Journal of Human Resource Management*, 24(19), 3681–3696.

Neuliep, J. W. (2018). *Intercultural communication: A contextual approach* (7th Ed.). Thousand Oaks, CA: Sage.

Yurur, S., Koc, E., Taskin, C., and Boz, H. (2020). Factors influencing intercultural sensitivity of hospitality employees. *International Journal of Hospitality and Tourism Administration*, 1–19.

References

Adler, N. J. (1997). *International dimensions of organizational behavior* (3rd ed.). Cincinnati, OH: South-Western.

Allen, M., Preiss, R. W., Gayle, B. M., and Burrell, N. (Eds.). (2001). *Interpersonal communication research: Advances through meta-analysis*. Abingdon: Routledge.

Ang, S., Van Dyne, L., Koh, C., Ng, K. Y., Templer, K. J., Tay, C., and Chandrasekar, N. A. (2007). Cultural intelligence: Its measurement and effects on cultural judgment and decision making, cultural adaptation and task performance. *Management and Organization Review*, 3(3), 335–371.

Arasaratnam, L. A. (2009). The development of a new instrument of intercultural communication competence. *Journal of Intercultural Communication*, 29(2), 137–163.

Ashton-James, C. E., and Chartrand, T. L. (2009). Social cues for creativity: The impact of behavioral mimicry on convergent and divergent thinking. *Journal of Experimental Social Psychology*, 45(4), 1036–1040.

Bailenson, J. N., and Yee, N. (2005). Digital chameleons: Automatic assimilation of non-verbal gestures in immersive virtual environments. *Psychological Science*, 16, 814–819.

Baum, T. and Devine, F. (2008). *Cultural awareness in the curriculum*. Higher Education Academy Network for Hospitality, Leisure, Sport and Tourism.

Baumeister, R. F., and Leary, M. R. (1995). The need to belong: Desire for interpersonal attachments as a fundamental human motivation. *Psychological Bulletin*, 117, 497–529.

Bennett, J. M., and Bennett, M. J. (2004). Developing intercultural sensitivity: An integrative approach to global and domestic diversity. In D. Landis, J. Bennett, and M. Bennett (Eds.), *Handbook of intercultural training* (3rd ed., pp. 147–165). Thousand Oaks, CA: Sage.

Berger, C. R. (1992). Communicating under uncertainty. In W. B. Gudykunst, and Y. Y. Kim (Eds.), *Readings on communicating with strangers* (pp. 5–15). New York: McGraw-Hill.

Berger, C. R., and Jordan, J. (1992). Planning sources, planning difficulty, and verbal fluency. *Communication Monographs*, 59, 130–149.

Bernieri, F. J., and Rosenthal, R. (1991). Interpersonal coordination: Behavior matching and interactional synchrony. In R. S. Feldman, and B. Rime (Eds.), *Fundamentals of non-verbal behavior* (pp. 401–432). Cambridge: Cambridge University Press

Biddle, B. J. (1986). Recent developments in role theory. *Annual Review of Sociology*, 12, 67–92.

Brickson, S. L. (2000). Impact of identity orientation on individual and organizational outcomes in demographically diverse settings. *Academy of Management Review*, 25(1), 82–101.

Byrne, D. (1971). *The attraction paradigm*. New York: Academic Press.

Cakici, C. and Guler, O. (2017). Emotional contagion and the influence of groups on service failures and recovery. In E. Koc (Ed.) *Service failures and recovery in tourism and hospitality* (pp. 135–159). Wallingford, Oxford: CABI.

Caligiuri, P.M. (2000). The big five personality characteristics as predictors of expatriates' desire to terminate the assignment and supervisor-rated performance. *Personnel Psychology*, 53, 67–88.

Chartrand, T. L., and Bargh, J. A. (1999). The chameleon effect: The perception-behavior link and social interaction. *Journal of Personality and Social Psychology*, 76, 893–910.
Chen, G. M. (2010). The impact of intercultural sensitivity on ethnocentrism and intercultural communication apprehension. *Intercultural Communication Studies*, 19(1), 1–9.
Chen, G. M., and Starosta, W. J. (2000). The development and validation of the intercultural communication sensitivity scale. *Human Communication*, 3, 1–15.
Cisler, J. M., Olatunji, B. O., Feldner, M. T., and Forsyth, J. P. (2010). Emotion regulation and the anxiety disorders: An integrative review. *Journal of Psychopathology and Behavioral Assessment*, 32, 68–82.
Costa, P. T., Jr and McCrae, R. R. (1992). Revised NEO *Personality Inventory (NEO-PR-R and NEO Five Factor Inventory (NEO-FFI): Professional manual.* Odessa, FL: Psychological Assessment Resources.
Cushner, K., and Chang, S. C. (2015). Developing intercultural competence through overseas student teaching: Checking our assumptions. *Intercultural Education*, 26(3), 165–178.
De Waal, B. (1995). *Motivations for video game play: A study of social, cultural and physiological factors* (Doctoral dissertation). School of Communication/Simon Fraser University.
Diefendorff, J. M., Croyle, M. H., and Gosserand, R. H. (2005). The dimensionality and antecedents of emotional labor strategies. *Journal of Vocational Behavior*, 66(2), 339–357.
Dutton, D., and Aron, A. (1974). Some evidence for heightened sexual attraction under conditions of high anxiety. *Journal of Personality and Social Psychology*, 20, 510–517.
Erber, R., and Erber, M. (2017). *Intimate relationships: Issues, theories, and research.* New York: Psychology Press.
Faraji-Rad, A., Samuelsen, B. M., and Warlop, L. (2015). On the persuasiveness of similar others: The role of mentalizing and the feeling of certainty. *Journal of Consumer Research*, 42(3), 458–471.
Finke, J. B., Behrje, A., and Schaechinger, H. (2018). Acute stress enhances pupillary responses to erotic nudes: Evidence for differential effects of sympathetic activation and cortisol. *Biological Psychology*, 137, 73–82.
Flavell, J.H. (1979). Metacognition and cognitive monitoring: A new area of cognitive developmental inquiry. *American Psychologist*, 34, 906–911.
Friedman, I. A. (2016). Being a teacher: Altruistic and narcissistic expectations of pre-service teachers. *Teachers and Teaching*, 22(5), 625–648.
Goodman, N. R. (1994). Cross-cultural training for the global executive. In R. W. Brislin and T. Yoshida (Eds.), *Improving intercultural interaction: Models for cross-cultural training programs* (pp. 34–54). Thousand Oaks, CA: Sage.
Gudykunst, W. B., and Ting-Toomey, S. (1998), *Culture and interpersonal communication cultural communication.* Thousand Oaks: Sage.
Guéguen, N. (2007). Courtship compliance: The effect of touch on women's behavior. *Social Influence*, 2(2), 81–97.
Harari, Y. N. (2016). *Homo Deus: A brief history of tomorrow.* London: Random House.
Hatfield, E., Cacioppo, J. T., and Rapson, L. R. (1992). Primitive emotional contagion. In M. S. Clark (Ed.), *Review of personality and social psychology: Emotion and social behavior* (Vol. 14, pp. 151–177). Newbury Park, CA: Sage.
Hewstone, M., and Ward, C. X. (1985). Ethnocentrism and causal attribution in Southeast Asia. *Journal of Personality and Social Psychology*, 48, 614–623.
Hochschild, A. (1983). *The managed heart.* Berkeley: University of California Press.

Hoffman, M. L. (1984). Interaction of affect and cognition in empathy. In C. E. Izard and R. B. Kagan (Eds.), *Emotions, cognition, and behavior* (pp. 103–131). Cambridge: Cambridge University Press.

Holt-Lunstad, J., Smith, T. B., Baker, M., Harris, T., and Stephenson, D. (2015). Loneliness and social isolation as risk factors for mortality: a meta-analytic review. *Perspectives on Psychological Science*, 10(2), 227–237.

Hopkins, S. A., Hopkins, W. E., and Hoffman, K. D. (2005). Domestic inter-cultural service encounters: An integrated model. *Managing Service Quality: An International Journal*, 15(4), 329–343.

Ihtiyar, A., Ahmad, F. S., and Baroto, M. B. (2013). Impact of intercultural competence on service reliability and customer satisfaction in the grocery retailing. *Procedia – Social and Behavioral Sciences*, 99(6), 373–381.

Inoue, K., Yagi, Y., and Sato, N. (2018). The mere exposure effect for visual image. *Memory and Cognition*, 46(2), 181–190.

Irimias, A. and Franch, M. (2019). Developing intercultural sensitivity as an emotional ability. In E. Koc (Ed.), *Emotional intelligence in tourism and hospitality* (pp. 95–107). Wallingford, Oxford: CABI.

Jones, J. T., Pelham, B. W., Carvallo, M., and Mirenberg, M. C. (2004). How do I love thee? Let me count the Js: implicit egotism and interpersonal attraction. *Journal of Personality and Social Psychology*, 87(5), 665.

Kashdan, T. B., Farmer, A. S., Adams, L. M., Ferssizidis, P., McKnight, P. E., and Nezlek, J. B. (2013). Distinguishing healthy adults from people with social anxiety disorder: Evidence for the value of experiential avoidance and positive emotions in everyday social interactions. *Journal of Abnormal Psychology*, 122(3), 645.

Kassing, J. W. (1997). Development of the intercultural willingness to communicate scale. *Communication Research Reports*, 14, 399–407.

Khan, M., Ro, H., Gregory, A. M., and Hara, T. (2016). Gender dynamics from an arab perspective: intercultural service encounters. *Cornell Hospitality Quarterly*, 57(1), 51–65.

Kim, Y. Y. (1990). Explaining Interethnic Conflict: An Interdisciplinary Overview. Paper presented at the annual convention of the Speech Communication Association, Chicago, IL.

Kim, M. G., Wang, C., and Mattila, A. S. (2010). The relationship between consumer complaining behavior and service recovery: an integrative review. *International Journal of Contemporary Hospitality Management*, 22(7), 975–991.

Koc, E. (2006). Total quality management and business excellence in services: The implications of all-inclusive pricing system on internal and external customer satisfaction in the Turkish tourism market. *Total Quality Management and Business Excellence*, 17(7), 857–877.

Koc, E. (2007). Assessing all-inclusive pricing from the perspective of the main stakeholders in the Turkish tourism industry. In A. G. Woodside (Ed.), *Advances in culture, tourism and hospitality research* (Vol. 1, pp. 273–288). Bingley, UK: Emerald Group Publishing.

Koc, E. (2010). Services and conflict management: Cultural and European integration perspectives. *International Journal of Intercultural Relations*, 34(1), 88–96.

Koc, E. (2013). Power distance and its implications for upward communication and empowerment: Crisis management and recovery in hospitality services. *The International Journal of Human Resource Management*, 24(19), 3681–3696.

Koc, E. (2016). *Tüketici Davranışı ve Pazarlama Stratejileri: Global ve Yerel Yaklaşım* (Vol. 7). Ankara, Turkey: Baskı, Seçkin Yayınları.

Koc, E. (2017). *Service failures and recovery in tourism and hospitality: A practical manual.* Wallingford, Oxford: CABI.

Koc, E. (2018). Turkish tourism and hospitality students' social anxiety and avoidance. *Journal of Hospitality and Tourism Education*, 31(1), 49–54.

Koc, E. (2020). Do women make better in tourism and hospitality? a conceptual review from a customer satisfaction and service quality perspective. *Journal of Quality Assurance in Hospitality and Tourism*, 1–28.

Koc, E., and Boz, H. (2020). Development of hospitality and tourism employees' emotional intelligence through developing their emotion recognition abilities. *Journal of Hospitality Marketing and Management*, 1–18.

Kramer, MW. (1999). Motivation to reduce uncertainty: A reconceptualization of uncertainty reduction theory. *Management Communication Quarterly*, 13(2), 305.

Lakin, J. L., Jefferis, V. E., Cheng, C. M., and Chartrand, T. L. (2003). The chameleon effect as social glue: Evidence for the evolutionary significance of nonconscious mimicry. *Journal of Non-verbal Behavior*, 27, 145–162.

Liebowitz, M. R., Gorman, J. M., Fryer, A. J., and Klein, D. F. (1985). Social phobia: Review of a neglected anxiety disorder. *Archives of General Psychiatry*, 42, 729–736.

MacKenzie, M. J., and Baumeister, R. F. (2019). Motivated gratitude and the need to belong: Social exclusion increases gratitude for people low in trait entitlement. *Motivation and Emotion*, 43(3), 412–433.

Magnini, V. P., Hyun, S., Kim, B., and Uysal, M. (2013). The influences of collectivism in hospitality work settings. *International Journal of Contemporary Hospitality Management*, 25(6), 844–864.

Navarrete, C. D., Fessler, D. M., and Eng, S. J. (2007). Elevated ethnocentrism in the first trimester of pregnancy. *Evolution and Human Behavior*, 28(1), 60–65.

Neuliep, J. W. (2018). Intercultural communication: A contextual approach (7th ed.). Thousand Oaks, CA: Sage.

Neuliep, J. W., and McCroskey, J. C. (1997). The development of intercultural and interethnic communication apprehension scales. *Communication Research Reports*, 14, 145–156.

Noja, G. G., Petrović, N., and Cristea, M. (2018). Turning points in migrants' labour market integration in Europe and benefit spillovers for Romania and Serbia: the role of socio-psychological credentials. *Zbornik Radova Ekonomski Fakultet u Rijeka*, 36(2), 489–518.

Olszanowski, M., Wróbel, M., and Hess, U. (2019). Mimicking and sharing emotions: a re-examination of the link between facial mimicry and emotional contagion. *Cognition and Emotion*, 1–10.

Oswald, P. A. (2002). The interactive effects of affective demeanor, cognitive processes and perspective-taking focus on helping behavior. *The Journal of Social Psychology*, 142, 120–132.

Pelham, B. W., Carvallo, M. C., DeHart, T., and Jones, J. T. (2003). Assessing the validity of implicit egotism: A reply to Gallucci (2003). *Journal of Personality and Social Psychology*, 85, 800–807.

Peng, R. Z., and Wu, W. P. (2016). Measuring intercultural contact and its effects on intercultural competence: A structural equation modeling approach. *International Journal of Intercultural Relations*, 53, 16–27.

Reisinger, Y., and Turner, L. (2002). Cultural differences between Asian tourist markets and Australian hosts, part 1. *Journal of Travel Research*, 40, 295–315.

Rivera, D. (2019). Developing intercultural sensitivity as an emotional ability. In E. Koc (Ed.) *Emotional Intelligence in Tourism and Hospitality* (pp. 75–94). Wallingford, Oxford: CABI.

Sampson, D. L., and Smith, A. R. (1957). A scale to measure world-minded attitudes. *Journal of Social Psychology*, 45, 99–106.

Sharma, P., Tam, J. L. M., and Kim, N. (2009). Demystifying intercultural service encounters: Toward a comprehensive conceptual framework. *Journal of Service Research*, 12(2), 227–242.

Sharma, P., Tam, J. L., and Kim, N. (2015). Service role and outcome as moderators in intercultural service encounters. *Journal of Service Management*, 26(1), 137–155.

Sharma, P., Tam, J. L., Kim, N., Zhan, W., and Su, Y. (2018). Intercultural service encounters (ICSEs): Challenges and opportunities for international services marketers. In *Advances in Global Marketing* (pp. 449–469). Cham: Springer.

Sizoo, S. (2008). Analysis of employee performance during cross-cultural service encounters at luxury hotels in Hawaii, London and Florida. *Asia Pacific Journal of Tourism Research*, 13(2), 113–128.

Sizoo, S., Iskat, W., Plank, R., and Serrie, H. (2003). Cross-cultural service encounters in the hospitality industry and the effect of intercultural sensitivity on employee performance. *International Journal of Hospitality and Tourism Administration*, 4(2), 61–77.

Solomon, M. R., Surprenant, C., Czepiel, J. A., and Gutman, E. G. (1985), A role theory perspective on dyadic interactions: the service encounter. *Journal of Marketing*, 49, 99–111.

Stauss, B. (2016). Retrospective: "culture shocks" in inter-cultural service encounters? *Journal of Services Marketing*, 30, 4.

Stel, M., Van Baaren, R. B., and Vonk, R. (2008). Effects of mimicking: Acting prosocially by being emotionally moved. *European Journal of Social Psychology*, 38(6), 965–976.

Sternberg, R. J. (1985). *Beyond IQ: A triarchic theory of human intelligence.* Cambridge: Cambridge University Press.

Sternberg, R. J. (1997). The concept of intelligence and its role in lifelong learning. *American Psychologist*, 52, 1030–1037.

Swanson, H. L. (1990). Influence of metacognitive knowledge and aptitude on problem solving. *Journal of Educational Psychology*, 82(2), 306–314.

Tajfel, H. (1974). Social identity and intergroup behaviour. *Social Science Information*, 13(2), 65–93.

Tajfel, H., Billig, M., Bundy, R. P., and Flament, C. (1971). Social categorization and intergroup behaviour. *European Journal of Social Psychology*, 1, 149–178.

Tan, J., Ariely, D., and Hare, B. (2017). Bonobos respond prosocially toward members of other groups. *Scientific Reports*, 7(1), 1–11.

Tanner, R. J., Ferraro, R., Chartrand, T. L., Bettman, J. R., and Baaren, R. V. (2007). Of chameleons and consumption: The impact of mimicry on choice and preferences. *Journal of Consumer Research*, 34(6), 754–766.

Thomas, D. C., Elron, E., Stahl, G., Ekelund, B. Z., Ravlin, E. C., Cerdin, J. L., ... and Maznevski, M. (2008). Cultural intelligence: Domain and assessment. *International Journal of Cross Cultural Management*, 8(2), 123–143.

Ting-Toomey, S. (1999). *Communicating across cultures*. New York: Guilford Press.

Van Baaren, R. B., Maddux, W. W., Chartrand, T. L., De Bouter, C., and Van Knippenberg, A. (2003). It takes two to mimic: Behavioral consequences of self-construals. *Journal of Personality and Social Psychology*, 84, 1093–1102.

Van Dyne, L., Ang, S., and Koh, C. (2015). Development and validation of the CQS: The cultural intelligence scale. In *Handbook of cultural intelligence* (pp. 34–56). Abingdon. Routledge.

Villi, B., and Koc, E. (2018). Employee attractiveness and customers' service failure perceptions. *Journal of Hospitality Marketing and Management*, 27(1), 41–60.

Wang, W., and Zhou, M. (2016). Validation of the short form of the intercultural sensitivity scale (ISS-15). *International Journal of Intercultural Relations*, 55, 1–7.

Weber, K., Sparks, B., and Hsu, C. H. (2016). The effects of acculturation, social distinctiveness, and social presence in a service failure situation. *International Journal of Hospitality Management*, 56, 44–55.

Westerman, D. L., Lanska, M., and Olds, J. M. (2015). The effect of processing fluency on impressions of familiarity and liking. *Journal of Experimental Psychology: Learning, Memory, and Cognition*, 41(2), 426.

Wiens, K. J. (2016). Leading through burnout: The influence of emotional intelligence on the ability of executive level physician leaders to cope with occupational stress and burnout (Unpublished doctoral dissertation). University of Pennsylvania, Philadelphia.

Wilson-Wünsch, B. R. and Decosta, N. P. L. (2019). Development of personal expertise in tourism and hospitality professions: cognitive knowledge, personality and learning style. In E. Koc (Ed.), *Emotional intelligence in tourism and hospitality* (pp. 62–74). Wallingford, Oxford: CABI.

Wiseman, R. L., Hammer, M. R., and Nishida, H. (1989). Predictors of intercultural communication competence. *International Journal of Intercultural Relations*, 13, 349–370.

Wolfe, J. M., Kluender, K. R., Levi, D. M., Bartoshuk, L. M., Herz, R. S., Klatzky, R. L., ... and Merfeld, D. M. (2006). *Sensation and perception*. Sunderland, MA: Sinauer.

Yurur, S., Koc, E., Taskin, C., and Boz, H. (2020). Factors influencing intercultural sensitivity of hospitality employees. I*nternational Journal of Hospitality and Tourism Administration*, 1–19.

Chapter 4

Culture and context in communication

Learning Objectives

After reading this chapter, you should be able to:

- explain the main characteristics of high context and low context cultures;
- explain how high- and low-context cultural background influence tourism and hospitality operations in terms of association, interaction, territoriality and space, and learning;
- explain the influence of monochronic and polychronic cultural orientation of people on their attitudes towards various issues;
- understand the concept of in-group collectivism and how it may influence behaviour of people in organisations.

Introduction

In his book *The Silent Language* (1959), anthropologist Edward Hall viewed culture as a form of communication, and he differentiated cultures in relation to the context that underlines all communication messages. According to the concept of high and low context developed by Hall (1976) the two main types of communication are a) explicit (overt), verbal, open, and direct, and b) implicit, indirect, and non-verbal. Cultures that are characterised by explicit and verbal are low-context cultures, whereas cultures which are characterised by implicit and non-verbal communication are high-context cultures (Hall, 1976). While explicit and verbal communication in low-context cultures depends on the "what", or content, implicit (overt) communication in high-context cultures takes into account a variety of factors, and depends on the "how, why, when, where, to whom, and how", as well as non-verbal cues (Manrai et al., 2019). However, this does not mean that communication in low-context cultures is not more thorough. It is just that their communication contains less apparent direct presentation that is made up of non-verbal nuances (Yen et al., 2016). While high-context is associated with collectivism dimension of culture, low context is associated with individualism dimension.

As emphasised in Chapters 1 and 3, tourism and hospitality operations necessitate intense and frequent interactions between customers and employees, employees and employees, employees and managers. Hence, awareness and knowledge of the concept of high and low context, and its implications on the above interactions would be valuable for the efficient and effective marketing and management of tourism and hospitality businesses. On an individual basis, an employee's intercultural abilities in cross-cultural communication have become of paramount importance in today's multicultural business environments (Noja et al., 2018).

This chapter explains the characteristics of high- and low-context cultures in relation to tourism and hospitality, and the implications of related concepts such as space, time, and in-group collectivism for interaction and communication.

High- and low-context cultures

As briefly mentioned in the Introduction section, high- and low-context dimensions are about the extent to which messages are explicit, and the context is important in communication. Table 4.1 lists of some of the high- and low-context cultures (Hall, 1976, 1983; Hall and Hall, 1990), and their basic characteristics (van Everdingen and Waarts, 2003; Ting-Toomey and Dorjee, 2018). According to Tung (1995) about 70% of the world population can be classified as high-context.

Table 4.1 High- and low-context countries and their main characteristics

Low-Context (Specific) Cultures (West Europeans, Scandinavians, North Americans)		*High-Context (Diffuse) Cultures (Central Europeans, Southeast Asians, Arabs, the Mediterranneans, Latins, Africans)*	
Countries	*Characteristics*	*Countries*	*Characteristics*
Germany Austria Switzerland Australia Denmark South Africa Norway United States Canada (English)	Messages are made explicitly (overtly), and most of the meaning is created in the communication message (verbal or written) Emphasis is more on the content of the message Interpretation of the messages depends on the content (words) of the verbal or written message	Japan Korea China India Turkey Mexico India Hungary Argentina	Messages are implicit, and most of the message may be created through the context Emphasis is more on the context of the message Interpretation of messages depends on contextual factors

Table 4.1 continued

Low-Context (Specific) Cultures (West Europeans, Scandinavians, North Americans)		*High-Context (Diffuse) Cultures (Central Europeans, Southeast Asians, Arabs, the Mediterranneans, Latins, Africans)*	
Countries	*Characteristics*	*Countries*	*Characteristics*
Finland Sweden Israel United Kingdom Belgium Netherlands Luxembourg	Messages include all the details and the speaker (or the writer) is responsible for the message clarity. Search for and the use of information that is based on reports, the internet, and databases Individual achievement and task-oriented Competitive and task-oriented Contracts tend to be longer and detailed	Romania Brazil Greece Indonesia Russia Malaysia Ukraine Taiwan Uruguay Czechia Spain Portugal Italy France	The details are embedded in the context and the listener is responsible for understanding the message Search for and the use of information is based on personal sources Team achievement and relationship-oriented Cooperative and team-oriented Shorter contracts since less information is required

Exercise

Determine whether your country is a high- or low context culture. Also, find colleagues who are the opposite to you. Based on the experiences of you and your colleagues, discuss the extent to which the characteristics in Table 4.1 represent your culture. From a dyadic perspective (organisational behaviour and human resource management – marketing and consumer behaviour) what would be the advantages and disadvantages, and implications of your cultural characteristics in managing tourism and hospitality businesses? When considering the implications think about the likely influences on the marketing mix elements (7Ps) and the service quality (SERVQUAL) dimensions.

The cultural dimensions explained throughout this book (e.g., power distance, uncertainty avoidance, indulgence, masculinity and individualism, developed by Hofstede et al., 2010) have scores for countries, which make comparisons between countries possible. However, the high and low context cultural orientation countries (or cultures) are grouped broadly (without specific scores[1]) as high-or low context. Hall (1976) provides only a broad continuum of countries as shown in Figure 4.1.

The high- and low-context cultures in Figure 4.1 fall on a continuum that describes how a person communicates with others, and the extent to which they use contextual factors. Figure 4.2 shows the use of verbal and non-verbal (contextual) elements used in

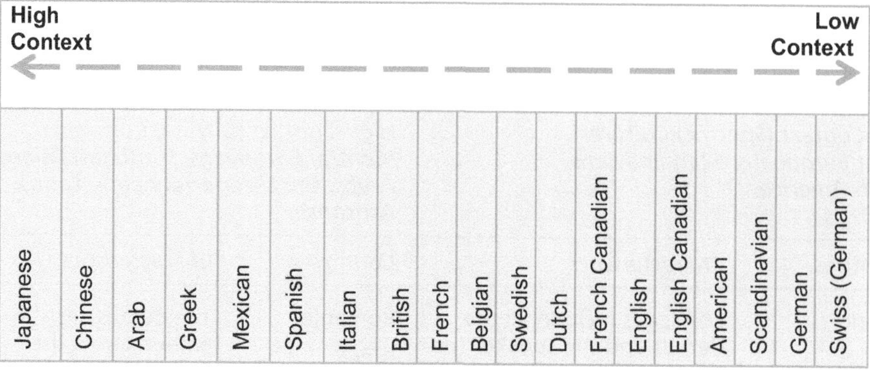

Figure 4.1 High- and low-context cultures continuum

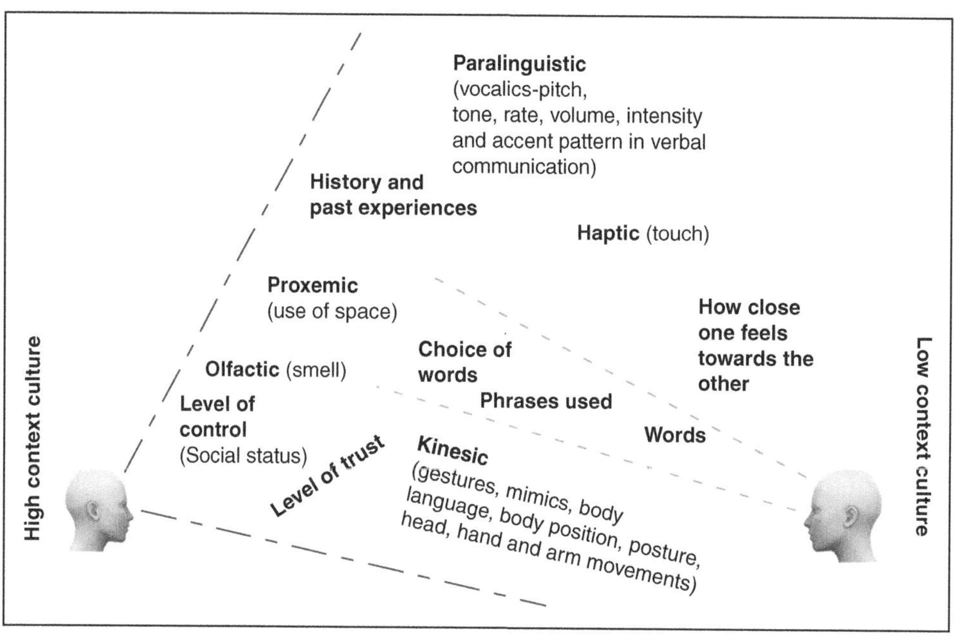

Figure 4.2 Communication in high- and low-context cultures

communication by high- and low-context people. Contextual factors comprise factors such as paralinguistic (vocalics – pitch, tone, rate, volume, intensity, and accent pattern in verbal communication), kinesic (gestures, mimics, body language, body position, posture, head, hand, and arm movements), haptic (touch), olfactic (smell), and proxemics (use of space), history and past experiences, trust, and social status, as well as verbal elements (words, vocabulary, choice, and use of words and phrases).

Figure 4.2 shows that in high-context cultures, referred to as diffuse cultures by Trompenaars and Hampden-Turner (1998), communication requires more than simply a verbal or written message. The message depends on various non-verbal and contextual cues that convey information and the recipient is expected to "read between the lines" (Hall, 1998; Chen et al., 2011). According to Hall (1998: 61) "high-context communication is one in which most of the information is already in the person, while very little is in the coded, explicit, transmitted part of the message". The focus tends to be in relationships and indirect communication. As opposed to high-context cultures, in low-context cultures, referred to as specifity cultures by Trompenaars and Hampden-Turner (1998), "the mass of the information is vested in the explicit code" (Hall, 2000: 281), that is, the message itself means everything (Chen et al., 2011). In low context, the meaning is expressed precisely by the words themselves (Gong, 2009: 87), making reading between the lines unnecessary (Chen et al., 2011).

Although the high- and low-context cultures mainly refer to nations (cultures) and language groups, it has also been applied to corporations, other cultural groups, offline communication settings, individuals, and professions (Würtz, 2005). For instance, while marketing and human resource management jobs are considered as high-context jobs, production and engineering jobs are considered as low-context jobs. The following Activity box provides a self-report questionnaire to measure one's high- or low-context orientation.

Activity

Low- and high-context communication scale

Measure your personal high or low context scale score by filling in in the below questionnaire.

Important Note: *Throughout the book, there are a number of self-report scales/tests like the one below. Please save your personal test score records (especially the ones relating to cultural awareness, cultural competence, ethnocentrism, cultural intelligence, etc.) to make comparisons later After studying the whole book you are advised to go back and redo all of these tests once more. By doing this you can compare your scores with the ones you had earlier on. This is expected to enable you to see the changes taken place as a result of the learning experience.*

Instructions

The following scale has 32 statements regarding how you feel about communicating in different ways. In the blank column to the left of each item, indicate the degree (1–9) to which you agree or disagree with each statement. If you are unsure or think that an item does not apply to you, enter a 5 in the column.

Strongly Disagree 1 2 3 4 5 6 7 8 9 Strongly Agree

Please keep in mind that there is no right or wrong response for each statement. In order to avoid biased responses, you are recommended to record your initial response without elaborating too much on the statements.

	Items	*Value (1 to 9)*
1	I catch on to what others mean, even when they do not say it directly.	
2	I show respect to superiors, even if I dislike them.	
3	I use my feelings to determine whether to trust another person.	
4	I find silence awkward in conversation.	
5	I communicate in an indirect fashion.	
6	I use many colourful words when I talk.	
7	In an argument, I insist on very precise definitions.	
8	I avoid clear-cut expressions of feelings when I communicate with others.	
9	I am good at figuring out what others think of me.	
10	My verbal and non-verbal speech tends to be very dramatic.	
11	I listen attentively, even when others are talking in an uninteresting manner.	
12	I maintain harmony in my communication with others.	
13	Feelings are a valuable source of information.	
14	When pressed for an opinion, I respond with an ambiguous statement/position.	
15	I try to adjust myself to the feelings of the person with whom I am communicating.	
16	I actively use a lot of facial expressions when I talk.	
17	My feelings tell me how to act in a given situation.	
18	I am able to distinguish between a sincere invitation and one intended as a gesture of politeness.	
19	I believe that exaggerating stories makes conversation fun.	
20	I orient people through my emotions.	
21	I find myself initiating conversations with strangers while waiting in line.	
22	As a rule, I openly express my feelings and emotions.	
23	I feel uncomfortable and awkward in social situations where everybody else is talking except me.	
24	I readily reveal personal things about myself.	
25	I like to be accurate when I communicate.	
26	I can read another person "like a book".	
27	I use silence to avoid upsetting others when I communicate.	

	Items	*Value (1 to 9)*
28	I openly show my disagreement with others.	
29	I am a very precise communicator.	
30	I can sit with another person, not say anything, and still be comfortable.	
31	I think that untalkative people are boring.	
32	I am an extremely open communicator.	

Scoring: Reverse your score for items 4, 6, 7, 10, 16, 19, 21, 22, 23, 24, 25, 28, 29, 31, and 32. If your original score was 1, reverse it to a 9; if your original score was a 2, reverse it to an 8; and so on. After reversing the scores for those 15 items, simply sum the 32 items. Lower scores indicate low-context communication. Higher scores indicate high-context communication.

Source: Gudykunst et al. (1996). Reprinted with permission from S. Ting-Toomey,

NB: Halverson's (1993) Cultural Context Inventory could also be filled in to test personal high- and low-context orientation.

Characteristics and implications of high- and low-context cultures

According to Halverson (1993), the main differences between high- and low-context cultures can be looked at from the perspective of association, learning, interaction, territoriality, and space. As a characteristic of high- and low- context cultures, temporality will be explained in Chapter 11, where long- and short-term orientations are discussed, so it will not be covered here.

Association

In high-context cultures, relationships tend to be stable and last longer. The relationships are deep and very much depend on trust. On the other hand, in low-context cultures, relationships tend to be superficial, and may begin and end quickly. This means that the functioning of work teams in high-context cultures may take longer as members need to build trust first among themselves. While in low-context cultures relationships tend to be many, looser and short-lived, in high-context cultures people engage in fewer, tighter and more long-term relationships.

A study by Lee et al. (2015) of American (low-context) and Japanese (high-context) restaurant customers showed that American customers' perception of service effectiveness, emotional response, and intention to revisit increased with more frequent check-backs. American customers felt that they received more prompt and responsive service when the service employee (the waiter) checked back on them often. On the other hand, the perceptions of service effectiveness, emotional response, and the intention to revisit by Japanese customers were not influenced by the server check-back style. This meant that for the Japanese customers the number of check-backs did not influence their perceptions. Lee et al.'s research showed that frequent check-backs increased high-context customers' (from Europe and the United States) positive emotional response, and their intention to revisit. Additionally, immediacy behaviours such as smiling and direct eye contact and attentiveness appealed more positively to American customers' emotions, which, in turn, increased their intention to revisit the restaurant.

Mattila (1999) puts forward that tourists from high-context cultures place more emphasis on interpersonal relationships (functional quality) when they evaluate the service. On the contrary, customers from low-context cultures tend to put more emphasis on efficiency and time saving (technical quality). While technical quality is concerned with what the customer actually receives from the service transaction, functional quality is to do with the service approach or the manner in which the customer receives the service from the service provider (Koc, 2015, 2017). While technical quality relates more to reliability, functional quality relates more to responsiveness and empathy as service quality dimensions (Gronroos, 2007; Koc, 2006). While tourism and hospitality customers from low-context cultures tend to focus their service quality evaluations on task completion and efficient delivery, customers from high-context cultures focus on the quality of interactions between employees and customers (Mattila, 2000; Yuksel and Yuksel, 2001). According to Mattila (1999), tourists from high-context cultures tend to provide significantly lower ratings to the service encounter and overall service quality as they have higher service expectations. They place more importance on contextual cues in making their service quality evaluations.

In addition, while in high-context cultures achieving productivity and goals, and getting things done very much depends on the relationships among group members, and the group processes, in low-context cultures achieving productivity and goals, and getting things done primarily depend on concentrating on the procedures and objectives. This means that while the workplace in a high-context culture has a social atmosphere, the low-context workplace may be quite mechanistic. Würtz's (2005) previously mentioned association of marketing and human resource management jobs with high-context and production and engineering jobs with low-context may be remembered here.

Moreover, while in high-context cultures people's identity is rooted in the groups they belong to (e.g., family, work, culture), in low-context cultures their identity is rooted in themselves and their accomplishments. Finally, while in high-context cultures social relationships and authority are structured, hierarchical, and centralised, the social structure tends to be decentralised. Chapter 6 explains how the lack of empowerment among employees and a lack of direct communication between subordinates and managers can cause delays in the recovery of service failures in tourism and hospitality (Koc, 2013).

Learning

People in high-context cultures tend to learn from multiple sources of information and their thinking proceeds from general to specific. Learning occurs by observing others,[2] as people tend to model or demonstrate and then engage in the practice. In these cultures, a group orientation in learning is preferred, and accuracy is emphasised.

On the other hand, in low-context cultures, instead of multiple sources, one source of information tends to be used, and their thinking proceeds from specific to general. In low-context cultures, learning occurs by following the explicit and open directions and explanations of others. As opposed to high-context cultures, in low-context learning environments, an individual orientation is preferred, and the speed tends to be more valued in learning.

Managers in tourism and establishment businesses can design their formal and informal training according to the cultural background of their employees to increase the efficiency and effectiveness of learning activities. For instance, as high-context employees would prefer learning by observing (social learning) (Koc, 2016), training sessions may use videos, scenarios, and anecdotes. As low-context cultures learn more often by reading and listening (cognitive learning) (Koc, 2016), they may be given detailed explanations and instructions.

Koc's (2020) comparative gender study in tourism and hospitality showed that women were superior to men in terms of screening out information in relation to the environment (context). His study showed women were superior to men in terms of spatial elaboration, structural inconsistencies, order, structural interrelationships, remembering objects, locations, design, colour, design and appearance, furniture, changing contexts, facial expressions, mimics, body language, noticing changes in the environment (context). Hence, women may have a more high-contextual orientation in terms of information processing, decision making, and learning. This also correlates with men tending to have a tunnel vision (long–narrow) (which was helpful for chasing and hunting animals), and women tending to have a more peripheral vision (a wider arc of peripheral vision, useful for them due to their gatherer and nest defender roles), as will be explained in Chapter 8.

Koc (2020) concluded that women (as employees, managers, and entrepreneurs) may perform better in tourism and hospitality as the contextual factors constitute an important element of the services marketing mix (physical evidence) and service quality (tangibles). However, caution must be made, as collection and analysis of more information may lead to information overload, a state in which the amount of information an individual must process exceeds the individual's information processing resources and abilities (O'Reilly, 1980), and eventually lead to intuitive decision making. Another study by Koc (2002) showed that due to their communal orientation, women as tourism and hospitality customers were more involved in the holiday purchase decisions, and collected and analysed more information than men. On the other hand, men, due to their agentic orientation, used information more selectively and depended on shortcuts and heuristics in their decision making, and ended up collecting and analysing fewer information cues in their decision making (Meyers-Levy and Loken, 2015).

Another perspective that may relate to high- and low-context in terms of information collection, decision making, and learning could be personality orientations of people. Introverts tend to be more responsive to external stimuli (contextual factors) than extroverts as they perceive situations more intensely, due to cortical arousal (Eysenck and Eysenck, 1967; Pazda and Thornstenson, 2018). For instance, research shows that introverts are more likely to produce a large amount of saliva in response to lemon than extroverts (Eysenck and Eysenck, 1967; Pazda and Thornstenson, 2018). Based on the above explanations, the relationship between high- and low-context orientation, gender, and personality factors such as introversion and extroversion may be further investigated. These studies may shed more light on the understanding of customers and service employees in tourism and hospitality.

Interaction

As explained earlier, in high-context cultures non-verbal elements of communication such as the tone of the voice, gestures, facial expressions, and eye movements are considered to be important in communication. As high-context cultures depend very much on non-verbal behaviours, emotional contagion (Cakici and Guler, 2017) may be more common in these cultures. Hence, negative emotional/facial expressions of one service employee may be more likely to influence other employees.

Additionally, it may be expected that tourism and hospitality employees from a high-context culture may have better emotion/facial expression recognition abilities. However, Boz and Koc's (2020) study showed that though they were high-context, Turkish tourism and hospitality employees' facial expression recognition abilities were not high, and employees had inflated self-efficacy beliefs regarding their facial expression abilities. As will be explained in Chapter 5, this may be because in the Turkish tourism and hospitality industry many unqualified people are employed without sufficient training who may be asked to work long hours for very little pay. It must be stated here that facial expression abilities can be developed and improved. Koc and Boz's (2019) experimental study showed that a brief online emotion/facial expression training lasting less than a minute made significant improvements in service employees' emotion/facial expression recognition abilities, in terms of their speed of recognition and the rate of accuracy.

In addition, as mentioned previously, high-context cultures messages tend to be rather implicit and indirect, and indirect and implicit messages may be a hindrance, for example, in service recovery efforts requiring the engagement of managers. In low-context cultures, non-verbal elements are not important, and in general, messages tend to be explicit and open. A study of the communication needs of medical tourists by Ngamvichaikit and Beise-Zee (2014) showed that people from low-context cultures preferred direct and explicit information.

Exercise

Study the following quotes and the poem by Sara Teasdale. Consider how these quotes and the poem may relate to intercultural communication (verbal, body language, and mimics) taking place between tourism and hospitality staff and customers who are from different cultures.

> The human body is the best picture of the human soul.
>
> Ludwig Wittgenstein

> The body never lies.
>
> Martha Graham

> The single biggest problem in communication is the illusion that it has taken place.
>
> George Bernard Shaw

> Effective communication is 20% what you know and 80% how you feel about what you know.
>
> Jim Rohn

> There are four ways, and only four ways, in which we have contact with the world. We are evaluated and classified by these four contacts: what we do, how we look, what we say, and how we say it.
>
> Dale Carnegie
>
> When the eyes say one thing, and the tongue another, a practiced man relies on the language of the first.
>
> Ralph Waldo Emerson
>
> 60% of all human communication is non-verbal body language; 30% is your tone, so that means 90% of what you're saying ain't coming out of your mouth.
>
> Alex Hitchens
>
> Stephen kissed me in the spring,
> Robin in the fall,
> But Colin only looked at me
> And never kissed at all.
> Stephen's kiss was lost in jest,
> Robin's lost in play,
> But the kiss in Colin's eyes
> Haunts me night and day.
>
> Sara Teasdale (1884–1993)

Tourism and hospitality customers from high-context cultures tend to be more impatient and annoyed when people (e.g., service staff) overload them with verbal and written information (Becker, 2000), as they feel that understanding is achieved by mutual trust fostered through a shared knowledge of core cultural values (Gudykunst and Ting-Toomey, 1988). As in collectivist cultures, communication in high-context cultures is more often implied through non-verbal activity and tends to be more intuitive and more visual than in low-context, individualistic cultures. In service encounters, conflicts may arise as high-context cultures value patience and empathy, while low-context cultures value straight talk, assertiveness, and honesty (Stewart et al., 2001; Chen et al., 2011). The behaviours of a customer or service employee from a low-context culture may be interpreted as ignorant, rude, or incompetent by a customer or a service employee who is from a high-context culture. This interpretation may be due to the fact that a person from a low-context culture may ask a lot of questions (implying that he does not understand), act in a confrontational manner, and be unable to carry out many tasks simultaneously.

According to Ting-Toomey (2005), face is an important element of communication, and there are four types of face people pay attention when they communicate:

- Face-restoration or self-negative-face is the need of individuals to give themselves the freedom and space to protect themselves from other's infringement on their autonomy.

- Face-saving or other negative-face is the need to signal respect for the other person's need for freedom, space, and dissociation.
- Face-assertion or self-positive-face is the need to defend and protect one's need for inclusion and association.
- Face-giving or other positive-face is the need to defend and support the other person's need for inclusion and association.

Individuals from high-context cultures tend to focus on face-giving, protecting the other person's reputation and striving for inclusion, while individuals from low-context cultures tend to employ face-restoration, defending self-face concerns and signalling the need for autonomy (Ting-Toomey, 1988). Likewise, people from high-context cultures may be more likely to engage in obliging, compromising, and avoiding conflict management styles (Ting-Toomey, 1988), while people from low-context cultures may tend to use integrating and dominating conflict management styles (Ting-Toomey, 1988).

Differences between high- and low-context cultures can also be detected in advertising messages in different countries. Würtz's (2005) study compared McDonald's online advertising in Japan, China, Korea, Hong Kong, Pakistan, Germany, Denmark, Sweden, Norway, Finland, and the United States, and found that there were more colours, movements, and sounds (representing the context) in high-context country advertisements. On the other hand, in low-context countries, she found that the advertising focused more on verbal information and linear processes.

Callow and Schiffman's (2002) study, which examined the degree to which consumers infer meaning from images in advertising, found that messages evoked more implicit meanings in high-context rather than in low-context cultures. As people from high-context cultures are more used to implicit messages, and for which it is necessary to use cues from the context to decode the message, they may be able to understand metaphors more easily. On the other hand, in low-context cultures, as people are used to messages that are direct and simple, they may find interpreting metaphors relatively more demanding (Hornikx and le Pair, 2017).

Le Pair and Van Mulken's (2008) study which investigated the perceived complexity and appreciation of advertisements with metaphors in France, Spain (both relatively high-context cultures), and the Netherlands (a relatively low-context culture) found that the Dutch showed a less liking for advertisements which contained metaphors, that is, which were complex. Hornikx and le Pair (2017) also found that customers from high-context cultures found visual metaphors less complex than customers who were from low-context cultures, and high-context customers had more liking for visual metaphors than low-context customers. Based on the above research findings, tourism and hospitality managers are recommended to segment their markets according to the cultural backgrounds of their customers and design their marketing communication messages and their websites based on this segmentation. Managers are also recommended to increase their employees' intercultural sensitivity and competencies so that they can adjust their communication styles to customers with different cultural characteristics (Irimias and Franch, 2019; Wilson-Wünsch and Decosta, 2019).

Apart from the promotion (marketing communications), contextual factors may also influence other marketing mix elements, such as product, place, process, and physical evidence in tourism and hospitality marketing. Becker (2000) showed that customers from high-context cultures had more sensory involvement in eating, entertaining, and socialising.

In addition, as opposed to low-context cultures, communication in high-context cultures is viewed as an art form, or a way of engaging someone, rather than a way of exchanging information, ideas, and opinions. This may also cause delays in serving customers, a late response to service failures, and eventually cause service quality problems in terms of responsiveness, empathy and reliability dimensions (Koc, 2019, 2020).

Moreover, in high-context cultures, disagreement with someone tends to be personalised, and people tend to be sensitive towards conflict expressed by others through their non-verbal communication (Koc, 2010). On the other hand, in low-context cultures, disagreement is not personalised, and people tend to focus on rational solutions, not on individuals per se. In a low-context culture, people may express their annoyance and irritation more easily with the behaviour of someone.

In situations of failure and problems, while people from high-context cultures tend to have an internal locus of control, and attribute failures to themselves, people from low-context cultures would have an external locus of control and tend to attribute to external factors and others. For instance, as a high-context culture, Japan has also a traditionally flexhumble culture. Individuals in Japan attribute success to external factors, and failure to internal factors (Bergiel et al., 2012). While the internal locus of control in high-context cultures would result in reserved and inward reactions in situations of failure and conflict, people in low-context cultures would be more likely to demonstrate visible, external and outward reactions in situations of failure and conflict. This may mean that groups in high-context would be more likely to be harmonious with a strong sense of family and have a high level of cohesion. Hence, in these cultures, relationships and bonds tend to be deeper and long-lasting, and people tend to be more committed to relationships than tasks.

On the other hand, relationships in low-context cultures tend to be more superficial and fragile with a low level of loyalty. In low-context cultures, there would be flexible grouping patterns, and changes occur when needed. Moreover, in low-context cultures, while there is a little distinction between in- and out-group, in high-context cultures there would be a strong distinction, and a strong sense of in-group (i.e., in-group collectivism) (Koc, 2016).

In high-context communication, people may be quite content and comfortable with silence as they do not rely on verbal communication as the main source of information (Neuliep, 2018). As a matter of fact, silence in high-context cultures may convey a meaning of mutual understanding. A Turkish proverb states that "If words are silver, the silence is golden." Traditionally, in Turkey adults praise children who are quiet and silent as "uslu", meaning clever. Again, as a high-context culture, Japanese, in general, feel that expressing personal and intimate details can be best made non-verbally and intuitively (Iwao, 1993). Würtz (2005) argues that silence is also a contextual element conveying meaning in a high-context culture, as well as other contextual factors, such as gestures, facial expressions, body language, proximity, and other non-verbal expressions.

However, in low-context cultures, silence can be quite uncomfortable and people who do not talk are perceived negatively. When someone is quiet in a transaction, people from low-context cultures may feel that something is missing or wrong (Neuliep, 2018). For instance, tourism and hospitality customers from a low-context culture may perceive a silent service employee who is from a high-context culture, as being unhappy, sulking, and negative, while the employee may be trying to serve customers as unobtrusively as possible.

In-group collectivism

As a characteristic of high-context cultures, in-group collectivism is the extent to which individuals express pride, loyalty, and cohesiveness in their teams, families, and friends (House et al., 2004: 12). In-group collectivism, also referred to as family collectivism (as opposed to broad collectivism as a cultural dimension will be explained in Chapters 9 and 12, in relation to universalism and particularism dimension) results in extreme favouring of the in-group. High-context cultures tend to be particularistic, rather than universalistic (see Chapter 12). In the instance of in-group collectivism, people behave subjectively, tend to do extreme favours, walk the extra mile, even break the rules, regulations and the law for the good of the in-group members, while demonstrating a standard behaviour towards other people, that is, people who are out-group, outside the in-group. While in low-context cultures the difference (or the gap) of behaviour towards in- and out-group is minimal, in high-context cultures this difference (or the gap) of behaviour tends to be significant.

CASE STUDY

In-group collectivism in a high-context culture

In the 1990s an American professor had to attend a conference in Turkey. However, as he thought there would be plenty of rooms at the conference hotel, he did not book his room early enough at the hotel (inconsistent with his individualistic and masculinity background – see Chapters 8 and 9). However, when he contacted the conference hotel, it was full and there were no rooms available. When he contacted his long-time colleague and friend from Turkey for potential assistance, he immediately invited his former colleague to stay in his house with his family during the conference. At first, the American professor declined the offer. But, upon the insistence of his Turkish colleague he accepted the stay at his friend's house, as he felt that his friend would have resented it if he had declined his offer.

On a Friday afternoon, the American professor arrived at the airport in Istanbul. The conference was to start on Monday morning. The Turkish friend picked up the American professor at the airport in his car and took him to his house to meet his family. The American professor related this experience on Friday, Saturday, and Sunday as follows:

> My friend and his family treated me as if I was the king. Every meal was highly extravagant and completely different than the one before and they always insisted that I should eat more. They served high-quality wine. They always checked whether I needed anything else. They gave me the largest and most comfortable room in the house. Everybody was extremely kind, smiling and hospitable all the time. They wanted to give me cushions to put behind my back when I sat down so as to make me comfortable. They took me around to a nice pub around the house. They did not let me spend a cent. When I wanted

to pay they held my hand firmly showed me that they would be offended if I had paid.

On Monday, my friend had an important and urgent business to attend on the European side of Istanbul. As he had to leave the house at 6:00 a.m. in the morning he was unable to take me to the conference hotel. He apologised a few times for not being able to take me to the hotel personally. He suggested arranging another friend, or his family members to take me to the conference hotel. I kindly declined his offers and insisted that I could go on my own as he had given me detailed directions to the hotel.

When I left the house at 8:00 on Monday morning, I thought I had plenty of time to reach the conference hotel as it was only five kilometres away from where my Turkish friend and his family lived. However, I faced a different atmosphere than the one I experienced over the weekend with my friend and his family.

I had to go across the street and take a taxi there for the conference hotel. But none of the cars seemed to stop so that I could go across the street. After, waiting for about 8 minutes, I caught a chance to go across the street. It was a risk crossing as the cars did not stop when I was trying cross. When I reached the other side of the road no taxis I hailed seemed to stop. After ten minutes of waiting, a taxi pulled by. But a gentleman ushered and jumped into the taxi before me, although I was there earlier than him. I am used to these kinds behaviours as I come from a metropolitan city, New York. And Istanbul was a large metropolitan city too. But I was bewildered at the differences of treatment I had over the weekend with my friend and his family and the treatment I had outside, in the street. I was like an invisible man in the street. I learned that I had to be quick to get into the taxi. I arrived at the hotel at 9:05, much later than I thought.

Task

What was the reason for the differences in behaviour above? What does the above case study tell about in-group collectivism?

Hence, in high-context cultures, subjective and emotional behaviour, as opposed to rational and objective, may be more prevalent and result in nepotism, a lack of performance orientation, and groupthink. As explained in Chapter 7, groupthink results in a team valuing consensus and cohesion more than the quality of decision making and the actual efficiency and effectiveness of the team (Janis and Janis, 1982). This may mean that tourism and hospitality establishments in high-context cultures may lack rationality and subjectivity, resulting in the loss of efficiency and effectiveness, and eventually loss of a competitive edge. It should also be cautioned that in high-context tourism and hospitality establishments, group cohesion exercises such as company dinners and company picnics, as they tend to increase in-group collectivism, may result in employees asking for favours and expecting leniency from their managers.

CASE STUDY

Turkey and Japan as two high-context cultures

In spite of marked differences, as high-context, high-power distance, high-uncertainty avoidance, restraint (to some extent) and collectivist cultures, Turkey and Japan have some cultural similarities. These two cultures tend to have strong high-context characteristics. For instance, a Japanese tea ceremony is an example of a high-context message. Almost every moment, gesture, and action has some importance to those who understand the "code" being used (Ting-Toomey and Dorjee, 2018).

Having come to Turkey for a period of one month for a project, but ended up living in the country for 28 years, Japanese architect and businessman Yoshinori Moriwaki stated on a TV programme that Turks and Japanese are rather similar in terms of various aspects of culture, and how they communicate. Yoshinori Moriwaki's following statements explain the similarities of relationships and communication as follows:

> When I go and work in a European country I don't usually get as warm a welcome as I get over here in Turkey. Turks place importance on relationships significantly. You can establish strong bonds with them.
>
> When you go to a European country [i.e., a low-context culture], let's say the salt on the table is away from you. And you ask someone to pass you the salt. If one of the words you use is incorrect, it is not understood. However, in Turkey even if you use a letter (not even a word) the Turkish person shows many things on the table and says, "This one? That one?" He helps you until you find the salt. This is the characteristics of Turkish people, they are warm and friendly.

Author's note: Based on the above brief anecdote and the explanations in this chapter, tourism and hospitality customers from high-context cultures may evaluate service personnel from high-context cultures as being helpful and responsive.

Territoriality and space

Space refers to the study of physical space and people. In high-context cultures space between people tends to be treated as communal, whilst, in low-context cultures as people view privacy to be an important issue, space tends to be compartmentalised. This means that, as opposed to low-context cultures, people in high-context cultures tend to stand close to each other and share the same space. Sorokowska et al. (2017) measured social and interpersonal distances in centimetres between people with participants from 42 countries.

According to Hall (1963), personal space is the region surrounding a person that they consider as psychologically theirs. In general, people value their personal space and

Table 4.2 Proxemics and the types of space

Distance	*Explanation*	*Centimetres*
Intimate distance (close person)	Reserved for lovers, children, close family members, friends, and pets	0–46 cm
Personal distance (acquaintance)	Used in conversations with friends, to chat with associates, and in group discussions	46–122 cm
Social distance (stranger)	Reserved for strangers, newly formed groups, and new acquaintance	122–240 cm
Public distance (audience)	Reserved for larger audiences	240 cm plus

Adapted from Hall (1963).

feel discomfort, anger, or anxiety when their personal space is violated. Proxemics is about the distance people feel comfortable with in relation to others. According to Hall (1963), proxemics deals with four distances as provided in Table 4.2 (for a comparison of personal distance in cultures, see the Information zone box "Territoriality and Space" in Chapter 9).

As tourism and hospitality staff from a high-context cultures (e.g., India, Turkey, or Romania) tend to stand close to each other and share the same space, people from low-context cultures (e.g., from the United States or Germany) may feel uncomfortable or unsafe in these instances. Tourism and hospitality staff from high-context cultures need to be reminded not to get to close to the customers during the service encounters. Additionally, service staff, from high-context cultures, who may work and stand too close to one another, may be viewed as unprofessional or idle by customers (Pearson, 2015) from a low context culture. The Covid-19 pandemic in 2020 throughout the world is expected to have a permanent influence on the physical and social distance people have between themselves in terms of extending these distances.

Exercise

Visit the Cultural Atlas webpages (https://culturalatlas.sbs.com.au) to compare the communication characteristics of your country together with countries of your choice. What sort of differences and peculiarities are there? Consider and determine to what extent may high- or low-context orientation of these countries be influential in the formation of differences in their communication patterns?

Conclusion

This chapter explored how cultural context orientation may influence communication and interaction. Based on the concept of context, the chapter studied how high- and low-context cultures can be analysed in terms of association, interaction, territoriality and space, temporality, and learning. Contextual implications of interaction, territoriality and space, temporality, and learning have been explained in relation to tourism and hospitality marketing and management. It is seen that people tend to prefer interacting with others in the form they are used to, which is mainly based on their high- or low-context cultural orientation. The design of marketing mix elements, the concentration of service quality dimensions, and internal communications may need adaptation based on the cultural context of the people involved in the interaction.

Questions

1. What are the main differences between high- and low-context cultures? Name five countries which are high context and five countries low context?
2. How may high- and low-context influence intercultural communication, the design of marketing mix elements, and the service quality dimensions in tourism and hospitality? Discuss.
3. What is proxemics? How may proxemics relate to tourism and hospitality service encounters? What sorts of problems may arise in terms of proxemics when service employees behave according their cultural orientation?
4. Explain the concept of in-group collectivism? How may in-group collectivism influence interactions in a multicultural business environment?
5. Explain and discuss Peter Drucker's quote "The most important thing in communication is hearing what isn't said" from the perspective of high- and low-context cultures.

Research question /ideas to pursue for researchers

As stated in this chapter, people from high-context cultures depend more on body language, mimics, etc. when communicating. Hence, people from high-context cultures may be expected to recognise, understand mimics, body language, and facial expressions better, more easily, and correctly. By using the facial expression (emotional expressions) photos a set of seven emotions, including one which is neutral, of the same person, from Karolinska Institute (https://kdef.se/home/aboutKDEF.html), compare facial expression recognition abilities of tourism and hospitality employees from two countries, one being high context and the other one being low context.

Karolinska Institute stores 4,900 facial (emotional) expressions whose validity reliability have been tested previously (Lundqvist et al., 1998; Goeleven et al., 2008). As the recognition of emotions/facial expressions constitute a substantial proportion of emotional intelligence (Boz and Koc, 2020), would people from high-context cultures be expected to have a higher level of emotional intelligence? Or would there be other factors influencing emotional intelligence scores of people?

Also as explained in this chapter, while people from high-context cultures tend to concentrate more on functional quality, people from low-context cultures tend to concentrate more on technical quality. As Würtz (2005) reports, apart from countries and national scale, the concept of high- and low-context has been used in relation to individuals. By using the personal high- and low-context scale, customers' individual high- and low-context orientations, their attitudes towards various functional and technical quality attributes may be investigated.

Notes

1 Although the model of high- and low-context cultures is a popular framework in intercultural studies, there have been some criticisms of it, based on the fact that it lacks empirical validation.

2 After having lived in Turkey for a long period, Hugh Pope, the author of several books on Turkish culture and identity, such as *Sons of the Conquerors* (2005), describes Turkish people (a high-context culture) as people who prefer learning by observing and listening, rather than reading and investigating.

Recommended further reading

Hall, E. T. (1959). *The silent language*. Garden City, NY: Doubleday.

Hall, E. T. (1976). *Beyond culture*. Garden City, NY: Anchor Press.

Hall, E.T. (1983). *The dance of life: The other dimension of time*. Garden City, NY: Anchor Press/Doubleday.

Hall, E. T., and M. R. Hall. (1990). *Understanding cultural differences: Germans, French and Americans*. Boston, MA: Intercultural Press.

Jeong, J. Y., and Crompton, J. L. (2018). Do subjects from high and low context cultures attribute different meanings to tourism services with 9-ending prices?. *Tourism Management*, 64, 110–118.

Manrai, L. A., Manrai, A. K., Lascu, D., and Friedeborn, S. (2019). Determinants and effects of cultural context: A review, conceptual model, and propositions. *Journal of Global Marketing*, 32(2), 67–82.

Neuliep, J. W. (2018). *Intercultural communication: A contextual approach* (7th ed.). Thousand Oaks, CA: Sage.

Ting-Toomey, S., and Dorjee, T. (2018). Communicating Across Cultures. New York: Guilford Publications.

Trompenaars A., and Hampden-Turner C. (1998). *Riding the waves of cultural diversity in global business*. Boston, MA: Nicholas Brealey Publishing.

References

Becker, C. (2000). Service recovery strategies: The impact of cultural differences. *Journal of Hospitality and Tourism Research*, 24(4), 526–538.

Bergiel, E. B., Bergiel, B. J., and Upson, J. W. (2012). Revisiting Hofstede's dimensions: Examining the cultural convergence of the United States and Japan. *American Journal of Management*, 12(1), 69–79.

Boz, H., and Koc, E. (2020). Service quality, emotion recognition, emotional intelligence and Dunning Kruger syndrome. *Total Quality Management and Business Excellence*, 1–14.

Cakici, C., and Guler, O. (2017). Emotional Contagion and the influence of groups on service failures and recovery. In E. Koc (Ed.). *Service failures and recovery in tourism and hospitality* (pp. 135–159). Wallingford, Oxford: CABI.

Callow, M., and Schiffman, L. G. (2002). Implicit meaning in visual print advertisements: A cross-cultural examination of the contextual communication effect. *International Journal of Advertising*, 21(2), 259–277.

Chen, P. J., Okumus, F., Hua, N., and Nusair, K. (2011). Developing effective communication strategies for the Spanish and Haitian-Creole-speaking workforce in hotel companies. *Worldwide Hospitality and Tourism Themes*, 3(4), 335–353.

Eysenck, S. B., and Eysenck, H. J. (1967). Salivary response to lemon juice as a measure of introversion. *Perceptual and MOTOR SKILLS*, 24(3_suppl), 1047–1053.

Goeleven, E., De Raedt, R., Leyman, L., and Verschuere, B. (2008). The Karolinska directed emotional faces: A validation study. *Cognition and Emotion*, 22(6), 1094–1118.

Gong, W. (2009), National culture and global diffusion of business-to-consumer e-commerce. *Cross cultural management: An international journal*, 16(1), 83–101.

Gronroos, C. (2007). *Service management and marketing: Customer management in service competition* (Vol. 3). Chichester: Wiley.

Gudykunst, W. B., and Ting-Toomey, S. (1988). *Culture and interpersonal communication*. Newbury Park, CA: Sage.

Gudykunst, W. B., Matsumoto, Y., Ting-Toomey, S., Nishida, T., Kim, K., and Heyman, S. (1996). The influence of cultural individualism-collectivism, self construals, and individual values on communication styles across cultures. *Human Communication Research*, 22(4), 510–543.

Hall, E. T. (1959). *The silent language*. Garden City, NY: Doubleday.

Hall, E. T. (1963). A system for the notation of proxemic behavior. *American Anthropologist*, 65(5), 1003–1026.

Hall, E. T. (1976). *Beyond culture*. Garden City, NY: Anchor Press.

Hall E.T. (1983). *The dance of life: The other dimension of time*. Garden City, NY: Anchor Press/Doubleday

Hall, E. T. (1998). The power of hidden differences. In M. Bennett (Ed.), *Basic concepts of intercultural communication: selected readings* (pp. 53–67). Yarmouth: Intercultural Press.

Hall, E. T. (2000). Monochronic and polychronic time. *Intercultural Communication: A Reader*, 9, 280–286.

Hall, E. T., and M. R. Hall. (1990). *Understanding cultural differences: Germans, French and Americans*. Boston, MA: Intercultural Press.

Halverson, C. B. (1993). *Cultural context inventory. The 1993 annual: Developing human resources*. San Francisco, CA: Pfeiffer.

Hofstede, G., Hofstede, G. J., and Minkov, M. (2010). *Cultures and organizations: Software of the mind* (rev. and expanded 3rd ed.). New York: McGraw-Hill.

Hornikx, J., and le Pair, R. (2017). The influence of high-/low-context culture on perceived Ad complexity and liking. *Journal of Global Marketing*, 30(4), 228–237.

House, R. J., Hanges, P. J., Javidan, M., Dorfman, P. W., and Gupta, V. (2004). *Culture, leadership and organizations: The GLOBE study of 62 Societies*. London: Sage.

Irimias, A., and Franch, M. (2019) Developing intercultural sensitivity as an emotional ability. In E. Koc (Ed.), *Emotional intelligence in tourism and hospitality* (pp. 95–107). Wallingford, Oxford: CABI.

Iwao, S. (1993). *The Japanese woman: Traditional image and changing reality*. Cambridge, MA: Harvard University Press.

Janis, I. L., and Janis, I. L. (1982). *Groupthink: Psychological studies of policy decisions and fiascoes* (Vol. 349). Boston: Houghton Mifflin.

Koc, E. (2002). The impact of gender in marketing communications: The role of cognitive and affective cues. *Journal of Marketing Communications*, 8(4), 257–275.

Koc, E. (2006). Total quality management and business excellence in services: The implications of all-inclusive pricing system on internal and external customer satisfaction in the Turkish tourism market. *Total Quality Management and Business Excellence*, 17(7), 857–877.

Koc, E. (2010). Services and conflict management: Cultural and European integration perspectives. *International Journal of Intercultural Relations*, 34(1), 88–96.

Koc, E. (2013). Power distance and its implications for upward communication and empowerment: Crisis management and recovery in hospitality services. *The International Journal of Human Resource Management*, 24(19), 3681–3696.

Koc, E. (2015). *Hizmet Pazarlaması ve Yönetimi, 1*. Ankara: Baskı, Seçkin Yayıncılık.

Koc, E. (2016). *Tüketici Davranışı ve Pazarlama Stratejileri: Global ve Yerel Yaklaşım* (Vol. 7). Ankara, Turkey: Baskı, Seçkin Yayınları.

Koc, E. (2017). *Service failures and recovery in tourism and hospitality: A practical manual*. Wallingford, Oxford: CABI.

Koc, E. (2019). Service failures and recovery in hospitality and tourism: a review of literature and recommendations for future research. *Journal of Hospitality Marketing and Management*, 28(5), 513–537.

Koc, E. (2020). Do women make better in tourism and hospitality? A conceptual review from a customer satisfaction and service quality perspective. *Journal of Quality Assurance in Hospitality and Tourism*, 1–28.

Koc, E., and Boz, H. (2019). Development of hospitality and tourism employees' emotional intelligence through developing their emotion recognition abilities. *Journal of Hospitality Marketing and Management*, 1–18.

Lee, H. E., Hwang, J. H., and Bennett, K. (2015). Understanding culture on the effectiveness of restaurant servers' check-back style. *International Journal of Contemporary Hospitality Management*, 27(8), 1905–1926.

Le Pair, R., and Van Mulken, M. (2008). Perceived complexity and appreciation of visual metaphors by consumers with different cultural backgrounds. In F. Costa Pereira, J. Veríssimo, and P. Neijens (Eds), New *trends in advertising research* (pp. 279-290). Lisbon: Sílabo.

Lundqvist, D., Flykt, A., and Öhman, A. (1998). *The Karolinska Directed Emotional Faces – KDEF*. Stockholm: Karolinska Institutet.

Manrai, L. A., Manrai, A. K., Lascu, D., and Friedeborn, S. (2019). Determinants and effects of cultural context: A review, conceptual model, and propositions. *Journal of Global Marketing*, 32(2), 67–82.

Mattila, A. S. (1999). The role of culture and purchase motivation in service encounter evaluations. *Journal of Services Marketing*, 13(4/5), 376–389.

Mattila, A. S. (2000). The impact of culture and gender on customer evaluations of service encounters. *Journal of Hospitality and Tourism Research*, 24, 263–273.

Meyers-Levy, J., and Loken, B. (2015). Revisiting gender differences: What we know and what lies ahead. *Journal of Consumer Psychology*, 25(1), 129–149.

Neuliep, J. W. (2018). *Intercultural communication: A contextual approach* (7th Ed.). Thousand Oaks, CA: Sage

Ngamvichaikit, A., and Beise-Zee, R. (2014). Communication needs of medical tourists: An exploratory study in Thailand. *International Journal of Pharmaceutical and Healthcare Marketing*, 8(1), 98–117.

Noja, G. G., Petrović, N., and Cristea, M. (2018). Turning points in migrants' labour market integration in Europe and benefit spillovers for Romania and Serbia: the role of socio-psychological credentials. *Zbornik Radova Ekonomski Fakultet u Rijeka*, 36(2), 489–518.

O'Reilly, C. A. (1980). Individuals and information overload in organizations: Is more necessarily better? *Academy of Management Journal*, 23(4), 684–696.

Pazda, A. D., and Thorstenson, C. A. (2018). Extraversion predicts a preference for high-chroma colors. *Personality and Individual Differences*, 127, 133–138.

Pearson Education. (2015). Foundations of restaurant management and culinary arts. http://www.pearsonschool.com/index.cfm.

Pope, H. (2005). Sons of the conquerors: The rise of the Turkic world. New York: Overlook Press.

Sorokowska, A., Sorokowski, P., Hilpert, P., Cantarero, K., Frackowiak, T., Ahmadi, K., ... and Blumen, S. (2017). Preferred interpersonal distances: a global comparison. *Journal of Cross-Cultural Psychology*, 48(4), 577–592.

Stewart, C. M., Shields, S. F., and Sen, N. (2001). Diversity in on-line discussions: A study of cultural and gender differences in listervs. In C. Ess and F. Sudweeks (Eds), *Culture, technology, communication: Towards an intercultural global village* (pp. 161–186). Albany, NJ: State University of New York Press.

Ting-Toomey, S. (1988). Intercultural conflict styles: A face-negotiation theory. In Y. Y. Kim and W. Gudykunst (Eds.), *Theories in intercultural communication* (pp. 213–235). Newbury Park, CA: Wadsworth.

Ting-Toomey, S. (2005). The matrix of face: An updated face-negotiation theory. *Theorizing about Intercultural Communication*, 71–92.

Ting-Toomey, S., and Dorjee, T. (2018). Communicating across cultures. New York: Guilford Publications.

Trompenaars A. and Hampden-Turner C. (1998). Riding the waves of cultural diversity in global business. Boston, MA: Nicholas Brealey Publishing

Tung, R. (1995). International organizational behaviour. In F. Luthans (Ed.), *Virtual OB* (pp. 487–518). New York: McGraw-Hill.

Van Everdingen, Y. M., and Waarts, E. (2003). The effect of national culture on the adoption of innovations. *Marketing Letters*, 14(3), 217–232.

Wilson-Wünsch, B. R., and Decosta, N. P. L. (2019). Development of personal expertise in tourism and hospitality professions: cognitive knowledge, personality and learning style. In E. Koc (Ed.), *Emotional intelligence in tourism and hospitality* (pp. 62–74). Wallingford, Oxford: CABI.

Würtz, E. (2005). Intercultural communication on web sites: A cross-cultural analysis of web sites from high-context cultures and low-context cultures. *Journal of Computer-Mediated Communication*. 11(1), 274–299.

Yen, C. L., Singal, M., and Murrmann, S. K. (2016). Cultural context orientation and recruitment message strategy: Evidence from hospitality students in the United States and Taiwan. *Journal of Human Resources in Hospitality and Tourism*, 15(3), 325–345.

Yuksel, A., and Yuksel, F. (2001). Measurement and management issues in customer satisfaction research: Review, critique and research agenda: part two. *Journal of Travel and Tourism Marketing*, 10(4), 81–111.

Chapter 5

The influence of indulgence and restraint on tourism and hospitality

Learning Objectives

After reading this chapter, you should be able to:

- explain the main characteristics of indulgence and restraint cultures;
- understand the concept of indulgence and restraint on tourism and hospitality customers;
- explain how restraint may influence tourism and hospitality staff in delivering high-quality service customers;
- explain the concept of emotional labour and how it may relate to the attitudes of employees from an indulgence and restraint culture;
- explain the components of customer participation and its potential relationship with indulgence and restraint.

Introduction

This chapter explains and discusses the dyadic influence of indulgence and restraint dimension of culture on the marketing and management of tourism and hospitality businesses. The indulgence and restraint dimension has been developed as the last dimension and hence it is the least researched dimension of all. However, as it appears to be one of the most relevant dimensions, it is explained first in the book. Hence, inferences have been made based on various other research findings. The chapter explores the influence of indulgence and restraint in tourism on hospitality under the headings of marketing mix elements, service quality, and service orientation. The potential relationships between indulgence and restraint and concepts such as emotional labour and customer participation are investigated.

The concept of restraint and indulgence

Information zone

Khayyam on indulgence

Coming from a short-term oriented culture (Iran) Omar Khayyam's following poems on indulgence, drinking wine, enjoying life, and having fun contribute to the understanding of the concept of indulgence.

Ho heart, if the times make you said
Suddenly, your pure soul will part of your body
Lay down on the grass and live joyfully for a few days
Before the grass out from your clay (remains)

* * *

When once you hear the roses are in bloom,
The is the time, my love, to pour the wine;
Houris and palaces and Heaven and Hell-
These are but fairy-tales, forget them all.

* * *

And lately by the Tavern Door agape,
Come stealing through the Dusk an Angel Shape
Bearing a Vessel on his Shoulder; and
He bid me taste of it; and It was–the Grape!

* * *

There are no sorrows wine cannot allay,
There are no sins wine cannot wash away,
There are no riddles wine knows not to read,
There are no debts wine is too poor to pay.

* * *

Would you forget a woman, drink red wine;
Would you remember her, then drink red wine!
Is your heart breaking just to see her face?
Gaze deep within this mirror of red wine.

* * *

Youth, like a magic bird, has flown away
He sang a little morning-hour in May
Sang to the rose, his love, that too is gone--
Whither is more than you or I can say.

* * *

> The wine-cup is a wistful magic glass,
> Wherein all day old faces smile and pass,
> Dead lips press ours upon its scented brim,
> Old voices whisper many a sweet "alas!"
>
> Omar Khayyam was a Persian astronomer, philosopher, mathematician, and poet who lived between 1048 and 1131. The poems attributed to him, written in the form of quatrains (Rubaiyat), became widely known in the Western world after Edward FitzGerald's translation in 1859, titled *Rubaiyat of Omar Khayyam*.

According to Koc et al. (2017) and Koc (2020), although probably the most relevant of all the cultural dimensions for tourism and hospitality marketing and management, indulgence and restraint appear to be the least studied dimension by researchers of all the six dimensions developed by Geert Hofstede. Intrigued by Inglehart's (1997) analysis of well-being versus survival dimension, the indulgence and restraint was first coined by Minkov (2009) and was added as a cultural variable to Hofstede's cultural dimensions (Hofstede et al., 2010). The idea behind the formulation of indulgence and restraint dimension was to cover the certain societal differences which the World Values Survey (WVS) revealed. Indulgence and restraint dimension was based on 1995–2004 WVS data from 93 societies in the world which showed that there was a correlation between *relationships* and *happiness* in a society. Table 5.1 shows the restraint and indulgence scores for 72 selected countries in the world, where a lower score indicates that a particular country is more restraint oriented, and a higher score indicates that a country is more indulgence oriented.

According to Hofstede et al. (2010), indulgence reflects a tendency to allow the gratification of basic and natural desires and enjoyment in life, while restraint, that is, a lack of indulgence, is the belief that basic and natural desires and enjoyment in life need to be controlled and regulated by social norms. Indulgence cultures allow hedonistic behaviour and encourage pleasure, enjoyment, spending consumption, sexual gratification, and general merriment. On the other hand, restraint cultures have strict social norms and encourage the control of such hedonistic gratifications.

Information zone

Tulip as a symbol of abundance, indulgence, and hedonism

Tulip (or tulipa) comes from the Turkish word *turban* (hair dress) and was first brought to Asia Minor and then to Europe by Seljuck and Ottoman Turks. The commercial cultivation of tulip started in the Ottoman Empire during the eleventh century. The first tulip bulbs were sent to Europe in the sixteenth century, causing a craze in Europe. In the Netherlands around 1630, this craze was called Tulip Mania.

In the Ottoman Empire, the era or period between 1718 and 1730 is called the Tulip Period, which triggered the Ottoman Renaissance. The tulip, which represented abundance, indulgence, and hedonism, became an inspiration for many Ottoman paintings, calligraphies, songs, and poems in that period.

Table 5.1 Indulgence and restraint values in selected countries

Rank	*Country*	*Restraint Score*	*Rank*	*Country*	*Restraint Score*	*Rank*	*Country*	*Restraint Score*
1	Egypt	**4**	*25*	Indonesia	**38**	*49*	Austria	***63***
2	Latvia	**13**	*26*	Germany	**40**	*50*	South Africa	***63***
3	Albania	**15**	*27*	Iran	**40**	*51*	Ireland	***65***
4	Bulgaria	**16**	*28*	Japan	**42**	*52*	Malta	***66***
5	Estonia	**16**	*29*	Philippines	**42**	*53*	Switzerland	***66***
6	Lithuania	**16**	*30*	Jordan	**43**	*54*	Iceland	***67***
7	Iraq	**17**	*31*	Spain	**44**	*55*	Canada	***68***
8	Ukraine	**18**	*32*	Thailand	**45**	*56*	Chile	***68***
9	Bangladesh	**20**	*33*	Peru	**46**	*57*	The Netherlands	***68***
10	Romania	**20**	*34*	Singapore	**46**	*58*	United States	***68***
11	Russia	**20**	*35*	France	**48**	*59*	United Kingdom	***69***
12	China	**24**	*36*	Slovenia	**48**	*60*	Denmark	***70***
13	Lebanon	**25**	*37*	Turkey	**49**	*61*	Australia	***71***
14	Morocco	**25**	*38*	Greece	**50**	*62*	Ghana	***72***
15	India	**26**	*39*	S. Arabia	**52**	*63*	New Zealand	***75***
16	Serbia	**28**	*40*	Uruguay	**53**	*64*	Sweden	***78***
17	Slovakia	**28**	*41*	Dominica	**54**	*65*	Mozambique	***80***
18	Czechia	**29**	*42*	Norway	**55**	*66*	Trinidad	***80***
19	Poland	**29**	*43*	Luxembourg	**56**	*67*	Colombia	***83***
20	Italy	**30**	*44*	Belgium	**57**	*68*	Nigeria	***84***
21	Croatia	**33**	*45*	Finland	**57**	*69*	Angola	***86***
22	Portugal	**33**	*46*	Malaysia	**57**	*70*	El Salvador	***89***
23	Libya	**34**	*47*	Brazil	**59**	*71*	Mexico	***97***
24	Vietnam	**35**	*48*	Argentina	**62**	*72*	Venezuela	***100***

Source: Hofstede (2020). Used with permission.

Indulgence and restraint paradigm explains why people in poorer countries may be happier than people living in a richer country (Hofstede et al., 2010). Hofstede et al. (2010: 286) claim that due to their indulgence and restraint orientations, poorer people in the Philippines may be, in general, happier than people of Hong Kong, who are relatively richer. However, it should be kept in mind that there is a relationship between happiness or at least some degree of satisfaction with life, and money, as well. For instance, Cylus et al.'s (2014) study showed that a one-dollar increase in unemployment benefit programmes may reduce suicide rates significantly.

High levels of restraint may cause members of a society (e.g., people in countries such as Egypt, Russia, Romania, China, Serbia, Poland, and to some extent Japan and Turkey) tend to be moderate in their decision making and have (or let themselves to have) limited wants and desires. Table 5.2 provides a basic summary of the main characteristics of restraint and indulgence explained by Hofstede et al. (2010: 297). Based on these characteristics, a number of potential implications for tourism and hospitality may be outlined. As the indulgence and restraint dimension of culture has been largely ignored so far, the implications provided in the left-hand column of Table 5.2 are inferences made based on the cultural characteristics. Future research may concentrate on this dimension to explore the potential implications of indulgence and restraint on tourism and hospitality operations.

In addition to the characteristics provided in Table 5.2, some other characteristics of indulgence and restraint may be mentioned, which may not have such as direct influence on tourism and hospitality activities. For instance, in indulgence cultures, while people may have less moral discipline, and less strict sexual norms (especially in wealthy countries), in restraint cultures they may have more moral discipline and stricter sexual norms (Hofstede et al., 2010). Moreover, in indulgence countries while freedom of speech may be viewed as relatively more important and maintaining order may not be given a high priority (e.g., lower numbers of police officers per 100,000 people), in restraint cultures freedom of speech may not be viewed as relatively important and maintaining order may be given a high priority (e.g., higher numbers of police officers per 100,000 people). According to Minkov (2009), nations that placed constraints on their people's freedom to indulge had a lower percentage of happy people. Hamid's (2016) study of Chinese (a restraint culture) websites found that web pages had a rather low percentage of pictures of people laughing, and a high percentage of people with serious-looking faces.

Based on the above, Dukes (2016) put forward that in a high indulgence society people would show expression of opinions more readily than a culture that restrains itself. This may mean that people from indulgence cultures are more likely to make formal complaints and engage in eWoM communications. Ruiz-Equihua et al. (2019) found that tourism and hospitality customers from indulgence countries were more likely to engage in eWOM and reacted more positively towards it, and had higher booking intentions than restrained countries, regardless of the valence of the online review. On the other hand, customers from restraint cultures were less likely to write online reviews (engage in eWOM), and if they did, they tended to produce more negative online reviews, as they were more pessimistic. Ruiz-Equihua et al. (2019) recommended that managers of tourism and hospitality establishments serving customers from indulgent countries should encourage their customers to write online reviews.

Table 5.2 Basic summary of the main characteristics of indulgence and restraint cultures

Indulgence Cultures e.g., Venezuela, Mexico, Sweden, New Zealand, Australia, Denmark, United Kingdom, United States, Argentina, Brazil, Belgium, Luxembourg	*Restraint Cultures e.g., Egypt, Bulgaria, Estonia, Iraq, Ukraine, Romania, Russia, China, Serbia, Slovakia, Poland and Italy.*	*Potential Implications for Tourism and Hospitality*
Perception of personal life control	A perception of helplessness – "what happens to me is not my own doing" kind of mentality	Restraint – the attribution of service failures to external factors by service personnel. Procrastination of problems. Reluctance to take initiative action.
Higher importance of leisure and fun	Lower importance of leisure and fun	Plenty of implications for both restraint and indulgence cultures. Indulgence – a higher level of involvement of tourists with holidays. Collection and processing of more information relating to tourism and hospitality products and services. Emphasising fun, hedonism and happiness themes in marketing mix elements (e.g., in marketing communications) may be more relevant. Restraint – a lower level of service orientation of employees and the service business in general.
Higher importance of having friends; more extroverted personalities	Lower importance of having friends; more neurotic personalities	Indulgence – marketing communications messages showing friends enjoying themselves may be effective. Restraint – staff may lack social and teamwork skills tourism and hospitality operations require.
More likely to remember positive emotions	Less likely to remember positive emotions	Restraint – the tendency of customers to evaluate tourism and hospitality experiences more negatively. Negative attitude towards service recovery efforts. The service recovery paradox may not occur in many instances. Indulgence – the tendency of customers to evaluate tourism and hospitality experiences more positively.

Table 5.2 continued

Indulgence Cultures e.g., Venezuela, Mexico, Sweden, New Zealand, Australia, Denmark, United Kingdom, United States, Argentina, Brazil, Belgium, Luxembourg	*Restraint Cultures e.g., Egypt, Bulgaria, Estonia, Iraq, Ukraine, Romania, Russia, China, Serbia, Slovakia, Poland and Italy.*	*Potential Implications for Tourism and Hospitality*
Positive attitude and optimism	Cynicism and pessimism	Indulgence – positive attitudes of employees towards change and development initiatives by management. Restraint – a cynical attitude of employees towards change and development initiatives by management.
Thrift is not very important	Thrift is important	Restraint – over-emphasis on thrift may result in allocating a smaller budget by customers for tourism and hospitality activities.
Smiling as a norm; loose society	Smiling as a suspect; tight society	Indulgence – service employees may establish rapport and social relationships with customers more easily. Customers may feel more relaxed when served by smiling service personnel.
A higher percentage of people who feel healthier and happier. More people participating in activities in sports.	A lower percentage of people who feel healthier and happier. Fewer people participating in actively in sports.	Indulgence – service employees who feel happier and healthier may provide a better service. Sports-based tourism activities (e.g., golf tourism and skiing) may be more developed. Restraint – service employees who may not feel happy and healthy may not provide a good-quality service. Sports-based tourism activities (e.g., golf tourism and skiing) may not be highly developed.
More satisfying family life; "household tasks should be shared between partners" view is prevalent	Less satisfying family life; unequal sharing of household tasks may not be seen as a problem	Indulgence – engaging in tourism and hospitality activities as a family may be more common. This may have several implications for all marketing mix elements and service quality dimensions. Restraint – engaging in tourism and hospitality activities as a family may not be so common. This may have several implications for all marketing mix elements and service quality dimensions.

Source: Hofstede et al. (2010).

CASE STUDY

Pessimism, optimism and problem solving

Jung-Beeman et al. (2004), who carried out research in the area of the neuroscience of insight, found that when people were in a good mood they were significantly better at solving hard problems that required insight than people who were bad tempered, irritable, and depressed. Happy people tend to solve 20% more word puzzles than unhappy people. This can be due to the fact that brain areas associated with executive control, such as the prefrontal cortex and the anterior cingulate cortex (ACC), are not highly preoccupied with managing the emotional life. In other words, when they are happy, people do not worry about why they are unhappy, which means that they are freer to solve the problem at hand.

Based on these characteristics, it may be speculated that, in general, people from indulgence cultures may be better at solving problems than people from restraint cultures.

Watch the short video at https://bit.ly/2OpPpyl. The video shows the influence of positive thinking on getting successful results.

Exercise

Find your country's indulgence and restraint score in Table 5.1 to determine whether it is an indulgence or restraint culture. Also look at the figures of the countries which are at the other end of the continuum, that is, the ones which have a significantly different indulgence and restraint orientations from your own country. Find colleagues who are from the countries at the other end of the indulgence and restraint continuum. Sit down with your colleagues and study the basic main characteristics of indulgence and restraint cultures explained earlier. Determine the extent to which these characteristics apply to your countries. Discuss the potential implications of these characteristics for tourism and hospitality activities and operations.

The relationship between restraint and indulgence and tourism and hospitality operations

Indulgence and restraint may influence tourism and hospitality customers and service employees in a number of ways as shown in the incidents in Table 5.3.

Table 5.3 Potential tourism and hospitality incidents relating to indulgence and restraint

Indulgence Culture	*Restraint Culture*
A tourist from an indulgence culture may know more about the features and history of Basilica Cistern (Istanbul) than a local shopkeeper who may have run a shop in the area catering for international tourists for many years.	After its opening a five-star luxury hotel in Antalya, Turkey (a relatively restraint culture), though the hotel may have excellent physical facilities amenities, hotel management may employ former construction workers, who worked in the construction of the hotel, as a waiter who has little or no training in service delivery.
As tourism and hospitality customers from an indulgence culture may be more knowledgeable and skilled about the service, they may have a more positive attitude towards participating in the service.	A waiter in a restaurant in a restraint culture may not know that the guest would be served from the right-hand side.
Tourism and hospitality customers from an indulgence culture may evaluate a service more positively as they are more likely to remember positive emotions.	Service recovery paradox[1] may be experienced more infrequently by tourism and hospitality customers from a restraint culture as they are more likely to remember negative emotions.
Service employees from an indulgence culture may have a relatively higher level of service orientation as they have an inherent understanding and feeling of fun, leisure, and hedonic experiences.	A manager of tourism and hospitality business from a restraint culture may employ fewer and less skilled staff.

Marketing mix elements

As briefly mentioned in Table 5.2, indulgence and restraint may influence marketing mix elements in a number of ways. The main influences of indulgence and restraint on tourism and hospitality may relate to marketing mix elements, service quality, and service orientation. As indulgence cultures allow hedonistic behaviour and encourage pleasure, enjoyment, spending consumption, sexual gratification, and general merriment (Hofstede et al., 2010), tourism and hospitality businesses marketing their products and services to customers from an indulgence culture may position their products around these themes.

For instance, as an airline company, Emirates adopts a breakaway positioning strategy (Koc, 2016), that is, markets itself as if it is an extremely luxury restaurant or a hotel, rather than as another airline. Breakaway positioning encourages customers to perceive the product or service in a completely different category, rather than just an alternative to others (Moon, 2005). Emirates, which is consistently ranked as one of the world's best, and is generally considered as one of the most luxurious airlines, uses sensory stimuli to entice their customers by emphasising how their highly exquisite and delicious 12450 recipes are prepared by award-winning 1,800 chefs.

The marketing mix elements of Emirates convey messages to reflect its positioning as shown in Table 5.4.

Table 5.4 Indulgence indicators in the marketing mix elements of emirates

Marketing Mix Elements	*Examples*	*Messages Conveyed*
Product	Some 12,450 recipes prepared by 1800 award-winning chefs.	
	Highly skilled chefs produce extremely delightful and beautiful recipes which are like intricate works of art.	
	Emirates chauffeur service – to pick up the customers at their front doors.	
	Meals are served on-demand and customers can choose from a huge selection of foods, accompanied by the fine selection of wines. During the flight, the customers can use the inflight lounge/bar area.	
	There is also an easy connection for phone and email.	
Price	High prices reflect exclusivity and luxury.	Exclusivity
Place	Airport lounges and offices designed and decorated in such a way to exude the feeling of comfort, luxury, and exclusivity.	Prestige
Promotion	Advertisements show how their chefs pay attention to detail.	
	Advertisements emphasise the inflight entertainment system and promote the extensive network of global destinations.	Luxury
People	Award-winning chefs.	Hedonism
	Beautiful and handsome flight attendants with a healthy body mass index scores.	Delight
	Staff smiling and responsive all the time.	
	Stylish looking fashion design uniforms.	Pleasure
	Flight attendants attend eight weeks of training before they start.	
	After 12 to 18 months, crew members can advance from economy class to business class.	Deliciousness
Process	Customers are fast-tracked through security to go straight to the luxury lounges.	Comfort
	The lounges are situated nearby the gate. When the flight is ready the customers simply have to walk down a flight of stairs to embark on the plane.	Ease
	The customers can change their seats anytime they like before the flight.	
Physical Evidence	All fleet comprise wide-body aircrafts.	
	On the plane, there would be a massive television screen and the award-winning ICE (Information, Communication and Entertainment) system with up to 1,400 channels showing the latest films, television, music, news, and even live sporting events. Customers can browse the entertainment options and build a playlist of everything they plan to watch and listen to during their flights.	
	Flatbed seats.	

As another example, the following case study (based on the notes from Mathieu's (1999) paper titled "Economic citizenship and the rhetoric of gourmet coffee", shows how Starbucks, as a hospitality firm, has been able to develop its marketing image and positioning in the market. The case study explains how Starbucks designed its marketing mix elements (7Ps) to develop its hedonistic and pleasure-oriented image in the market.

Starbucks claim that drinking its coffee is a transcendent gourmet experience and that they train their baristas to convey the feeling of "unique coffee experience". In line with these features of indulgence, the customer involves herself/himself in the indulgence-related terminology and learns Starbucks' terminology. As mentioned in the case, Starbucks assures its customers that if a shot of espresso is not served within 10 seconds of brewing, it is poured out. While this message enhances the dedication to hedonistic pleasures and indulgence, it actually valorises wastefulness as a virtue (Mathieu, 1999) (a symbolism of indulgence), not thrift (a symbolism of restraint).

Exercise

Watch a few sessions of the TV show *Amazing Hotels* (presented by Giles Coren and Monica Galetti) on YouTube. Take down notes and explain how 7Ps (marketing mix elements) and service quality dimensions are designed to satisfy indulgent customers in luxury hotels.

CASE STUDY

Indulgence at Starbucks

Between the fifteenth and nineteenth centuries, coffee and tobacco were among the most important pleasures in the Ottoman culture. Coffee and tobacco was offered and consumed almost everywhere from coffee houses to mansions and palaces. Coffee was an essential element of hospitality and entertaining accommodating guests.

Founded in Seattle, Washington in 1971, Starbucks, today with about its 30,000 stores and about 400,000 employees all over the world is the largest coffee chain in the world. Starbucks' net income exceeded $ 6 billion in 2019.

Mathieu's (1999) paper "Economic citizenship and the rhetoric of gourmet coffee" published in *Rhetoric Review* provides some cues to understand the hedonic and indulgence related aspects of Starbucks. The following notes have been extracted from Mathieu (1999):

- When we consume Starbucks, we consume justifying narratives along with the products.
- Starbucks attempts to persuade consumers that drinking its coffee is a transcendent gourmet experience (unique coffee experience).
- The language and images of Starbucks bolster the assertion that its beverages are not merely coffee; rather they are made from unique ingredients and prepared to highest standards.
- Behind it bustles an often-frantic, highly energetic staff of workers, called baristas; this term, which is Italian for "bartender", has become an industry standard for people who make espresso. The baristas wear matching uniforms consisting of green aprons and logoed baseball caps or visors. All orders are communicated and passed along verbally, in a system of call-and-response. The orders rapidly repeated back and forth take on a strange cadence, given the denseness of the terminology: "doppio con panna", "double tall skinny iced decaf no-whip skim mocha". With all the scenery and action, set to the hiss and sputter of the espresso machine, a Starbucks store contains all the elements of a theatrical performance.
- Consumers are encouraged not to think of the people who plant, harvest, and transport coffee but instead to see only the performing baristas who take centre stage, enacting the service of making coffee.
- Starbucks attempts to persuade consumers that drinking its coffee is a transcendent gourmet experience. The language and images of Starbucks bolster the assertion that its beverages are not merely coffee; rather they are made from incomparable ingredients and prepared to exacting standards. Therefore, the language used to describe the drinks must be completely different. This belief is reinforced by stamping one of two slogans on its disposable cups. One, "The Weather Changes Our Grind",
- Other examples of medical language include "the right dose", "extraction", "method", "variables", "experiment", "optimum temperature", "results", and "critical." By detailing the meticulous steps involved in coffee brewing, Starbucks spins a narrative that a successful cup is always elusive.
- Coffee is positioned no longer as a drink, but as a drug that must be administered by skilled professionals in its proper "dose". The company can then justify its elaborate rituals and higher prices all in the name of good science, and firmly establish its authority.
- Starbucks' discourse, crucially, does not rely on the language of technology and science alone. At the same time as emphasising strict brewing procedures, Starbucks promises how sensual and refined an experience drinking its coffee will be. To capture this element of eroticism and connoisseurship, Starbucks echoes language commonly used to describe sexuality, wine-tasting, art, philosophy, and European imperialism. As an erotic experience, espresso drinking is presented as a momentary thrill, one which will leave the drinker almost painfully wanting more. This is achieved by the use of phrases like "savoured momentarily", "burst of flavour sensed throughout the mouth", "fleeting flavor", and "rewarding the drinker."
- In addition to being an erotic thrill, gourmet coffee is portrayed as a pleasure to be appreciated by aficionados with highly refined taste. Europe, especially Italy, is referred to time and again as a romantic world of connoisseurs who should be emulated. The basis for Starbucks' language is Italian: barista, doppio, chiaro, ristretto, machiatto, and con panna are all Italian-based drink names while sizes are short, tall, or grande. References are made to the "authentic", "Italian coffee culture", "aficionados", "in France

tells customers that a variation in weather can drastically change the taste of a cup of coffee. At the same time, the message assures consumers that Starbucks adjusts its grinding technique in order to offer a consistent cup: "Our coffee preparation is so exacting that the grind of our coffee is constantly monitored. Even a change in weather can precipitate a change in our grind. It's our guarantee that your next cup of Starbucks will be as good as your last."

- Assurance that Starbucks will provide the drinker with a perfect cup of coffee in any weather lives on long past the actual drink. A second message gives espresso drinkers the "10 second rule" strictly followed by baristas. If a shot of espresso is not served within 10 seconds of brewing, it is poured out. Again, this message of efficiency, which actually valorises wastefulness as a virtue, becomes an integral part of the product served by Starbucks.
- Starbucks' logo, a ubiquitous image that even passers-by recognise and consume. Starbucks' logo is an ambiguous female Siren or mermaid. Her hair is long, her body is curvy, and her mouth is open. Her arms are spread out to her side, and what appears to be her tail is spread wide, disappearing behind her crowned head. If logos are predominantly graphic abstractions, they allow the consumer to interpret them according to his or her fantasies (Willis, 1991). This sexualised logo is a form of visual rhetoric, appearing on store signs and disposable cups as a constant reminder of the company and its products, perhaps appealing to the majority-male Starbucks' repeat customers (Gower, 1994).

and Italy", "Milan and Turin." Throughout many brochures, coffee-drinking is compared to wine connoisseurship. "The World of Coffee" includes a glossary of coffee-tasting terminology, with terms reminiscent of wine-tasting, like "earthy", "briny", "mellow", "tangy" and even "winy—a desirable flavor reminiscent of fine red wine". To drink Starbucks and to speak the language allows the consumer to define him- or herself as someone with refined tastes, without requiring the massive costs of fine art or wine collecting. It allows consumers to partake in a fast-food version of a European connoisseur tradition.

- When depicting coffee producers, Starbucks presents romanticised images while promoting its own work with aid organisations such as CARE. Starbucks donates two dollars to CARE from the purchase of a special "CARE sampler" of coffees from Kenya, Guatemala, Sumatra, and Java. The company also boasts other financial donations to global charities as well as donation of its "old" coffee beans to local charities. The advertisement of these donation practices, as well as a health-care package available to part-time employees at its retail stores, allows Starbucks to create a reputation as an ethical, global-friendly coffee purveyor.
- Deciding to make a purchase at Starbucks, one is faced with another inducement to scotosis in the form of Starbucks' specialised terminology. Starbucks offers its consumers an overwhelming array of drink choices; including all sizes and different options, the drink selections number in the dozens. Because many different drinks are available, one can entertain the illusion that a drink choice is tailored specifically to one's individual desires – control.

- Closely related to the technological language (and procedures), the "Espresso: What You Need to Know" brochure contains numerous references to science and medicine. The very title assumes the dire, medical tone more commonly associated with an informational brochure on venereal-disease prevention than one for a coffee shop.
- The drink names at Starbucks exemplify functionalised language. Such cumbersome language once repeated often enough, becomes just another "natural" part of the purchasing ritual. According to Marcuse (1991), "the ritualized concept is made immune against contradiction".

Exercise

As Howard Schultz, the founding CEO of Starbucks, put it the company expects its employees to pour their hearts into it (the cup). Study the again the previous case study (Indulgence at Starbucks) and the following service orientation scale. Based on the following, prepare a presentation to explain how Starbucks ensures service orientation for its hedonistic and indulgence-based coffee experience:

The main tenets of "The Starbucks Experience" expects the following from its employees:

- "Make it your own" – customisation of the experience (e.g., things like writing the names of the customers on the cup).
- "Everything matters" – focusing on every aspect of the job. Never losing focus on the customer's experience and point of view.
- "Surprise and delight" – doing the unexpected to make buying a cup of coffee a unique and enjoyable experience.
- "Embrace resistance" – learning from mistakes.
- "Leave your mark" – doing the job in a way that your customers remember the individual Starbucks employee.

Starbucks distributes a company pamphlet called the "Green Apron Book" which puts an emphasis on the following five principles:

- "Be welcoming"
- "Be genuine"
- "Be considerate"
- "Be knowledgeable"
- "Be involved".

According to Koc et al. (2017) people with a high level of restraint are more likely to define a discipline for each behaviour and try to keep themselves generally disinterested in the opposite (Bathaee, 2011). Additionally, a low level of indulgence (i.e., restraint) is correlated with a feeling of pessimism and negativism as restraint and limitations in these societies tend to foster negative feelings and a lack of trust (Hofstede et al., 2010; Marcu et al., 2018; Noja et al., 2018). This, in turn, may prevent or delay a customer's attention to new and alternative options, and cause the customers to lower their evaluations of a product, and in the end reduce their level of satisfaction (Koc et al., 2017).

CASE STUDY

Gratification in restraint cultures

As explained earlier, while indulgence cultures tend to allow hedonistic behaviour and encourage pleasure, enjoyment, spending consumption, sexual gratification and general merriment, restraint cultures tend to have strict social norms and encourage the control of such hedonistic gratifications. Using Freud's components of personality analogy indulgence cultures may be said to resemble id (uncontrolled bodily urges of food, sex, etc.), while restraint cultures may be said to resemble to superego (society's rules and norms to control behaviour).

As a restraint culture, people in Japan (especially women) are embarrassed to have other people hear the sounds of the more private bodily functions. Women used to use the flush in the toilets a few times so that others do not hear their bodily functions. As this resulted in the wasting of a lot of water, most ladies' rooms in department stores and office buildings in Japan are equipped with a device called Otohime (originally the brand name of a product developed by Toto Ltd) that emits the sound of a toilet flushing. At the opposite end in Holland, an indulgence culture, one may find see-through toilets in crowded squares. The Dutch do not feel restrained by the presence of others when they go to the toilet.

As thrift is another feature of restraint cultures, such as Japan, though people are relatively rich, they may tend to be frugal and refrain from spending unless it is really necessary. Turkey has a culture with a relatively low level of indulgence, yet the level of conspicuous consumption is high due to the high level of power distance; wastefulness, as the opposite of thrift, is still viewed as a vice. Koc (2016) reports that trade-in (bringing the old one for a discount) campaigns are widely used by marketers in Turkey to persuade customers to buy new products. When customers bring in their old products to get new ones, they feel that they are being thrifty, that is, not wasteful.

Again in Turkey when people laugh and enjoy themselves for a while they tend to say that "We have laughed much. Hope we don't cry now." This may be because they feel that indulging themselves is wrong. Also when somebody used to laugh heavily and loudly, it was said "Don't laugh like a woman" or worse, degradingly, "Don't laugh like a flippant or floozy woman." In addition, families used to have their dinners and lunches in complete silence. Talking and laughing during eating were unacceptable. Further, Turks may tend to have a pessimistic approach towards events in life. For example, when the businessmen are asked how the business is going, although they may be doing well and prospering, they tend to refrain from saying positive things, and at best they may say "not bad". Students in Turkey, even after undertaking a good exam, refrain from saying that it was good until the results are announced. People also make these negative comments as they believe (superstitiously) that making positive comments would cause other people to envy them, which in turn may cause results being really negative.

Additionally, in Turkey, traditionally before a wedding the groom was expected to go through a number of painful experiences (e.g., drinking salty coffee) before he was able to get married. A groom also had to pay a significant amount in fees (several times more than the usual fee) and tips to people such as tailors, hairdressers, and those in the registry offices, and go through various pranks people played. This was as if they had to pay a price or suffer before in order to be able to experience happiness.

In Turkey, traditionally the night before the wedding, called henna night, is a night for ladies, a kind of bachelorette party in the Western countries (but with the whole family instead). This ceremony is a time to celebrate the bride and saying goodbye to her family. During this time, the bride is the centre of her family, and she moves on to be the wife of her groom and becomes the centre of her groom's family. The groom attends the ceremony for a short while in the middle when the henna is placed on the bride's hands. Hence, it is called henna night. Through the singing of local traditional songs, with the theme of leaving parents' home, the bride is made to cry. As a restraint cultural norm, the bride is expected to cry, as otherwise it would mean that she did not love her family, and she was too happy to marry and leave her parents and the family.

Moreover, in Turkey when people visited other families with their children, they used to warn their children to make sure that they rejected the food and beverage offerings made by the host family. Appearing greedy was the wrong thing. Although some of these traditions and related rituals changed significantly through time, some of the restraint culture characteristics still appear to be strongly embedded in the Turkish culture.

When McDonald's opened its first restaurant in Moscow in the 1990s, it trained its staff to smile at the customers when they came to the restaurant. Later, the McDonald's managers found out that Russian customers (a restraint culture) were shocked by those broad smiles and took those smiles with suspicion, as Russians never smiled to a stranger. They thought something was wrong with the service personnel (Hofstede et al., 2010; Humphrey, 2018).

Service quality

Service quality dimensions

As shown in Table 5.2, customers from restraint cultures tend to attach less value to fun, leisure and other desires, and hedonic activities. Considering how tourism and hospitality products and services primarily offer hedonic experiences, indulgence and restraint dimension may have strong implications for various aspects of tourism and hospitality (Koc, 2017a). These implications may relate to customers, employees, managers, and society as a whole (e.g., attitudes of locals towards tourists and guests). Koc (2017a) puts forward that indulgence may have significant implications for tourism and hospitality service encounters in general, and service failures and recoveries in particular. Koc et al.

(2017) argue that as restraint cultures attach less value and importance to fun, leisure and hedonistic activities, employees and managers of tourism and hospitality businesses in restraint cultures may find it difficult to internalise the tourism and hospitality activities to the extent required by customers. Hence, staff and managers in these businesses may be unable to manage service encounters efficiently and effectively and may fail to develop and deliver better touristic products/services, and destinations. From a service quality perspective, a restraint orientation may have important potential implications for service quality gaps (see the following Information zone).

Information zone

Potential implications of restraint for service quality gaps

Service Quality Gap	*Explanations*	*Implications for Service Business from a Restraint Culture*
The Knowledge or Perception Gap	Difference between what customers expect and what managers think customers expect from the service business. The service business does not know exactly what customers expect.	Service employees may not understand and interpret customers' expectations correctly. Service employees may view customer expectations as unnecessarily high, exaggerated, and senseless. Service employees and managers may fail to pay sufficient attention to customers' expectations.
The Standards or Policy Gap	Difference between service businesses' understanding of the customer needs and the translation of that understanding into service delivery policies and standards.	Service managers may find it difficult to translate customer expectations into standards, procedures, processes, and policies. Service managers may fail to establish rigorous human resource management policies, procedures and strategies.
The Delivery Gap	Difference between service quality standards and specifications and the actual service delivered to the customers.	Service employees may be unable to perform according to the standards set due to the lack of knowledge and abilities. Service employees may view standards as unnecessarily high, or useless.

Service Quality Gap	*Explanations*	*Implications for Service Business from a Restraint Culture*
		Service managers may be unable to design and implement training programmes to ensure performance according to the standards set. Service managers may fail to establish cohesive teams to deliver a unified service to customers.
The Communications Gap	Difference between what is communicated to the customer and the actual service delivered.	Unnecessarily high and wrong customer expectations may be established through marketing communications messages.
The Customer Gap	Difference between customer expectations and customer perceptions. Customers may not always understand what the service has done for them or they may misinterpret the service quality.	Ideally, the customers' expectations need to be almost identical to the customers' perceptions. Based on the above inabilities there may be a gap between customers' expectations and perceptions.

As previously mentioned, people from high indulgence cultures would be more likely to remember positive emotions and experiences, while customers from restraint cultures are more likely to remember negative experiences. This may mean that the indulgence-restraint orientation of customers may have significant implications in terms of the post-service evaluations of customers. For instance, Koc et al.'s (2020) study showed that service recovery paradox did not take place among Russian tourists (a restraint culture) having holidays in Antalya, Turkey, due to the fact that they were more likely to remember the negative experiences. Service recovery paradox can be defined as "a situation in which a customer has experienced a problem which has been satisfactorily resolved, and where the consumer subsequently rates their satisfaction to be equal to or greater than that in which no problem had occurred" (McCollough and Bharadwaj, 1992: 119), that is, customer's post-failure satisfaction is greater than pre-failure satisfaction. Moreover, when customers experience a satisfactory recovery, their loyalty tends to increase, which is consistent with the service recovery paradox (Smith and Bolton, 1998; Baker, 2017; Kim, 2017; Koc 2017a).

While the optimism in indulgence-oriented cultures usually causes a perception of more personal life control, the pessimism in restraint cultures causes a perception of helplessness (Hofstede et al., 2010). The service employees from a restraint culture may feel helplessness when faced with service failures, may externally attribute the causes of the failure, and may be reluctant to take the necessary initiative to recover the failure. Additionally, the feeling of cynicism (Hofstede et al., 2010) among service personnel may result in a lack of empathy for customers during service failures, and an apathy towards management's change and development attempts. Moreover, research in organisational behaviour shows that cynicism results in a decline in job satisfaction, organisational commitment, organisational trust, organisational citizenship behaviour, and increases job alienation and employee burnout (Abraham, 2000; Brandes and Das, 2006; Bedeian, 2007; Brandes et al., 2008). This may mean that employees from a restraint culture may have reduced levels of job satisfaction, organisational commitment, organisational trust, organisational citizenship behaviour, and increased job alienation and employee burnout compared with employees from an indulgence culture working in the same tourism and hospitality business. The consequences of the cynicism of employees may have a significant influence on customer satisfaction as the above consequences of cynicism may influence the quality of the service provided by these service employees.

In addtion, pessimism may have important implications for both customers and employees in tourism and hospitality. For instance, pessimist customers may be more likely to have a high level of risk aversion, which may result in a low level of variety-seeking behaviour. Likewise, neophobia (fear of eating new or unfamiliar foods) and neophilia (tendency to like and try new foods) may also be influenced by the indulgence and restraint orientation of customers. From an organisational behaviour perspective, the pessimism of employees reduces their motivation (Bunjak et al., 2019), and results in a lack of creativity (i.e., in solving customer problems) (Rego et al., 2018). This means that employee pessimism, just like cynicism, may have detrimental effects on employee–customer interactions and the delivery of a high level of service quality.

Verduyn and Lavrijsen (2015) found that sadness and anger were the longest-lasting emotions in mind. As people from a restraint culture are more likely to remember negative feelings (such as sadness and anger), these emotions may be more likely to last longer in the minds of customers and employees who are from a restraint culture. Future research may investigate and compare the duration of negative emotions remaining in the minds of employees and customers from indulgence and restraint cultures in relation to various aspects of tourism and hospitality operations.

Emotional labour

The lack of the ability of service employees from restraint cultures to internalise the tourism and hospitality activities to the extent required by the customers may also cause other problems in terms of the emotions employees demonstrate. Service employees are expected to control their feelings to express organisationally expected emotions through facial and bodily displays, and verbal communication (Ashforth and Humprey, 1993). According to Hochschild (1983: 7), the concept of emotional labour can be defined as "the management of feelings to create a publicly observable facial and bodily display".

As briefly explained in Chapter 3, the two main dimensions of emotional labour are *surface acting* and *deep acting* (Hochschild, 1983; Diefendorff et al., 2005). Surface acting is the act of service employees hiding their real feelings and showing different emotional exhibitions (i.e., faking and feigning their emotions and behaviour) towards customers, peers and managers (Koc, 2017a). This means that in surface acting employees pretend to have certain emotions they do not have at a particular time moment (Ashforth and Humphrey, 1993; Basim and Begenirbas, 2012). Employees use words, mimics, and body language to show the positive emotions they are expected to demonstrate towards customers, peers, and managers.

On the other hand, in *deep acting*, service employees try to feel those emotions that they are expected/required to feel and *internalise* the emotions due to the role expectations. In deep acting, emotions of employees are actively encouraged, suppressed, or shaped (Basim and Begenirbas, 2012). In other words, when service employees engage in deep acting they put themselves in the customer's (or peer's or manager's) place before exhibiting a behaviour, and act on the basis of what is expected of them (Yilmaz et al., 2015; Koc and Bozkurt, 2017).

When service employees fake their (surface acting), they will eventually feel emotionally exhausted and reduce their job satisfaction (Morris and Feldman, 1996; Koc, 2017a). Based on role conflict theory, it is assumed that there are two positive correlations between emotional dissonance, emotional exhaustion, emotional effort, and job satisfaction. When service employees display a fake emotion (surface acting), they tend to experience a higher level of emotional exhaustion and a lower level of job satisfaction (leading to stress and job burnout). Service employees who display genuine emotion (deep acting) will experience a lower of level emotional exhaustion and higher level of job satisfaction (Chu, 2002; Koc and Bozkurt, 2017).

Compared with surface acting, deep acting requires more ability, knowledge, and skills (to internalise the service) than surface acting. The previous explanations may be interpreted that service employees from a restraint culture may be more likely to engage in surface acting, that is, fake, feign their emotions, and pretend to have certain emotions they do not have at a particular time moment) and feel more emotional dissonance. This may mean that service employees from a restraint culture may be more likely to experience job stress and burnout.

However, employees' own culture is not the only determinant of their behaviours. The employees' outward responses may be seriously influenced by the culture of the customers with whom they interact. Yurur et al. (2011) found that employees' emotional behaviours are significantly influenced by the behaviour of customers. For instance, as employees from a restraint culture feel that indulging themselves is wrong, they may be irritated by the hedonistically oriented behaviours (pleasure, enjoyment, spending consumption, sexual gratification behaviours) of customers from an indulgence culture during the consumption of tourism and hospitality services.

Job stress occurs when work demands exceed an employee's coping abilities (Koc, 2006). However, when the employees experience prolonged periods of work demands beyond their coping abilities, they may find themselves in a situation of learned helplessness and eventually burnout syndrome (Maslach et al., 2001). Employee burnout has a number of important consequences such as deterioration of job performance, job dissatisfaction, a shifting of time spent on work-related activities to non-work related activities, diminished organisational commitment, and increased absenteeism and turnover intentions (Chen et al., 2012; Jung et al., 2012; Yurur and Unlu, 2011). All these consequences may have serious implications for service quality dimensions. A tourism and hospitality business with employees who are stressed and possibly experiencing burnout syndrome may find it difficult to score high in terms of reliability, responsiveness, assurance, and empathy.

As a final note on emotional labour, it should be remembered that people from indulgence cultures tend to be more extrovert and are more likely to express their opinions, feelings, and emotions; people from restraint cultures tend to be more introvert and are more likely to refrain from expressing their opinions, feelings, and emotions. This may further exacerbate the problem of emotional dissonance at work among service employees who are from a restraint culture.

As stated previously, customers from an indulgence culture tend to place more value on leisure and fun, and hence their level of involvement in the purchase (pre-purchase, purchase, and post-purchase), use and consumption stages of tourism and hospitality products and services may be high (Koc, 2017a). Money and Crotts (2003) found that as a restraint culture people in Japan tended to leave travel arrangements to professionals rather than do themselves, that is, they were not highly involved with their holiday arrangements.

As involvement may cause customers to engage in more intensive effort to collect and analyse information, customers from indulgence cultures may be more sophisticated and astute, and hence may develop more specific expectations regarding the tourism and hospitality products (Koc et al., 2017; Khosrowjerdi et al., 2020).

Exercise

Tables 5.2 and 5.4 show that people from indulgence cultures tend to attach more importance to leisure, fun, and hedonism.

In a group of three or more, carry out an internet search to find out the country backgrounds of the world's top twenty a) hotels, b) restaurants, c) fast-food chains, d) leisure and entertainment businesses, e) coffee chains. Prepare a top twenty businesses lists for each category together with the countries they come from. Study the list and the countries.

What have you found? Are they all from indulgence countries? You have probably found that all of these businesses do not come from a variety of indulgence countries and plenty of them are particularly from one county: the United States.

Look at your top twenty businesses lists for each category again. Consider and discuss the likely influence of factors, other than a country's indulgence and restraint orientation of a country, such as such as the population, wealth, history, and development of these nations to explain each country's background of businesses in your top twenty lists.

Customer participation in tourism and hospitality services

The notion of placement of importance to fun may also have implications for customer participation in tourism and hospitality services. Customer participation/co-creation/involvement can be defined as the extent to which a customer is involved in producing and delivering a service (Cermak et al., 2011; Koc et al., 2017). As customer participation requires knowledge, ability, skills, and willingness to participate in the service, customers from a restraint culture may be less likely to participate in the service. Customer participation may have several benefits for both customers and service businesses (Koc et al., 2017) such as increased productivity and decreased costs, improved service quality, increased enjoyment of the service and customer loyalty, greater repurchase intentions, and word of mouth referrals (Bendapudi and Leone, 2003; Cermak et al., 2011; Prentice, 2013; Koc et al., 2017).

Customer participation may be in the form of physical, mental, or emotional participation (Cermak et al., 2011). Mental participation/inputs, or the cognitive labour, of customers, involves gathering analysing, synthesising, comparing, memorising, and calculating activities in relation to the service (Koc et al., 2017). Physical inputs are to do with the body of the customer and her/his actions with tangible elements of service such as carrying (e.g., customers picking up their own food from an open buffet restaurant in a hotel to carry it to their table), moving, organising, and tidying up of things (Lovelock 2001; Koc et al., 2017). Lastly, emotional inputs may be in the form of all the emotions felt by customers while participating in a service setting such as being patient, being keen to receive the service, and forming positive expectations in terms of the consequences of the service (Koc et al., 2017).

Based on the tendency of placing less importance on fun, leisure, and pleasure and being less involved in tourism and hospitality activities, customers from a restraint culture may be expected to be less likely to participate in any the forms of customer participation in tourism and hospitality services. On the other hand, customers from an indulgence culture may be more able, and willing to participate in such services.

Moreover, in indulgence cultures, while the gender roles may be loosely prescribed, in restraint cultures the gender roles may be more strictly prescribed (Hofstede et al., 2010). According to the World Tourism Organisation's (UNWTO) Global Report on Tourism (2011: 43), "even in areas where women in tourism perform better than women in other sectors of the economy, women still lag far behind men". The report demonstrates that even in the tourism industry, there is widespread and systematic discrimination against women (Women First, 2010; Koc, 2020). The jobs women carry out in tourism and hospitality can often be classified as physically exhausting, stressful, low paid, and demeaning (Hoel and Einarsen, 2003). The jobs women hold in tourism and hospitality can often be regarded as *dirty work* (Guerrier and Adib, 2003; Pritchard, 2014), as they are usually carried out in unsocial and exploitative working conditions with limited training and career opportunities (Hoel and Einarsen, 2003; Koc, 2020). Hence, women's employment in tourism and hospitality tend to be both vertically and horizontally segregated, women employees holding jobs that are subordinated and with low levels of income (Obadic and Maric, 2009; Kogovsek and Kogovsek, 2015). Koc's (2020) study analysed findings from various disciplines such as anthropology, biology, psychology, sociology, services marketing and management, and tourism and hospitality marketing and management and showed that women may be more able to provide and oversee a better quality of service (in terms of all aspects of service quality dimensions, that is, tangibles, reliability, responsiveness, assurance, and empathy), and in general be better service oriented than men. Koc (2020) summarised women's characteristics, which may be relevant for offering and ensuring a better quality of service in tourism and hospitality as seen in Table 5.5.

Service orientation

As shown in the previous Information zone and Table 5.4, due to the lesser value attached to fun, leisure, and pleasure in restraint cultures, service employees may be unable to provide a high-quality service. They may lack certain knowledge, skills, and abilities without being aware of it. Boz and Koc's (2019) study showed that a significant proportion of tourism and hospitality employees in Turkey (not a very high indulgence

Table 5.5 SERVQUAL and women's key areas of aptitude

SERVQUAL Dimension	*Women's Key Areas of Aptitude*
Tangibles	Spatial elaboration, structural inconsistencies, order, structural interrelationships, remembering, objects, locations, design, colour, design and appearance, furniture, changing contexts, facial expressions, mimics, body language, noticing changes
Reliability	Dependability, consistency, work under pressure, stress, multitasking, noticing changes, competence, changing contexts, detailed information, adaptability, patience, caring, self-discipline
Responsiveness	Facial expressions, stimuli, aversive stimuli, mimics, body language, noticing changes, understanding emotions, smiling, helpfulness, positive emotions
Assurance	Courtesy, trust, establish trust, trustworthiness, honesty, security, confidence, ethics, morals, ethical, credibility
Empathy	Empathy, helpfulness, sensitivity, understanding, egocentricity

Source: Koc (2020).

culture with an indulgence score of 49) had some difficulties recognising facial expressions of customers though they had inflated self-efficacy beliefs, that is, they thought they had the sufficient level of skills in terms of recognising facial expressions of customers. Employees with high or inflated self-efficacy beliefs (as in Dunning Kruger syndrome) do not tend to believe that they lack a skill, hence do not tend to be motivated to spend time, resources (e.g., to spend money on training programmes), energy, and effort to learn and/or improve that particular skill.

As customers from an indulgence-oriented culture collect and analyse more information regarding their holidays, they may be expected to be more interested in authenticity and the relevancy of the features of the touristic product or destination (Koc, 2017b). As mentioned previously, due to their high level of involvement, customers from a high indulgence culture may tend to be more knowledgeable about their holiday and leisure experiences. For instance, customers/tourists from an indulgence culture would know that a cultural trip to rural India would entail fewer luxuries, hence, they would alter their expectations accordingly, though it may be a high-end holiday in terms of its price. According to Koc (2015), Turkish domestic tourists tended to be less satisfied with their holidays compared with tourists from the Netherlands, the UK, and Denmark who stayed in the same resort hotels. The indulgence figures for Turkey, the Netherlands, the UK, and Denmark are respectively, 49, 68, 69, and 70.

In addition, from a supply side perspective, as people from indulgence cultures tend to be more involved in leisure and pleasure activities, service employees in these cultures may be in a better position to understand and internalise customers' expectations and thus have a deeper understanding of their needs, wants, and expectations. This, in turn, may mean that people from indulgence cultures may be able to design tourism and hospitality products and services more efficiently and effectively than people from restraint cultures.

It may also be put forward that, due to an inability to understand and internalise fun and leisure activities, tourism and hospitality service personnel, managers, and the business as a whole in restraint cultures may lack the basic skills to display service-oriented behaviours. Koc (2017b) reports that in restraint cultures service failures and a lack of mechanisms to recover failures are more likely to occur.

The service orientation scale (Lytle et al., 1998) provided in the following Activity box may be used to assess the level of service orientation in a tourism and hospitality business. The scale measures the service orientation of a business in terms of nine dimensions comprising customer treatment, employee empowerment, service technology, service failure prevention, service failure recovery, service standards communication, servant leadership, service rewards, and service training. A service business may use the scale to understand which areas of the service orientation they are good at and which parts of the service-orientation they are not so good at. Based on this understanding, training and other interventions may be designed and implemented to achieve a higher level of service orientation.

Activity

Service Orientation Scale (SERV* OR)

Complete the following Service Orientation Scale for the tourism and hospitality business for your work (work in the past) or any tourism and hospitality business you are familiar with. The scale was designed tested by Lytle et al. (1998). The original test measures service quality orientation for managers to evaluate their own businesses. In the following scale, the subjective personal pronouns of "we", objective pronouns of "us", and possessive pronouns of "our and ours" were transformed into they, them, their, and theirs respectively.

Please read the statements below and indicate how much each statement describes the business in the blank section on the left of each statement, from 1 to 5 as follows:

(5) strongly agree (4) agree (3) neutral (2) disagree (1) strongly disagree

Customer Treatment

______ **1.** Employees care for customers as they would like to be cared for.

______ **2.** Employees go the "extra mile" for customers.

______ **3.** They are noticeably more friendly and courteous than the competitors' employees.

______ **4.** Employees go out of their way to reduce inconveniences for customers

Employee Empowerment

______ **5.** Decisions are made "close to the customer". In other words, employees often make important customer decisions without seeking management approval.

______ **6.** Employees have the freedom and authority to act independently in order to provide excellent service.

Service Technology

______ **7.** The business enhances the service capabilities through the use of "state of the art" technology.

______ **8.** Technology is used to build and develop higher levels of service quality.

______ **9.** We use high levels of technology to support the efforts of men and women on the front line.

Service Failure Prevention

______ **10.** Employees go out of their way to prevent customer problems.

______ **11.** They go out of our way to "head off" or prevent customer problems rather than reacting to problems once they have occurred.

______ They actively listen to their customers.

Service Failure Recovery

______ **13.** They have an excellent customer complaint handling system for service follow-up.

______ **14.** They have established problem-solving groups to enhance our ability to resolve service breakdowns.

______ **15.** They provide follow-up service calls to confirm that services are being provided properly.

______ **16.** They provide every customer with an explicit service guarantee.

Service Standards Communication

______ **17.** They do not wait for customers to complain, we use internal standards to pinpoint failures before we receive customer complaints.

______ **18.** Every effort is made to explain the results of customer research to every employee in understandable terms.

______ **19.** Every employee understands all the service standards that have been instituted by all departments.

______ **20.** They have a developed chain of objectives linking together every branch in support of the corporate vision.

______ **21.** Service performance measures are communicated openly with all employees regardless of position or function.

______ **22.** There is a true commitment to service, not just lip service.

______ **23.** Customers are viewed as opportunities to serve rather than as sources of revenue.

______ **24.** It is believed that fundamentally, the organisation exists to serve the needs of its customers.

Servant Leadership

______ **25.** Management constantly communicates the importance of service.

______ **26.** Management regularly spends time "in the field" or "on the floor" with customers and front-line employees.

_____ **27.** Management is constantly measuring service quality.
_____ **28.** Management shows that they care about service by constantly giving of themselves.
_____ **29.** Management provides resources, not just "lip service" to enhance employee ability to provide excellent service.
_____ **30.** Managers give personal input and leadership into creating quality service.

Service Rewards
_____ **31.** Management provides excellent incentives and rewards at all levels for service quality, not just productivity.
_____ **32.** This organisation noticeably celebrates excellent service.

Service Training
_____ **33.** Every employee receives personal skills training that enhances their ability to deliver high-quality service.
_____ **34.** They spend much time and effort in simulated training activities that help them provide higher levels of service when actually encountering the customer.
_____ **35.** During training sessions, they work through exercises to identify and improve attitudes towards customers

Source: Lytle et al. (1998).

Truong and King's (2010) study showed that the attitudes and behaviours of service personnel significantly influenced the perception, satisfaction, and loyalty of guests. However, the expectations, perceptions, and service quality evaluations (the overall and individual emphasis on service quality dimensions) of tourism and hospitality customers may be significantly influenced by cultural similarity and dissimilarity (Weiermeier, 2000; Tasci and Severt, 2017). Guests with higher cultural dissimilarity with hosts may be less demanding and less critical on service quality dimensions (Weiermeier, 2000; Tasci and Severt, 2017). In addition, the increased experience of international tourism and hospitality activity by customers increases their level of tolerance towards service quality problems (Weiermair and Fuchs, 2000; Tasci and Severt, 2017).

Conclusion

This chapter explains the potential influences of indulgence and restraint, a recently added and largely overlooked dimension, on tourism and hospitality operations. The indulgence and restraint paradigm is particularly relevant for tourism and hospitality as this dimension influences people's attitude towards fun, leisure, and pleasure. As tourism and hospitality services are mainly based on hedonistic drives, cultural orientations of individuals, as consumers, employees, managers, and members of society may determine their attitudes and behaviours towards various aspects of tourism and hospitality. This chapter demonstrates that, apart from its influence on the design and implementation of marketing mix elements, indulgence and restraint may influence service quality and service orientation of service employees and tourism and hospitality businesses as a whole.

Questions

1. Explain the key characteristics of indulgence and restraint culture. Form a group of six people including yourself – three being from indulgence and the other three from a restraint culture. Discuss whether the characteristics explained in this chapter apply to people in your group. Try to discover cultural examples in terms of traditions, proverbs, norms, attitudes, and behavioural patterns to explain your case.
2. Study Herzberg's Two Factor theory of motivation and explain how dissatisfaction and demotivation of staff from a restraint culture can be eliminated and how they can be motivated to provide a high quality of service.
3. Make a list of ten indulgence and ten restraint countries. Assume that you are a manager of a tourism or a hospitality business marketing your services to these countries. Prepare a report that could be used in the design of marketing mix elements for each segment.
4. Likewise, prepare a report that could be used to ensure a high level of service quality for each segment.
5. In a group of three, prepare a training programme outline for tourism and hospitality staff from a restraint culture.
6. Explain the potential relationships between service orientation (of service employees and the service business as a whole) and the indulgence and restraint dimension.
7. Explain the potential relationship between emotional labour and the indulgence and restraint dimension.
8. Explain and discuss Fulke Greville's quote "They that seldom take pleasure, seldom give pleasure" in relation to cultural variable of indulgence from both service providers' and customers' perspectives.

Research questions/ideas to pursue for researchers

As stated previously, people from restraint cultures attach less value and importance to fun, leisure, and hedonistic activities. Hence, employees and managers of tourism and hospitality businesses in restraint cultures may find it difficult to internalise the tourism and hospitality activities to the extent required by the customers. By using the Service Orientation Scale (SERV* OR) developed by Lytle et al. (1998) the service orientations of tourism and hospitality businesses from indulgence and restraint cultures can be compared to see the whether there are differences. If there are differences, which aspects of the dimensions of service orientation do they relate to? Based on the findings, policy implications and recommendations may be offered to the practitioners.

Note

1 The concept of service recovery paradox and the pertaining research is explained later in this chapter.

Recommended further reading

Hofstede, G. Hofstede, G.J., and Minkov, M. (2010). Cultures and organizations: Software of the mind (3rd ed.). New York: McGraw-Hill.

Koc, E., Ar, A. A., and Aydin, G. (2017). The potential implications of indulgence and restraint on service encounters in tourism and hospitality. *Ecoforum Journal*, 6(3), 1–6.

Mathieu, P. (1999). Economic citizenship and the rhetoric of gourmet coffee. *Rhetoric Review*, 18(1), 112–127.

Minkov, M. (2009). Predictors of differences in subjective wellbeing across 97 nations. *Cross-Cultural Research*, 43, 152–179.

Ruiz-Equihua, D., Romero, J., and Casaló, L. V. (2019). Better the devil you know? The moderating role of brand familiarity and indulgence vs. restraint cultural dimension on eWOM influence in the hospitality industry. *Journal of Hospitality Marketing and Management*, 1–19.

References

Abraham, R. (2000). Organizational cynicism bases and consequences: Generic, social and general. *Psychology Monographs*, 126(3), 269–292.

Ashforth, B., and Humphrey, R. (1993). Emotional labor in service roles: The influence of identity. *Academy of Management Review*, 18(1), 88–115.

Baker, M. (2017). Service failures and recovery: Theories and models. In E. Koc (Ed.), *Service failures and recovery in tourism and hospitality* (pp. 27–41). Wallingford, Oxford: CABI.

Basim, N., and Begenirbas, M. (2012). Çalısmayasamındaduygusalemek: Birölçekuyarlamacalısması [Emotional labor in work life: a study of scale adaptation]. *Yönetim ve Ekonomi*, 19(1), 77–90.

Bathaee, A. (2011). Culture affects consumer behavior: Theoretical reflections and an illustrative example with Germany and Iran, Working paper (No. 02/2011). Ernst Moritz Arndt University of Greifswald, Faculty of Law and Economics.

Bedeian, A. (2007). Even if the tower is ivory, it isn't white: Understanding the consequences of faculty cynicism. *Academy of Management Learning and Education*, 6, 9-32.

Bendapudi, N., and Leone, R. P. (2003). Psychological implications of customer participation in co-production. *Journal of Marketing*, 67(1), 14–28.

Brandes, P., and Das, D. (2006). Locating behaviour cynicism at work: Construct issues and performance implications. *Employee Health, Coping and Methodologies*, 5, 233–266.

Brandes, P., Castro, S., James, M. S. L., Martinez, A., Matherly, T., Ferris, G. and Hochwarter, W. (2008). Organizational cynicism on work effort following a layoff. *Journal of Leadership and Organizational Studies*, 14(3), 233–240.

Boz, H., and Koc, E. (2019). Service quality, emotion recognition, emotional intelligence and Dunning Kruger syndrome. *Total Quality Management and Business Excellence*, 1–14.

Bunjak, A., Černe, M., and Wong, S. I. (2019). Leader–follower pessimism (in) congruence and job satisfaction: The role of followers' identification with a leader. *Leadership and Organization Development Journal*, 40(3), 381–398.

Cermak, D. S., File, K. M., and Prince, R. A. (2011). Customer participation in service specification and delivery. *Journal of Applied Business Research*, 10(2), 90–97.

Chen, Z., Sun, H., Lam, W., Hu, Q., Huo, Y., and Zhong, J. A. (2012). Chinese hotel employees in the smiling masks: Roles of job satisfaction, burnout, and supervisory support in relationships between emotional labor and performance. *The International Journal of Human Resource Management*, 23(4), 826–845.

Chu, K. H. L. (2002). *The effects of emotional labor on employee work outcomes* (Doctoral dissertation). Virginia Polytechnic Institute and State University.

Cylus, J., Glymour, M. M., and Avendano, M. (2014). Do generous unemployment benefit programs reduce suicide rates? A state fixed-effect analysis covering 1968–2008. *American Journal of Epidemiology*, 180(1), 45–52.

Diefendorff, J. M., Croyle, M. H., and Gosserand, R. H. (2005). The dimensionality and antecedents of emotional labor strategies. *Journal of Vocational Behavior*, 66(2), 339–357.

Dukes, H. (2016). *Cultural effects on wellness as it applies to society and the individual: An international comparison of Germany and the United States of America* (Unpublished PhD thesis).

Gower, T. (1994). Starbucks Nation: A Caffeinated Juggernaut Gives Competitors the Jitters. *Seattle Weekly*, 10 August.

Guerrier, Y., and Adib, A. (2003). Work at leisure and leisure at work: A study of the emotional labour of tour reps. *Human Relations*, 56(11), 1399–1417.

Hamid, M. A. (2016). Does culture impact choice of pictures for websites: An analysis of Chinese cultural dimensions on websites of Chinese universities. *New Media and Mass Communication*, (45), 34–45.

Hochschild, A. (1983). *The managed heart: Commercialization of human feeling*. Berkeley: University of California Press.

Hoel, H., and Einarsen, S. (2003). *Violence at work in catering, hotels and tourism*. Geneva: International Labour Office.

Hofstede, G. (2020). Cultural dimensions. https://www.hofstede-insights.com/product/compare-countries/ (accessed 20 January 2020).

Hofstede, G., Hofstede, G. J., and Minkov, M. (2010), *Cultures and organizations: Software of the mind* (rev. and expanded 3rd ed.). New York: McGraw-Hill.

Humphrey, C. (2018). To smile and not to smile: mythic gesture at the Russia-China border. *Social Analysis*, 62(1), 31–54.

Inglehart, R. (1997). *Modernization and postmodernization: Cultural, economic and political change in 43 societies*. Princeton, NJ: Princeton University Press.

Jung, H. S., Yoon, H. H., and Kim, Y. J. (2012). Effects of culinary employees' role stress on burnout and turnover intention in hotel industry: moderating effects on employees' tenure. *The Service Industries Journal*, 32(13), 2145–2165.

Jung-Beeman, M., Bowden, E. M., Haberman, J., Frymiare, J. L., Arambel-Liu, S., Greenblatt, R., … Kounis, J. (2004). Neural activity observed in people solving verbal problems with insight. *PLOS Biol.*, 2, 500–510.

Khosrowjerdi, M., Sundqvist, A., and Byström, K. (2020). Cultural patterns of information source use: A global study of 47 countries. *Journal of the Association for Information Science and Technology*, 71(6), 711–724.

Kim, J. H. (2017). Memorable service experiences: A service failure and recovery perspective. In E. Koc (Ed.), *Service failures and recovery in tourism and hospitality: A practical manual* (pp. 56–69). Wallingford, Oxford: CABI.

Koc, E. (2006). Total quality management and business excellence in services: The implications of all-inclusive pricing system on internal and external customer satisfaction in the Turkish tourism market. *Total Quality Management and Business Excellence*, 17(7), 857–877.

Koc, E. (2015). *Hizmet Pazarlaması ve Yönetimi, 1*. Ankara: Baskı, Seçkin Yayıncılık.

Koc, E. (2016). *Tüketici Davranışı ve Pazarlama Stratejileri: Global ve Yerel Yaklaşım* (Vol. 7). Ankara, Turkey: Baskı, Seçkin Yayınları.

Koc, E. (2017a). *Service failures and recovery in tourism and hospitality: A practical manual*. Wallingford, Oxford: CABI.

Koc. E. (2017b). Cross-cultural aspects of service failures and recovery. In E. Koc (Ed.), *Service failures and recovery in tourism and hospitality: A practical manual* (pp. 197–213). Wallingford, Oxford: CABI.

Koc, E. (2020). Do women make better in tourism and hospitality? A conceptual review from a customer satisfaction and service quality perspective. *Journal of Quality Assurance in Hospitality and Tourism*, 1–28.

Koc, E., and Bozkurt, G. A. (2017). Hospitality employees' future expectations: Dissatisfaction, stress, and burnout. *International Journal of Hospitality and Tourism Administration*, 18(4), 459–473.

Koc, E., Ar, A. A., and Aydin, G. (2017). The potential implications of indulgence and restraint on service encounters in tourism and hospitality. *Ecoforum Journal*, 6(3), 1–6. http://www.ecoforumjournal.ro/index.php/eco/article/view/657

Koc, E., Ulukoy, M., Kilic, R., Yumusak, S., and Bahar, R. (2017). Service recovery paradox in restraint cultures: An implementation in tourism sector. *Journal of Empirical Economics and Social Sciences*, 2(1), 82–91.

Koc, E., Yilmaz, O., and Boz, H. (2020). Service recovery paradox in restraint cultures: An implementation in tourism sector. *Journal of Empiricial Economics and Social Sciences*. Article in Press.

Kogovsek, M., and Kogovsek, M. (2015). Hospitality and tourism gender issues remain unsolved: A call for research. *Quaestus*, 6, 194.

Lovelock, C.H. (2001), *Services marketing, people, technology, strategy* (4th ed.). Upper Saddle River, NJ: Prentice-Hall.

Lytle, R. S., Hom, P. W., and Mokwa, M. P. (1998). SERV* OR: A managerial measure of organizational service-orientation. *Journal of Retailing*, 74(4), 455–489.

Marcu, N., Siminică, M., Noja, G. G., Cristea, M., and Dobrotă, C. E. (2018). Migrants' integration on the European labor market: A spatial bootstrap, SEM and network approach. *Sustainability*, 10(12), 1–21.

Marcuse, H. (1991). *One-dimensional man: Studies in the ideology of advanced industrial society. 1964*. Boston: Beacon.

Maslach, C., Schaufeli, W. B., and Leiter, M. P. (2001). Job burnout. *Annual Review of Psychology*, 52, 397–422.

Mathieu, P. (1999). Economic citizenship and the rhetoric of gourmet coffee. *Rhetoric Review*, 18(1), 112–127. shorturl.at/qER78.

McCollough, M.A. and S.G. Bharadwaj (1992) The Recovery Paradox: An Examination of Consumer Satisfaction in Relation to Disconfirmation, Service Quality and Attribution based Theory, in C.T. Allen et al. (Eds.), Marketing Theory and Applications, Chicago, IL: American Marketing Association.

Minkov, M. (2009). Predictors of differences in subjective wellbeing across 97 nations. *Cross-Cultural Research*, 43, 152–179.

Money, R. B., and Crotts, J. C. (2003). The effect of uncertainty avoidance on information search, planning, and purchases of international travel vacations. *Tourism Management*, 24(2), 191–202.

Moon Y. (2005). Break free from the product lifecycle. *Harvard Business Review*, 83(5), 86–94.

Morris, J. A., and Feldman, D. C. (1996). The dimensions, antecedents, and consequences of emotional labor. *Academy of Management Review*, 21(4), 986–1010.

Noja, G. G., Petrović, N., and Cristea, M. (2018). Turning points in migrants' labour market integration in Europe and benefit spillovers for Romania and Serbia: the role of socio-psychological credentials. *Zbornik Radova Ekonomski Fakultet u Rijeka*, 36(2), 489–518.

Obadic, A., and Maric, I. (2009). The significance of tourism as an employment generator of female labour force. *Ekonomska misao i praksa*, 18(1), 93.

Prentice, C. (2013). Service quality perceptions and customer loyalty in casinos. *International Journal of Contemporary Hospitality Management*, 25(1), 49–64.

Pritchard, A. (2014). Gender and feminist perspectives in tourism research. In A. Alan, C. Lew, H. Michael, and Allan M. Williams (Eds), *The Wiley Blackwell Companion to Tourism* (pp. 314–324). Oxford: Wiley-Blackwell.

Rego, A., Cunha, M. P. E., Reis Júnior, D., Anastácio, C., and Savagnago, M. (2018). The optimism-pessimism ratio as predictor of employee creativity: the promise of duality. *European Journal of Innovation Management*, 21(3), 423–442.

Ruiz-Equihua, D., Romero, J., and Casaló, L. V. (2019). Better the devil you know? The moderating role of brand familiarity and indulgence vs. restraint cultural dimension on eWOM influence in the hospitality industry. *Journal of Hospitality Marketing and Management*, 1–19.

Smith, A. K., and Bolton, R. N. (1998). An experimental investigation of customer reactions to service failure and recovery encounters paradox or peril? *Journal of Service Research*, 1(1), 65–81.

Tasci, A. D., and Severt, D. (2017). A triple lens measurement of host–guest perceptions for sustainable gaze in tourism. *Journal of Sustainable Tourism*, 25(6), 711–731.

Truong, T.-H., and King, B. (2010). Cultural values and service quality: Host and guest perspectives. *Tourism, Culture and Communication*, 10, 15–32.

UNWTO (United Nations World Tourism Organization) (2011). Global Report on Women in Tourism 2010. UNWTO and UN Women. http://ethics.unwto.org/en/content/global-report-women-tourism -2010.

Verduyn, P., and Lavrijsen, S. (2015). Which emotions last longest and why: The role of event importance and rumination. *Motivation and Emotion*, 39(1), 119–127.

Weiermair, K. (2000). Tourists' perceptions towards and satisfaction with service quality in the cross-cultural service encounter: Implications for hospitality and tourism management. *Managing Service Quality*, 10(6), 397–409.

Weiermair, K., and Fuchs, M. (2000). The impact of cultural distance on perceived service quality gaps: The case of alpine tourism. *Journal of Quality Assurance in Hospitality & Tourism*, 1(2), 59–75.

Willis, S. (1991). *A primer for everyday life*. London: Routledge.

Women First (2010). The case for change: Women working in hospitality, leisure, travel and tourism. www.people1st.co.uk/webfiles/Business%20and%20Training%20Support/Women%201st/Women_1st_Case_For_Change_Executive_Summary_November_2010.pdf.

Yilmaz, K., Altinkurt, Y., Guner, M., and Sen, B. (2015). The Relationship between Teachers' Emotional Labor and Burnout Level. *Eurasian Journal of Educational Research*, 59, 75–90.

Yurur, S., and Unlu, O. (2011). Duygusal Emek, Duygusal Tukenme ve İşten Ayrılma Niyeti İlişkisi, ISGUC *The Journal of Industrial Relations and Human Resources*, 13 (2).

Yurur, S. Gumus, M., and Hamarat, B. (2011). Çalışan-Müşteri İlişkiklerinde Algılanan Adalet/Adaletsizliğin Duygusal Emek Davranışlarına Etkisi, *Journal of Yaşar University*, 23(6), 3826–3839.

Chapter 6

Power distance as a cultural variable

Learning Objectives

After reading this chapter, you should be able to:

- understand the concept of power distance and its influence on people and organisations;
- explain the influence of power distance on the marketing mix of tourism and hospitality businesses;
- discuss the relationship between power distance and service quality dimensions in tourism and hospitality;
- understand the concept of employee empowerment and its influence on tourism and hospitality employees and customers;
- explain the relationship between service quality, communication, interaction, and decision making in tourism and hospitality businesses.

Introduction

This chapter explains and discusses the influence of power distance as a cultural variable on tourism and hospitality establishments by explaining its various implications for customers, employees, managers, and systems. The chapter first explains the concept of power distance as a cultural variable. Then, supported by several international research findings, the influences of power distance on tourism and hospitality operations are explained and discussed in terms of marketing mix elements, service quality, staff training, communication, interaction, decision making, and empowerment.

The concept of power distance as a cultural variable

As one of the often studied cultural variable *power distance* can be defined as the extent to which less powerful members of a society expect and accept the unequal distribution of power and privileges (Javidan et al., 2005; Hofstede, 2010). In other words, it is the extent to which members of a society expect and agree that power and privileges should be stratified and concentrated at higher levels (Javidan et al., 2005). Power distance also determines one's perceived social distance and reliance on others and influences how individuals behave in social relationships (Daniels and Greguras, 2014).

The Power Distance Index (PDI) measures the degree to which power differences within societies, organisations, and institutions (e.g., the family) are accepted by less powerful members. Hofstede (1980) derived the power distance scores of 50 countries from the answers given by IBM employees in the same type of positions to the same questions. The PDI primarily centres around three questions asked to less powerful members (e.g., subordinates in an organisation):

1. How frequently, in your experience, are you afraid to express disagreement with your managers? (The respondents are expected a mean score on a 1–5 scale from "very frequently" to "very seldom".)
2. Your perception of your superior's decision-making style. (A percentage of all respondents who chose the description of either an autocratic or a paternalistic style out of four possible styles in addition to a "none of these alternatives" option.)
3. Your *preference* for your superior's decision-making style. (A percentage of all respondents preferred an autocratic or paternalistic, i.e., non-consultative) style.)

Table 6.1 shows the power distance index scores (PDI) for 72 selected countries in the world. A higher value indicates that a country has a high (large) power distance. According to Table 6.1, countries such as Malaysia, Guatemala, Panama, the Philippines, Russia, Romania, Mexico, Venezuela, China, Egypt, Brazil, France, Poland, Turkey, and India appear to have a relatively high level of power distance, while countries such as Austria, Israel, Finland, Sweden, Denmark, the Netherlands, and the United States appear to have a relatively low level of power distance. It should be noted that although geographically Asian and Arab countries have a high level of power distance, European countries such as Romania, France, Belgium, Poland, and Greece tend to have a relatively high power distance as well.

Information zone

The origins of power distance scores

The origins of a culture's power distance score may be influenced by its language, geography, history, political system, demographics, and economy. In general, Romance languages (e.g., Spanish, Portuguese, French, Italian, and Romanian) appear to have higher power distance scores, with Germanic languages (Indo-European family of languages spoken by the Germanic peoples such as German, English, Dutch, Danish, Norwegian, and Swedish). This difference may be attributable to the Roman Empire and its single power centre. Hofstede and Minkov (2010) put forward that people in a society develop mental programmes to survive, then the ensuing political and social systems became part of the culture.

Countries with Germanic languages were never fully absorbed by the Roman Empire and they typically tend to have lower power distance scores. According to Hofstede (1980), other determinants of PDI are related to population size and geographic latitude. Larger populations (e.g., China, India, and Turkey – because of the Ottoman Empire) may be assumed to depend on a more authoritative system of administration that is less accessible than do smaller populations. However, there may be exceptions to this, such as the United States. In terms of the geographical latitude, societies which live in lower latitudes depend more heavily on agriculture due to their abundant natural resources and climate. In lower latitudes, competition with other groups of people for the same territory (e.g., for arable and well-watered pieces of land) is strong and the establishment of a hierarchical society increases the chances for peaceful survival. In societies located at higher altitudes, nature and the climate appear to be less suitable for agriculture and hence people had to create and sustain the industry and had to engage in agriculture to a relatively limited extent. This meant that people were less dependent on powerful rulers. A high level of industry led to less traditional agriculture enabled the development of more knowledge and modern technology (Clark, 2013).

As another determinant of power distance, the political system has been influenced by the consequences of population size and the latitude as explained previously. In traditionally democratic societies, there appears to be less power distance. Additionally, quite often the degree of power distance may also be related to the wealth of a country. In societies where education is more accessible to everyone, the establishment of a middle class became more possible. In societies where the level of education is low, people tend to prefer a more authoritarian system of administration. In high-power distance societies income and wealth tend to be less equally distributed resulting in fewer very rich people and many extremely poor people (Clark, 2013). Some of the countries with a high level of power distance have the highest percentage of people earning a minimum wage. The following table shows power distance scores and the percentage of people earning minimum wage or less.

Country	*Power Distance Score*	*Percentage of People Earning Minimum Wage or Less*	*Country*	*Power Distance Score*	*Percentage of People Earning Minimum Wage or Less*
Turkey	66	43	Bulgaria	70	8.8
Slovenia	71	19.1	France	68	8.7
Romania	90	15.7	Greece	60	7.7
Poland	68	11.7	Netherlands	38	3.0

Source: EUROSTAT (2020) Mimum wage statistics. shorturl.at/ltwJV (accessed 10 January 2020).

Table 6.1 Power distance scores of selected countries in the world

RANK	*Country*	*PDI Score*	RANK	*Country*	*PDI Score*	RANK	*Country*	*PDI Score*	RANK	*Country*	*PDI Score*
1	Malaysia	**104**	18	Indonesia	**78**	35	Tanzania	**64**	52	Hungary	**46**
2	Guatemala	**95**	19	Ghana	**77**	36	Thailand	**64**	53	Jamaica	**45**
3	Panama	**95**	20	India	**77**	37	Zambia	**64**	54	United States	**40**
4	Philippines	**94**	21	Nigeria	**77**	38	Chile	**63**	55	Netherlands	**38**
5	Russia	**93**	22	Singapore	**74**	39	Portugal	**63**	56	Australia	**36**
6	Romania	**90**	23	Bulgaria	**70**	40	Uruguay	**61**	57	Costa Rica	**35**
7	Mexico	**81**	24	Brazil	**69**	41	Greece	**60**	58	Germany	**35**
8	Venezuela	**81**	25	France	**68**	42	South Korea	**60**	59	United Kingdom	**35**
9	China	**80**	26	Hong Kong	**68**	43	Iran	**58**	60	Switzerland	**34**
10	Egypt	**80**	27	Poland	**68**	44	Taiwan	**58**	61	Finland	**33**
11	Iraq	**80**	28	Colombia	**67**	45	Czech Republic	**57**	62	Norway	**31**
12	Kuwait	**80**	29	El Salvador	**66**	46	Spain	**57**	63	Sweden	**31**
13	Lebanon	**80**	30	Turkey	**66**	47	Pakistan	**55**	64	Ireland	**28**
14	Libya	**80**	31	Belgium	**65**	48	Japan	**54**	65	New Zealand	**22**
15	Saudi Arabia	**80**	32	Ethiopia	**64**	49	Italy	**50**	66	Denmark	**18**
16	United Arab Emirates	**80**	33	Kenya	**64**	50	Argentina	**49**	67	Israel	**13**
17	Ecuador	**78**	34	Peru	**64**	51	South Africa	**49**	68	Austria	**11**

Source: Hofstede (2020). Used with permission.

People from high-power distance cultures expect and accept differences in wealth, social status, and prestige (Schumann et al., 2010). From an organisational perspective, junior or subordinate members of staff working in an organisation in a high-power distance culture are expected to show respect and loyalty to their seniors. Subordinates follow the instructions of authority figures (e.g., immediate supervisors or managers), and their behaviors tend to be guided by their role as subordinates (Noja et al., 2018). Subordinates in high-power distance cultures tend to imitate the behaviour of their superiors. Hence, negative behaviours of superiors have a trickle-down effect on the subordinates (Hon and Lu, 2016).

According to GLOBE study (House et al., 2004: 536), in high-power distance cultures power is usually seen as providing social order, relational harmony, and role stability, while in low-power distance cultures power is quite often seen as a source of corruption, coercion, and dominance. The quote "The more corrupt the state, the more numerous the laws" by Gaius Cornelius Tacitus, a Roman historian who lived between *c.* 56 and *c.* 120, explains succinctly the potential relationship which may exist between corruption and bureaucracy.

Based on the previous research (Hofstede, 1991, 2001; Patterson et al., 2006; Botero and Van Dyne, 2009; Reisinger and Crotts, 2010; Chen et al., 2011; Bisel et al., 2012; Koc, 2013) the characteristics of power distance cultures may be summarised as in Table 6.2.

While people in low-power distance cultures people may recognise and respect *earned power*, that is, the power which is based on an individual's accomplishments, drive, hard work, motivation, and effort, they may resent those whose power is decreed by birth or wealth or formal authority (i.e., the *positional power*) (Hofstede, 1980; Neuliep, 2018). Employees in low-power distance cultures expect leaders to rely on informal rules and to consult employees more often than those in high-power distance cultures (Daniels and Greguras, 2014).

Exercise

Study Tables 6.1 and 6.2. Determine whether your country is a high-power distance culture or not. Also, find colleagues who are from the countries at the other end of the high- and low-power distance continuum. Based on the experiences of you and colleagues, discuss the extent to which the above-explained characteristics represent your culture. From a dyadic perspective (organisational behaviour and human resource management – marketing and consumer behaviour) what would be the advantages and disadvantages, and implications of your cultural characteristics in managing tourism and hospitality businesses? When considering the implications, think about the likely influences on the marketing mix elements (7Ps) and the service quality (SERVQUAL) dimensions.

Table 6.2 Characteristics of high and low power distance cultures

High (Large) Power Distance Cultures e.g., Russia, Romania, Malaysia, Mexico, Guatemala, Venezuela, China, Egypt, Brazil, France, Poland, Turkey, and India	*Low (Small) Power Distance Cultures e.g., Austria, Israel, Finland, Sweden, Denmark, the Netherlands, and the United States*
Highly centralised power and traditional hierarchy.	Decentralised power and flatter hierarchy.
Highly hierarchical and bureaucratic – people are ranked within society by strict roles. People are not equal and everybody has a *rightful* place.	Less hierarchical and bureaucratic. There is a more egalitarian view of people.
More emphasis is given to managers' hierarchical status in the organisation. Managers are expected to know most things.	More emphasis is given to managers' ability, knowledge, and expertise. Managers are not expected to know most things.
Inequalities among the members of an organisation are considered to be more appropriate.	Inequalities among the members of an organisation are not considered as appropriate.
There is a greater reliance by the less powerful members on those people who have power.	Less powerful members are not very much dependent on their superiors.
Tend to value things like tradition, which keeps society stable and prevent massive changes to power relations. Traditions play a role to keep society stable and prevent massive changes in power relations.	Tend to value innovation and novelty rather than tradition.
Legitimacy may be considered as irrelevant.	Legitimacy is sought after in most of the interactions and dealings with people.
Superiors tend to make decisions.	Subordinates can also make decisions.
The less powerful members (e.g., lower-ranking staff/subordinates in organisations) are unable to express their opinions easily. People are afraid to disagree with their superiors.	The less powerful members express their opinions easily and are able to refute the ideas of their superiors when disagreement occurs. People are not afraid to disagree with their superiors.
Prefer decision-making styles that are autonomous or autocratic, and which rarely include others. Subordinates depend on the superiors.	Prefer decision-making styles that are democratic, consultative and participative. There tends to be interdependence between superiors and subordinates.
Statuses and titles are more important.	Statuses and titles are less important.
The emotional distance between superiors and subordinates is relatively large. Superior and subordinate interaction is very limited.	The emotional distance between superiors and subordinates is relatively small. Superior and subordinate interaction is common.
Inequality is expected and accepted.	Inequality is perceived negatively.

Table 6.2 continued

High (Large) Power Distance Cultures e.g., Russia, Romania, Malaysia, Mexico, Guatemala, Venezuela, China, Egypt, Brazil, France, Poland, Turkey, and India	*Low (Small) Power Distance Cultures e.g., Austria, Israel, Finland, Sweden, Denmark, the Netherlands, and the United States*
Referent and coercive power expected, accepted and obeyed. Obedience tends to be valued and people are expected to engage more in obedient, peaceful, cooperative communication strategies that allow compromise with or collaboration with others as they are afraid of disagreeing with others and deviating from what is expected of them.	Legitimate power and expertise are respected. Obedience is not sought after.
Subordinates are likely to be separated from the superiors by wide differentials in salary, privileges and status symbols.	Subordinates may not be separated from the superiors by wide differentials in salary, privileges and status symbols.
Conformity and having a willingness to subordinate themselves to autocratic and paternalistic managers are prevalent practices.	Conformity and willingness to subordination by less powerful members are not sought after.

Source: adapted from Hofstede et al. (2010).

CASE STUDY

Authority and obedience experiments: the perils of obedience

Milgram (1963) examined justifications for the acts of genocide offered by those accused at the World War II Nuremberg War Criminal trials. The accused people based their defence often on "obedience" – that they were just following orders from their superiors. Milgram chose the participants for the experiment by advertising for male participants to take part in a study on "learning" at Yale University. Forty male participants took part in the experiments, aged between 20 and 50, unskilled professionals from the New Haven area. The participants were paid $4.50 for taking part.

Milgram (1963) was interested in finding out how far people would go in obeying an instruction even if it involved harming another person severely. In the experiment procedure, the participant was paired with another person (a confederate). They drew lots (straws) to determine who would be the "learner" and who would be the "teacher". The draw was fixed so that the participant became the teacher, and the learner (the confederate) became the learner in each individual experiment.

The learner (the confederate) was taken into a room and had electrodes tied around his arms, and the teacher (the participant) went into the next room accompanied by a researcher dressed in a gray lab coat. Two rooms were used in the Yale Interaction Laboratory – one being for the learner (with an electric chair), and the other one being for the teacher and the researcher/experimenter with an electric shock generator. The room for the participant contained an electric shock generator and a row of switches with marking ranging from 15 volts (slight shock) to 450 volts (danger – severe shock).

The learner (confederate) was strapped to a chair with electrodes. After he has learned a list of word pairs, the "teacher" (participant) tested him by naming a word and asking the learner to recall its partner/pair from a list of four possible choices. The teacher (the participant) was told to administer an electric shock every time the learner made a mistake, increasing the level of shock each time.

The teacher (participant) was told to administer an electric shock each time the learner made a mistake, increasing the level of shock each time. As mentioned above, there were 30 switches on the shock generator marked from 15 volts (slight shock) to 450 (danger – severe shock).

The learner (confederate) gave mainly wrong answers (on purpose), and for each of these, the teacher/participant had to give him an electric shock. When the teacher refused to administer a shock, the experimenter was to give a series of orders/prods to ensure they continued such as: a) Prod 1 – please continue; b) Prod 2 – the experiment requires you to continue; c) Prod 3 – it is absolutely essential that you continue; and d) Prod 4 – you have no other choice but to continue.

The results of the experiment showed that 65% of participants (teachers) continued to the highest level of 450 volts. All the participants continued to 300 volts. This meant that ordinary people tended to follow orders given by an authority figure, even to the extent of killing an innocent human being. People were likely to obey orders from other people if they recognise their authority as morally right and/or legally based.

Activity

Self-Assessment Power Distance Scale

Important Note: Throughout the book there are several self-report scales/tests like the one below. Please save your personal test score records (especially the ones relating to cultural awareness, cultural competence, ethnocentrism, cultural intelligence, etc.) in order to make comparisons later. After studying the whole book, you are advised to go back and redo all these tests once more. By doing this you can compare these scores with your earlier ones. This is expected to help you to see the changes that have taken place as a result of the learning experience.

Instructions: The following are ten statements regarding issues you may encounter at work, in the classroom, and at home. Indicate in the blank box to the left of each statement the degree to which you (1) strongly agree, (2) agree, (3) are unsure, (4) disagree, or (5) strongly disagree with the statement.

For example, if you strongly disagree with the first statement, place a 5 in the blank. You are recommended to complete the test as quickly as possible as it is important to indicate your initial response.

For items 4, 5, 6, 8, and 9 (*items in italic*), reverse your responses. That is, if your original response score was 1, reverse it to 5. If your original response score was 2, reverse it to 4, and so on.

Item	*Statements*	*Scores (1) strongly agree (5) strongly disagree*
1	Within a business, employees should feel comfortable expressing disagreements to their managers.	
2	Within a class, students should be allowed to express their points of view towards a subject without being punished by their teacher/professor	
3	At home, children should be allowed to openly disagree with their parents.	
4	*The primary purpose of a manager is to monitor the work of the employees to check whether they are doing their jobs appropriately.*	
5	*Authority is essential for the efficient running of a business, class, or home.*	
6	*At work, people are more productive when they are closely supervised by those in charge.*	
7	*In problem-solving situations within organisations, input from employees is important.*	
8	*Generally, employees, students, and children should be seen and not heard.*	
9	*Obedience to managers, teachers, and parents is good.*	
10	Managers, teachers, and parents should be considered equal to their workers, students, and children.	
TOTAL		

Scoring: add up your 10 responses. This sum is your power distance score. Higher scores mean a higher level of power distance.

Source: Hofstede and Minkov (2010). Used with permission.

The dyadic influence of power distance on tourism and hospitality operations

Owing to the inseparability nature of production and consumption of tourism and hospitality services, and the intense and continuous interactions between customers and staff, understanding the influence of power distance on service encounters is of paramount importance. From a dyadic perspective power distance appears to influence particularly almost all marketing mix elements, service quality (including service quality dimensions), communication, interaction and decision making, and empowerment.

Marketing mix elements

Consumer behavior research shows that customers from a high-power distance culture tend to accept hierarchical structures in the society, as well as differential prestige, power, social acceptability, and wealth among its members (Lam et al., 2009; Schumann et al. 2010). Therefore, marketing cues conveyed through all marketing mix elements are expected to conform to and reflect these differences (Koc, 2017a). For instance, Correia et al. (2011) found that power distance was the most influential cultural factor influencing tourists' holiday product and destination choice decisions. In making their holiday product and holiday decisions, tourists heavily relied on quality and brand image.

Information zone

Power distance may have a significant influence on the design and implementation of marketing mix elements. The following table provides a summary of the examples to show the influence of power distance on marketing mix elements.

Product **(The services/ products customers buy to satisfy their needs)**	Harris et al. (2005) found that customers from a higher power distance country had more positive attitudes to hedonic services than respondents in a lower power distance culture. Tourism and hospitality customers from a high power distance culture tend to have significantly high service expectations, are more difficult to please, and are more likely to evaluate service quality negatively (Ladhari et al., 2011; Gao et al., 2018).
Price **(Monetary and non-monetary costs to customers)**	In contrast with low power distance, customers from a high power distance culture have a greater tendency to use price to judge the quality, as they have a greater need for structure, making them more likely to discriminate between brands and ranking them based on price (Lalwani and Forcum, 2016). Power distance negatively impacts the enjoyment of bargain-hunting behaviour (Bathaee, 2011).

Place (Location, availability, and access to the service)	Mattila (1999) found that the hedonic dimension of consumption (i.e., website aesthetics) is more important for customers from low power distance than for those from a high power distance culture. Chen and Gursoy (2000) found that French tourists (high power distance) were more likely to use proprietary communication channels such as promotional materials (brochures) of hotels or airlines as principal sources of information compared with German tourists (low power distance), who tended to use third-party communication channels such as the independent travel guide.
Promotion (Planned marketing communi-cations messages delivered through advertising, public relations, sales promotion, and personal selling)	As a high power distance culture, in Japan advertisements are more likely to be associated with fear and rules/formality (Zhao, 2017). Cheong et al. (2010) found that the advertising appeals of *ornamental, status*, and *dear* were more frequently found in Chinese food advertisements (a relatively high power distance culture) compared with the United States (a relatively low power distance culture). Swaminathan (2012) found that the appeals of ornamental, vain, dear, and status were positively correlated, while the appeals of cheap, humility, nurturance, and plain were negatively correlated with power distance. According to De Mooij (2019) cultures with a small power distance often use humour in their advertisements, as they are not afraid to parody themselves and see youth as independent and individualistic which is why it is idealised. In large power distance cultures, status symbols are used more frequently. Messages that use expensive symbols and promote higher social status are likely to influence the power, wealth, and elitism aspirations of high power distance individuals (Nath et al., 2016).
Physical Evidence (All tangible elements of the service.	The availability of facilities that signal the sense of exclusivity, elitism and higher place in the society such as *spas, golden beaches*, or *rock-climbing facilities* are more likely to attract customers form a high power distance culture (Nath et al., 2016).
Process (All processes that make up the service such as ordering, booking, consumption, and payment)	Customers from a high power distance culture expect a more personalised service (Davis et al., 2009). In the event of service failures, customers from a high power distance culture are less likely to make a formal complaint (Yuksel et al., 2006). As a result of this, businesses need to establish systems and means to identify the dissatisfaction of customers from these countries. Heung and Lam's (2003) research showed that the Chinese customers (i.e., people from a high-power distance culture) tended to adopt an unassertive style of communication approach

	when they encountered failures. When a failure is recovered, Chinese customers are more likely to end up being silent and avoid further friction. Hospitality customers from a low power distance culture (e.g., the United States) tend to discourage formalities in their interactions with the service employees as they see themselves equal with them. Hence, communication initiated by service employees is not perceived as negatively. On the other hand, tourism and hospitality customers from a high power distance culture (e.g., Japan) are more likely to view a service employee's attempts to initiate communication negatively, as they see themselves superior compared with the service employees (Lee, 2015).
People ***(The skills, abilities, and knowledge of staff)***	In the event of service failures, customers from a high power distance culture expect the apology to come from a high-status employee (e.g., a manager) rather than a lower-level employee (e.g., a receptionist, waiter) (Patterson et al., 2006). Mueller et al.'s (2003) research in restaurants showed that when an apology is made by a higher status employee (i.e., a manager) customer satisfaction with the recovery tended to be much higher.

As previously explained, tourism and hospitality customers from a low-power distance (e.g., countries such as Austria, Denmark, Switzerland, and the United States) see themselves equal with service employees, they may be more positive towards participating (co-production) of the service. On the other hand, tourism and hospitality customers from a high power distance culture (e.g., countries such as Russia, Mexico, China and to some extent Japan) may be more unwilling to participate in the service. The concept of customer participation is explained in Chapter 10.

Exercise

According to Pollay and Gallagher (1990) and Cheong et al. (2010), the three advertising appeals which are related to high power distance cultures are ornamental, status, and dear (see following table). In addition, Swaminathan (2012) found that the appeals of ornamental, vain, dear, and status were positively correlated while the appeals of cheap, humility, nurturance, and plain were negatively correlated.

Appeal	*Description*
Ornamental	Beautiful, decorative, adorned, embellished, detailed, designed, styled

Appeal	*Description*
Status	Dominance, exhibitionism, pride in ownership, wealth (including the sudden wealth of prizes), trend-setting, to seek compliments
Dear	Expensive, valuable, highly regarded, extravagant, exorbitant, luxurious, priceless

Task

Each of the above appeals may have important implications, not only for advertising (as a promotional element) but also for all the other marketing mix elements of tourism and hospitality establishments. Prepare a marketing mix (7Ps) table for a tourism or hospitality business and write down for each marketing mix element things to do and not to do.

As people from a high power distance culture emphasise differences in social class and distribution of power, wealth, and prestige (Hofstede et al., 2010), customers from this culture tend to favour products and services that indicate their social elitism. Tourism and hospitality research shows that compared with low power distance culture customers, customers from a high power distance culture tend to prefer destinations, hotels, restaurants, and services that enhance their credibility of belonging to a superior social class, higher prestige, and wealth (Crotts and Erdmann, 2000; Weiermair, 2000; Nath et al., 2016).

As high power distance cultures may also be extremely competitive (Han and Heather, 2001), they tend to seek novelty through their tourism and hospitality activities (Manrai and Manrai, 2011). While these customers may participate in standard package holidays and structured leisure and pleasure activities due to their collectivist orientation, their motivation to participate in tourism and hospitality activities may be driven by adventure and novelty seeking.

As higher price represents superior service quality, customers from a high power distance culture are expected to be happy with the delivery of service depending on the price paid, that is, they are generally more comfortable with the manifestation of the inequality (Nath et al., 2016). Tourism and hospitality businesses that use fewer service promises, concentrating on only the must-have elements such as safety, security, and hygiene, are found to be less appealing to tourism and hospitality customers from high power distance cultures. Tourism and hospitality customers from a high power distance culture tend to have a significantly high-level of service expectation, they are more difficult to please, and are more likely to evaluate service quality negatively (Mattila, 1999; Ladhari et al., 2011; Nath et al., 2011; Ergun and Kitapci, 2018; Gao et al., 2018), compared with customers from low power distance cultures. Turkish tourists (relatively high power distance culture) tended to be less satisfied with their holidays compared with tourists from the Netherlands, the UK and Denmark (relatively low power distance), who stayed at the same holiday establishment in Turkey (Koc, 2018).

Activity Box

A tourism and hospitality business aiming to attract customers from a high-power distance culture is recommended to:

- use authority figures to endorse its service/products
- display official stamps and certifications
- include cultural and national symbols, where appropriate
- emphasise order within the website
- have a clear hierarchy of content

On the other hand, a tourism and hospitality business aiming to attract customers from a low power distance culture is recommended to:

- be transparent and provide its customers with full disclosure (e.g., as to how it uses customer data)
- use earned media (ratings, likes, testimonials, etc.) to endorse its service/products
- base the reputation of the business on professional and academic merit
- use a looser structure throughout to allow users to explore the site for themselves
- provide equal access to areas of the site, regardless of social status (though some sections may be made subscription-based, etc.)

Task

Based on the information provided here, take down notes for two specific tourism or hospitality businesses (e.g., an online travel agency and a restaurant) aiming to attract a) customers from a high power distance culture, and b) customers from a low power distance culture to be used in designing their websites.

In a high power distance cultures, less powerful members are expected to show respect for people who have more status. In Turkey, a high power distance culture, the words "sister" and "brother" become different words depending on the age of the person (see the following Information zone).

Information zone

In a high power distance culture, less powerful members are expected to show respect for people who have more status. In Turkey, a relatively high power distance culture, the words "sister" and "brother" become different words depending on the age of the person. In Turkey an older sister is called "*abla*" (different from a sister who is the same age or younger – who is called "*kız kardeş*") and an older brother is called "*ağabey*" (abi – short form) (different from a brother who is the same age or younger – who is called "erkek kardeş"). This kind of acknowledgement, a sign of power distance, also used to indicate fondness, is also used (a rather informal form) to address strangers. When age difference is higher, a person may address the other person as uncle, aunt, grandmother, and grandfather, although they may be strangers.

Traditionally, in Turkey elders are approached first and treated with more respect during greetings. It is especially respectful to kiss them on their right hand and then place it to your own forehead. As opposed to low power distance countries such as the United States and the United Kingdom, in Turkey, the titles such as the professor or associate professor continue to be held, even after leaving the university, or during retirement.

In Turkey, age traditionally has been influential in appointments and promotions. For instance, no matter what the performance of a person, an employee has to be at a certain age for them to be appointed to a managerial position. At universities, for associate professors to be appointed as a full professor, in addition to their publications record, they have to serve a minimum of five years as an associate professor. In seniority-based systems, there may be problems in terms of the performance orientation (explained in Chapter 12) of individual employees. In a seniority-based system, additional measures are needed to ensure efficiency and effectiveness.

In Japan, performance appraisal, rewarding, recruitment, and promotions are based on age, seniority, and ability. In the traditional Japanese human resource management system, there is no built-in layoff system, and it is rather difficult to discharge an employee. If a business wishes to discharge an employee, the business is expected to pay at least 60% (in some cases 100%) of her/his annual salary.

Professor Ouchi, after studying American and Japanese systems of human resource management practices, offered a synthesised system (Theory Z) in his book *Theory Z: How American Business Can Meet the Japanese Challenge*. The book basically synthesised a high power distance culture (Japan), and a low power distance culture (the United States) human resource management practices. For certain aspects of human resource management, Ouchi (1981) advocated either the American or Japanese system. On the other hand, for certain aspects, Ouchi (1981) advocated a middle-path strategy. For instance, based on the fact that in Japan there has been traditionally lifetime employment, and in the United States there has been short-term employment, Ouchi offered long-term employment.

Service quality

A low level of power distance culture among tourism and hospitality employees is believed to be disadvantageous in terms of the quality of the services provided, as power distance results in an unbalanced organisational structure (Nazarian et al.,

2017), a less participative stance in decision making, a greater reliance on rules and procedures, excessively high levels of subordinate submissiveness, a reluctance to take responsibilities outside the immediate scope of one's job, and a lack of informal communication (Yilmaz et al., 2005; Radojevic et al., 2019). Radojevic et al. (2019) suggest that from the supply side perspective a low power distance may be regarded as advantageous for providing high-quality tourism and hospitality services. Hence, tourism and hospitality businesses are recommended to establish better performance monitoring and management systems and run training programmes in order to increase the ability, knowledge, and skills of employees to ensure the delivery of a high-quality service. For instance, increasing service employees' intercultural sensitivity (as explained in Chapter 3) would significantly influence the quality of the service delivered by the staff.

As previously explained, customers from high power distance cultures are more difficult to please and they evaluate services more negatively (Ladhari et al., 2011; Nath et al., 2011; Ergun and Kitapci, 2018; Gao et al., 2018). Tsang and Ap (2007) and Manrai and Manrai (2011) explain that high power distance would increase the social position between the customer and service provider, and increase the quality expectations of tourists and their likelihood of providing a negative evaluation. Also, a high level of power distance increases reliance on relational service quality attributes such as empathy (including courtesy), and responsiveness.

In terms of the *tangibles* element of service quality, Huang et al. (1996) and Cho (2001) found that hotel guests from a country with larger power distance were more likely to perceive unsatisfactory goods and services as a fact of life and were less likely to complain. However, tourism and hospitality customers from a high power distance culture place a much higher value on tangibles (Donthu and Yoo, 1998; Hsieh and Tsai, 2009; Bhattacharyya and Borhart, 2018). According to Furrer et al. (2000), high power distance cultures emphasise the importance of tangible objects as the grandeur of the tangible objects shows the extent to which the service providers respect "the power of the superiority", and represents the people's statuses in the hierarchy. Cho (2001) and Nath et al. (2016) explain the emphasis of tangible elements as they signal high status, exclusivity, and elitism. On the other hand, as the grandeur of tangible objects, the higher status may not matter much for low power distance cultures, they may place less importance on the tangibles dimension of the service quality.

Research by Furrer et al. (2000) and Kueh and Ho Voon (2007) found that the relationships between power distance and *reliability* and *responsiveness* dimensions of service quality were negative. This means that customers with high power distance orientation tended to have lower expectations of service reliability and responsiveness. On the other hand, tourism and hospitality employees from a low-power distance culture had a high level of expectation for responsiveness and reliability (Donthu and Yoo, 1998). Furrer et al. (2000) also found that power distance is negatively correlated with *empathy* and positively correlated with *assurance* and tangibles. They put forward that in a high power distance culture the service employees depend on the customers, and, consequently, customers tend to have superior power. On the other hand, customers expect the service employees to have less power which causes them to have high level of service expectations. Hsieh and Tsai's (2009) study confirms the above as Taiwanese tourists (relatively high power distance) had higher service quality expectations than American tourists (relatively low power distance).

CASE STUDY

Tourism and hospitality jobs in Turkey

As a high power distance culture, in Turkey service jobs (tourism and hospitality jobs – for example, working as a waiter) are considered as lower status jobs and people carrying out these jobs may not be respected quite often. Most people (especially males) work as service employees only if they are desperate, and are unable to find any other jobs. Hence, tourism and hospitality jobs are viewed, especially by men, as temporary, not permanent jobs.

Male tourism and hospitality employees may leave their jobs at short notice as soon as they find other jobs. These employees may leave their service jobs to work as labourers in manufacturing and other businesses, and in many instances for lower wages and harder working conditions. In some cases, office jobs, which are called "desk jobs" with lower wages are also preferred. The main motivation behind male tourism and hospitality employees to leave their jobs is to improve their status. They would like to gain more respect with their new jobs from other people in general, and from their girlfriends, perspective wives, and their families in particular. In the Turkish society, many parents are prepared to endure financial and other hardships just to be able to provide their children with good education, so that their children in the future have higher status jobs in the society.

As service employees come in and go out quite frequently, in Turkey, service businesses experience a high level of employee turnover. It is often difficult to find new recruits and make replacements for service businesses. As a result, managers in tourism and hospitality businesses usually engage in compromising behaviour, and quite often recruit people who may not be appropriate for the tourism and hospitality job in terms of their knowledge, ability, skills, education, and experience. As managers are aware that service employees view service jobs as temporary, they are unwilling to spend time, effort and financial resources on the recruitment, orientation, and training of staff. Moreover, staff who lack the necessary abilities, skills, knowledge, and experience may be overstressed as they may be unable to provide service at the required level.

In Turkey, many tourism and hospitality businesses face serious reliability problems in terms of service quality. This is because a) it is often difficult to make replacements for service employees who are not suitable to carry out the tasks – in terms of their abilities, knowledge, skills, and attitudes, b) due to high levels of employee turnover there may be continually inexperienced and unskilled staff serving the customers, and c) time and other resources spent on recruitment, orientation, and training of staff may be viewed as a waste as employees may view these jobs as temporary.

Task

Develop a training programme to train staff to change their perceptions of tourism and hospitality jobs in a high power distance culture. Would training of staff be sufficient to change their perceptions? What else can be made?

Hseih and Tsai (2009) found that both American (relatively low power distance culture) and Taiwanese (relatively high power distance culture) tourists had high expectations regarding the responsiveness dimension of service quality. Both American and Taiwanese tourists expected a prompt for different reasons. American tourists are impatient with time and could not stand waiting. On the other hand, Taiwanese tourists, due to high power distance, believed that they were higher in status compared with service providers, they deserved excellent service and the service personnel should be able to respond to the customers even when they were busy.

In service recovery situations following a service failure, when offering an apology to a customer, customers from high power distance cultures attach more significance to the status of the employee. In other words, they prefer an apology to be made by a manager, rather than a lower-ranking staff such as a receptionist or a waiter in the instance of a service failure (Patterson et al., 2006; Koc, 2016). Orsingher et al. (2010) found that if the employee who manages the complaint is perceived low in status, the influence of interactional and procedural justice on satisfaction with complaint handling was lower in high power distance cultures. In other words, these customers feel that their complaint has not been handled fairly. This means that while customers from a lower power distance culture attach more weighting to distributive justice (i.e., how fair the compensation received was), customers from a high power distance culture tend to attach greater importance to procedural justice (i.e., how fair the process was), and interactional justice (i.e., how fair the customer was treated) during the service recovery process (Koc, 2017a). However, a more general stream of research on power distance shows that when making evaluations of authorities, people from low power distance cultures place more value on the quality of their treatment by authorities, while people from high power distance cultures place more value on the favorability of their outcomes (Tyler et al., 2000).

Customers from a larger power distance culture are more likely to perceive unsatisfactory goods and services as a fact of life and are less likely to complain when encountered with service failures (Au et al., 2010). Swanson et al. (2011) found that power distance was negatively associated with the customer complaining directly to the service provider. In other words, customers from a high power distance culture are less likely to make a direct complaint to the service provider. Hence, tourism and hospitality establishments serving customers from high power distance cultures are recommended to encourage their customers to make a complaint so as to identify and solve problems.

From a service quality prospective, customers who are members of a low power distance culture tend to attach more significant weighting to reliability and responsiveness dimensions of service quality (Donthu and Yoo, 1998). Furrer et al.'s (2000) studies are somewhat supportive of Donthu and Yoo (1998), who found that power distance was negatively correlated with reliability, responsiveness, and empathy and positively correlated with assurance and tangibles dimensions. Tsaur et al. (2005) compared Asian, English and European tourists who visited the UK and found similar results to the above. Again, Dash et al.'s (2009) study findings, though in the banking industry, supports the above research studies in terms of the influence of power distance on service quality dimensions.

Exercise

Read the article "The Best and Worst Airlines and Airports of 2019" (on Bloomberg website – shorturl.at/bdqEY). Explain and discuss what sort of factors in the marketing mix elements and service quality dimensions make an airport good or bad.

Communication, interaction, and decision making

Activity

Power distance and non-verbal communication

In high power distance cultures, the amount of non-verbal interaction between subordinates and superiors may be restricted (Neuliep, 2018). According to Andersen et al. (2003), in large power distance cultures people without power (lower in rank/hierarchy) are expected to express only positive emotions (e.g., smile more often), when they interact with people who have power (higher in rank/hierarchy). Power distance may also influence paralinguistic cues[1] people in culture may use (Neuliep, 2018).

Paralinguistics cues refer to the aspects of spoken communication that do not involve words such as body language, gestures, facial expressions, tone and pitch of voice. Paralinguistic cues used in communication are extremely important as they can change the message conveyed significantly. People in low power distance cultures are generally less aware of their vocalics (e.g., volume, intensity) than are people in high power distance cultures. Vocalics, the non-verbal uses of the voice (such as the pitch, tone, rate, volume, and accent pattern) reveal emotions and provide cues as to how the message should be interpreted (DeFleur and DeFleur, 2016).

Andersen et al. (2003) point out that North Americans (low power distance culture) are often perceived as noisy, exaggerated, and childlike. Oculesics, which is to do with the way the eyes are used during communication, may also be influenced by power distance. In high power distance cultures, subordinates are taught to avoid eye contact, often as a sign of respect for those in superior positions. Direct eye contact or gaze by the subordinates can be interpreted as a threat or a challenge to the person in authority.

Additionally, in high power distance cultures, when a person of high status hands something to a person of lower status, the lower status person quite often may tend to use both hands to receive the item, recognising her/his lower status (Neuliep, 2018). Subordinates in high power distance cultures are expected to be skilled in decoding non-verbal behaviour, especially the non-verbal behaviour of their superiors (Andersen et al., 2003).

Based on the information provided here, write a short essay to explain how power distance may influence the communication taking place between customers and employees, and between employees in tourism and hospitality operations during the following occasions:

- A service employee from a low power distance culture responding to a dissatisfied customer from a high power distance culture.
- A service employee from a high power distance culture responding to a dissatisfied customer from a low power distance culture.
- A service employee from a low power distance culture reporting a service failure to her/his superior who is from a high power distance culture.
- A waiter, from a low power distance culture, telling the chef, who is from a high power distance culture, that a customer's specific requirements have not been taken into account when the meal was prepared.

Task

Visit two international restaurants in your country, one being a high power distance (e.g., Japanese or Mexican) and the other one being low power distance (e.g., German or Swiss). Make sure that these restaurants employ mainly service staff and managers who are nationals of these respective countries. Observe their interactions, verbal and non-verbal communications with their peers and managers and take down notes. Discuss whether their patterns of interaction conform to the explanations given here or not. If there are discrepancies, think of other factors that may have influenced their interaction, apart from their power distance orientation.

As explained above in the Activity box, in high power distance cultures the amount of non-verbal interaction between subordinates and superiors may be restricted (Neuliep, 2018), and subordinates may be expected to show only positive emotions when they interact with their superiors (Andersen et al., 2003). Boz and Koc's (2020) study in Turkey (a relatively high power distance) tourism and hospitality staff, in general, had a problem of recognising facial expressions of customers, and they had inflated self-efficacy beliefs (may be referred to as Dunning Kruger syndrome) regarding their abilities to recognise facial expressions of customers. Boz and Koc's study (2020) found a major difference between self-report and ability-based measures of tourism and hospitality staff in terms of their abilities regarding facial expression/emotion recognition. Based on the above explanations, it may be recommended that in high power distance cultures managers may be trained to better understand actual emotions of staff (and also customers) to detect and solve problems as early as possible.

In relatively higher power distance cultures, recruitment for upper-level management may be carried out internally by superiors by promoting the subordinates they trust and they have known for a long time (Rao, 2009). As subordinates are aware that their career development is dependent on their relationships with their superiors, they may tend to avoid the questioning of the authority of superiors, and as well as disagreeing with them. There may be serious ethical and efficiency implications of this system of subordinate–superior relationships. Davis and Ruhe (2003), Seleim and Bontis (2009) and Nam (2018) found that corruption and nepotism were more likely to occur in high power distance cultures.

This may mean that in high power distance organisations recruitment, performance appraisal and reward systems may be based on the level of obedience or submission of staff, rather than their actual performance, competency, and merit. Consequently, coupled with the presence of bureaucracy and the hierarchical systems, it may be claimed that there are serious efficiency and effectiveness problems in organisations in high power distance cultures.

In a high power distance, culture employees are afraid to express opinions that differ from those of superiors and they tend to take a passive stance in the decision-making process (Khatri, 2009; Valverde Moreno et al., 2019). It must be borne in mind that employee participation in decision making not only increases job satisfaction and motivation (Tariq et al., 2016; Gallie et al., 2017), but also the quality of the decisions made in an organisation (Kim et al., 2010). Boopathi (2014) compared Finnish (low power distance) and Indian (high power distance) tourism establishments and put forward that in Finland, subordinates, and people in general, are interdependent and they have rather limited dependency on people who have high status and power in the organisation. In low power distance cultures, even junior members of staff can make decisions without consulting their superiors and Finnish managers do not underestimate their employees' capabilities in terms of making decisions.

Staff training

The previous explanations show that in addition to all training initiatives including the design and implementation of empowerment programmes require special attention in high power distance cultures. Regarding training initiatives, it should also be noted that employees from a low power distance culture value learner-centred learning and training initiatives, while employees from a high power distance culture tend to value trainer-centred learning approach (Baum, 2006). In high power distance cultures, training effectiveness is believed to be dependent on the knowledge and expertise of the trainer (Baum, 2006). There is plenty of research showing the importance of active participation of staff members in the training and learning activities (Felstead et al., 2010; Inanc et al., 2015; Gallie et al., 2017), especially in skill development training initiatives compared with training initiatives aimed at the information or knowledge transfer.

Information zone

Reducing cultural differences among employees through service scripts

Nguyen et al. (2014) and Baker (2017) recommend the use of service scripts in reducing the differences among service employees and standardising their behaviours in tourism and hospitality businesses.

Service scripts show what actions an employee needs to take during a service encounter and the general rules and procedures to follow during each step of the service process (Walsh et al., 2012). Moreover, service scripts have an overall influence on the interactions and communication between employees by controlling what employees are expected to say and do (Abelson, 1981).

For example, Ritz Carlton gave its employees a 20-item checklist of rules to follow when interacting with hotel guests (Nguyen et al., 2014). The use of service scripts can be an effective tool in controlling employee behaviours as the standardisation of the service encounter allows tourism and hospitality businesses to control and overcome various differences in employees' skills, abilities, and attitudes (Rafaeli et al., 2008) which may be conditioned by their cultural characteristics (Koc, 2017b).

Empowerment

Empowerment can be defined as a discretionary construct that the management of the business provides employees with discretion and autonomy over their tasks (Hsieh and Chao, 2004). Empowerment encourages service personnel to use their own judgement to make prompt decisions (Humborstad et al., 2008) so that an individual frontline service personnel can deliver high-quality service as a discretionary effort (Hancer and George, 2003). Hence, empowerment has important implications, not only in terms of rapid recovery of service failures but also for responsiveness, reliability and assurance dimensions of service quality in relation to the service provided by a tourism and hospitality business (Koc, 2013). A lack of empowerment resulting as a consequence a high level of power distance may also cause a knowledge gap in terms of the service quality gaps (see Chapter 1) identified by Parasuraman et al. (1991). The knowledge gap is the difference between what customers expect and what managers think customers expect from the service business. In other words, in the case of this gap, the management of the service business does not know exactly what the customers expect. In a high power distance culture, as the relationships and communication are based on a hierarchical system, the subordinates may not frequently and freely interact with their superiors. As a result customers' expectations and changes in customers' expectations may not be conveyed to senior management in a timely manner to make alterations and adjustments in service elements and processes.

While a lack of empowerment may cause customer dissatisfaction and result in customer switching behaviour on the part of customers, it may also result in despair, demotivation, high-level stress and burnout on the part of the service employees (Surachartkumtonkun et al., 2013; Guchait et al., 2014). Conversely, empowerment reduces problems at work, and increases employee's motivation, consequently contributing to business success (Ashness and Lashley, 1995; Shaw et al., 2006). Hocutt and Stone's (1998) model shows the importance of employee empowerment on employee job satisfaction, responsiveness, empathy, and customer satisfaction (Figure 6.1).

In terms of service personnel relationships, employees in a high power distance culture may be more likely to resort to avoiding and accommodating strategies (much like a paper over the cracks approach) in situations of conflict (Koc, 2010), which result in causing a delay in diagnosing and handling of conflicts among service personnel and ending up with more major problems in future. Power distance also influences the way service personnel to behave and interact with their peers, subordinates, and superiors. For instance, Koc's (2013) study[2] on service failures and recovery found that hospitality employees in the UK, a country with a relatively low power distance score, responded to the same service failure scenarios more quickly and directly than the hospitality employees in Turkey, a country with a relatively high power distance score. While Turkish employees used mitigated speech in communicating the service problem to their superiors, the UK employees used a more direct approach when they communicated the problem to their supervisors. Mitigated speech as a linguistic term can be described as deferential or indirect speech; opposite of direct communication, involving the avoidance of the use of explicit statements (Koc,

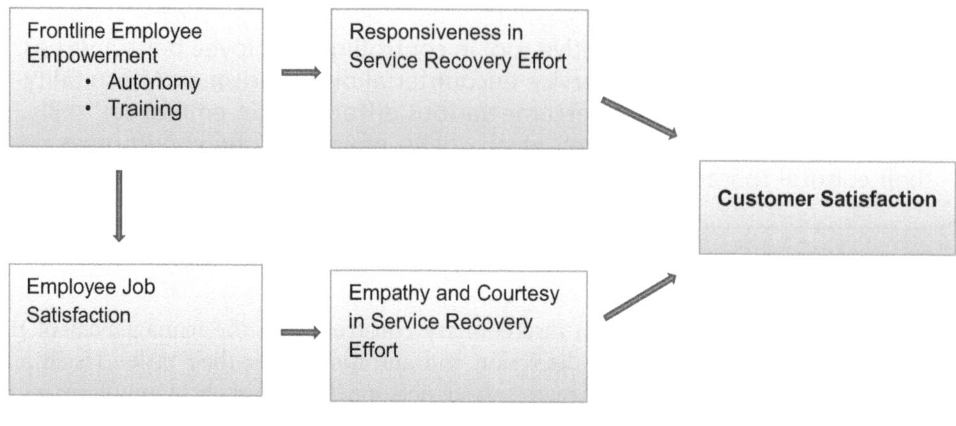

Figure 6.1 Employee empowerment and service recovery
Source: Hocutt and Stone (1998).

2013). This study shows the need for the development of empowerment among service personnel and establishing a more direct and informal communications system between subordinates and superiors in a high power distance culture.

As junior members of staff in high power distance cultures would not have the authority to make and implement a wide variety of decisions without consulting their superiors, that is, they would lack empowerment (Koc, 2013), to a large extent they would be dependent on their superiors. Sriramesh and Vercic's (2009) study found that employees from a high power distance culture tended to lose respect for a manager who consult them before making decisions. In high power cultures, less powerful people are expected to be dependent on more powerful people (Neuliep, 2018). Subordinates comply with their leader rather than challenge them or try to arrive at their own solutions in dealing with conflict. On the other hand, in low power distance cultures the inequalities among the members of society tend to be minimal while decentralisation of activities is more likely. In addition, in low-power distance societies, subordinates are expected to be consulted by superiors and privileges and status symbols appear to be less evident.

CASE STUDY

Power distance and airline crashes: communication between subordinates and superiors

Human failures play a significant role in airplane crashes. According to Wiegman et al (2005), skill errors are the most common type of failure reported in the Federal Aviation Administration (FAA) database, as nearly 80%of all accidents were associated with at least one skill error.

Fischer and Orasanu (1999) and Orasanu et al. (1997) studied the causes of passenger plane crashes and claimed that the tone of communication between pilots of different ranks (between subordinates and supervisors) may have detrimental effects. While in low power distance countries, such as Denmark, Sweden, Austria, the Netherlands and the United States, the subordinates' (first officers' – second pilots' or co-pilots') communication with their immediate supervisor (captains, that is, the legal commander of passenger airplanes), to a large extent is direct, that is, not mitigated. Subordinates can easily express disagreement with their superiors and tell them when something is wrong. However, in high power distance cultures, for example, Soth Korea, China, Mexico, Venezuela (first officers' – second pilots' or co-pilots') communication with their immediate supervisors (captains, that is, the legal commander of passenger airplanes), to a large extent is indirect, that is, mitigated. In high power distance cultures subordinates generally tend to be uncomfortable in approaching and interacting with their superiors, they find it difficult to express disagreement with their superiors and tell them that something may be wrong.

In the study of plane crashes, Fischer and Orasanu (1999) found that in high power cultures while captains felt comfortable giving orders and telling staff what to do, the first officer (second pilot), charged with the monitoring of the environment and plane conditions, found it difficult to provide clear and direct messages regarding the courses of actions to be taken under conditions of emergency. Fischer and Orasanu (1999) argue that mitigated and indirect statements by first officers were not taken seriously by the captains. Furthermore, their subordinates' indirect and mitigated messages caused additional confusion in the cockpit during emergencies. In another study, Tam and Duley (2005) found that although Taiwanese and Korean pilots stated that they preferred relationships where an authority figure conferred with subordinates about decisions, in actual life, these pilots had to operate in cockpits where an autocratic captain had the sole discretion in making decisions.

Fischer and Orasanu (1999) claim that many airplane crashes of the Korean Air in the 1970s, 1980s, and 1990s were attributable to a lack of clear, direct and non-mitigated communication between first officers and the captains. Mitigated statements were not very helpful in an airplane cockpit on a stormy night with an exhausted pilot trying to land at an airport with insufficient facilities. Later, Korean Airlines' established a series of training programmes to improve communication between the subordinates and the superiors. By requiring Korean Air pilots to communicate in English, safety engineers were able to enhance communication and substantially reduce the likelihood of plane crashes.

Task

Based on this case study think of three tourism or hospitality service encounter scenarios where the level of service quality may be in jeopardy as a result of the high level of power distance. Describe the likely negative consequences which may occur and offer courses of action so that these incidents do not take place in the future.

References

Fischer, U., and Orasanu, J. (1999). Say it again Sam! Effective communication strategies to mitigate pilot error. *Proceedings of the 10th International Symposium on Aviation Psychology*.Columbus, OH.

Gladwell, M. (2008). *Outliers: The story of success*. New York: Little, Brown and Company.

Orasanu, J., Davison, J., and Fischer, U. (1997). What did he say? Culture and language barriers to efficient communication in global aviation. *International Symposium on Aviation Psychology*, 673–678.

Wiegmann, D. A., Shappell, S. A., Boquet, A., Detwiler, C., Holcomb, K., and Faaborg, T. (2005). *Human error and general aviation accidents: A comprehensive, fine-grained analysis using HFACS* (Final Tech. Rep. No. AHFD-05–08/FAA-05–03). Washington, DC: Federal Aviation Administration.

This case study explains the importance of empowerment of staff and the communication between subordinates and supervisors. Service employees in a high power distance culture may lack initiative and empowerment to deliver a high-quality service or adjust service to the specific requirements of a customer (Koc, 2013).

In Ritz Carlton hotels each service employee has the authority (is empowered) to spend up to $2,000 to turn a dissatisfied customer into a satisfied one (Dimitriou, 2017). Several studies show the importance of speed of recovery and empowerment in service failure recoveries in tourism and hospitality (e.g., Hocutt and Stone, 1998; Schumacher and Komppula, 2016).

The importance of understanding employee's facial expressions by managers was mentioned previously. The recognition of facial expressions is equally important from the perspective of customers. Owing to the inseparability nature of services, a simultaneous understanding of customers' emotions relating to various aspects of service is important to make changes and corrections to the service. For the empowerment to work better, the frontline service employees need to be able to understand the true emotions of customers by recognising facial expressions and their non-verbal behaviours accurately and quickly (Kele et al., 2017; Bello and Bello, 2017; Li et al., 2017; Koc and Boz, 2019).

Apart from the employee actions and empowerment, tangibles and service atmosphere may also have an important influence on the perception of responsiveness as a service quality dimension. For instance, Bilgili et al.'s (2020) study showed that the red colour of lighting significantly increased Turkish hospitality customers' waiting time perceptions in the restaurants. As explained in Chapter 1, people from different cultures tend to attach different meanings to colours. Hence, the influence of colour or the colour of lighting in the service atmosphere may be perceived differently by cultures in terms of waiting time in tourism and hospitality services. Timely service and the amount of waiting time are important determinants of the perception of responsiveness as a service quality dimension. Table 6.3 demonstrates how certain factors may increase the perception of waiting time by the customers in general

Table 6.3 Customer waiting situations in tourism and hospitality

Customer Waiting Situations	*Examples and Strategies*
A person's boredom is related to her/his paying attention to the elapses time. When a person is not engaged, the amount of time elapsed is felt longer than the time elapses when she/he is engaged.	Placement of TV sets, provision of free wi-fi, making newspapers, magazines available can make people engaged and reduce the perception of elapsed time in waiting environments such as the reception area.
Pre-process (for instance ordering of the meal) and post-process (paying for the bill) waiting times are perceived to be longer than the actual service process.	As restaurant customers wait for their main course, they may be offered appetisers or even samplers. This does not only keep them engaged as they wait, but also makes them feel appreciated.
Waiting in anxiety may increase the perception of the waiting time.	Tourism and hospitality establishments may reduce their customers' risk perceptions by providing information and allowing customers to have more control over various aspects of the service.
Unpredictable and uninformed waiting time is perceived to be longer than the informed and predictable waiting time. If the customers do not know why they are waiting, they tend to perceive the elapsed time as longer.	If customers are informed how long, on average, they may need to wait, then they tend to wait more calmly to be served. Restaurant menus may provide an average duration of time it takes of each dish to serve, for all or some of the exceptional food items which may take longer than usual food items.
Waits believed to be unfair tend to cause customers to perceive the waiting time to be longer than waits believed to be fair.	Appropriate systems need to be established so that customers feel that they are not being kept waiting unnecessarily. In a restaurant, a customer whose food is served later than the customer sitting at the next table, who happened to order later, may be explained that the dish s/he ordered takes longer to prepare.
When the perceived value of the service increases (i.e., an exceptional service) customers tend to not mind the waiting time as much they do for ordinary services.	According to Fillon (2016), estimation of how long diners will have to wait for the privilege of eating at the top ten restaurants in 2016 was as follows:

Table 6.3 continued

Customer Waiting Situations	*Examples and Strategies*

Rank	*Restaurant and Location*	*Booking Needed Before*	*Rank*	*Restaurant and Location*	*Booking Needed Before*
1	Osteria Francescana (Modena, Italy)	At least 3 and a half months	**6**	Mirazur (Menton, France)	Up to 1 year
2	El Celler de Can Roca (Girona, Spain)	11 months	**7**	Mugaritz (Errenteria, Spain)	3 to 6 months
3	Eleven Madison Park (New York City)	2 to 3 weeks	**8**	Narisawa (Tokyo)	At least 2 months
4	Central (Lima, Peru)	At least 2 months	**9**	Steirereck (Vienna, Austria)	1 month
5	Noma (Copenhagen) at least 3 months	At least 3 months	**10**	Asador Etxebarri (Axpe, Spain)	1 to 3 months

	For an up-to-date list of the world's best restaurants please visit: shorturl.at/DHUV7l
Physically uncomfortable waiting is perceived to be lasting longer than comfortable waiting.	Waiting and service areas at airport lounges, planes, hotels, or restaurants can be equipped with comfortable furniture.
Solitary waits may be perceived to be lasting longer than group waits.	Waiting areas may be arranged in a way that customers may see each other, while at the same time not being disturbed by the presence of others.
Those customers who use a service seldom tend to perceive the duration of the waiting time longer than the regular customers.	Customers may be appropriately informed about the average time that they may have to wait.

Source: adapted from Koc (2015) and Dalgic et al. (2017).

CASE STUDIES

How to change customers' waiting time perceptions in tourism and hospitality

Case study 1

Some of the guests at a 3-star hotel complained about the amount of time they waited for the lifts to arrive. Hotel management did not know how to solve the problem as a) the cost of building an additional lift was high and would interrupt the service at the hotel, and b) there was no room available to build an additional lift.

After prolonged discussions with staff, the management of the hotel decided to put decorative mirrors by the side of the present lifts. The idea behind the solution was that while people waiting they kept looking at themselves in the mirror and did not pay as much attention to the passing time as they did before. The number of complaints by customers about the lift waiting times decreased significantly after the solution implemented.

Case study 2

Passengers using a specific route at the Houston Airport complained about the time they had to wait for their luggage. Extra baggage handlers were hired which reduced the waiting times to eight minutes. However, complaints continued. A study carried out by the airport management showed that passengers spent one minute walking to the baggage claim area, to be followed by seven minutes of waiting to claim their luggage, which was not too long. Then, the airport management devised a new solution. They changed the arrival gate, which took passengers longer to come to the baggage claim area. The complaints stopped as passengers were able to collect their luggage almost as soon as they walked to the baggage claim area. Although the actual waiting was the same, customers' satisfaction increased as a result of this change.

Source: Adapted from Koc (2015).

As a final note, the influence of generation changes can be mentioned here. Important changes are taking place as societies evolve from Generation X to Y and Z. Generation Z is the cohort after the Millenials, defined as those born from the mid-1990s to the early 2000s. Although members of Generation Z, in general, tend to have a global perspective and look for management without hierarchy (and bureaucracy) (Dixon et al., 2013), Millenials and Generation Z members in high power distance cultures still tend to be attracted to status and pursuit for career advancement (Ismail and Lu, 2014), are more concerned with money, prestige, and promotional opportunity compared with individuals in low power distance societies (Colakoglu and Caligiuri, 2012). These people are more still likely to set career goals as being at the upper levels of the organisational hierarchy. This may mean that as generations evolve in societies the influence of cultural characteristics, such as power distance, may still continue to influence the members of a society in a similar fashion as they did in the past.

Conclusion

This chapter explains the influence of power distance on tourism and hospitality service encounters. Research findings show that power distance influences the decisions relating to the design and implementation of marketing mix elements, service quality dimensions, and the relationship and systems within tourism and hospitality establishments. By gaining a deeper understanding of power distance as a cultural variable, tourism and hospitality managers can increase efficiency and effectiveness of their operations, and be more able to establish competitive advantage in the market.

Questions

1. What are the key characteristics of high and power distance cultures?
2. In addition to your own country, find at least five high power distance and five low distance countries. What do high and low power distance countries have in common?
3. What is empowerment? With which of the service quality dimensions can empowerment be associated? What are the implications of empowerment and customer participation for both the customers and the employees in tourism and hospitality?
4. Explain how power distance may influence each marketing mix element.
5. Explain and discuss the research findings on power distance relating to service quality in general and each service quality dimension in particular.
6. How does power distance influence the relationship and communication between staff and the relationship and communication with customers?
7. Explain and discuss Aristotle's (384–322 bce) quote "The worst form of inequality is to try to make unequal things equal" from the perspective of power distance.

Research questions/ideas to pursue for researchers

Customers in high power distance cultures view themselves as superior compared with the service employees who serve them and tend to avoid interaction with them unless it is necessary (Lee, 2015). On the other hand, in low power distance cultures customers tend to see service employees equal and be comfortable interacting with them. As customer participation (co-production) in services may increase the interaction of customers with the service employees, the attitudes of customers towards customer participation in tourism and hospitality services may vary in high and low power distance cultures. This notion may be investigated in a comparative study.

Notes

1 In primates, showing the teeth, especially teeth held together, is almost always a sign of submission and the human smile may have probably evolved from that. When chimpanzees smile they do it by covering their top teeth and showing their bottom teeth. A human smile is seen as a threatening expression to chimpanzees. When the chimpanzees are afraid or when they are trying to be intimidating, they tend to show all their top teeth and do what we call a "fear grimace."

2 The main thrust of this study came from an anecdote explained in Chapter 7 of Gladwell's (2008) book *Outliers: The Story of Succes*. This anecdote, explained in the above case study, shows the significant influence of power distance in communication and its likely drastic consequences.

Recommended further reading

Daniels, M. A., and Greguras, G. J. (2014). Exploring the nature of power distance implications for micro-and macro-level theories, processes, and outcomes. *Journal of Management*, 40(5), 1202–1229.

Gao, B., Li, X., Liu, S., and Fang, D. (2018). How power distance affects online hotel ratings: the positive moderating roles of hotel chain and reviewers' travel experience. *Tourism Management*, 65, 176–186.

Hofstede, G. (2010). *Cultures and organizations: Software of the mind* (3rd ed.). New York: McGraw-Hill.

Hsieh, A. T., and Tsai, C. W. (2009). Does national culture really matter? Hotel service perceptions by Taiwan and American tourists. *International Journal of Culture, Tourism and Hospitality Research*, 3(1), 54–69.

Koc, E. (2013). Power distance and its implications for upward communication and empowerment: Crisis management and recovery in hospitality services. *The International Journal of Human Resource Management*, 24(19), 3681–3696.

References

Abelson, R. F. (1981) Psychological status of the script concept. *American Psychologist*, 36, 715–729.

Andersen, P. A., Hecht, M. L., Hoobler, G. D., and Smallwood, M. (2003). Non-verbal communication across cultures. In W. B. Gudykunst (Ed.), *Cross-Cultural and Intercultural Communication* (pp. 73–90). Thousand Oaks, CA: Sage.

Ashness, D., and. Lashley, C. (1995). Empowering service workers at Harvester Restaurants. Personnel Review. *Empowerment Methods and Techniques for Sport Managers*, 24(8), 17–32.

Au, N., Law, R., and Buhalis, D. (2010). The impact of culture on e-complaints: Evidence from the Chinese consumers in hospitality organizations. In U. Gretzel, R. Law, and M.

Fuchs (Eds.), *Information and communication technologies in tourism 2010* (pp. 285–296). Vienna, Switzerland: Springer-Verlag.

Bathaee, A. (2011). Culture affects consumer behavior: Theoretical reflections and an illustrative example with Germany and Iran. Working paper (No. 02/2011). Ernst Moritz Arndt University of Greifswald, Faculty of Law and Economics.

Baker, M. (2017). Service failures and recovery: Theories and models. In E. Koc (Ed.), *Service failures and recovery in tourism and hospitality* (pp. 27–41). Wallingford, Oxford: CABI.

Baum, T. (2006). *Human resource management for tourism, hospitality and leisure: an international perspective*. London: Thomson Learning.

Bello, Y. O., and Bello, M. B. (2017). Employees' empowerment, service quality and customers' satisfaction in hotel industry. *Strategic Journal of Business and Change Management*, 4(4), 1001–1019.

Bhattacharyya, K., and Borhart, A. (2018). National cultural values on service quality: A typology for global dining experience in the 21st century. *Journal of Service Science Research*, 10(1), 1–24.

Bilgili, B., Ozkul, E., and Koc, E. (2020). The influence of colour of lighting on customers' waiting time perceptions. *Total Quality Management and Business Excellence*, 31(9–10), 1098–1111.

Bisel, R. S., Messersmith, A. S., and Kelley, K. M. (2012). Supervisor-subordinate communication hierarchical mum effect meets organizational learning. *Journal of Business Communication*, 49, 2, 128–147.

Boopathi, S. N. (2014). A detailed comparison of Finland and India through Hofstede and Globe study. *Global Review of Research in Tourism, Hospitality and Leisure Management (GRRTHLM) An Online International Research Journal*, 1(1), 72–101.

Botero, C. I., and Van Dyne, L. (2009). Employee voice behavior: Interactive effects of lmx and power-distance in the United States and Colombia. *Management Communication Quarterly*, 23(1), 84–104.

Boz, H., and Koc, E. (2020). Service quality, emotion recognition, emotional intelligence and Dunning Kruger syndrome. *Total Quality Management and Business Excellence*, 1–14.

Cakici, C. and Guler, O. (2017). Emotional Contagion and the Influence of Groups on Service Failures and Recovery. In E. Koc (Ed.), *Service failures and recovery in tourism and hospitality* (pp. 135–159). Wallingford, Oxford: CABI.

Chen, J. S., and D. Gursoy. (2000). Cross-cultural comparison of the information sources by first-time and repeat travelers and its marketing implications. *Hospitality Management*, 19, 191–203.

Chen, P.J., Okumus, F., Huan, N., and Khaldoon, N. (2011), Developing effective communication strategies for the Spanish and Haitian-Creole-speaking workforce in hotel companies. *Worldwide Hospitality and Tourism Themes*, 3, 4, 335–353.

Cheong, Y., Kim, K., and Zheng, L. (2010). Advertising appeals as a reflection of culture: a cross-cultural analysis of food advertising appeals in China and the US. *Asian Journal of Communication*, 20(1), 1–16.

Cho, H. (2001), The effects of market and organizational factors on international news coverage in local Japanese daily newspapers, *Keio Communication Review*, 23, 107–123.

Clark, S. (2013). *Organizational behavior and human resource management practices: A comparison between the United States and Brazil based on Hofstede's cultural framework* (Unpublished thesis). Honors College, San Marcos, Texas.

Colakoglu, S., and Caligiuri, P. (2012). Cultural influences on Mllennial MBA students' career goals: Evidence from 23 countries. In Ng et al. (Eds), *Managing the new workforce: International perspective on the millennial generation* (pp. 262–280). Cheltenham, UK: Edward Elgar.

Correia, A., Kozak, M., and Ferradeira, J. (2011). Impact of culture on tourist decision-making styles. *International Journal of Tourism Research*, 13(5), 433–446.

Crotts, J. C. and Erdmann, R. (2000). Does national culture influence consumers' evaluation of travel services? A test of Hofstede's model of cross-cultural differences. *Managing Service Quality*, 10(6), 410–419.

Dalgic, A., Toksoz D., and Birdir, K. (2017). The role of empowerment, internal communication, waiting time and speed in service recovery. In E. Koc (Ed.), *Service failures and recovery in tourism and hospitality* (pp. 181–196). Wallingford, Oxford: CABI.

Daniels, M. A., and Greguras, G. J. (2014). Exploring the nature of power distance implications for micro-and macro-level theories, processes, and outcomes. *Journal of Management*, 40(5), 1202–1229.

Dash, S., Bruning, E., and Acharya, M. (2009). The effect of power distance and individualism on service quality expectations in banking: A two-country individual-and national-cultural comparison. *International Journal of Bank Marketing*, 27(5), 336–358.

Davis, J. H., and Ruhe, J. A. (2003). Perceptions of country corruption: Antecedents and outcomes. *Journal of Business Ethics*, 43(4), 275–288.

Davis, P., Lu, V., and Crouch R. (2009). Importance of service quality across different services types: An exploratory study of Australian and Chinese consumers. *Proceedings of the Australian and New Zealand Marketing Academy (ANZMAC) Annual Conference: Sustainable management and marketing conference*, pp. 1–9.

De Mooij, M. (2019). *Consumer behavior and culture: Consequences for global marketing and advertising*. Thousand Oaks, CA: Sage.

DeFleur, M. L., and DeFleur, M. H. (2016). *Mass communication theories: Explaining origins, processes, and effects*. Abingdon: Routledge.

Dimitriou, C. (2017). Understanding and dealing with service failures in tourism and hospitality. In E. Koc (Ed.), *Service failures and recovery in tourism and hospitality* (pp. 9–26). Wallingford, Oxford: CABI

Dixon, G., Mercado, A., and Knowles, B. (2013). Followers and generations in the workplace. *Engineering Management Journal*, 25(4), 62–73.

Donthu, N. and Yoo, B. (1998), Cultural influences on service quality expectations. *Journal of Service Research*, 1(2), 178–186.

Ergun, G. S., and Kitapci, O. (2018). The impact of cultural dimensions on customer complaint behaviours: an exploratory study in Antalya/Manavgat tourism region. *International Journal of Culture, Tourism and Hospitality Research*, 12(1), 59–79.

EUROSTAT (2020) Mimum wage statistics. shorturl.at/ltwJV (accessed 10 January 2020).

Felstead, A., Gallie, D., Green, F., and Zhou, Y. (2010). Employee involvement, the quality of training and the learning environment: An individual level analysis. *The International Journal of Human Resource Management*, 21(10), 1667–1688.

Fillon, W. (2016). How to get a table at the world's top 10 restaurants: better plan ahead. *Eater*. https://www.eater.com/2016/6/14/11931452/reservations-50-best-restaurants-osteria-francescana-el-celler-de-can-roca-noma (accessed 1 December 2019).

Fischer, U. and Orasanu, J. (1999), Say it again Sam! Effective communication strategies to mitigate pilot error. *Proceedings of the 10th International Symposium on Aviation Psychology*. Columbus, OH.

Furrer, O., Liu, B. S. C., and Sudharshan, D. (2000). The relationships between culture and service quality perceptions: Basis for crosscultural market segmentation and resource allocation. *Journal of Service Research*, 2(4), 355–371.

Gallie, D., Zhou, Y., Felstead, A., Green, F., and Henseke, G. (2017). The implications of direct participation for organisational commitment, job satisfaction and affective psychological well-being: A longitudinal analysis. *Industrial Relations Journal*, 48(2), 174–191.

Gao, B., Li, X., Liu, S., and Fang, D. (2018). How power distance affects online hotel ratings: the positive moderating roles of hotel chain and reviewers' travel experience. *Tourism Management*, 65, 176–186.

Gladwell, M. (2008). *Outliers: The story of success*. New York: Little, Brown and Company.

Guchait, P., Paşamehmetoğlu, A., and Dawson, M. (2014). Perceived supervisor and co-worker support for error management: Impact on perceived psychological safety and service recovery performance. *International Journal of Hospitality Management*, 41, 28–37.

Han, B., and Heather, J. (2001). Korean Tourists' Characteristics in Guam. *Journal of Photo-Geographers*, 11(1), 69–83.

Hancer, M., and George, R. T. (2003). Job satisfaction of restaurant employees: an empirical investigation using the Minnesota satisfaction questionnaire. *Journal of Hospitality & Tourism Research*, 27(1), 85–100.

Harris, P., Rettie, R., and Cheung, C. K. (2005). Adoption and usage of m-commerce: A cross-cultural comparison of Hong Kong and the United Kingdom. *Journal of Electronic Commerce Research*, 6(3), 210–224.

Heung, V.C.S., and Lam, T. (2003). Customer complaint behaviour towards hotel restaurant services. *International Journal of Contemporary Hospitality Management*, 15(5), 285–289.

Hocutt, M. A., and Stone, T. H. (1998). The impact of employee empowerment on the quality of a service recovery effort. *Journal of Quality Management*, 3(1), 117–132.

Hofstede, G. (1980). *Culture's consequences: International differences in work-related values*. Beverly Hills, CA: Sage.

Hofstede, G. (1991). *Cultures and organization: Software of the mind*. New York: McGraw-Hill.

Hofstede, G. H. (2001). *Culture's consequences: Comparing values, behaviors, institutions, and organizations across nations*. Thousand Oaks, CA: Sage.

Hofstede, G., (2010). *Cultures and organizations: Software of the mind* (3rd ed.). New York: McGraw-Hill.

Hofstede, G. (2020). Cultural dimensions. https://www.hofstede-insights.com/product/compare-countries/ (accessed 20 January 2020).

Hofstede, G. J., and Minkov, M. (2010). Cultures and ORganizations: Software of the mind (3rd rev. ed.). New York: McGraw-Hill.

Hofstede, G., Hofstede, G. J., and Minkov, M. (2010). *Cultures and organizations: Software of the mind*. New York: McGraw-Hill.

Hon, A. H., and Lu, L. (2016). When will the trickle-down effect of abusive supervision be alleviated? The moderating roles of power distance and traditional cultures. *Cornell Hospitality Quarterly*, 57(4), 421–433.

House, R. J., Hanges, P. J., Javidan, M., Dorfman, P. W., and Gupta, V. (2004). *Culture, leadership and organizations: The GLOBE study of 62 societies*. Thousand Oaks: Sage.

Hsieh, A. T. and Chao, H. Y. (2004), A reassessment of the relationship between job specialization, job rotation and job burnout: example of Taiwan's high-technology industry. *International Journal of Human Resource Management*, 15, 1108–1123.

Hsieh, A. T., and Tsai, C. W. (2009). Does national culture really matter? Hotel service perceptions by Taiwan and American tourists. *International Journal of Culture, Tourism and Hospitality Research*, 3(1), 54–69.

Huang, J. H., Huang, C. T., and Wu, S. (1996). National character and response to unsatisfactory hotel service. *International Journal of Hospitality Management*, 15(3), 229–243.

Humborstad, S. I. W., Humborstad, B., Whitfield, R., and Perry, C. (2008). Implementation of empowerment in Chinese high power-distance organizations. *The International Journal of Human Resource Management*, 19, 1349–1364.

Inanc, H., Zhou, Y., Gallie, D., Felstead, A., and Green, F. (2015). Direct participation and employee learning at work. *Work and Occupations*, 42(4), 447–475.

Ismail, M., and Lu, H. S. (2014). Cultural values and career goals of the millennial generation: An integrated conceptual framework. *Journal of International Management Studies*, 9(1), 38–49.

Javidan, M., Stahl, G. K., Brodbeck, F., and Wilderom, C. P. (2005). Cross-border transfer of knowledge: Cultural lessons from Project GLOBE. *Academy of Management Perspectives*, 19(2), 59–76.

Kele, A. T. B. A., Mohsin, A., and Lengler, J. (2017). How willing/unwilling are luxury hotels' staff to be empowered? A case of East Malaysia. *Tourism Management Perspectives*, 22, 44–53.

Khatri, N. (2009). Consequences of power distance orientation in organisations. *Vision*, 13(1), 1–9.

Kim, J., MacDuffie, J. P., and Pil, F. K. (2010). Employee voice and organizational performance: Team versus representative influence. *Human Relations*, 63(3), 371–394.

Koc, E. (2010). Services and conflict management: Cultural and European integration perspectives. *International Journal of Intercultural Relations*, 34(1), 88–96.

Koc, E. (2013). Power distance and its implications for upward communication and empowerment: Crisis management and recovery in hospitality services. *The International Journal of Human Resource Management*, 24(19), 3681–3696.

Koc, E. (2015). *Hizmet Pazarlaması ve Yönetimi, 1*. Ankara: Baskı, Seçkin Yayıncılık.

Koc, E. (2016). Food consumption in all-inclusive holidays: illusion of control as an antecedent of inversionary consumption. *Journal of Gastronomy and Tourism*, 2(2), 107–116.

Koc, E. (2017a). *Service failures and recovery in tourism and hospitality: A practical manual.* Wallingford, Oxford: CABI.

Koc. E. (2017b) Cross-cultural aspects of service failures and recovery. In E. Koc (Ed.), *Service failures and recovery in tourism and hospitality: A practical manual* (pp. 197–213). Wallingford, Oxford: CABI.

Koc, E. (2018). *Hizmet Pazarlaması ve Yönetimi, 3*. Ankara: Baskı, Seçkin Yayıncılık.

Kueh, K., and Ho Voon, B. (2007). Culture and service quality expectations: Evidence from Generation Y consumers in Malaysia. *Managing Service Quality: An International Journal*, 17(6), 656–680.

Ladhari, R., Pons, F., Bressolles, G., and Zins, M. (2011). Culture and personal values: How they influence perceived service quality. *Journal of Business Research*, 64(9), 951–957.

Lalwani, A. K., and Forcum, L. (2016). Does a dollar get you a dollar's worth of merchandise? The impact of power distance belief on price-quality judgments. *Journal of Consumer Research*, 43(2), 317–333.

Lam, D., Lee, A., and Mizerski, R. (2009). The effect of cultural values on word-of-mouth communication. *Journal of International Marketing*, 17(3), 55–70.

Lee, H. E. (2015). Does a server's attentiveness matter? Understanding intercultural service encounters in restaurants. *International Journal of Hospitality Management*, 50, 134–144.

Li, C., Cui, G., and Peng, L. (2017). The signaling effect of management response in engaging customers: A study of the hotel industry. *Tourism Management*, 62, 42–53.

Manrai, L. A., and Manrai, A. (2011). Hofstede's cultural dimensions and tourist behaviors: A review and conceptual framework. *Journal of Economics, Finance and Administrative Science*, 16(31), 23.

Mattila, A. (1999). Culture in evaluating services. *Journal of Service Research*, 1(3), 250–261.

Milgram, S. (1963). Behavioral study of obedience. *Journal of Abnormal and Social Psychology*, 67, 371–378.

Mueller, R. D., Palmer, A., Mack, R., and McMullan, R. (2003). Service in the restaurant industry: an American and Irish comparison of service failures and recovery strategies. *International Journal of Hospitality Management*, 22, 395–418.

Nam, T. (2018). Examining the anti-corruption effect of e-government and the moderating effect of national culture: A cross-country study. *Government Information Quarterly*, 35(2), 273–282.

Nath, P., Devlin, J., and Reid, V. (2016). Expectation formation in case of newer hotels: The role of advertising, price, and culture. *Journal of Travel Research*, 55(2), 261–275.

Nazarian, A., Atkinson, P., and Foroudi, P. (2017). Influence of national culture and balanced organizational culture on the hotel industry's performance. *International Journal of Hospitality Management*, 63, 22–32.

Neuliep, J. W. (2018). *Intercultural communication: A contextual approach* (7th ed.). Thousand Oaks, CA: Sage.

Nguyen, H., Groth, M., Walsh, G., and Hennig-Thurau, T. (2014). The impact of service scripts on customer citizenship behavior and the moderating role of employee customer orientation. *Psychology and Marketing*, 31(12), 1096–1109.

Noja, G. G., Petrović, N., and Cristea, M. (2018). Turning points in migrants' labour market integration in Europe and benefit spillovers for Romania and Serbia: the role of socio-psychological credentials. *Zbornik Radova Ekonomski Fakultet u Rijeka*, 36(2), 489–518.

Orasanu, J., Davison, J., and Fischer, U. (1997). What did he say? culture and language barriers to efficient communication in global aviation. *International Symposium on Aviation Psychology*, 673–678.

Orsingher, C., Valentini, S., and de Angelis, M. (2010). A meta-analysis of satisfaction with complaint handling in services. *Journal of the Academy of Marketing Science*, 38(2), 169–186.

Ouchi, W. G. (1981). *Theory Z: How American business can meet the Japanese challenge.* Reading, MA: AddisonWesley.

Parasuraman, A., Berry, L. L., and Zeithaml, V. A. (1991). Refinement and reassessment of the SERVQUAL scale. *Journal of Retailing*, (Winter), 420–450.

Patterson, P.F., Cowley, E., and Prasongsukarn, K. (2006). Service failure recovery: The moderating impact of individual-level cultural value orientation on perceptions of justice. *International Journal of Research in Marketing*, 23(3), 263–277.

Pollay, R. W., and Gallagher, K. (1990). Advertising and cultural values: Reflections in the distorted mirror. *International Journal of Advertising*, 9(4), 359–372.

Radojevic, T., Stanisic, N., and Stanic, N. (2019). The culture of hospitality: From anecdote to evidence. *Annals of Tourism Research*, 79, 102789.

Rafaeli, A., Ziklik, L., and Douce, L. (2008). The impact of call center employees' customer orientation behaviors on service quality. *Journal of Service Research*, 10, 239–255.

Rao, P. (2009). The role of national culture on Mexican staffing practices. *Employee Relations*, 31(3), 295–311.

Reisinger, Y., and Crotts, J. C. (2010). Applying Hofstede's national culture measures in tourism research: Illuminating issues of divergence and convergence. *Journal of Travel Research*, 49(2), 153–164.

Schumacher, S., and Komppula, R. (2016). Frontline employees' perspectives and the role of empowerment. *European Journal of Tourism, Hospitality and Recreation*, 7(2), 117–127.

Schumann, J. H., Wangenheim, F. V., Stringfellow, A., Yang, Z., Blazevic, V., Praxmarer, S., ... Jimenez, F. R. (2010). Cross-cultural differences in the effect of received word-of-mouth referral in relational service exchange. *Journal of International Marketing*, 18(3), 62–80.

Seleim, A., and Bontis, N. (2009). The relationship between culture and corruption: a cross-national study. *Journal of Intellectual Capital*, 10(1), 165–184.

Shaw, D., Newholm, T., and Dickinson, R. (2006) Consumption as voting: An exploration of consumer empowerment. *European Journal of Marketing*, 40(9/10), 1049–1067.

Sriramesh, K., and Vercic, D. eds. (2009). *The Global Public Relations Handbook* (rev. and expanded ed.). Abindgon: Routledge.

Surachartkumtonkun, J., Patterson, P. G., and McColl-Kennedy, J. R. (2013). Customer rage back-story: Linking needs-based cognitive appraisal to service failure type. *Journal of Retailing*, 89(1), 72–87.

Swaminathan, F. (2012). The uncommon sense of advertising–understanding contemporary advertising appeals in press of top advertisers in India. *Proceedings of the LCBR European Marketing Conference.*

Swanson, S. R., Frankel, R., Sagan, M., and Johansen, D. L. (2011). Private and public voice: Exploring cultural influence. *Managing Service Quality: An International Journal*, 21(3), 216–239.

Tam, L., and Duley, J. (2005). Beyond the West: Cultural gaps in aviation human factors research. *Proceedings of the mini-conference on human factors in complex sociotechnical systems*, April 25–28, New Jersey.

Tariq, S., Jan, F. A., and Ahmad, M. S. (2016). Green employee empowerment: A systematic literature review on state-of-art in green human resource management. *Quality and Quantity*, 50(1), 237–269.

Tsang, N. K., and Ap, J. (2007). Tourists' perceptions of relational quality service attributes: a cross-cultural study. *Journal of Travel Research*, 45, 355–363.

Tsaur, S. H., Lin, C. T., and Wu, C. S. (2005). Cultural differences of service quality and behavioral intention in tourist hotels. *Journal of Hospitality and Leisure Marketing*, 13(1), 41–63.

Tyler, T. R., Lind, E. A., and Huo, Y. J. (2000). Cultural values and authority relations: The psychology of conflict resolution across cultures. *Psychology, Public Policy, and Law*, 6(4), 1138–1163.

Valverde Moreno, M., Torres-Jiménez, M., Lucia-Casademunt, A. M., and Muñoz-Ocaña, Y. (2019). Cross cultural analysis of direct employee participation: dealing with gender and cultural values. *Frontiers in Psychology*, 10, 723.

Walsh, G., Gouthier, M., Gremler, D. D., and Brach, S. (2012). What the eye does not see, the mind cannot reject: Can call center location explain differences in customer evaluations? *International Business Review*, 21, 957–967.

Weiermair, K. (2000). Tourists' perceptions towards and satisfaction with service quality in the cross-cultural service encounter: Implications for hospitality and tourism management. *Managing Service Quality*, 10(6), 397–409.

Wiegmann, D. A., Shappell, S. A., Boquet, A., Detwiler, C., Holcomb, K., and Faaborg, T. (2005). *Human error and general aviation accidents: A comprehensive, fine-grained analysis using HFACS* (Final Tech. Rep. No. AHFD-05–08/FAA-05–03). Washington, DC: Federal Aviation Administration.

Yilmaz, K., Altinkurt, Y., Guner, M., and Sen, B. (2015). The Relationship between Teachers' Emotional Labor and Burnout Level. *Eurasian Journal of Educational Research*, 59, 75–90.

Yuksel, A., Kilinc, U.K. and Yuksel, F. (2006), Cross-national analysis of hotel customers' attitudes toward complaining and their complaining behaviors. *Tourism Management*, 27(1), 11–24.

Zhao, D. (2017). The effects of culture on international advertising appeals: A cross-cultural content analysis of US and Japanese global brands. *Professional Projects from the College of Journalism and Mass Communications*, 15, 13–14.

Chapter 7

Uncertainty avoidance as a cultural variable

Learning Objectives

After reading this chapter, you should be able to:

- explain the main characteristics of low- and high-uncertainty avoidance cultures;
- explain the main types of risks tourism and hospitality customers may perceive and how uncertainty avoidance may influence their preferences;
- understand the concept of risk and its influence on tourism and hospitality customers and employees;
- understand the concept of control and its role and potential in the design of marketing strategies.

Introduction

All main service characteristics of *inseparability, heterogeneity, intangibility*, and *perishability* may contribute towards increasing customers' perception of risk (Parasuraman, Zeithaml, and Berry, 1988), eventually resulting in concerns regarding the reliability of the service. Reliability can be defined as the ability of a tourism and hospitality business to keep its promises (Parasuraman et al., 1988). When a customer has concerns regarding reliability, s/he may refrain from purchasing a particular tourism and hospitality product or service.

Irimiás et al. (2017) point out that although films could influence destination development by reducing unfamiliarity (*risk*) towards a destination and increasing interest towards it, in some cases, they may cause unreal expectations, resulting in service failures due to the gap between the features of the actual destination and the features of the destination as depicted in films. They also point out that this difference causes a decline in revisit intentions while increasing the likelihood of negative word-of-mouth (WOM) communication.

On the part of the customers, touristic products and services, in particular, involve committing large sums of money on something which cannot be seen or tested before the purchase. Although tourism and travel activities of individuals may represent a relatively smaller proportion of time in a year, they may involve the spending of large sums of money. For example, a week's holiday may represent less than 2% of the time duration in a 52-week year, while the amount of money spent on this holiday may be as high as 10%, or more of a tourist's annual income (Koc, 2000). Additionally, tourism decisions may involve large emotional investments as the whole family may look forward to their holidays. The consumption of tourism and hospitality services depends largely on emotions, and may refer to idealised experiences that generally involve a prolonged cognitive process (Seabra et al., 2013). Hence, in the case of tourism and hospitality, the fear of failure can be high, as the opportunity cost (time risk) may be irreversible. If a holiday goes wrong, many people may not have another opportunity to go on holiday in the near future (Koc, 2000). In addition, holidays often involve encounters with the unknown in terms of destinations, accommodation, transport, food, people, etc.

These uncertainties and ambiguities, when coupled with the uncertainty-avoidance orientations of customers, and employees, may have several implications for perception of risk on tourism and hospitality activities. Based on this background, this chapter explains and discusses the influence of uncertainty-avoidance orientations of customers, employees, and managers in tourism and hospitality. It is one of the most widely researched cultural dimensions in tourism and hospitality (Koc, 2017a, 2017b) as "uncertainty avoidance" is the most influential determinant of travel and tourism planning behaviour (Money and Crotts, 2003).

The chapter first explains the uncertainty avoidance as a cultural dimension. Then, based on the research findings, the implications of uncertainty avoidance for tourism and hospitality establishments from the perspective of both marketing (consumer behaviour) and management (organisational behaviour and human resource management) are explained. The chapter also explains the types of risks which may be encountered in tourism and hospitality and the concept of control as a risk reduction strategy.

Information zone

Risk, fear, and social behaviour

Kenrick and Griskevicius (2013) argue that exposure to fear (risk) increases individuals' likelihood of engaging in social behaviour, that is, being with or part of a group, and conforming to the group. After having watched a horror movie, people tended to like advertisements/commercials more that implied togetherness and being with a crowd of people. It was also seen that the participants tended to avoid advertisements/commercials and products which implied being alone. On the contrary, after watching a romantic movie, people tended to act with the motivation of being alone and preferred advertisements/commercials and products which implied being alone. Just like with animals, fear (risk) causes human beings to be with a group or to be a part of a group, while cues relating to romantic relations cause them to prefer to be alone. Likewise, Greenberg et al.'s (1990) research showed that when people were reminded that they were mortal (i.e., fear of death), their tendency to become closer to people from the same religion increased and showed ethnocentric behaviours towards people from other religions. Hence, it may be stated that fear (risk) can make people be more ethnocentric.[1]

The concept of uncertainty avoidance

According to Hofstede (2001: xx), uncertainty avoidance refers to the degree of comfort members of a society feel in unfamiliar or unstructured situations and the degree to which "a society tries to control the uncontrollable". People from high-uncertainty avoidance cultures tend to feel uncomfortable and threatened in unstructured, uncertain, and unfamiliar situations and they value structure and predictability (Hofstede, 2001; Litvin et al., 2004).

Table 7.1 shows the uncertainty avoidance index scores (UAI) for 72 selected countries in the world. A higher value indicates that a country has a high level of uncertainty avoidance. According to Table 7.1 countries such as Greece, Portugal, Belgium, Russia, Japan, Romania, Turkey, and Mexico appear to have a relatively high level of uncertainty avoidance, while countries such as Singapore, Sweden, Hong Kong, United Kingdom, United States, Norway, and New Zealand appear to have a relatively low-level uncertainty avoidance.

The fundamental issue in relation to the concept of uncertainty deals with whether uncertainty should be controlled (high-uncertainty avoidance cultures) or just let it happen (low-uncertainty avoidance cultures) (McCornack and Ortiz, 2017). Countries having a high level of uncertainty avoidance believe and behave in a strict manner and tend to avoid unconventional ways of thinking and behaving. Table 7.2 provides a summary of the comparison of the main characteristics of low- and high-uncertainty cultures (Hofstede et al., 2010).

Exercise

Find the uncertainty avoidance score of your country in Table 7.1, and determine whether it is a high- or low- (or medium)-uncertainty avoidance culture. Also look at the figures of the countries that are at the other end of the continuum, that is, the ones which have significantly different uncertainty-avoidance orientations from your own country. Find colleagues who are from the countries at the other end of the uncertainty-avoidance continuum. Sit down with your colleagues and study the basic main features of uncertainty-avoidance cultures as explained in Table 7.2. Determine the extent to which these characteristics apply to your countries. Think about and discuss the potential implications of these characteristics on tourism and hospitality activities and operations.

Table 7.1 Uncertainty avoidance scores of selected countries in the world

Rank	*Country*	*UAI Score*	*Rank*	*Country*	*UAI Score*	*Rank*	*Country*	*UAI Score*
1	Singapore	**8**	25	Sierra Leone	**54**	49	Israel	**81**
2	Jamaica	**13**	26	Switzerland	**58**	50	Mexico	**82**
3	Denmark	**23**	27	Iran	**59**	51	Hungary	**82**
4	Hong Kong	**29**	28	Finland	**59**	52	Turkey	**85**
5	Sweden	**29**	29	Thailand	**64**	53	South Korea	**85**
6	United Kingdom	**35**	30	Germany	**65**	54	Bulgaria	**85**
7	Ireland	**35**	31	Ecuador	**67**	55	Panama	**86**
8	Malaysia	**36**	32	Egypt	**68**	56	France	**86**
9	China	**40**	33	Iraq	**68**	57	Chile	**86**
10	India	**40**	34	Kuwait	**68**	58	Spain	**86**
11	Philippines	**44**	35	Lebanon	**68**	59	Argentina	**86**
12	United States	**46**	36	Libya	**68**	60	Costa Rica	**86**
13	Indonesia	**48**	37	Estonia	**60**	61	Peru	**87**
14	South Africa	**49**	38	Saudi Arabia	**68**	62	Romania	**90**
15	New Zealand	**49**	39	United Arab Emirates	**68**	63	Japan	**92**
16	Norway	**50**	40	Taiwan	**69**	64	Serbia	**92**
17	Australia	**51**	41	Pakistan	**70**	65	Poland	**93**
18	Ethiopia	**52**	42	Austria	**70**	66	El Salvador	**94**
19	Kenya	**52**	43	Czechia	**74**	67	Belgium	**94**
20	Tanzania	**52**	44	Italy	**75**	68	Russia	**95**
21	Zambia	**52**	45	Venezuela	**76**	69	Uruguay	**100**
22	Netherlands	**53**	46	Brazil	**76**	70	Guatemala	**101**
23	Ghana	**54**	47	Croatia	**80**	71	Portugal	**104**
24	Nigeria	**54**	48	Colombia	**80**	72	Greece	**112**

Source: Hofstede (2020). Used with permission.

The influence of personal factors on uncertainty avoidance and attachment on uncertainty

The level of uncertainty (risk aversion) avoidance of an individual may depend on her/his personal factors (see following Information zone: Toxoplasma gondii and the section on risk and control), personality traits, and his/her attachment style. In terms of the big five personality traits (openness to experience, conscientiousness, extraversion,

Table 7.2 Basic summary of the main characteristics of low and high-uncertainty avoidance cultures

Low-uncertainty Avoidance Cultures E.g., Singapore, Sweden, Hong Kong, United Kingdom, United States, Norway, and New Zealand	*High-uncertainty Avoidance Cultures E.g., Greece, Portugal, Belgium, Russia, Japan, Romania, Turkey, and Mexico*
Comfortable in ambiguous, uncertain and unfamiliar situations. Ambiguity is tolerated. More prepared to take risks. Risks are perceived as opportunities.	Not comfortable in ambiguous, uncertain and unfamiliar situations. Predictability and clarity are preferred. Concerned about safety and security. Less prepared to take risks. Risks are perceived as threats.
Uncertainty is the fact of life. "Take things as they come" kind of attitude.	"Uncertainty in life is threatening and must be reduced" kind of attitude.
"What is different is curious."	"What is different is dangerous."
Fewer rules. "If the rules/laws cannot be adhered to, they should be changed" attitude.	More formal rules. "If the rules/laws cannot be adhered to, we are doing something wrong" attitude.
Uncertainty is considered normal.	Uncertainty is considered a threat.
Employees are comfortable with unstructured work processes.	Employees are comfortable with structured work processes.
Relaxed. Employees experience a low level of stress. People appear to be easy-going and in control.	Anxiety and stress. Employees experience a high level of stress. People appear to be busy, aggressive.
Low time-consciousness.	High time-consciousness.
Conflicts are accepted. Deviance is not a threat. More tolerant. Deviant behaviour is tolerated.	Conflicts and deviances are seen as a threat. Deviant behaviour is suppressed. Less tolerant.
Competition and conflict can be constructive.	Competition and conflict can be destructive. Always try to establish consensus.
Strong belief in generalists and common sense.	Strong beliefs in experts and knowledge.
Emotions are not shown.	Showing emotions is acceptable.
Employees tend to appear quiet, easy-going, indolent, controlled, and/or lazy.	Employees tend to appear busy, emotional, aggressive, and/or active.
Higher labour turnover.	Low labour turnover.
Open-ended learning.	Structured learning.
Flexible. More willing to take risks.	Rigid. Not willing to take risks.
Managers are more interpersonally oriented.	Managers are more task-oriented.

Table 7.2 continued

Low-uncertainty Avoidance Cultures E.g., Singapore, Sweden, Hong Kong, United Kingdom, United States, Norway, and New Zealand	*High-uncertainty Avoidance Cultures E.g., Greece, Portugal, Belgium, Russia, Japan, Romania, Turkey, and Mexico*
The leader is a facilitator.	The leader is the expert.
Innovation and achievement are important. Tolerance for and less resistance to change and innovation. High tolerance of deviant and new ideas.	Precision and security are important. Resistance to change. No tolerance for new and strange behaviour.
Politicians and managers can be young people.	Politicians and managers tend to be older.
Loose social norms.	Rigid social norms.
Academic qualifications are less relevant than experience.	Academic qualifications are more relevant than experience.

Source: Hofstede et al. (2010).

agreeableness, and neuroticism), research shows low avoidance correlates with higher levels of extraversion and openness to experience and lower levels of conscientiousness (Tok, 2011; McGhee et al., 2012). High-level neuroticism may have a significant influence on risk-taking behaviours of people (Tok, 2011; Merritt and Tharp, 2013). However, other sub-traits of personality may influence risk-taking and uncertainty-avoidance behaviour under specific circumstances. For instance, Gupta et al. (2006) found that disinhibition, boredom susceptibility, cheerfulness, and excitability, as well as low levels of conformity and self-discipline, were strongly associated with gambling (i.e., risk-taking). Researchers have found a significant relationship between sensation seeking and risk-taking in tourism and hospitality activities (e.g., adventure holidays) (Pizam et al. 2004; Reisenger and Mavondo, 2006; Gray and Wilson, 2009; Williams and Baláž, 2013)

An individual's attachment to her/his mother (or the main caregiver) (through contact and proximity) during the first two to three years of life may have a lifelong influence on wide variety of social aspects of life (including success) including trust in other people and risk aversion (Bowlby, 1988, 2008).

Ainsworth (1964) identified three types, or styles, of attachment as a) secure attachment, b) insecure-avoidant, and c) insecure ambivalent/resistant.

1. *Secure attachment.* Securely attached individuals tend to trust others, be more interdependent, highly self-efficacious – the belief in one's ability to complete tasks and reach goals – less anxious and more satisfied with their relationships. Securely attached people tend to be open, and can easily form healthy, strong relationships. They do not fear being rejected. People with secure attachment styles are comfortable displaying interest and affection. They also tend to be comfortable being alone and independent. They do not find it difficult to correctly prioritise their relationships

within their life and tend to draw clear boundaries and maintain them (Bowlby, 2008; Felton and Lowett, 2013).

2. *Insecure avoidant*. These people tend to shut down feelings in order not to experience the pain of loss. They tend to be fearful, but extremely independent, self-directed, and usually uncomfortable with intimacy. They have problems in terms of commitments and develop strategies to avoid intimate situations (Bowlby, 2008; Howe, 2011).
3. *Insecure ambivalent/resistant*. Insecure ambivalent/resistant people tend to cling to people (or objects) and experience an inconsolable state of grief when they lose who/what they cling to. They tend to be nervous and stressed about their relationships, and need constant reassurance and affection from other people (e.g., their partners). They find it difficult to trust other people. They are more likely to engage in unhealthy or abusive relationships. They may behave irrationally, sporadically, and in an overly emotional manner. They tend to blame other people (especially the opposite sex) being cold and heartless (Bowlby, 2008; Gibson and Gibson, 2015).

Li et al. (2019), who found that insecure attachment styles increase consumers' risk-taking behaviours, argue that attachment theory can shed light on understanding customers relational consumption patterns (Simpson et al., 2012); how they respond to advertising (David and Bearden, 2017); how they are influenced by pricing strategies (David et al., 2017); and their relationship with brand personalities (Thomson et al., 2012).

Research shows that insecurely attached people tend to be more risk-taking individuals (Bogaert and Sadava, 2002; Taubman-Ben-Ari and Mikulincer, 2007; Li et al., 2019). The reason being that such individuals grew up in unpredictable environments (e.g., inconsistent parents) and became unable to forecast the future reliably (Belsky et al., 2012; Li et al., 2019). The risk-sensitivity theory puts forward that individuals make risk-sensitive decisions depending on their needs. In other words, they are more likely to take risks if they are unlikely to meet their needs through safer, low-risk means (Kacelnik and Bateson, 1996, 1997; Mishra et al., 2017; Li et al., 2019). Hence, when people need something, they shift from risk-aversion to risk-taking, as risky choices, although slim, may offer a chance to satisfy their needs (Mishra et al., 2014; Li et al., 2019).

Exercise

Visit the web page link at https://www.psychologytoday.com/intl/tests/relationships/relationship-attachment-style-test and complete the Revised Adult Attachment Scale (Collins and Read, 1996) to determine your attachment style.

Then, visit the web page at https://www.ncbi.nlm.nih.gov/pmc/articles/PMC4364085/ and read the following article:

Sheinbaum, T., Kwapil, T. R., Ballespí, S., Mitjavila, M., Chun, C. A., Silvia, P. J., and Barrantes-Vidal, N. (2015). Attachment style predicts affect, cognitive appraisals, and social functioning in daily life. *Frontiers in Psychology*, 6, 296.

Do you agree with most of the characteristics explained there regarding your attachment style? If not, please explain why this may be the case?

Information zone

Touch and attachment

American psychologist Harry Harlow (1958) studied the effects of maternal separation, dependency and social isolation on mental and social development. Harlow et al. (1965) carried out a series of experiments on rhesus monkeys and observed how isolation and separation could influence the subjects in the later years of their lives.

In Harlow et al.'s (1965) experiments, infant rhesus monkeys were taken away from their mothers and raised in a laboratory setting. One of the groups of infant monkeys was placed in separate cages away from their peers. The infant monkeys who were socially isolated showed disturbed behaviours, for example, staring blankly, circling their cages, and engaging in self-mutilation. Later, when the isolated infant monkeys were re-introduced to the group, they were not sure how to interact with the others. Many of them tended to stay separate from the group, and some of them even died after a short while as they refused to eat.

The experiments showed that even without complete isolation, the infant monkeys raised without their mothers developed social deficits, showing reclusive tendencies and clinging to their cloth diapers. Harlow and his colleagues were interested in exploring the infant monkey's attachment to the cloth diapers, thinking that touching the soft material may simulate the comfort provided by a mother's touch. Based on this observation, Harlow and his colleagues designed the surrogate mother experiment. In their study, they took infant monkeys from their biological mothers and gave them two inanimate surrogate mothers: a) one was a simple construction of wire and wood, and b) the second was covered in foam rubber and soft terry cloth. The infant monkeys were assigned to one of two conditions. In the first case, the wire mother had a milk bottle and the cloth mother did not; in the second case, the cloth mother had the food while the wire mother had none.

In both conditions, Harlow et al. found that the infant monkeys tended to spend significantly more time with the terry cloth mother (soft) than they did with the wire mother (hard). In the instance when the wire mother had food, the infant monkeys came to the wire mother to feed themselves and after that immediately returned and clung to their soft terry cloth surrogate mothers. The study also demonstrated that infant monkeys turned to inanimate soft terry cloth surrogate mothers for comfort when they were faced with new and scary (and hence risky) situations. When infant monkeys were placed in a novel environment, they started to explore the environment. However, when they were startled (perceived some level of risk), they ran back to their surrogate mothers for a while and then continued to explore the area. In the absence of the surrogate mothers, the infant monkeys tended to be petrified with fear and huddled in a ball and sucked their thumbs. When an alarming noise-making toy was placed in the cage, if the infant monkeys had their surrogate mothers with them, they tended to explore and attack the toy. However, when the surrogate mother was not present, the monkeys tended to cower in fear.

Harlow's experiments showed the effects of love, belonging, attachment, and touch on social behaviours, risk perceptions, and risk-taking behaviours, social development, and learning.

Sonneveld and Schifferstein's (2008) research showed that softness and smoothness in the service atmosphere (i.e., of furniture) increased arousal, pleasure, and consumption tendencies. Guéguen's (2006) study showed the importance of touching on risk reduction and persuasion in two experiments. In the first experiment, a young male confederate asked young women to dance with them when slow songs were played in a nightclub. When making his request, the confederate touched (or not) the young woman on her forearm for one or two seconds. In the second experiment, a young male confederate approached young women individually in the street and asked their phone numbers. As in the first experiment, the requests were made by a light touch or not on the young woman's arm. In both experiments, it was seen that the touch increased compliance with the young man's request, as it decreased risk, and increased liking. In similar research, Lynn et al. (1998) found that waiters who touched their customers lightly for a short while received 20% more tips.

However, people's responses (positive or negative) to touch, and personal distance are influenced by their cultural orientations (see Chapter 9). Argyle (1986) argues that the degree of physical contact varies across cultures. Although there are certain similarities between touch and the amount of personal space, they may work differently (Sophonsiri, 2008). For instance, in Western cultures, people tend to prefer to have a wider personal distance from their exchange partners, but they may not mind touching or being touched by their exchange partners. On the other hand, in Eastern cultures, it is more polite for people from Eastern cultures to stand closer to their exchange partners, but it may be inappropriate for their exchange partners to touch them or for them to touch their exchange partners (Sophonsiri, 2008). For instance, Sophonsiri reports that unexpected body contact is commonly perceived by Thais as inappropriate, though it may be easily forgiven.

It needs to be noted that care must be taken that a violation of a certain part of the body can be severe as each body part may be perceived to have a different status in a hierarchy, and the touching opposite sex (e.g., in Islamic countries) may have serious implications.

NB: As Harlow et al.'s (1965) experiments involved cruelty to animals they have been widely criticised.

CASE STUDY

Romanian orphans

In Romania, abortion was legal between the years of 1957 and 1966. However, from 1967 to 1990 abortion was severely restricted, in an effort of the Communist leadership (Nicolae Ceauşescu) to increase the country's population. However, Ceausescu's government was unable to provide much of its promised assistance to families, leaving many families in difficult situations. As a result, significant numbers of children were abandoned to orphanages. The orphanages were infamous for institutionalised neglect and abuse. Also in the orphanages, the children had no physical contact and developed attachment disorders. As a result of Ceausescu's policy, there were also many children living in the streets of Romania. Several of the children from the orphanages were later adopted from the orphanages by American families and taken to the US. As these children did not have physical contact and were not loved in the orphanages, they were aggressive and exhibited behaviours similar to sociopaths (Stout, 2006).

Uncertainty avoidance and tourism and hospitality

As mentioned previously, the perception of risk and uncertainty may have implications for tourism and hospitality establishments, from both perspective marketing (consumer behaviour) and management (organisational behaviour and human resource management).

The implications of uncertainty avoidance for marketing

The characteristics of high and low-uncertainty avoidance cultures provided in Table 7.2 may have a number of important marketing and management implications for the tourism and hospitality establishments. For instance, the fact that people in high-uncertainty avoidance cultures tend to feel uncomfortable and threatened in unstructured, uncertain, and unfamiliar situations (Noja et al., 2018), value structure and predictability (Hofstede, 2001; Litvin et al., 2004), and avoid risks may influence their behaviour both as customers and as employees. Research shows that tourists from high-uncertainty avoidance cultures (e.g., the Japanese) engage in significantly more risk- or uncertainty-reducing behaviours such as purchasing more often prepaid tour packages, travel in larger groups, stay for shorter periods, and visit fewer destinations than tourists from low-uncertainty avoidance culture (e.g., German) counterparts when engaging in international tourism activities (Money and Crotts, 2003; Reisinger and Crotts, 2010; Koc, 2013).

Manrai and Manrai (2011) add that the Japanese, as high-uncertainty avoidance people have a preference/choice for own cuisine, traveling in groups, preference/choice of safe activities, rigid planning of the trips, satisfaction in seeing "staged" events, etc. The design of tourism and hospitality activities aimed at high-uncertainty avoidance cultures necessitate taking personal, social, financial, and safety risks into account, as well as attention to personal details.

Money and Crotts (2003) also argue that tourists from a higher level of uncertainty-avoidance cultures would be inclined to collect more information. Japanese, who are famous for their group mentality, may probably feel that there is less chance of being disappointed when they have travelled as a large group. As explained in Chapter 3 (while explaining the concepts of intercultural competence and intercultural sensitivity), from an anthropological perspective people formed social relationships with other people with the instinct to survive and prosper (Harari, 2016; Erber and Erber, 2017). Even, the primitive human beings knew by instinct that they could not survive on their own and needed to establish relationships with others to cope with the risks and uncertainties in the environment. It was also mentioned that studies showed that loneliness and social isolation are important risk factors for mortality even in today's modern world (Holt-Lunstad et al., 2015). However, after the Covid-19 epidemic in 2020, being together with a group on a holiday may be shunned by people from a wide variety of cultural backgrounds, including the Japanese. People may opt for more individual holidays.

Frias et al.'s (2012) research is supportive of Money and Crotts's (2003) and Reisinger and Crotts's (2010) studies. Frias et al.'s (2012) study found that tourists from the UK (a low-uncertainty avoidance culture) did not associate online information with higher risk. On the other hand, customers from high-uncertainty avoidance cultures (France, Belgium, and Italy) were more likely to use low-risk information sources (travel agencies). Those tourists with high-uncertainty avoidance orientation and using low-risk information sources were more likely to develop more positive images of the destinations, while the ones who used online information sources developed less positive images of the destinations. This means that tourism and hospitality businesses may be advised to use more personal channels of communication and distribution when they target customers from high-uncertainty avoidance cultures.

As will be explained later, tourism and hospitality establishments targeting customers from high-uncertainty avoidance cultures may be recommended to design their marketing mix elements according to the customers' cultural characteristics. For instance, pre-paid (all-inclusive) package holidays with fewer destinations (product element of their marketing mix) with special rates and discounts to groups (product, price, and promotion elements of the marketing mix) may be more effective for tourists from high-uncertainty avoidance cultures. Koc (2006) argues that given the fact that tourism and hospitality products are intangible, cannot be tested beforehand, and involve encounters with the unknown in terms of destinations, accommodation, transport, food, etc., all-inclusive customers who are risk-averse are more likely to purchase package holidays to reduce their perception of risk.

Information zone

Reducing customers' risk perception through marketing communications

According to Mittal (1999), intangibility of services (e.g., tourism and hospitality) increases the risk perceptions of customers and presents difficulties in communicating with them. Coupled with the cross-cultural differences, the intangibility feature of tourism and hospitality services can make additional demands on tourism and hospitality managers' abilities.

According to Mittal (1999), difficulties associated with intangibility are a) incorporeal existence, b) abstractness, c) generality, d) non-searchability, and e) mental impalpability.

- *Incorporeal existence.* This is the core property of intangibility. It is about not being made of physical matter, and not occupying physical space. This prevents the showing of the service to the customer and making them feel the service difficult, if not impossible.

- *Abstractness.* Service benefits such as peace of mind, joy, fun, happiness, and financial benefits are abstract and do not correspond directly with objects, making them difficult to visualise and understand.
- *Generality.* As opposed to specifity, generality refers to a class of things, persons, events, or properties. On the other hand, specificity refers to particular objects, people, or events. Most services and service promises are described in generalities (wonderful experience, your dream holiday), making them difficult to differentiate from those of competitors.
- *Non-searchability.* Based on David and Karni's (1973) classification of three attributes of products (search, experience, and credence), it is not possible to understand the value of the services beforehand by searching and evaluating by using the available information, as they are in general non-searchable. As in the case of tourism and hospitality services (e.g., a holiday or a restaurant service), the service often cannot be previewed or inspected in advance of purchase. Credence attributes can neither be searched nor experienced as they depend on faith and the reputation of the provider. As in the case of medical tourism service, the customer has not much to do apart from developing beliefs that he has been cured, and her/his problem has been solved.
- *Mental impalpability.* This is about the inability to mentally grasp the intangible aspects of a product or service because as it may be too complex, abstract, or not previously experienced. Impalpability is to do with a lack of prior exposure, familiarity, or knowledge necessary for making a proper evaluation and assessment. A customer may find it difficult to *understand why a meal consisting of meat, vegetables,* ***and salad*** may cost as much as two thousand dollars in the Spanish restaurant SubliMotion.

Based on the above difficulties, Mittal (1999) offers the following strategies to minimise the negative influences of intangibility.

Intangibility Problem	*Marketing Communications Strategy*	*Explanations*	*Examples*
Incorporeal existence	Physical representation	Show the physical components of service. Focus on the tangibles. Use brand icons to make service tangible. Use association, physical representation, documentation, and visualisation.	Show photos, videos of the rooms, swimming pool of the hotel. Show photos, videos of dishes, kitchen and dining hall of the restaurant.
Generality	System documentation performance	Objectively document physical-system capacity.	Demonstrate the results of customer satisfaction surveys.

Intangibility Problem	*Marketing Communications Strategy*	*Explanations*	*Examples*
	documentation Service-performance episode	Objective claims: document and cite past performance statistics. Subjective claims: present an actual service-delivery incident.	
Non-searchability	Consumption documentation Reputation Obtain and present customer testimonials Cite independently audited performance documentation	Obtain and present customer testimonials. Cite independently audited performance. Feature service employees in communication.	Present positive customer testimonials on the websites, for example, the Marriott. Follow-up negative comments on online platforms and solve problems.
Abstractness	Service-consumption episode	Capture and display typical customers benefiting from the service	Show the photos, videos of happy and satisfied customers, customers having fun, and enjoying tourism and hospitality services.
Mental Impalpability	Service-process episode Case-history episode Service-consumption episode	Present a vivid documentary on the step-by-step service process. Present an actual case history of what the firm did for a specific client. An articulate narration or depiction of a customer's subjective experience. Use narrative to demonstrate the service experience. Use interactive imagery.	Emirates uses sensory stimuli to convince customers how their exquisite and delicious 12,450 recipes are prepared by their 1,800 award-winning chefs.

Source: adapted from Mittal (1999).

Exercise

According to Albers-Miller and Gelb (1996), the three advertising appeals related to uncertainty avoidance are safety, tamed, and durable (see the following table).

Appeal	*Description*
Safety	Carefulness, guarantees, caution, stability, guarantee
Tamed	Compliant, faithful, reliable, responsible, domesticated, docile, civilized
Durable	Long-lasting, permanent, stable, strong, powerful, tough, enduring

Task

Each of the above appeals may have important implications, not only for advertising (as a promotional element) but also for all the other marketing mix elements of tourism and hospitality establishments. Prepare a marketing mix (7Ps) table for a tourism or hospitality business and write down for each marketing mix element things to do and not to do in relation with the above themes.

As mentioned in the previous exercise, using marketing communications messages that comprise cues relating to safety may prove to be beneficial for customers from high-uncertainty avoidance cultures. However, as Rittichainuwat's (2013) study found, safety measures may scare tourists and increase their risk perceptions. Rittichainuwat showed that an increase in safety measures tended to frighten about 33% of tourists. Only about 14% of tourists stated that they would not be discouraged, while the remaining proportion of tourists were neutral. This may be to do with priming (Koc, 2016), or co-variance bias, as safety measures, or safety cues may act as signals to remind tourists of the risks that may be present.

Money and Crotts (2003) found that customers from Japan were more likely to seek information from channel members such as travel agencies. Tourism and hospitality customers from high-uncertainty avoidance cultures are more likely to avoid online purchases than customers from a low-uncertainty avoidance culture (Lim et al., 2004; Sabiote-Ortiz et al., 2016). In general, for customers, the perceived risk of using an online medium for making purchases is greater than a traditional channel (Suki and Suki, 2007). Sabiote-Ortiz et al. (2016) report that travel agencies tend to cause lower levels of uncertainty for customers because of their personal interaction, and the control that the tourists feel regarding the medium they are using.

Moreover, as it is explained in Chapter 5, Japanese are also from a restraint culture (as opposed to indulgence), and are not inclined to be highly involved in fun, leisure, and pleasure activities such as tourism and hospitality. Using travel agencies may be a good risk-reduction strategy, as depending on other sources (e.g., a tourist looking at websites, making analyses and comparisons) may be a risky thing to do when the person is not highly involved. The findings and the discussion presented above may have implications for the promotion and place (distribution) elements of marketing in tourism and hospitality.

Seo et. al. (2018) studied the behavioural intentions of international visitors towards local restaurants in South Korea. They argue that tourists/customers who were from high-uncertainty avoidance cultures tended to rely more on attitude and past experience (as a risk reduction strategy) for behavioural intention (as a risk reduction strategy) when choosing a restaurant, while tourists/customers from low-uncertainty avoidance cultures were more likely to rely more on actual knowledge of the relevant attributes of a situation. However, as the information regarding a particular local South Korean restaurant was unavailable to tourists/customers to make rational decisions, they tended to depend on subjective knowledge (such as knowing the name of the dish, cooking methods), as a kind of heuristics, when choosing a particular restaurant.

Another study on customers and uncertainty avoidance by Ndubisi et al. (2012) found that customer loyalty tended to be low in countries with low level of risk avoidance. In high-uncertainty avoidance cultures, customers tend to cling to service providers who satisfy them and tend to be loyal to them. Their motivation to avoid risks is higher than their motivation to seek variety. Hence, when they are satisfied with one service provider, they do not search for alternatives that may not provide what the current one offers.

In general, customers frequently engage in variety-seeking behaviour in the purchase of hedonic experiences like tourism and hospitality (Bigné et al., 2009). As high-uncertainty avoidance cultures are less likely to engage in variety-seeking behaviour, targeting tourism and hospitality customers from high-uncertainty avoidance cultures may allow businesses a longer-planning horizon.

The emphasis on stability by tourism and hospitality customers from high-uncertainty avoidance cultures may lead to status quo bias and preference for maintaining current status or situation (Samuelson and Zeckhauser, 1988). One of the most influential factors on status quo bias is the cognitive misperception of loss aversion (Samuelson and Zeckhauser, 1988; Samioğlu, 2020), that is, the belief that losses loom larger than gains in value perception (Kahneman et al., 1991), which is based on the survival motive. Losses may endanger survival. According to Kahneman and Tversky's (1989) prospect theory, people tend to attach more weight to fear of loss than they do to hope of gain. In general, people are risk/loss averse and they dislike losses more than equivalent gains. In general, the amount of sadness, a person feels when losing 100 Euros is significantly more than the happiness s/he has when finding/winning 100 Euros. Again, the amount of sadness or anger is higher when somebody forgets to take an umbrella on a rainy day is higher than when taking an umbrella but it does not rain.

People are more willing to take risks to avoid a loss due to the biased weighting of probabilities and loss aversion. When a service failure occurs (of course, depending on the level of the failure), customers may feel that they have lost something. However, when the service recovery takes place they realise that they have not lost. As a consequence, customers become relaxed and happier than they were before encountering the service failure, that is, experiences service recovery paradox (see Chapter 5).

According to research, unexpected gains cause more pleasure than expected gains, and unexpected losses cause more pain than those that are expected (Mellers et al., 1997). This is why service recovery paradox and customer delightment, that is, surprising customers by exceeding their expectations and thus creating a positive emotional reaction, occurs. What customer delightment and service recovery paradox have in common is that they both happen unexpectedly, that is, they surprise customers, and both have positive consequences for customers. Mellers et al. (1997) discovered that a surprising $9 win was more enjoyable than an expected $17 win, and likewise, a surprising $9 loss was more painful than an expected $17 loss.

It was mentioned previously that customers from high-uncertainty avoidance cultures tended to value predictability and stability, and they were more likely to behave under the influence of status quo bias. These customers tend to avoid variety-seeking behaviour, and engage in general tourism activities (GIT), as opposed to special tourism activities (SIT) (Koc and Altinay, 2007).

Also, customers from high-uncertainty avoidance cultures are more likely to stick to the standard, national cuisine restaurants, and have more neophobia (fear of eating new or unfamiliar foods). Also, customer trust and loyalty would be higher in countries with high-uncertainty avoidance (Ndubisi et al., 2012). On the other hand, as customers from low-uncertainty avoidance cultures tend to value innovation and originality, they may engage in variety-seeking behaviour more often, be less loyal towards brands, be more likely to engage in special interest tourism, and be more likely to have neophilia (tendency to like and try new foods). For instance, Lam et al.'s (2005) research showed that customers from high-uncertainty avoidance cultures had a significant tendency towards brand loyalty, as switching meant more uncertainties and risk. Interestingly, Tsaur et al.'s (2005) research showed that tourists from high-uncertainty avoidance cultures had a higher intention to praise the service provider if they experienced positive service quality. Even if they experienced a problem, they showed a lower intention to switch to another service provider, and to engage in negative word of mouth communications, or to complain. This may be to do with the fact that these customers may believe that switching may involve more uncertainties and risks, and hence, may prefer to not to switch.

Based on Cohen's (1972) original typology of four tourist roles, Lepp and Gibson (2003) identified two tourist segments based on the perception of risk. Lepp and Gibson (2003) combined the "organised mass tourist" and the "independent mass tourist" into one group as people who prefer familiarity with the destination (Seabra et al., 2013). On the other hand, the "drifters" and the "explorers" tend to be motivated by novelty as they associate less amount of risk with novelty. Tourists who have a tendency to take risks and seek thrills may engage in high energy and outdoor activities (e.g., wilderness hiking and river rafting) and therefore prefer active and spontaneous vacations (Chen and Jiang, 2019). On the other hand, those who have a high level of risk perception may favour slow-paced and indoor activities (e.g., visiting friends and relatives and shopping) (Pizam and Jeong, 1996; Chen and Jiang, 2019), stay at their holiday home, or take part in General Interest Tourism (e.g., sun, sand, and sea tourism) (Koc and Altinay, 2017).

Another feature of uncertainty avoidance that may influence the design and implementation of marketing mix elements is to do with how in high and low-uncertainty avoidance cultures people treat their children. Zein (2015) argues that while in low-uncertainty avoidance cultures children are left alone to play, in high-uncertainty avoidance cultures children are meticulously looked after, and are never let out of sight. The above may have significant implications for the design of tangibles (e.g., the location of children's swimming pool) and various sub-elements of the tourism and hospitality services targeted at famlies.

In terms of the price element in the marketing mix, Sabiote-Ortiz et al. (2016) found that the pricing level that tourism and hospitality establishments determine for a service had a direct influence on the perceived risk perceptions of tourists from high-uncertainty cultures. These tourists were more likely to make price-service quality associations. In a similar vein, Mattila and Choi (2006) found that presenting information on a hotel's pricing policy had a positive effect on Korean customers' (high-uncertainty avoidance) satisfaction levels, while American customers (low avoidance) were relatively unaffected by such information.

Dolnicar (2007) identified risk perception as one of the most important segmentation variables in tourism and hospitality. Taskin et al.'s (2017) study, which used EEG and eye tracker analysis, showed that risk caused holidaymakers to pay more attention to verbal cues when considering travelling to conflict-ridden destinations, rather than the visual cues, which normally tended to attract more customer attention.

Managers of tourism and hospitality establishments need to consider the implications of the above-presented findings in the design and implementation of their marketing mix strategies. A failure in the design and implementation of efficient and effective marketing mix elements may cause service quality gaps. As the first service quality gap, the knowledge gap is the difference between what customers expect and what managers think customers expect from the service business. For instance, the manager of a hotel or restaurant may redesign its menu and think that adding more new, original, and exotic recipes to the menu may please the customers, while customers from high-uncertainty avoidance cultures may not like these changes.

Exercise

Read the short discussion on predictability, status quo bias and variety-seeking behaviour again. Think about the potential marketing mix (7Ps) implications of this discussion and prepare a report highlighting how a tourism and hospitality business catering for customers from a) high-uncertainty avoidance culture, and b) low-uncertainty avoidance culture may design its marketing mix elements.

The implications of uncertainty avoidance for management

Hofstede (2011) put forward that people in high-uncertainty avoidance societies are more likely to avoid changing jobs, while people in low-uncertainty avoidance societies may feel more at ease with changing jobs. The managers in international tourism and hospitality can make mistakes if they base their decisions on employee turnover rates or figures alone. Employee turnover rates may be relatively low in their operations in high-uncertainty avoidance cultures, but this may not necessarily mean that employees are happy and motivated there.

In general, people from high-uncertainty avoidance cultures tend to have a high level of stress and place a high value on control and rigid rules (Hofstede, 2010). Also, people in high-uncertainty avoidance cultures tend to depend on formalised policies and procedures, they tend to show resistance to change and have an intolerance for untraditional ways of behaving. Nedeljković et al.'s (2012) research in Serbia (a country with a high level of uncertainty avoidance, power distance, and restraint) is supportive of the above. They found that employees, in general, tended to agree with company rules, valued employment stability (intention to stay with the same business for a long period of time), though they experienced higher levels of job stress.

Owing to the general service characteristics, particularly heterogeneity, tourism and hospitality operations require constant change and adaptation to customer and market demands. Tourism and hospitality businesses in high-uncertainty cultures with rigid rules and modus operandi may disappoint customers, especially those from a low-uncertainty avoidance culture, who may see that problems could be solved with minor changes and adaptations. Kale and Barnes (1992) argue that strong resistance to change can be detected in countries with high levels of uncertainty avoidance, while in cultures with a low level of uncertainty avoidance there was a much lower level of resistance to change. This is to do with the close link between change and uncertainty (Peng and Lin, 2009). In high-uncertainty avoidance cultures, adapting to changes taking place in the environment and markets may be slow, and problems relating to establishing and sustaining competitive advantage may arise. Radojevic et al. (2019) argue that low avoidance, which may be associated with an employee's tendency to try new things, can be instrumental in making their organisations highly agile and competitive and allowing the employees to provide high-quality service.

The rigidity and adherence to rules and regulations in high-uncertainty avoidance cultures resemble the hierarchical and bureaucratic higher power distance cultures. Hence, high-uncertainty avoidance may be associated with a high level of power distance. Hofstede (2001) reports that older people in high-uncertainty avoidance cultures are respected and feared, and when children are being taught the beliefs of their culture, they are not allowed to question them. This may also show the relationship between high-uncertainty avoidance and high-power distance.

In low-uncertainty avoidance cultures, uncertain situations do not cause employees a significant amount of anxiety so that their need for avoiding risks tend to be low (Hofstede, 1984). In this case, the rules and norms of the authority in the tourism and hospitality businesses can be perceived as having minor importance for regulating and formalising employees' modes of behaviour (García-Cabrera and García-Soto, 2011) and employees could exert their personal self-control, and discretionary behaviour to undertake actions to balance work and family. Consequently, this is expected to lead to an increased perception of well-being. This is due to the fact that their a low level of uncertainty avoidance values would make them comfortable with adopting a risk approach (García-Cabrera and García-Soto, 2011).

Early research in the field by Baker and Carson (1975) showed that employees who had low levels of uncertainty avoidance saw no need to attach with their team, while those who had high levels of uncertainty tended to show a high level of attachment to their teams. This finding shows the relationship between uncertainty avoidance and collectivism as mentioned earlier. Also, based on Baker and Carson's (1975) statement, it may be put forward that group cohesion and harmony may be high in high-uncertainty avoidance cultures. However, given rigid rules and regulations in high-uncertainty cultures, the group cohesion may lead to groupthink. Groupthink is a situation where a team places more emphasis on consensus and cohesion that efficiency and effectiveness (Janis and Janis, 1982).

Hofstede (2011) also reports that in high-uncertainty avoidance cultures the use of formality in interactions with others is rather prevalent, which also corresponds with high-power distance. Formality in interactions in tourism and hospitality service encounters may cause service quality problems relating to empathy and responsiveness for customers, especially during a service recovery process. Moreover, formality in interaction, especially during the service recovery process, may make customers feel that they have not been properly and fairly treated, that is, there is a lack of interactional justice (Baker, 2017).

Another issue relating to interactions is that while people in low-uncertainty avoidance cultures do not appear to have any difficulty with interacting with people who are different from them, people in high-uncertainty avoidance cultures may have difficulties with interacting with people who are different from them (Hofstede, 2001). Actually, people in high-uncertainty avoidance cultures, to a certain extent, may show signs of xenophobia, fear of people who are different to them. This may mean that employees from high-uncertainty avoidance cultures may be more likely to have a low level of intercultural sensitivity and intercultural competence, and a high level of social anxiety and social avoidance regarding intercultural communication.

To support this view, Zein (2015) argues that while in low-uncertainty avoidance cultures children are encouraged to mix with others of different cultures and social class, in high-uncertainty cultures children are taught to mix with those of their own culture and social class. This may mean people in high-uncertainty avoidance cultures grow up with less intercultural sensitivity and intercultural competence and with strong beliefs in social class and hierarchy. Hence, as mentioned previously, there may be a relatively strong relationship between uncertainty avoidance and power distance.

Koc's (2018) study found that a significant proportion of students studying tourism and hospitality at Turkish universities had a high level of social anxiety and social avoidance. Considering that these students will be serving international customers, Turkish tourism and hospitality programmes need to redesign their programmes to reduce social anxiety and avoidance, while increasing intercultural sensitivity and intercultural competence of their students.

Kelly et al. (2017) emphasises the growing role and potential of self-service technologies in both backstage and front stage operations in tourism and hospitality. Research shows that cultures with high-individualism and indulgence, low-power distance, low-uncertainty avoidance present characteristics such as freedom, taste for risk, independence, adaptability, propensity to change, pursuit of objectives, assertiveness or importance of leisure that relate them positively with technological acceptance (Hofstede, 2011; Khan and Cox, 2017; Coves et al., 2018). On the other hand, cultures that are collective and have high-uncertainty avoidance and power distance are not inclined to adopt technological innovations easily (Steenkamp et al., 1999; Hofstede, 2011 Coves et al., 2018).

Risk and the concept of control

In basic terms, the risk is the possibility or probability of harm or damage – that is, of a loss, an injury, an unwanted outcome, or an undesired result (Häyry and Takala, 1998). Uncertainty may be interpreted as unanticipated, and possibly unpleasant consequences. As mentioned previously, due to the many unknowns and uncertainties (regarding destinations, transportation, accommodation, food, and recipes), and the inherent service characteristics of intangibility, heterogeneity and inseparability, tourism and hospitality decisions may involve high levels of risk for customers.

From a broad perspective, customers find the purchasing of services riskier than the purchasing of tangible products (Nordin et al., 2011; Dorothea and Benkenstein, 2014). The cultural distance between the service provider and customer increases the perception of risk (Shenkar, 2001; Litvin et al., 2004). Ahmed and Krohn (1993) put forward that there is a large number of Japanese-owned hotels in Hawaii, as many Japanese believe that only the Japanese can fully meet the needs of other Japanese.

Information zone

Toxoplasma gondii: a parasite reducing perception of fear and risk

Toxoplasma gondii is a parasite that infects most species of warm-blooded animals, including cats, rats, dogs, and human beings. Toxoplasma gondii, often referred to as toxo, in order to travel throughout the body of the organism, hijacks the white blood cells, which are designed to destroy foreign invaders, such as viruses and parasites. Toxo parasites not only use the white cells to ride or travel within the body of the organism but also turns them into small chemical factories to produce a neurotransmitter reducing fear memory through dysfunctioning of the cortex and amygdala in the brain. The amygdala is a section of the brain that is responsible for detecting fear and preparing for emergency events.

As a result organisms (e.g., rats, cats, dogs, and human beings) do not feel fear or danger and tend to be more comfortable to engage in risk-taking behaviours (Flegr, 2010, 2013). Toxoplasma gondii-infected organisms when exposed to danger do not tend to engage in behaviour to avoid or prevent danger. Instead of the feeling of fear and risk, the infected organisms feel lethargic, impulsive, sexually aroused and engaged in risk-taking behaviour (Barragan and Sibley, 2003; Flegr, 2010).

As well as causing schizophrenia among people (Barragan and Sibley, 2003; Flegr, 2010, 2013), Ling et al. (2011) found that toxoplasma infection increased suicides among women. Empirical research also found that toxoplasma gondii infection caused traffic accidents as it increased risk-taking behaviours (Kocazeybek et al., 2009; Flegr, 2013). Johnson et al.'s (2018) research discovered that toxoplasma gondii infection was even a consistent positive predictor of entrepreneurial activity and entrepreneurial intentions at the national scale.

Based on the above, it may be put forward that people with toxoplasma gondii to be more likely to take part in individualistic and adventurous holidays with activities such as mountaineering, paragliding, parasailing, rafting, etc. Therefore, in addition to the research provided at the end of the chapter, in the future, researchers may investigate the concept of status quo bias and risk-taking behaviours of tourism and hospitality customers, employees, and managers in relation to toxoplasma gondii parasite infections.

Types of risk

The main types of risk customers may feel are monetary (losing or wasting income), functional (does not meet the need), physical (personal illness or injury), social (is unfashionable or lowers status), and psychological (damages self-esteem or engenders guilt) (Solomon et al., 2012). In general, the risk associated with tourism and hospitality products can be outlined as in Table 7.3.

Table 7.3 Types of risk in tourism and hospitality

Risk Type	*Some of the Key Issues*	*Questions/Queries*
Physiological – physical risk	Health, well-being, safety, security, hygiene, threat	Is it safe as the chalets are so far away from the nearest village? Would the food served in the restaurant be fresh and hygienically produced? Would it be safe to walk in the streets when I visit the destination? Do they have a swimming pool for children?
Financial or monetary risk	Losing or wasting money, being cheated or swindled	Can I afford that much or should I go for a cheaper hotel? How much the dinner would cost? Would there be extras? Would I be wasting my money? Is it sensible to pay for the local trips beforehand?
Social risk	Fashionable, popular, high, showing off, class, prestige, old-fashioned, tasteless, low class, humiliating	Would people be impressed when they see my photo in Instagram – eating at this restaurant? Would it look prestigious to go on this cruise?
Ego or psychological risk	Self-esteem, content, happy, guilt, regret	Will I feel as good as I want to feel? Is the business socially responsible?
The performance or functional risk	Performance, waiting time, ingredients, contents	Is it really all-inclusive? Do they really use all those ingredients? Are the menu items as delicious as they look in the photos they put on their website?
Time risk	Wasting time, irreversible, reversible, revocable, irrevocable, money-back guarantee	Would I get my money back? What if all turns out to be bad? Would I be wasting my time?

Adapted from Koc (2015).

Exercise

Study the types of risk in Table 7.3 again. By considering the tourism or hospitality business you work for (or worked for in the past or you are familiar with), develop marketing mix strategies to reduce the risk perception of customers for each type of risk.

Concept of control

All human beings need to have some degree of control in any situation to reduce uncertainty and increase predictability (Ding et al., 2016; Koc and Boz, 2017) as fewer risks and uncertainty foster survival. In fact, the motivation to reduce risk and increasing predictability have been so important as to be viewed as constituting the main pillars of today's modern society. The main thrust of the move from a hunter-gatherer society to agrarian (agricultural) society, circa 8000 BCE in Mesopotamia, was due to the need to reduce risk people faced, and to increase the predictability of the future (Harari, 2016; Koc and Boz, 2017). As the uncertainties and lack of predictability were threats to the survival of human beings, they tried to establish systems, mechanisms, and ways of life to control as many things as possible. Miller's (1979) "minimax hypothesis" puts forward that people are motivated to minimise the maximum danger for themselves. This means that someone who has control over a dangerous event ensures experiencing a lower level of maximum danger than someone else who does not have control (Koc and Boz, 2017).

Likewise, Kahneman and Tversky's (1979) prospect theory resembles Miller's (1979) minimax hypothesis, in that they put forward that people attach significantly more value to not losing than winning. This is because losing may endanger human beings' primary goal of sustaining survival.

Against this background, Averill (1973) offered three types of control, namely, cognitive, behavioural, and decisional. *Cognitive control* is about having sufficient information about the future, and being confident about the future so that no negative surprises would occur (Faranda, 2001; Koc and Boz, 2017). From a tourism and hospitality perspective, a customer may be said to have control if s/has been informed accordingly and appropriately about all necessary details comprising prices, payments, etc. For instance, tourists with a high level of risk aversion (uncertainty avoidance) may purchase all-inclusive packages so that they will not have to pay anything in addition to the pre-paid amount (Koc, 2013). Likewise, a restaurant clearly displaying its menu and prices and allowing its potential customers to see it would be providing the customers with the means to have cognitive control.

As the second type of control, *decisional control* is about customers' ability to make their own decisions, to have sufficient alternatives, and to be able to alter the product/service according to their needs, without the intrusion of others (Koc, 2013; Koc and Boz, 2017). In other words, decisional control is about people's ability to make decisions themselves without the pressure or intrusion of others. The provision of several alternatives regarding the service and being able to make free choices on all-inclusive package holidays (e.g., the ability to choose what to eat in the open buffet restaurant) increases decisional control of the customers as they would have the freedom to choose. Burger King's "Have it Your Way" slogan emphasises decisional control.

As described in Chapter 5, Starbucks offers its consumers a wide array of drink choices, various sizes and different options. As many different drinks are available at Starbucks, it is possible to have the illusion that a drink choice is tailored specifically to one's individual desires (Mathieu, 1999).

The feeling of decisional control may usually cause a Pavlovian conditioning, a type of cognitive bias, or an attributional error, called illusion of control (Heider, 1958; Langer and Roth, 1975; Unzicker, 1999). Illusion of control can be defined as the tendency of a person to overestimate her/his ability in terms controlling events and the attribution of positive qualities. The illusion of control is also called *illusory superiority*, or *optimism bias* (Lovallo and Kahneman, 2003). It often increases an individual's self-efficacy beliefs (Bandura, 1997), and results in increased value attachment to and liking for an individual's own choices (Weiner, 2000; McKenna and Albery, 2001). The illusion of control is also similar to the endowment effect, or *divestiture aversion* (Thaler, 1980), which is about attributing or attaching more value to things merely because people own them (Kahneman et al., 1991).

Finally, *behavioural control* is about enabling customers to influence a situation or event. For instance, when customers are given the option to cancel their reservation or holiday two days before their holiday, without any, or with a small fine, they will have behavioural control. Table 7.4 summarises the three types of control and offers strategies to provide more control to customers.

The concept of control has been studied by scholars from a wide variety of disciplines and perspectives. However, from a services marketing and management perspective,

Table 7.4 Types of control and strategies to provide control to customers

Type of Control	*Explanations and Examples*	*Strategies*
Cognitive Control	Predictability of future events, having sufficient information about future events and being free from negative surprises	Providing customers with detailed information about the various aspects and components of service, such as price and payment details
		Offering standard packages with standard prices (as in all-inclusive holidays)
		Ensuring the standardisation of services
Decisional Control	The ability to make free choices allows customers to have decisional control	Allowing customers to design the services according to their needs and wants
		Offering sufficient alternatives and choices for customers
		Allowing customers to make their choices freely
Behavioural Control	Enabling customers to cancel a transaction at any point in time without incurring any significant costs	Offering customers opportunities to cancel their purchase with a refund

Source: Koc (2017a).

the study of control has been mainly limited to topics such as customer co-production (Bendapudi and Leone, 2003; Esmark et al., 2016), the use of self-service technologies (Lee and Allaway, 2002; Robertson et al., 2016), consumer choice (Hui and Bateson, 1991; Koc, 2013, 2016), and risk perception (Yagil, 2002).

Koc's (2013, 2016) studies on all-inclusive package holidays showed that the decisional control in these holidays caused the illusion of control on the part of the customers. Customers tended to attach more value to the food they chose from the open buffet restaurants on these holidays and had increased liking for the food they chose. Consequently, people on these holidays consumed more food, in terms of both quantity and variety, than they did in their ordinary lives. This meant that all-inclusive holidays with open buffet restaurants had the potential to cause obesity for people who participated in these holidays.

As the three types of control (cognitive, decisional, and behavioural) provide customers with feelings of stability and predictability, customers may show a preference for service businesses that offer control to these customers. Koc and Boz (2017) developed two scales to measure a) willingness of customers to have control, and b) a service business' ability or willingness to offer control to its customers. Although these scales were developed for services in general, they are applied to tourism and hospitality as well.

Activity

Control scale: customers' willingness to have control

Measure your willingness to have control when you purchase and consume tourism and hospitality products and services. Although the scale developed by Koc and Boz (2017) measures willingness to have control for any service, fill in the following questionnaire by thinking about tourism or a hospitality service you purchase and consume.

Important Note: Throughout the book, there are a number of self-report scales/tests like the one below. Please save your personal test score records (especially the ones relating to cultural awareness, cultural competence, ethnocentrism, cultural intelligence, etc.) to make comparisons later After studying the whole book you are advised to go back and redo all of these tests once more. By doing this you can compare your scores with the ones you had earlier on. This is expected to enable you to see the changes taken place as a result of the learning experience.

Control scale instructions

Please read the following statements and indicate how much each statement describes you when you interact with people from other cultures by assigning a value from 1 to 5 in the blank section on the left of each statement as follows:

(5) strongly agree (4) agree (3) neutral (2) disagree (1) strongly disagree

Please keep in mind that there is no right or wrong response for each statement. In order to avoid biased responses, you are recommended to record your initial response without elaborating too much on the statements.

Dimensions	*Items*	*Value (1 to 5)*
Behavioural Control	When purchasing a service (e.g., a hospitality service in a hotel or a restaurant, a health service, transportation, GSM or banking service, etc.), it is important for me to be able to opt out of purchasing.	
	When I am in doubt that the service may not meet my expectations, it is important for me to reverse my decision to buy this service.	
	If and when I change my mind not to purchase a service, I would not like to be under any pressure (e.g., unapproving expressions or looks of service staff).	
	When purchasing a service, it is important for me to be able to opt out of purchasing that service at any stage of the purchasing process.	
	During the process of purchasing, if I feel that something is not right (e.g., regarding the quality of the service etc.) it is important for me to be able to change my mind and opt out of purchasing.	
	When buying a service, I would not wish to feel that I have to make the purchase just because the service staff have been helpful to me.	
	When buying a service, I would not like to pay any fees, charges or penalties when I want to opt out of purchasing.	
	When making my purchasing decision for a service, it is important for me to be entitled to return the service without paying any fees, charges or penalties.	
	When making my purchasing, if I wish to opt out of purchasing, I would like the fees, charges, or penalties to be minimum.	
Decisional Control	The services I buy by myself, without the influence of anyone else, would please me more.	
	It makes me uncomfortable when a service personnel attempts to help me without my request.	
	I would prefer to buy the service I choose rather than the one service staff recommends.	
	The willingness of the service business staff to alter a product or service to suit my requests would make me pleased.	
	It makes me uncomfortable when a service personnel attempts to steer me against my will.	

Dimensions	*Items*	*Value (1 to 5)*
	Unless I request, the presence of a service personnel around me when I make my purchasing decision would make me feel uncomfortable.	
	When buying a service, the pressure of service staff would make me feel uncomfortable.	
	I like the service I choose rather than the one offered by the service staff.	
	I prefer to buy self-service services as much as possible as other people will not attempt to influence my purchasing decision.	
Cognitive Control	When I buy a service, having the exact price information would make me feel more comfortable.	
	When I buy a service, having the exact price information, would influence my purchasing decision positively.	
	It is important for me to have the exact pricing information before purchasing a service.	
	After making a purchasing decision for a service, the likelihood of future negative surprises would make me feel uncomfortable.	
	It is disturbing for me to be unclear about the content/scope of the service when I buy a service.	
	During the purchase of a service, the fact that information about the service is not clear reduces my trust for the service.	
	The possibility of additional costs arising after the purchasing of a service would make me feel uncomfortable.	
	I prefer purchasing pre-paid services (e.g., package holidays) as they prevent experiencing negative surprises.	
	Before purchasing a service, I prefer to be given just the required amount of information with an overload of information.	
	It is important for me to have the price list before the purchasing of a service.	

Scoring: Please add up your scores for each section. Values in the following table show your willingness to have control under each dimension.

Willingness to Control	*Cognitive Control*	*Decisional Control*	*Behavioural Control*
Low	1–20 points	1–18 points	1–18 points
Medium	21–30 points	19–27 points	19–27 points
High	31–50 points	28–45 points	28–45 points

Source: Koc and Boz (2017).

Activity

Control scale: service business' ability or willingness to offer control to its customers

Measure the ability or willingness to offer control to customers by the tourism and hospitality business you work for (or worked for or familiar with). Although the scale developed by Koc and Boz (2017) measures willingness to have control for any service, fill in the questionnaire by assuming that you are filling the questionnaire for tourism or a hospitality business.

Control scale instructions

Please read the statements below and indicate how much each statement describes you when you interact with people from other cultures by assigning a value from 1 to 5 in the blank section on the left of each statement as follows:

(5) strongly agree (4) agree (3) neutral (2) disagree (1) strongly disagree

Please keep in mind that there is no right or wrong response for each statement. In order to avoid biased responses, you are recommended to record your initial response without elaborating too much on the statements.

Dimensions	*Items*	*Value (1 to 5)*
Behavioural Control	The service business does not ask for fees, charges, or penalties to be paid when the customers change their mind and opt out of purchasing.	
	The service business offers its customers the opportunity to opt out of purchasing at any time during the purchase.	
	The service business offers its customers the opportunity to opt out of purchasing without incurring any costs.	
	The service business does not pressure customers (e.g., in the form of unapproving expressions or looks of service staff) when customers changes their mind and opt out of purchasing.	
	As the service business has an online buying option it offers its customers the opportunity to cancel a purchase.	
Decisional Control	The service business provides a sufficient number of options for the customer.	
	Service personnel do not put pressure on their customers to influence their decisions.	
	The service business allows its customers to make adjustments to the service to suit the service to their needs.	

Dimensions	*Items*	*Value (1 to 5)*
	The service business offers various alternatives to its customers to assist them in making their decisions.	
	The service business does not exhaust its customers by providing unnecessary information.	
	Service personnel do not annoy their customers by being around the customers all the time when customers make their purchase decisions.	
Cognitive Control	The service business does its best to make sure that its customers do not have negative surprises.	
	The service business informs the customer regarding the scope and details of the service before customers make their purchase decision.	
	The service business predicts the potential uncertainties that may arise and informs the customer accordingly before the customer purchases the service.	
	The prices of the services offered by the service business are presented to the customer in a clear/understandable manner.	
	The service business provides the customer with a sufficient amount of information regarding the content of the service.	
	There is no ambiguity about the prices and the payment process regarding the services offered by the service business.	
	Customers who purchase services from the service business do not have any doubts regarding the price.	
	The customers do not have any anxiety regarding the price of the service.	

Scoring: add up your scores for each section. Values in the following table show the service business' ability or willingness to offer control to its customers.

Willingness to Control	*Cognitive Control*	*Decisional Control*	*Behavioural Control*
Low	1–16 points	1–12 points	1–10 points
Medium	17–24 points	13–18 points	11–15 points
High	25–40 points	19–30 points	16–25 points

SOURCE: Koc and Boz (2017).

Conclusion

This chapter explains the influence of uncertainty avoidance from both marketing (consumer behaviour) and management (organisational behaviour and human resource management) perspectives. As the chapter demonstrates, the tendency or willingness to take or avoid various types of risks (financial or monetary risk, social risk, ego or psychological risk, performance or functional risk, and time risk) can significantly influence marketing mix, service quality perceptions, and management strategies in tourism and hospitality. The concept of and types of control (cognitive, decisional, and behavioural) were explained as instruments to reduce risk and uncertainty and increase stability and predictability for the customers.

Questions

1. Prepare two reports based on the research findings presented in this chapter, a) to explain the influence of uncertainty avoidance on tourism and hospitality customers, and b) to explain the influence of uncertainty avoidance on tourism and hospitality employees.
2. What sort of differences would there be between customers from high and low uncertainty in terms of the design and emphasis on the marketing mix elements?
3. Explain the types of risks tourism and hospitality customers may feel. How can managers reduce the perceptions of these risks?
4. How would customers from high and low risk avoidance cultures differ in terms of variety-seeking behaviour, switching, and loyalty?
5. Why do people need control? What are the three types of control? What sort of strategies can be developed to provide control for the customers?
6. Explain and discuss Ennius's (239–169 bce) "Fortune favours the brave" from the perspective of risk aversion and control.

Research questions/ideas to pursue for researchers

As stated in this chapter, customers from high-uncertainty avoidance cultures may be more likely to have status quo bias and avoid variety-seeking behaviour. By using a status quo bias and variety-seeking behaviour scales, the motivations of holiday homeowners in high and low-uncertainty avoidance cultures may be compared. As holiday homes allow predictability and stability for the people, the main motivations for ownership of holiday homes in low-uncertainty avoidance cultures may be investigated. For example, with the increasing growth of the sharing economy (e.g., swapping holiday homes), it may be explored whether people from low-uncertainty avoidance cultures are more likely to swap holiday homes in different countries and if they do, how, as opposed to people from high-uncertainty cultures.

Note

1 As a consequence of Covid-19 epidemic, experienced by people in the world in 2020, people may not feel comfortable with touch and being in close physical distance with others and may avoid social relations to some ex tent.

Recommended further reading

Hofstede, G. Hofstede, G. J., and Minkov, M. (2010). Cultures and organizations: Software of the mind (3rd ed.). New York: McGraw-Hill.

Koc, E. (2013). Inversionary and liminoidal consumption: Gluttony on holidays and obesity. *Journal of Travel and Tourism Marketing*, 30(8), 825–838.

Koc, E., and Boz, H. (2017). Development of scales to measure customers' willingness to have control and the control offered by service businesses. *Ecoforum*, 6(3), 27–35.

Litvin, S. W., Crotts, J. C., and Hefner, F. L. (2004). Cross-cultural tourist behaviour: A replication and extension involving Hofstede's uncertainty avoidance dimension. *International Journal of Tourism Research*, 6(1), 29–37.

Lucia-Casademunt, A. M., García-Cabrera, A. M., and Cuéllar-Molina, D. G. (2015). National culture, work-life balance and employee well-being in European tourism firms: the moderating effect of uncertainty avoidance values. *Tourism and Management Studies*, 11(1), 62–69.

Reisinger, Y. (2009). Cross-cultural differences in tourist behaviour. In M. Kozak and A. Decrop (Eds), *Handbook of Tourist Behaviour: Theory and Practice* (pp. 237–255). New York: Routledge.

References

Ahmed, Z. U., and Krohn, F. B. (1993). Understanding the unique consumer behavior of Japanese tourists. *Journal of Travel and Tourism Marketing*, 1(3), 73–86.

Ainsworth, M. D. (1964). Patterns of attachment behavior shown by the infant in interaction with his mother. *Merrill-Palmer Quarterly of Behavior and Development,* 51–58.

Albers-Miller, N., and Gelb, B. (1996). Business advertising appeals as a mirror of cultural dimensions: A study of eleven countries. *Journal of Advertising*, 25, 57–70.

Argyle, M. (1986). Rules for social relationships in four cultures. *Australian Journal of Psychology*, 38(3), 309–318.

Averill, J. R. (1973). Personal control over aversive stimuli and its relationship to stress. *Psychological Bulletin*, 80(4), 286–303.

Baker, D., and Carson, K. (1975). The two faces of uncertainty avoidance: Attachment and adaptation. *Journal of Behavioral and Applied Management*, 12(2): 128–141.

Baker, M. (2017). Service failures and recovery: Theories and models. In E. Koc (Ed.), Service failures and recovery in tourism and hospitality (pp. 27–41). Wallingford, Oxford: CABI.

Barragan, A., and Sibley, L. D. (2003). Migration of Toxoplasma gondii across biological barriers. *Trends in Microbiology*, 11(9), 426–430.

Belsky, J., Schlomer, G. L., and Ellis, B. J. (2012). Beyond cumulative risk: Distinguishing harshness and unpredictability as determinants of parenting and early life history strategy. *Dev. Psychol.*, 48, 662–673.

Bendapudi, N., and Leone, R. P. (2003). Psychological implications of customer participation in co-production. *Journal of Marketing*, 67(1), 14–28.

Bigné, E. J., Sanchez, I., and Andreu, L. (2009). The role of variety seeking in short and long run revisit intentions in holiday destinations. *International Journal of Culture, Tourism and Hospitality Research*, 3(2), 103–115.

Bogaert, A. F., and Sadava, S. (2002). Adult attachment and sexual behavior. *Pers. Relationsh.*, 9, 191–204.

Bowlby, J. (1988). *A secure base: Parent-child attachment and healthy human development*. New York: Basic Books.

Bowlby, E. J. M. (2008). *Loss-sadness and depression: attachment and loss* (Vol. 3). London: Random House.

Chen, Y., and Jiang, K. (2019). Tourism management perspectives. *Tourism Management*, 30, 197–207.

Cohen, E. (1972). Towards a sociology of international tourism. *Sociological Research*, 39(3), 164–182.

Collins, N. L., and Read, S. J. (1996). Revised adult attachment scale. Unpublished instrument, scoring instructions and reliability information, Department of Psychology, University of California, Santa Barbara.

Coves Martínez, A. L., Sabiote-Ortiz, C. M., and Rey-Pino, J. M. (2018). The influence of cultural intelligence on intention of internet use. *Spanish Journal of Marketing-ESIC*, 22(2), 231–248.

Darby, M. R. and E. Karni (1973). Free competition and the optimal amount of fraud. *Journal of Law and Economics*, 16, 67–88.

David, M. E., and Bearden, W. O. (2017). The role of interpersonal attachment styles in shaping consumer preferences for products shown in relational advertisements. *Pers. Individ. Dif.*, 109, 44–50.

David, M. E., Bearden, W. O., and Haws, K. L. (2017). Priced just for me: The role of interpersonal attachment style on consumer responses to customized pricing. J. Consum. Behav., 16, 26–37.

Ding, Y., Ding, Y., Keh, H. T., and Keh, H. T. (2016). A re-examination of service standardization versus customization from the consumer's perspective. *Journal of Services Marketing*, 30(1), 16–28.

Dolnicar, S. (2007). Crises that scare tourists investigating tourists' travel-related concerns. In B. Prideaux, B. Laws, and K. Chon (Eds.), *Managing tourism crises* (pp. 98–109). London: CABI.

Dorothea Brack, A., and Benkenstein, M. (2014). Responses to other similar customers in a service setting–analyzing the moderating role of perceived performance risk. *Journal of Services Marketing*, 28(2), 138–146.

Erber, R., and Erber, M. (2017). *Intimate relationships: Issues, theories, and research*. New York: Psychology Press

Esmark, C. L., Noble, S. M., Bell, J. E., and Griffith, D. A. (2016). The effects of behavioral, cognitive, and decisional control in co-production service experiences. *Marketing Letters*, 27(3), 423–436.

Faranda, William T. (2001). A Scale to Measure the Cognitive Control Form of Perceived Control: Construction and Preliminary Assessment. Psychology and Marketing. 18 (12), 1259.

Felton, L., and Jowett, S. (2013). The mediating role of social environmental factors in the associations between attachment styles and basic needs satisfaction. *Journal of Sports Sciences*, 31(6), 618–628.

Flegr, J. (2010). Influence of latent toxoplasmosis on the phenotype of intermediate hosts. *Folia Parasitol*, 57(2), 81–87.

Flegr, J. (2013). Influence of latent Toxoplasma infection on human personality, physiology and morphology: pros and cons of the Toxoplasma–human model in studying the manipulation hypothesis. *Journal of Experimental Biology*, 216(1), 127–133.

Frías, D. M., Rodríguez, M. A., Alberto Castañeda, J., Sabiote, C. M., and Buhalis, D. (2012). The formation of a tourist destination's image via information sources: The moderating effect of culture. *International Journal of Tourism Research*, 14(5), 437–450.

García-Cabrera, A.M., and García-Soto, M.G. (2011). MNC commitment, OCB role definition and intent to leave in subsidiary top managers: The moderating effect of uncertainty avoidance values. *International Journal of Intercultural Relation*, 35, 641–657.

Gibson, A., and Gibson, N. (2015). *Human growth, behaviour and development: essential theory and application in social work*. Thousand Oaks, CA: Sage.

Gray, J. M., and Wilson, M. (2009). The relative risk perception of travel hazards'. *Environment and Behavior*, 41(2), 185–204.

Greenberg, J., Pyszczynski, T., Solomon, S., Rosenblatt, A., Veeder, M., Kirkland, S., and Lyon, D. (1990). Evidence for terror management theory II: The effects of mortality salience on reactions to those who threaten or bolster the cultural worldview. *Journal of Personality and Social Psychology*, 58(2), 308.

Guéguen, N. (2007). Courtship compliance: The effect of touch on women's behavior. *Social Influence*, 2(2), 81–97.

Gupta, R., Derevensky, J. L., and Ellenbogen, S. (2006). Personality characteristics and risk-taking tendencies among adolescent gamblers. *Canadian Journal of Behavioural Science/ Revue canadienne des sciences du comportement*, 38(3), 201.

Harari, Y. N. (2016). *Homo Deus: A Brief History of Tomorrow*. London: Random House.

Harlow, H. F. (1958). The nature of love. *American Psychologist*, 13, 573–685.

Harlow, H. F., Dodsworth, R. O., and Harlow, M. K. (1965). Total social isolation in monkeys. *Proceedings of the National Academy of Sciences of the United States of America*, 54(1), 90.

Häyry, M., and Takala, T. (1998). Genetic engineering and the risk of harm. *Medicine, Health Care and Philosophy*, 1, 61–64.

Heider, F. (1958). *The psychology of interpersonal relations*. New York: Wiley.

Hofstede, G. (1984). *Culture's consequences: International differences in work-related values*. Beverly Hills, CA: Sage.

Hofstede, G. (2001). Culture's consequences: Comparing values, behaviors, institutions and organizations across nations (2nd ed.). Thousand Oaks, CA: Sage.

Hofstede, G. (2011). Dimensionalizing cultures: The Hofstede model in context. *Online Readings in Psychology and Culture*, 2(1), 1–26.

Hofstede, G. (2020). Cultural dimensions. https://www.hofstede-insights.com/product/compare-countries/ (accessed 20 January 2020).

Hofstede, G., Hofstede, G. J., and Minkov, M. (2010). Cultures and organizations: Software of the mind (rev. and expanded 3rd ed.). New York: McGraw-Hill.

Holt-Lunstad, J., Smith, T. B., Baker, M., Harris, T., and Stephenson, D. (2015). Loneliness and social isolation as risk factors for mortality: A meta-analytic review. *Perspectives on Psychological Science*, 10(2), 227–237.

Howe, D. (2011). *Attachment across the lifecourse: A brief introduction*. Basingstoke: Macmillan International Higher Education.

Hui, M. K., and Bateson, J. E. (1991). Perceived control and the effects of crowding and consumer choice on the service experience. *Journal of Consumer Research*, 18(2), 174–184.

Irimiás, A., Michalkó, G., Timothy, D. J., and Franch, M. (2017). Disappointment in tourism and hospitality: The influence of films on destinations. In E. Koc (Ed.), *Service failures and recovery in tourism and hospitality: A practical manual* (pp. 214–227). Wallingford, Oxford: CABI

Janis, I. L., and Janis, I. L. (1982). *Groupthink: Psychological studies of policy decisions and fiascoes* (Vol. 349). Boston: Houghton Mifflin.

Johnson, S. K., Fitza, M. A., Lerner, D. A., Calhoun, D. M., Beldon, M. A., Chan, E. T., and Johnson, P. T. (2018). Risky business: linking Toxoplasma gondii infection and entrepreneurship behaviours across individuals and countries. *Proceedings of the Royal Society B: Biological Sciences*, 285(1883), 20180822.

Kacelnik, A., and Bateson, M. (1996). Risky theories: The effects of variance on foraging decisions. *American Zoologist*, 36, 343–402.

Kacelnik, A., and Bateson, M. (1997). Risk-sensitivity: Crossroads for theories of decision-making. *Trends Cogn. Sci.*, 1, 304–309.

Kahneman, D., and Tversky, A. (1979). Prospect theory: An analysis of decision under risk. *Econometrica: Journal of the Econometric Society*, 263–291.

Kahneman, D., Knetsch, J. L., and Thaler, R. H. (1991). Anomalies: The endowment effect, loss aversion, and status quo bias. *The Journal of Economic Perspectives*, 193–206.

Kale, S. H., and Barnes, J. W. (1992). Understanding the domain of cross-national buyer-seller interactions. *Journal of International Business Studies*, 23(First Quarter), 101–132.

Kelly, P., Lawlor, J., and Mulvey, M. (2017). Self-service technologies: Service failures and recovery. In E. Koc (Ed.), *Service failures and recovery in tourism and hospitality: A practical manual* (pp. 100–121). Wallingford, Oxford: CABI.

Kenrick, D. T. and Griskevicius, V. (2013). *The rational animal: How evolution made us smarter than we think*. New York: Basic Books.

Khan, R. and Cox, P. (2017). Country culture and national innovation. *Archives of Business Research*, 5(2), 85–101.

Koc, E. (2000). The role and potential of marketing communications in the Turkish domestic tourism market (Unpublished doctoral dissertation), Oxford Brookes University.

Koc, E. (2006). Total quality management and business excellence in services: The implications of all-inclusive pricing system on internal and external customer satisfaction in the Turkish tourism market. *Total Quality Management and Business Excellence*, 17(7), 857–877.

Koc, E. (2013). Inversionary and liminoidal consumption: Gluttony on holidays and obesity. *Journal of Travel and Tourism Marketing*, 30(8), 825 838.

Koc, E. (2015). *Hizmet Pazarlaması ve Yönetimi, 1*. Ankara: Baskı, Seçkin Yayıncılık.

Koc, E. (2016). Food consumption in all-inclusive holidays: illusion of control as an antecedent of inversionary consumption. *Journal of Gastronomy and Tourism*, 2(2), 107–116.

Koc, E. (2017a). *Service failures and recovery in tourism and hospitality: A practical manual*. Wallingford, Oxford: CABI.

Koc. E. (2017b). Cross-cultural aspects of service failures and recovery. In E. Koc (Ed.), *Service failures and recovery in tourism and hospitality: A practical manual* (pp. 197–213). Wallingford, Oxford: CABI.

Koc, E. (2018). Turkish tourism and hospitality students' social anxiety and avoidance. *Journal of Hospitality and Tourism Education*, 31(1), 49–54.

Koc, E., and Altinay, G. (2007). An analysis of seasonality in monthly per person tourist spending in Turkish inbound tourism from a market segmentation perspective. *Tourism Management*, 28(1), 227–237.

Koc, E., and Boz, H. (2017). Development of Scales to Measure Customers' Willingness to Have Control and the Control Offered by Service Businesses. *Ecoforum*, 6(3), 27–35.

Kocazeybek, B., Oner, Y. A., Turksoy, R., Babur, C., Cakan, H., Sahip, N., ... and Aslan, M. (2009). Higher prevalence of toxoplasmosis in victims of traffic accidents suggest increased risk of traffic accident in Toxoplasma-infected inhabitants of Istanbul and its *suburbs. Forensic Science International*, 187(1–3), 103–108.

Lam, Desmond C. S., and Lee, Alvin Y. C. (2005). The influence of cultural values on brand loyalty. *Proceedings of the Australia and New Zealand Marketing Association Conference 2005: Broadening the Boundaries* (pp. 163–171). Perth, WA: ANZMAC.

Langer, E. J., and Roth, J. (1975). Heads I win, tails it's chance: The illusion of control as a function of the sequence of outcomes in a purely chance task. *Journal of Personality and Social Psychology*, 32(6), 951.

Lee, J., and Allaway, A. (2002). Effects of personal control on adoption of self-service technology innovations. *Journal of Services Marketing*, 16(6), 553–572.

Lepp, A., and Gibson, H. (2003). Tourist roles, perceived risk and international tourism. *Annals of Tourism Research*, 30(3), 606–624.

Li, Y. J., Lu, S., Lan, J., and Jiang, F. (2019). Feel Safe to Take More Risks? Insecure Attachment Style Increases Consumer Risk-Taking Behavior. *Frontiers in Psychology*, 10, 874.

Lim, K. H., Leung, K., Sia, C. L., and Lee, M. K. O. (2004). Is e-commerce boundary-less? Effects of individualism-collectivism and uncertainty avoidance on internet shopping. *Journal of International Business Studies*, 35(6), 545–559.

Ling, V. J., Lester, D., Mortensen, P. B., Langenberg, P. W., and Postolache, T. T. (2011). Toxoplasma gondii seropositivity and suicide rates in women. *The Journal of Nervous and Mental Disease*, 199(7), 440.

Litvin, S. W., Crotts, J. C., and Hefner, F. L. (2004). Cross-cultural tourist behaviour: a replication and extension involving Hofstede's uncertainty avoidance dimension. *International Journal of Tourism Research*, 6(1), 29–37.

Lovallo, D. and Kahneman, D. (2003). Delusions of success. *Harvard Business Review*, July., 57–63.

Lynn, M., Le, J. M., and Sherwyn, D. (1998). Reach out and touch your customers. *Cornell Hotel and Restaurant Administration Quarterly*, 39, 60–65.

Manrai, L. A., and Manrai, A. (2011). Hofstede's cultural dimensions and tourist behaviors: A review and conceptual framework. *Journal of Economics, Finance and Administrative Science*, 16(31), 23.

Mathieu, P. (1999). Economic citizenship and the rhetoric of gourmet coffee. *Rhetoric Review*, 18(1), 112–127.

Mattila, A. S., and Choi, S. (2006). A cross-cultural comparison of perceived fairness and satisfaction in the context of hotel room pricing. *International Journal of Hospitality Management*, 25(1), 146–153.

McCornack, S., and Ortiz, J. (2017). *Choices and connections: An Introduction to communication* (2nd ed.). Bedford: St. Martin's.

McGhee, R. L., Ehrler, D. J., Buckhalt, J. A., and Phillips, C. (2012). The relation between five-factor personality traits and risk-taking behavior in preadolescents. *Psychology*, 3(08), 558.

McKenna, F. P., and Albery, I. P. (2001). Does unrealistic optimism change following a negative experience? *Journal of Applied Social Psychology*, 31(6), 1146–1157.

Mellers, B. A., Schwartz, A., Ho, K., and Ritov, I. (1997). decision affect theory: emotional reactions to the outcomes of risky options. *Psychological Science*, 8(6), 423–429.

Merritt, C. J., and Tharp, I. J. (2013). Personality, self-efficacy and risk-taking in parkour (free-running). *Psychology of Sport and Exercise*, 14(5), 608–611.

Miller, S. M. (1979). Controllability and human stress: Method, evidence and theory. *Behaviour Research and Therapy*, 17, 287–304.

Mishra, S., Barclay, P., and Lalumière, M. L. (2014). Competitive disadvantage facilitates risk taking. *Evol. Hum. Behav.*, 35, 126–132.

Mishra, S., Barclay, P., and Sparks, A. (2017). The relative state model: Integrating need-based and ability-based pathways to risk-taking. *Pers. Soc. Psychol. Rev.*, 21, 176–198.

Mittal, B. (1999). The advertising of services meeting the challenge of intangibility. *Journal of Service Research*, 2 (1), 98–116.

Money, B., and J. Crotts (2003). The effect of uncertainty avoidance on information search, planning and purchases of international travel vacations. *Tourism Management*, 24(2), 191–202.

Ndubisi, N. O., Malhotra, N. K., Ulas, D., and Ndubisi, G. C. (2012). Examining uncertainty avoidance, relationship quality, and customer loyalty in two cultures. *Journal of International Consumer Marketing*. 24(5), 320–337.

Nedeljković, M., Hadžić, O., and Čerović, S. (2012). Organizational changes and job satisfaction in the hospitality industry in Serbia. *UTMS Journal of Economics*, 3(2), 105–117.

Noja, G. G., Petrović, N., and Cristea, M. (2018). Turning points in migrants' labour market integration in Europe and benefit spillovers for Romania and Serbia: the role of socio-psychological credentials. *Zbornik Radova Ekonomski Fakultet u Rijeka*, 36(2), 489–518.

Nordin, F., Kindström, D., Kowalkowski, C., and Rehme, J. (2011). The risks of providing services: Differential risk effects of the service-development strategies of customisation, bundling, and range. *Journal of Service Management*, 22(3), 390–408.

Parasuraman, A., Zeithaml, V. A., and Berry, L. L. (1988). SERVQUAL: a multiple-item scale for measuring consumer perceptions of service quality. *Journal of Retailing*. 64(1), 12–40.

Peng, Y. S., and Lin, S. S. (2009). National culture, economic development, population growth and environmental performance: The mediating role of education. *Journal of Business Ethics*, 90(2), 203–219.

Pizam, A., and Jeong, G. H. (1996). Cross-cultural tourist behavior: Perceptions of Korean tour-guides. *Tourism Management*, 17(4), 277–286.

Pizam, A., Jeong, G. H., Reichel, A., van Boemmel, H., Lusson, J. M., Steynberg, L., ... and Montmany, N. (2004). The relationship between risk-taking, sensation-seeking, and the tourist behavior of young adults: A cross-cultural study. *Journal of Travel Research*, 42(3), 251–260.

Radojevic, T., Stanisic, N., and Stanic, N. (2019). The culture of hospitality: From anecdote to evidence. *Annals of Tourism Research*, 79, 102789.

Reisinger, Y., and Crotts, J. (2010). Applying Hofstede's national culture measures in tourism research: illuminating issues of divergence and convergence. *Journal of Travel Research*, 49(2): 153–164.

Reisinger, Y., and Mavondo, F. (2006). Cultural differences in travel risk perception. *Journal of Travel and Tourism Marketing*, 20(1), 13–31.

Rittichainuwat, B. N. (2013). Tourists' perceived risks toward overt safety measures. *Journal of Hospitality and Tourism Research*, 37(2), 199–216.

Robertson, N., Robertson, N., McDonald, H., McDonald, H., Leckie, C., Leckie, C., ... and McQuilken, L. (2016). Examining customer evaluations across different self-service technologies. *Journal of Services Marketing*, 30(1), 88–102

Sabiote-Ortiz, C. M., Frías-Jamilena, D. M., and Castañeda-García, J. A. (2016). Overall perceived value of a tourism service delivered via different media: A cross-cultural perspective. *Journal of Travel Research*, 55(1), 34–51.

Samioğlu, M (2020). Tüketici Satın Alma Karar Süreçlerini Etkileyen Sezgiseller: Marka Sadakati Eğiliminde Bilişsel Yanılgıların Rolü (Unpublished doctoral thesis). University of Istanbul.

Samuelson, W., and Zeckhauser, R. (1988). Status quo bias in decision making. *Journal of Risk and Uncertainty*, 1(1), 7–59.

Seabra, C., Dolnicar, S., Abrantes, J. L., and Kastenholz, E. (2013). Heterogeneity in risk and safety perceptions of international tourists. *Tourism Management*, 36, 502–510.

Seo, S., Kim, K., and Jang, J. (2018). Uncertainty avoidance as a moderator for influences on foreign resident dining out behaviors. *International Journal of Contemporary Hospitality Management*, 30(2), 900–918.

Shenkar O. (2001). Cultural distance revisited: towards a more rigorous conceptualization and measurement of cultural differences. *Journal of International Business Studies*, 32(3), 519–535.

Simpson, J. A., Griskevicius, V., and Rothman, A. J. (2012). Consumer decisions in relationships. *J. Consum. Psychol.*, 22, 304–314.

Solomon, M., Russell-Bennett, R., and Previte, J. (2012). *Consumer behaviour*. Frenchs Forest, Australia: Pearson Higher Education AU.

Sonneveld, M. H., and Schifferstein, H. N. J. (2008). The tactual experience of objects. In H. N. J. Schifferstein and P. Hekkert (Eds), Product Experience (pp. 41–67). London: Elsevier.

Sophonsiri, V. (2008). Developing host-guest relationships in Thai tourist resorts (Unpublished doctoral thesis). Victoria University, Melbourne, Australia.

Steenkamp, J.-B.E., ter Hofstede, F., and Wedel, M. (1999). A cross-national investigation into the individual and national cultural antecedents of consumer innovativeness. *The Journal of Marketing*, 63(2), 55–69.

Stout, M. (2006). *The sociopath next door*. New York: Broadway Books.

Suki, N., and Suki, N. (2007). Online buying innovativeness: Effects of perceived value, perceived risk and perceived enjoyment. *International Journal of Business and Society*, 8(2), 81–93.

Taskin, C., Koc, E., and Boz, H. (2017). Perceptual image of conflict-ridden destinations: An EEG and eye tracker analysis. *Business and Economics Research Journal*, 8(3), 533–553.

Taubman-Ben-Ari, O., and Mikulincer, M. (2007). The effects of dispositional attachment orientations and contextual priming of attachment security on reckless driving. *Transp. Res. F Traffic Psychol. Behav.*, 10, 123–138.

Thaler, R. (1980). Toward a positive theory of consumer choice. *Journal of Economic Behavior and Organization*, 1, 39–60.

Thomson, M., Whelan, J., and Johnson, A. R. (2012). Why brands should fear fearful consumers: how attachment style predicts retaliation. *J. Consum. Psychol.*, 22, 289–298.

Tok, S. (2011). The big five personality traits and risky sport participation. *Social Behavior and Personality: An International Journal*, 39(8), 1105–1111.

Tsaur, S. H., Lin, C. T., and Wu, C. S. (2005). Cultural differences of service quality and behavioral intention in tourist hotels. *Journal of Hospitality and Leisure Marketing*, 13(1), 41–63.

Unzicker, D. K. (1999). The psychology of being put on hold: An exploratory study of service quality. *Psychology and Marketing*, 164, 327–350.

Weiner, B. (2000). Intrapersonal and interpersonal theories of motivation from an attributional perspective. *Educational Psychology Review*, 121, 1–14.

Williams, A. M., and Baláž, V. (2013). Tourism, risk tolerance and competences: Travel organization and tourism hazards. *Tourism Management*, 35, 209–221.

Yagil, D. (2002). The relationship of customer satisfaction and service workers' perceived control: Examination of three models. *International Journal of Service Industry Management*, 13(4), 382–398.

Zein O. (2015). *Culture and project management, managing diversity in multicultural projects* (1st ed.). Farnham: Gower Publishing.

Chapter 8

Masculinity versus femininity, gender egalitarianism, and assertiveness

Learning Objectives

After reading this chapter, you should be able to:

- explain the main characteristics of masculine and feminine cultures;
- understand the concepts of gender egalitarianism and assertiveness and their relationship with culture;
- explain how masculinity, femininity, gender egalitarianism, and assertiveness relate to marketing and consumer behaviour (e.g., the design of marketing mix elements, responses to service failures);
- explain how masculinity, femininity, gender egalitarianism, and assertiveness relate to organisational behaviour and management aspects of tourism and hospitality operations.

Introduction

People are born into a sex group (i.e., become male or female) but learn to become masculine or feminine in the culture they grow up (Bem, 1974; Neuliep, 2018). In other words, while sex is innate, gender is learned.

This chapter explains and discusses the masculinity and femininity dimension of culture, together with the related concepts of assertiveness and egalitarianism. As explained in this chapter, masculinity and femininity influence how people perceive their environment and the way they collect, process, and analyse this information has significant implications for consumer behaviour, marketing management, human resource management, organisational behaviour, and management in tourism and hospitality.

In basic terms, masculinity refers to a preference for achievement, heroism, assertiveness, competitiveness, toughness, dominance, and material reward for success in a society (Hofstede et al., 2010). In a masculine society, people emphasise the nurturing of ambition and acquisition of wealth and men bear an image of importance in a social context. In masculine cultures, in general, people tend to be direct and confrontational.

CASE STUDY

Dutch directness

The directness of Dutch people is not a stereotype, as people in the Netherlands (especially in Amsterdam) tend to prefer a direct way of communicating in general. For instance, when they are invited for dinner, they may directly (and easily) tell the host that they did not like the dinner, or when their opinions are asked about one's new hairstyle they may directly say that it is not nice without being pretentious and diplomatic. Some people say that waiters in restaurants or cafes may even directly ask "What do you want?" instead of asking "What would you like to order?"

The Dutch believe that truthfulness comes before empathy and they do not conceal this. They do not feel intimidated in communication and do not communicate or act under very much control of the superego. As an egalitarian society in the Netherlands, people feel that they have the right to say whatever they want and be as direct as they want. If someone gets offended because of the truthfulness and directness, it is their fault. Many foreigners find the Dutch directness rude, harsh, or offending when they communicate with them for the first time (van der Horst, 2001).

According to Breukel (2020), the Dutch directness and straightforwardness emanate from the historical prevalence of Calvinism in the Netherlands (although at present the vast majority of Dutch people may not associate themselves with any religion). Calvinism dictated the individual responsibility for moral salvage from the sinful world through introspection, total honesty, soberness, rejection of 'pleasure' as well as the 'enjoyment' of wealth (Breukel, 2020).

It is mentioned below that because of impression management (see also Chapter 1), the data collected from the participants in tourism and hospitality studies (also in all social sciences) by traditional data collection methods may not reflect the truth. Triangulation in data collection and the use of neuromarketing tools in research are offered as a solution (Koc, 2014a, 2014b). It may be suggested that the truthfulness of data collected through rational methods of data collection (i.e., surveys and interviews) in the Netherlands can reflect the truth better.

The case study in Chapter 6 discussed the airplane crashes by Korean Airlines caused by indirect and mitigated communication. A research study showed that the way a service failure in a hotel may be communicated to superiors by subordinates differed in a low power-distance culture (the United Kingdom) from a high power-distance culture (Turkey) (Koc, 2013). Although the British may be quite indirect in social life (when they express their opinions, thoughts, and feelings except when they communicate with close friends), they may be rather direct in business communications due to the low power distance in the society.

On the other hand, femininity refers to preference cooperation, egalitarianism, communal and consensus orientation, modesty, caring for the weak, and the quality of life in a society (Hofstede et al., 2010). Although a country's masculinity–femininity score (see Table 8.1) is not related to its degree of economic development, the score is influenced by the rate of population living in poverty in that country (Hofstede, 2001). Table 8.2 shows income inequality among selected countries.

Apart from income equality and inequality, there may be a relationship between the language spoken in a country and the masculinity and femininity. Prewitt-Freilino et al.'s (2012) investigated the differences in gender equality in 111 countries with grammatical gender, natural gender, and genderless languages. Their research found that in countries where gendered languages are spoken there was evidence of less gender equality.

Table 8.1 Basic summary of the main characteristics of masculinity and femininity

Feminine Cultures *E.g., Sweden, Norway, Denmark, Netherlands, Finland, Chile, Portugal, Russia, Thailand, South Korea, Bulgaria, and Spain*	*Masculine Cultures* *E.g., Japan, Hungary, Austria, Venezuela, Switzerland, Italy, Mexico, United Kingdom, Germany, the United States, and Australia*
Gatherer	Hunter
Roles of women and men overlap, that is, egalitarian	Roles of women and men tend to be distinct, that is, unequal
Both men and women are expected to be tender and to be concerned with relationships	Women are expected to be tender and to take care of relationships
Caring for others and preservation are important	Material success and progress are important
Everybody is expected to be modest	Men are expected to be assertive, tough and ambitious
Small and slow are beautiful	Big and fast are beautiful
Communal orientation. Trying to be better than others neither socially nor materially rewarded	Success orientation. There are rewards (e.g., wealth and status) for the successful ones
Quality of life and serving others are dominant values	Being ambitious and the need to excel are dominant values
People tend to strive for consensus	People tend to be polarised
Decisiveness	Intuition
Cooperation	Competition
People work to live rather than live to work	People live to work rather than work to live
Gender egalitarianism, gender equality	Gender inequality
Relationship oriented	Ego oriented
Quality of life and people are important	Money and material things are important

Table 8.1 continued

Feminine Cultures *E.g., Sweden, Norway, Denmark, Netherlands, Finland, Chile, Portugal, Russia, Thailand, South Korea, Bulgaria, and Spain*	*Masculine Cultures* *E.g., Japan, Hungary, Austria, Venezuela, Switzerland, Italy, Mexico, United Kingdom, Germany, the United States, and Australia*
Environmental protection and social welfare in the country are important	The economic growth of the country is important
Conflicts can be solved through negotiation attitude. In conflict situations, people strive to compromise and negotiate	Conflicts can be solved through force attitude. Conflicts are fought out
Religion is less important in life	Religion is significantly important in life
The smaller gender wage gap	The larger gender wage gap
More women in management	Fewer women in management
Preference for fewer working hours	Preference for higher pay
Flexible family structure	Traditional family structure
Both boys and girls cry; neither fight	Girls cry boys don't; boys fight, girls don't
Failing at school is viewed as a minor accident	Failing at school is viewed as a disaster
People emphasise relationships	People emphasise achievement
The school system awards adaptation	The school system awards performance
At work, people tend to undersell themselves	At work, people tend to oversell themselves
Assertiveness is ridiculed	Assertiveness is appreciated
Unfortunate people are sympathised with	Successful people are admired for
Unisex is ideal	Ostentatious manliness is appreciated
Communication is about sharing	Communication is about sending the message
Communicate *with* attitude	Communicate *to* attitude

Source: Hofstede et al. (2010).

Exercise

Study and compare Tables 8.1 and 8.2. Is there a relationship between income equality and inequality, and masculinity and femininity? You will see that there are differences. What other factors may have played a role in the income equality and inequality level of a country?

Table 8.2 Income equality and inequality in selected countries in the world

Countries with Income Equality (or Low Inequality) (0 = Complete Equality; 1 = Complete Inequality)				*Countries Income Inequality (or Low Equality) 0 = Complete Equality; 1 = Complete Inequality)*			
Country	*Score*	*Country*	*Score*	*Country*	*Score*	*Country*	*Score*
Slovakia	0.24	Sweden	0.28	South Africa	0.62	Spain	0.34
Slovenia	0.24	Austria	0.28	Chile	0.42	Japan	0.34
Czechia	0.25	Poland	0.28	Mexico	0.46	Greece	0.33
Ireland	0.26	Netherlands	0.28	Turkey	0.40	Russia	0.33
Denmark	0.26	France	0.29	United States	0.39	Portugal	0.33
Norway	0.26	Germany	0.29	United Kingdom	0.36	Australia	0.33
Belgium	0.27	Switzerland	0.30	South Korea	0.35	Italy	0.33
Finland	0.27	Luxembourg	0.30	New Zealand	0.35	Estonia	0.33

Source: OECD (2015).

The concept of masculinity and femininity

Masculinity shows the extent to which social gender roles are distinct in a society, while in feminine societies gender roles tend to overlap (Hofstede et al., 2010). In masculine societies, males are conditioned to be assertive, tough, and focused on material success and possessions, while in feminine cultures, females are expected to be modest, tender, and focused on the quality of life (Hofstede et al., 2010). In feminine cultures, people value relationships, the welfare of others, friendly atmosphere, security of employment and nurturing (see Table 8.2), treatment of female equally in all aspects of social life, and balancing of family and work and family life (Reisinger and Movando, 2006). In terms of the balancing of work and family (or social life), Finland's (a highly feminine society) Prime Minister Sanna Marin supported a four-day working week, with six hours of work a day, stating that "I believe people deserve to spend more time with their families, loved ones, hobbies and other aspects of life such as culture" (*Independent*, 2020).

Table 8.3 shows the masculinity index scores (MAS) for 72 selected countries in the world. A higher value indicates that a country has a high level of masculinity, whilst a lower value shows femininity. According to the table, countries such as Sweden, Norway, the Netherlands, Denmark, Finland, Chile, and Portugal appear to have a relatively low level of masculinism, that is, they are feminine societies. On the other hand, countries such as Japan, Hungary, Sweden, Austria, Venezuela, Switzerland, Italy, Mexico, United Kingdom, Germany, and the United States appear to have high level masculinity.

Assertiveness and egalitarianism

Masculinity and femininity was distinguished in the GLOBE Project by House et al. (2004) and Minkov and Hofstede (2011) as two dimensions of assertiveness and

Table 8.3 Masculinity and femininity scores of selected countries in the world

Rank	*Country*	*MAS Scores*	*Rank*	*Country*	*MAS Scores*	*Rank*	*Country*	*MAS Scores*
1	Sweden	**5**	25	France	**43**	49	Argentina	***56***
2	Norway	**8**	26	Iran	**43**	50	Hong Kong	***57***
3	Netherlands	**14**	27	Serbia	**43**	51	Greece	***57***
4	Denmark	**16**	28	Panama	**44**	52	Czechia	***57***
5	Costa Rica	**21**	29	Turkey	**45**	53	New Zealand	***58***
6	Finland	**26**	30	Taiwan	**45**	54	Australia	***61***
7	Chile	**28**	31	Indonesia	**46**	55	United States	***62***
8	Estonia	**30**	32	Ghana	**46**	56	Ecuador	***63***
9	Portugal	**31**	33	Nigeria	**46**	57	South Africa	***63***
10	Thailand	**34**	34	Sierra Leone	**46**	58	Philippines	***64***
11	Russia	**36**	35	Israel	**47**	59	Poland	***64***
12	Guatemala	**37**	36	Singapore	**48**	60	Colombia	***64***
13	Uruguay	**38**	37	Brazil	**49**	61	China	***66***
14	South Korea	**39**	38	Malaysia	**50**	62	Germany	***66***
15	El Salvador	**40**	39	Pakistan	**50**	63	United Kingdom	***66***
16	Bulgaria	**40**	40	Egypt	**52**	64	Jamaica	***68***
17	Croatia	**40**	41	Iraq	**52**	65	Ireland	***68***
18	Ethiopia	**41**	42	Kuwait	**52**	66	Mexico	***69***
19	Kenya	**41**	43	Lebanon	**52**	67	Italy	***70***
20	Tanzania	**41**	44	Libya	**52**	68	Switzerland	***70***
21	Zambia	**41**	45	Saudi Arabia	**52**	69	Venezuela	***73***
22	Peru	**42**	46	United Arab Emirates	**52**	70	Austria	***79***
23	Spain	**42**	47	Belgium	**54**	71	Hungary	***88***
24	Romania	**42**	48	India	**56**	72	Japan	***95***

Source: Hofstede (2020). Used with permission.

gender equality, which are the two dominant values in a society (Bartosik-Purgat, 2014). Assertiveness can be defined as communicating in a way to express oneself freely (feelings, beliefs, and opinions) in a direct and honest manner (without being aggressive or passive) in interpersonal situations, while simultaneously respecting the rights and dignity of others (Koc, 2010). Nikolić (2014) found that self-motivation, as an element

Table 8.4 Assertive behaviours

Assertiveness is about …	*Assertiveness is not about …*
expressing your needs clearly and directly	relinquishing your right and responsibility to advocate
expressing your ideas without feeling guilty or intimidated	beating around the bush before stating your needs
sticking up for what you believe in	feeling too guilty or afraid to express your needs
knowing what your rights are and how to get them	agreeing with others when you would rather not
treating professionals as partners	leaving decisions to others because "they know best"
exhibiting self-confidence when communicating	reliance and dependence on others, giving in to defeat
self-reliance and independence	giving up when you run into "red tape"
persisting until you get what you need and deserve	making assumptions and decisions before you obtain all the facts

Source: Alberti and Emmons (2017).

of emotional intelligence, was the best predictor of assertiveness values. However, though assertiveness is associated with individualism and masculinity, women, in general, tend to have a higher level of emotional intelligence than men (Bradberry ve Greaves, 2005, 2009), most probably due to their higher scores in other dimensions of emotional intelligence such as self-awareness, social awareness, and social skills (Koc, 2019; Koc and Boz, 2020).

Alberti and Emmons (2017) distinguish behaviour that is assertive or not as shown in Table 8.4.

Information zone

Non-assertive and indirect communication in a feminine culture

Turkish culture is a non-assertive, high-context, and moderately feminine culture. The communication is usually non-confrontational, warm, and indirect. In general, people pay attention not to offend others, use an indirect way of communication, and usually beat around the bush. Criticism and disagreements are usually softened by the use of words "as if", "perhaps", "probably", "I guess", "sort of", and "may be" (Cultural Atlas, 2020). For example, "I guess, you may have overcharged me." This way of communication is less assertive, and it weakens the strength of negative or sensitive comments. As Turkish people, in general, are not assertive and confrontational, they avoid conflicts and disagreements. In many instances of conflict, they may ignore or conceal their disagreement. However, as relationships develop, they tend to be more direct in their communication.

Also, as Turkish people are highly risk-averse, that is, they do not like uncertainties and ambiguities, they often resort to uncertainty or ambiguity-reducing strategies in their communication. In their communication, they often use percentages and numbers to establish a sense of certainty, although in many instances this may result in exaggerations (e.g., "90% of people would do the same", "Not more than 5% of people would like this", "I have told you this forty times", "I have been waiting in this queue for two hours").

Egalitarianism, which is associated with femininity, is an overt display of justice, freedom, and the associated responsibilities accompanying these values (Kim et al., 2018). Gender egalitarianism is the equal treatment of men and women in terms of roles, responsibilities, and opportunities provided on a social or organisational level (Yukl, 2010). Gender egalitarianism is best predicted by gender, self-awareness, and social capability (Nikolić, 2014). Table 8.5 shows the assertiveness and gender egalitarianism scores of selected countries researched in the GLOBE project by House et al. (2004).

CASE STUDY

Capuchin monkeys expect equality

Brosnan and Waal's (2003) experiments showed that Capuchin monkeys cared for equality: equality for themselves and others. In experiments, two Capuchin monkeys were placed in proximate cages. In one of the cages, there was a basket with several tokens. There were two different tokens (their colours being different). Only one of the monkeys was able to select a token and deliver it to the researcher. The monkey which selected the token always received a food award. However, depending on the token, the other monkey received or did not receive a food reward. In other words, if the first monkey selected the "selfish" token, only s/he was able to get the food reward. However, if the first monkey chose the "prosocial" token, both of the monkeys were able to receive the food reward. It was surprising to see that if the non-selector monkey applied some pressure (e.g., by spitting water), the selector monkey decreased the selection of the prosocial token, that is, punishing the other monkey for the inappropriate behaviour (Brosnan and de Waal, 2003).

In another experiment, two monkeys were placed side by side in two different cages. The monkeys were given a simple task to do to receive a food reward. They had to give back a small rock they received from the researcher. When they gave the piece of rock to the researcher, they received a food reward. When the first monkey completed the task, s/he received a slice of cucumber as the food reward.

Table 8.5 Assertiveness and gender egalitarianism scores of selected countries

*Assertiveness Society Practices**

Rank	*Country*	*Score*	*Rank*	*Country*	*Score*
1	Nigeria	4.79	31	Ecuador	4.09
2	Hungary	4.79	32	Zambia	4.07
3	Germany[a]	4.73	33	Italy	4.07
4	Hong Kong	4.67	34	Zimbabwe	4.06
5	Austria	4.62	35	Poland	4.06
6	El Salvador	4.62	36	Canada[e]	4.05
7	South Africa[b]	4.60	37	Iran	4.04
8	Greece	4.58	38	Philippines	4.01
9	Germany[c]	4.55	39	Slovenia	4.00
10	U.S.	4.55	40	Ireland	3.92
11	Turkey	4.53	41	Taiwan	3.92
12	Morocco	4.52	42	Namibia	3.91
13	Switzerland	4.51	43	Egypt	3.91
14	Kazakhstan	4.46	44	Guatemala	3.89
15	Mexico	4.45	45	Malaysia	3.87
16	Spain	4.42	46	Indonesia	3.86
17	South Korea	4.40	47	Finland	3.81
18	South Africa[d]	4.36	48	Denmark	3.80
19	Venezuela	4.33	49	Bolivia	3.79
20	Netherlands	4.32	50	China	3.76
21	Australia	4.28	51	Costa Rica	3.75
22	Israel	4.23	52	India	3.73
23	Argentina	4.22	53	Russia	3.68
24	Brazil	4.20	54	Portugal	3.65
25	Colombia	4.20	55	Thailand	3.64
26	Georgia	4.18	56	Kuwait	3.63
27	Singapore	4.17	57	Japan	3.59
28	England	4.15	58	Switzerland[f]	3.47
29	France	4.13	59	New Zealand	3.42
30	Qatar	4.11	60	Sweden	3.38

Table 8.5 continued

*Gender Egalitarianism Society Practices**

Rank	*Country*	*Score*	*Rank*	*Country*	*Score*
1	Hungary	4.08	31	Thailand	3.35
2	Russia	4.07	32	U.S.	3.34
3	Poland	4.02	33	Brazil	3.31
4	Slovenia	3.96	34	South Africa[d]	3.27
5	Denmark	3.93	35	Indonesia	3.26
6	Namibia	3.88	36	Italy	3.24
7	Kazakhstan	3.84	37	New Zealand	3.22
8	Sweden	3.84	38	Ireland	3.21
9	Canada[a]	3.70	39	Japan	3.19
10	Singapore	3.70	40	Israel	3.19
11	Colombia	3.67	41	Taiwan	3.18
12	England	3.67	42	El Salvador	3.16
13	Portugal	3.66	43	Germany[e]	3.10
14	South Africa[b]	3.66	44	Austria	3.09
15	Philippines	3.64	45	Ecuador	3.07
16	France	3.64	46	Germany[f]	3.06
17	Mexico	3.64	47	China	3.05
19	Venezuela	3.62	49	Guatemala	3.02
20	Costa Rica	3.56	50	Nigeria	3.01
21	Georgia	3.55	51	Spain	3.01
22	Bolivia	3.55	52	Iran	2.99
23	Malaysia	3.51	53	Switzerland	2.97
24	Netherlands	3.50	54	India	2.90
25	Argentina	3.49	55	Turkey	2.89
26	Greece	3.48	56	Zambia	2.86
27	Hong Kong	3.47	57	Morocco	2.84
28	Switzerland[c]	3.42	58	Egypt	2.81
29	Australia	3.40	59	Kuwait	2.58
30	Finland	3.35	60	South Korea	2.50

Source: House et al. (2004).

* Higher scores indicate greater assertiveness. *Lower scores indicate greater male domination.

[a] Germany (East): Former GDR; [b] South Africa (White sample) [a] Canada (English-speaking); [b] South Africa (Black sample);

[c] Germany (West): Former FRG; [d] South Africa (Black sample); [c] Switzerland (French-speaking); [d] South Africa (White sample);

[e] Canada (English-speaking); [f] Switzerland (French-speaking) [e] Germany (West): Former FRG; [f] Germany (East): Former GDR

However, when the other monkey completed the task, s/he was given a large grape as the food reward. When the task was repeated, the monkey which received the slice of cucumber, threw the cucumber at the researcher as a sign of protest to inequality (Brosnan and de Waal, 2003).

On the other hand, assertiveness can be best predicted by self-motivation. In terms of the personality characteristics masculinity is predicted strongly as extraversion, conscientiousness, and, to a lesser degree, on agreeableness, and femininity was predicted strongly on agreeableness (Zheng and Zheng, 2011). As mentioned in the Introduction section, values such as equality, concern for the quality of life (i.e., people work to live rather than live to work), and helping weaker ones in the society appear to be dominant values in feminine cultures.

Exercise

Visit the web pages https://www.onlinepersonalitytests.org/disc/ and https://openpsychometrics.org/tests/ODAT/ and carry out the online personality tests (DISC – Dominance Influence Conscientiosuness Steadiness and The Big Five Personality Test) to understand yourself better.

Do you think the results of the tests describe you well? Discuss how your personality characteristics may influence your attitudes and behaviour as a) a tourism and hospitality customer, b) a tourism and hospitality employee or a manager. To which of the characteristics of cultural dimensions do your personality characteristics relate to?

However, a focus on achievements and success, competition (i.e., people live to work rather than work to live) tend to be the dominant values in masculine cultures. In masculine societies, higher managerial positions are usually occupied by men, with the belief that they are stronger and less susceptible to being influenced by emotions (Minkov and Hofstede, 2011). As a masculine society, in Japan only about 10% of top management positions and politicians and 3% of ambassadors are women (Lida, 2018).

Exercise

Study Tables 8.1 and 8.3. Determine whether your country is a masculine or a feminine one. In addition, find colleagues who are from the opposite cultural orientation. Based on you and your colleagues' experience, discuss the extent to which the above-explained characteristics represent your culture. From a dyadic perspective (organisational behaviour and human resource management – marketing and consumer behaviour), what would be the advantages and disadvantages, and implications of your cultural characteristics in managing tourism and hospitality businesses? When considering the implications, think about the likely influences on the marketing mix elements (7Ps) and the service quality (SERVQUAL) dimensions.

The Masculine and Feminine Self-Disclosure Scale (MFSDS)

Instructions: You are given a list of 42 topics below. This survey is concerned with the extent to which you would be willing to discuss these topics with different people. For each item, you will notice four columns. These columns represent the following people: (AA) a male friend, (BB) a female friend, (CC), a male clinician, and (DD) a female clinician. For these columns, you are to indicate how willing you would be to discuss each specific topic with each of the four specified persons. (0 meaning not at all willing to discuss this topic with and 4 meaning totally willing to discuss this topic with).

Item	*Statements*	*Scores (0) Not at all (4) Totally*			
		(AA)	*(BB)*	*(CC)*	*(DD)*
1	How self-sufficient you believe you are.				
2	How often you tell people you really like their friendship.				
3	The extent to which you speak up when you want something.				
4	How frequently you give up on tasks before actually completing them.				
5	How warm a person you believe you are.				
6	How autonomous you believe you are.				
7	How thoughtful you believe you are.				
8	How competitive you believe you are.				
9	How frequently you volunteer your time to "benefit" activities.				
10	How often you stop to help others pick up things they have dropped.				
11	How strongly you usually defend your own opinions.				
12	How kind you believe you are.				
13	How often you call up old friends just to see how they are.				
14	How gentle you believe you are.				

Item	*Statements*	*Scores* *(0) Not at all* *(4) Totally*			
15	How often you kiss or hug your family members.				
16	How forceful you believe you are				
17	How sympathetic you believe you are.				
18	How often you play to win in sports and other games.				
19	How often you put things off to do at a later time.				
20	How frequently you help others who are moving to a new location.				
21	How independent you believe you are.				
22	How often you change your mind when making a decision.				
23	The extent to which you usually direct a group's activity.				
24	How understanding of others you believe you are.				
25	How assertive you believe you are.				
26	How competitive you believe you are.				
27	How often you organise group projects.				
28	How concerned for others you believe you are.				
29	How often you hold hands with someone.				
30	How self-reliant you believe you are.				
31	How often you invite others over just to talk.				
32	How persistent you believe you are.				
33	How considerate of others you believe you are.				
34	The extent to which you work on tasks where you alone are responsible.				
35	How efficient you believe you are.				
36	How often you spend time with children.				
37	How tender you believe you are.				
38	How frequently you visit your relatives.				
39	How sensitive you believe you are.				
40	The extent to which you are typically the first to talk in a discussion group.				
41	How masculine you are.				
42	How feminine you are.				

Scoring: The Masculine and Feminine Self-Disclosure Scale (MFSDS) consists of six subscales for each disclosure recipient that is specified.

The labels and items for each of these six subscales are listed below. The other items on the MFSDS are treated as "filler" items.

1. Masculine Trait Scale (Items 1, 6, 21, 25, 30, 32, 35).
2. Masculine Behavior Scale (Items 3, 11, 22, 23, 27, 34, 40).
3. Feminine Trait Scale (Items 5, 12, 14, 17, 24, 33, 37).
4. Feminine Behavior Scale (Items 2, 10, 13, 15, 29, 31, 38).
5. "Global" Masculinity Scale (Item 41).
6. "Global" Femininity Scale (Item 42).

Source: Snell (2013).

The influence of masculinity and femininity, gender egalitarianism, and assertiveness on tourism and hospitality

Based on the characteristics explained earlier, masculinity and femininity may have significant implications for tourism and hospitality marketing and management. For instance, masculinity or femininity may influence the corporate social responsibility (CSR) of businesses. Kang et al. (2016) investigated the influence of national culture on positive and negative CSR in the hospitality industry with 365 observations between the years 1993 and 2011. Their research showed that masculinity had a negative and significant influence on positive CSR. This may be attributed to the fact that a business in a highly masculine culture tends to concentrate on its material gain and economic success, and hence it is less likely to perform socially responsible activities (i.e., positive CSR) that enhance quality of life in a society as a whole.

CSR appears to have a positive influence on customer satisfaction (Abbasi et al., 2016), repurchase intentions (Abbasi et al., 2016; Karimi et al., 2020), employee satisfaction (Sedlak, 1975; Carlini, 2015), organisational attachment, and organisational citizenship behaviours of employees (Carlini, 2015). Kim et al. (2018) found that organisational citizenship behaviours of employees were very much influenced by their cultural orientations. Kim et al (2018) recommended that in order to ensure the recruitment of tourism and hospitality staff with high levels of organisational citizenship behaviours, these businesses should target employees who are from cultures with a high power distance, low avoidance, low assertiveness, and high gender egalitarianism.

The implications of masculinity and femininity are explained in the following section under the headings of marketing mix elements, service quality, service quality dimensions, and manager–subordinate relationships, service failures and recovery, and loyalty.

Marketing mix elements

As masculinity and femininity orientations of people influence their values, preferences, attitudes, and behaviour, marketing mix elements targeted at masculine and feminine cultures need to demonstrate differences. Albers-Miller and Gelb (1996) developed advertising appeals relating to masculinity and femininity as shown in the following exercise.

Exercise

According to Albers-Miller and Gelb (1996) the advertising appeals which relate to a) masculinity are effective, convenient, and productivity and b) femininity are natural, frail, and modest (see the following table).

Orientation	*Appeal*	*Description*
Masculinity	Effective	Tasty (food), comfort, pragmatic, functional
	Convenient	Handy, quick, time-saving, accessible
	Productivity	Accomplishment, ambition, success, careers, being skilled, references to achievement, self-development, proficient
Femininity	Natural	References to the elements, vegetables, minerals, farming, organic, nutritious, purity of products
	Frail	Delicate, frail, dainty, sensitive, tender, susceptible, vulnerable, soft, genteel
	Modest	Naïve, innocent, reserved, shy, timid, coy, virtuous, pure, demure

Task

Each of the above appeals may have important implications, not only for advertising (as a promotional element) but also for all of the other marketing mix elements of tourism and hospitality establishments. Prepare a marketing mix (7Ps) table for a tourism or hospitality business and write down for each marketing mix element things to do and not to do.

In relation to restaurant services, Bhattacharyya and Borhart (2018) argue that masculine and feminine customers have different expectations when they dine. For instance, in terms of the people element of the marketing mix, masculine customers expect differentiated gender roles (for servers, ushers and cooks).

On the other hand, in terms of the product and process elements, masculine customers expect performance (quality of food, timely attendance, and delivery of food, etc.), and independence while dining. In contrast, customers from a feminine culture tend to value fluid gender roles (duality of service – providing equal rights to both males and females), quality of experience (ambiance, greeting, treating customers with a smile and respect, taking care of special needs), and interdependence. For the above reasons, Bhattacharyya and Borhart argue that franchised restaurants would be more suitable for customers from masculine cultures, while non-franchised restaurants would be more suitable for customers from feminine cultures. The franchised restaurants would have a) set personal responsibilities and b) a focus on time and achievement which may match masculine characteristics. In contrast, non-franchised restaurants would have a) shared responsibilities (e.g., among wait staff), and b) a focus on being empathetic and responsive which may match feminine characteristics.

In terms of the people element in the marketing mix, Bhattacharyya and Borhart state that in the United States employees tend to be competitive and assertive, while in Russia (a relatively feminine culture) employees tend to be rather passive. The passive roles in the Russian service industries require feminine traits of empathy and personalised care as people tend to focus on positive reinforcement and create relationships with others. People tend to place a higher value on services that provide a warm, friendly, and caring environment.

Pizam and Fleischer (2005) found that masculinity and femininity influenced the tourism product/service choices of tourists. According to Pizam and Fleischer, tourists from masculine countries (e.g., Ireland, Germany, Italy, United States, and South Africa) tended to prefer more dynamic and active tourist products, or activities than tourists who are from feminine countries (e.g., South Korea, Gabon, and Spain). Hence, a destination that wants to market its dynamic/active tourism products (e.g., hunting, fishing, rafting, sailing, and wilderness hiking) should promote these products to masculine and/or individualistic cultures (i.e., the United States, South Africa, and Ireland) as young people living in these cultures are among the most "active"-oriented individuals. These holiday products/activities appear to be the "proper" type of activities for highly successful, dominant, and assertive individuals. It is believed that future research may be carried out by using the VALS (Values, Attitudes, and Lifestyles) framework to shed more light onto the preferences of these customers. The VALS model is a psychographic consumer segmentation system owned by Strategic Business Insights, which segments customers into eight distinct groups of innovators, thinkers, achievers, experiencers, believers, strivers, makers, and survivors (Koc, 2016).

On the other hand, young adults who are from feminine cultures are more likely to prefer tourism products or activities that are softer, gentler, and people and culture oriented. It is believed that their feminine orientations explain why they prefer low energy and static holiday products, or activities such as visiting friends and relatives, shopping, attending cultural and arts festivals, going to the opera, ballet, and theatre, etc.

Studying gender differences in information processing of tourists, Koc (2002) found that women, due to their communal orientation collected and analysed more information (both cognitive and affective information), whilst men, due to their argentic orientation used and analysed very limited information (mainly cognitive information). Also due to their communal orientation, women tended to be more knowledgeable about the likes, dislikes, and preferences of all family members. In contrast, males tended to use shortcuts and heuristics in their decision-making such as credibility and attractiveness of the message or the sender. The research showed that a dummy travel agency with marketing communication messages adjusted to information processing styles of men and women was preferred more than the two of the most famous travel agencies.

Boz's (2015) research which used neuromarketing tools of EEG, eye tracker, and Galvanic skin response confirmed the above results. The study, which compared the results of a traditional survey with the results of neuromarketing research, reached interesting conclusions. In both stages of the study, participants were asked to choose a family holiday and to indicate the important features of a family holiday for them. The male participants (as husbands and fathers) indicated in the survey, that is, were self-aware, self-controlled, and engaged in impression management stated things such as availability of a swimming pool for children, appropriate entertainment for children, and so on. However, in the EEG and eye tracker study, the results showed that the same male participants focused on holidays that had attractive and sexy women images, that is, without any reference to the needs of children and the family as a whole. Koc and Boz's (2014a, 2014b) studies showed the need for triangulation (collection of data by using multiple methods) and the use of neuromarketing tools in tourism and hospitality research to ensure that research results reflected the truth (Boz et al., 2017).

CASE STUDY

How men and women see and perceive differently

Men's argentic, achievement, and success orientation may be related to vision and their anthropological hunter characteristics. According to Pease and Pease (2001) and Moss (2014) men tend to have tunnel vision (long–narrow), which was helpful for chasing and hunting animals during the hunter-gatherer phase of evolution. Men's ability to see peripherally (i.e., the ability to see objects that are not in the centre of one's visual field) is not as powerful as women.

Women were unable to chase animals, a process that may have taken hours, or sometimes even days. As women were likely to be pregnant or had to feed their babies, they were unable to go hunting. Instead, they became gatherers and collected seeds, nuts, fruits, and other edible plants around their caves and where they lived. Thus, women tend to have a wider arc of peripheral vision, probably because of their gatherer and nest-defender roles.

As men fixate their vision on their prey, they may tend to shut out other perceptual receptors to avoid distraction. As previously explained, men tend to collect and use limited information, and use shortcuts and algorithms, called heuristics, in their decision making. Perhaps, males' tendency to collect, process, and analyse less information than females may be attributable to their hunter origins. On the other hand, females' tendency to collect, process, and analyse more information may be due to their gatherer origins.

Crotts and Erdman's (2000) research on the airport and air flight service perceptions showed that customers with highly masculine orientations provided more negative evaluations in all aspects of the service due to their assertiveness and tendency to make more critical evaluations. Owing to their communal and egalitarian orientations, customers from feminine cultures (or with low levels of masculinity) tend to be less assertive, be less critical, and provide more positive evaluations of the service.

In relation to Crotts and Erdman's (2000) research, Table 8.6 shows the measured aspects of the service and which marketing mix element they relate to. This means that the

Table 8.6 Airport and air flight services and their relationship to marketing mix elements

Airport Services	*Related Marketing Mix Element*	*Air Flight Services*	*Related Marketing Mix Element*
Airport access	Physical evidence	Convenient schedules	Process, Product
Ground transportation	Physical evidence, process	Ticket price	Price
Terminal convenience	Physical evidence	Reservation service	Product, Process
Cleanliness	Product, Physical evidence	Check-in waiting time	Product, Process
Concession goods	Product	Check-in personnel	People, Product, Physical evidence
Concession prices	Price	Departure time	Product, Process
Terminal seating	Physical evidence	Flight attendants	People, Product, Physical evidence
International facilities	Product, Physical Evidence	Food and beverage	Product, process
Security	Product, People	Cabin cleanliness	Product
		Cabin noise level	Product
		Cabin layout	Physical evidence, Product
		Seat comfort	Physical evidence, Product
		Carry on storage	Physical evidence

same marketing mix elements targeted at masculine cultures may produce less satisfaction and that the design and the implementation of marketing mix elements targeted at highly masculine cultures need additional efforts on the part of service managers.

Pizam and Fleischer (2005) showed that tourists from medium power- distance/high-masculinity countries (e.g., Japan and Italy) tended to rate both the airport and airline attributes more critically than tourists who are from small power-distance/low, medium, and high masculinity countries (e.g., the UK, Germany, Australia, United States, Denmark, Netherlands, Norway, and Sweden).

Kwok and Uncles (2005) investigated the influence of masculinity and femininity on customers' responses towards sales promotions. They found that customers from feminine cultures were more responsive towards non-monetary sales promotions as the benefits of non-monetary sales promotions are more relationship-oriented. In contrast, customers from masculine cultures were more responsive to monetary sales promotions. On the whole, sales promotions with female identity (e.g., collection of coupons) tended to be less effective on men, especially those with more congruency (i.e., the men who wanted to be perceived as masculine).

As explained earlier, gender role differences tend to be greater in masculine cultures. This greater difference also reflects itself in areas such as having double standards regarding sexual norms (Hofstede, 2001). For instance, while in feminine countries premarital sex is socially acceptable for men and women, and "girls may take the initiative" (Hofstede, 1998: 174), in masculine countries, many women tend to have sex later in the relationship and are not expected to be sexually active (Hofstede, 2001). In other words, while feminine cultures do not tend to show significant moralistic attitudes towards sexuality, masculine cultures tend to demonstrate moralistic attitudes towards sexuality (Hofstede, 2001). According to Hofstede (1998), despite the sexual revolution, masculine cultures continue to show a stronger taboo on addressing sexual issues openly than people do in feminine cultures. According to Nelson and Paek (2005), such moralistic norms translate into what is appropriate, and not appropriate, and what to show and discuss in media. They found that masculinity was negatively related to sexuality and nudity presented in media. Based on these findings, it may be suggested that tourism and hospitality establishments targeting customers from masculine cultures need to make sure that the images they use in their advertisements and on their web pages do not demonstrate nudity and sexuality.

Masculinity and femininity may influence the place element (distribution channels) and promotion (marketing communications) (Park and Reisinger, 2012). DeMooij (2000) and Shiu and Dawson (2002) put forward that people from masculine societies tend to be involved in online activities (i.e., the use of the internet) more often for the purpose of work, while people from feminine cultures are more likely to use online activities for pleasure purposes. Based on this, tourism and hospitality businesses targeting customers from feminine cultures may put more emphasis on their online sources of information (as a distribution channel and promotion/marketing communications medium) as it may be easier to reach them in this way. Tourism and hospitality businesses targeting customers from masculine cultures may put more emphasis on other distribution channels and marketing communications medium. However, given the growth of the widespread use of the internet, the importance of online sources for customers from all cultural backgrounds is expected to increase.

Service quality, service quality dimensions, and manager–subordinate relationships

It was shown above that in masculine cultures (e.g., Japan) there are fewer women in high-status managerial positions. However, research shows that women's contribution to work has been significantly positive (Bart and McQueen, 2013). For instance, according to Joy et al.'s (2007) study management boards with female representation resulted in a 53% higher return on equity, a 66% higher return on invested capital, and a 42% higher return on sales. Additionally, having one female director on the management board tends to reduce the risk of bankruptcy by 20.2 % (Joy et al., 2007). Koc's (2020) study which analysed research findings from the disciplines of biology, anthropology, psychology, sociology, services marketing and management, and tourism and hospitality marketing and management showed that women tended to have superior characteristics across all service quality dimensions (tangibles, reliability, responsiveness, assurance, and empathy) (see Chapter 5 and Table 5.4). Women tourism and hospitality employees also appear to have a significantly higher intercultural sensitivity than their male counterparts (Yurur et al., 2020)

However, women's employment in tourism and hospitality is both vertically and horizontally segregated, and women tend to find employment in subordinated positions with a low level of income (Kogovsek and Kogovsek, 2015; Koc, 2020). In terms of vertical segregation, women frequently tend to hold lower levels of occupations with fewer opportunities to go higher up in the management hierarchy (Carvalho et al., 2018). On the other hand, in terms of horizontal segregation, women quite often have to work as receptionists, waitresses, room attendants, cleaners, travel agency salespersons (Remington and Kitterlin-Lynch, 2018). Tourism and hospitality may be seen as feminised industries in terms of the participation of women, but they are highly masculine since men and male values prevail in management positions. Costa et al. (2017) report that in tourism and hospitality women find it difficult to reconcile the professional life with personal life. Koc (2010) provides a comparison of male and female characteristics from organisational behaviour and teamwork perspectives (Table 8.7).

According to Cho (2001), tourism and hospitality customers from masculine cultures may consider objective service measures such as completeness of customer requests, and speed and accuracy (reliability) as important. On the other hand, customers from feminine cultures may view more subjective measures such as willingness to help customers in a friendly and honest manner (responsiveness and assurance), and concern for the problems of customers (empathy), as more important.

Table 8.7 Main differences between men and women at work

Males Tend to Engage in ...	*Research**	*Females Tend to Engage in ...*	*Research**
self-promotion or self-enhancement (the practice of boasting or emphasising one's best characteristics) more than women do	DuBrin, 1991; Lee et al., 1999; Strutton et al., 1995; Tannen, 1994; Meyers-Levy and Loken, 2015	more modesty (de-emphasising one's characteristics after a performance)	Heatherington et al., 1998; Jones and Wortman, 1973; Meyers-Levy and Loken, 2015
doing more favours for others (altruistic behaviours)	DuBrin, 1991; Higgins and Snyder, 1989; Strutton et al., 1995; Koc, 2002	opinion conformity (expressing opinions or behaviour similar to that of others), and flattery/compliments (praising others)	DuBrin, 1991; Eagley and Carli, 1981; Tannen, 1994; Koc, 2002; Meyers-Levy and Loken, 2015
more acclaiming or entitlement (taking responsibility for positive occurrences)	Lee et al., 1999; Meyers-Levy and Loken, 2015	less ingratiation than men do	Lee et al., 1999; Meyers-Levy and Loken, 2015

Source: Koc (2010).

* For more up-to-date references, see Meyers-Levy and Loken (2015) and Koc (2020).

As people from masculine cultures tend to be more assertive, they are more likely to provide assertive and critical evaluative responses to consumer satisfaction surveys and to evaluate tourism and hospitality services more negatively (Crotts and Erdmann, 2000). However, Crotts and Erdman's (2000) research showed that the proportion of female tourists from masculine cultures had a mitigating effect on negative and critical evaluations. In other words, women, even from masculine cultures, were not as critical and assertive as men in their evaluations of the main tangibles of the airport and air flight services.

Jansen-Verbeke's (1996) study of hotel managers showed that the level of masculinity influenced the frequency of meetings they have had with their subordinates and their relationships with them. As they are more assertive, managers with masculine orientation tended to have meetings less frequently. In addition, while managers with masculine orientation were more favourable (in terms of giving them more financial rewards) towards stronger subordinates, managers with feminine orientation were more favourable towards sensitive subordinates. The above findings appear to have implications for various human resource management activities (e.g., recruitment and selection, performance appraisal, and rewarding).

Moreover, based on the orientations of the managers, the focus on various service quality dimensions (e.g., reliability, responsiveness, empathy, and assurance) may vary in the tourism and hospitality business (Koc, 2006; Dimitriou, 2017). It may be expected that in tourism and hospitality businesses where the managers are more feminine oriented, there may be more emphasis on the empathy dimension of service quality, to be followed by responsiveness, assurance, and reliability. Bhattacharyya and Borhart (2018) put forward that masculinity had a negative influence on the empathy dimension in restaurants. On the other hand, in tourism and hospitality businesses where the managers are more masculine oriented, there may be more emphasis on the reliability dimension of service quality, to be followed by assurance, responsiveness, and empathy.

Based on the above explanations, when there is a mismatch between the cultural orientation of the manager and customer service quality gaps (especially Gap 1, and potentially, Gap 2 and 3) (see Chapter 1) problems may arise.

Masculinity and femininity may also influence staff training activities in tourism and hospitality businesses. Mitsis and Foley (2009) argue that as masculine people are goal-driven, they prefer a quick completion of training programmes and individual-centred training. In contrast, people who are feminine-oriented may view goals, knowledge, and experience as equally important and tend to prefer trainee-centred learning.

Service failures and service recovery

As it was explained previously, customers from feminine cultures were more responsive towards non-monetary sales promotions, whilst customers from masculine cultures were more responsive towards monetary sales promotions (Kwok and Uncles, 2005). Based on this finding, it may be expected that customers from masculine cultures may place greater significance on distributive justice (tangible outcomes, rewards) in the service recovery process, while customers from feminine cultures may place greater significance on procedural and interactional justice as they are more relationship-oriented (Baker, 2017).

Information zone

Testosterone, oestrogen and oxytocin and their relationship with masculinity and femininity

Testosterone, a steroid hormone produced primarily by the testes in men, is responsible for the development and maintenance of masculine features. The circulation of testosterone has been positively related to various social behaviours in males including dominance, status-seeking (Kemper, 1990; Mazur and Booth, 1998), economic risk-taking (Apicella et al., 2008), and competitiveness. Research also shows that there is a positive relationship between aggressiveness, violence, and crime (Dabbs et al., 1995; Chen et al., 2016; Hoskin, 2017; Anderson, 2019) and the testosterone hormone.

Kenrick and Griskkevicius (2013) also argue that the level of testosterone tends to be high in people who are decision makers in the finance sector, and gamblers in Las Vegas. According to Ellis et al. (2012) in countries where males get married and have children younger, men's level of testosterone decreases. As a result, their children appeared to have lived longer and were more like to stay away from criminal acts. Gettler et al.'s (2011) research shows that fatherhood reduces testosterone levels in males.

According to Kenrick and Griskkevicius (2013), the level of testosterone not only increases lust and libido but also rebellious and aggressive behaviours. The probability of young males' getting involved in crime is higher due to their higher levels of testosterone. It was seen that the injection of testosterone in people increased their lust and aggressiveness (Kenrick and Griskevicius, 2013).

A male primate's probability of mating with more female primates depends on his ability to compete and beat his rivals. Male-dominated primate groups are hierarchical, and aggression tends to be more prevalent than having social ties (Mlodinov, 2013). On the other hand, the basic strategy of females is to produce fewer offsprings so as to be able to feed and take good care of the infants. For this reason, females tend to establish good social skills not only with male primates but also with all others. According to Durante et al. (2011), in many countries during economic crises, while most women reduce their expenditure on necessities (food and drinks), they increase their spending on cosmetics.

In the city of Columbus (Georgia, United States) the average consumer debt is 2.7 times higher (a difference of $3,479 per customer) than in the nearby city of Macon in the same state. Griskevicius et al. (2012) suggest that this difference may be related to the ratio of single adult men to women in each city. While there are only 0.78 single men for every woman in Macon in Columbus, there are 1.18 single men for every woman. This means that in Columbus males tend to spend more on clothes, sports cars, etc. to be able to look attractive to women and to compete with other males (Buss et al., 1999; Sagarin, 2005; Griskevicius et al., 2012). In places where the ratio of men to women increases, males tend to decrease their savings as much as 42% and increase their credit card debts as much as 84% (Durante et al., 2011; Kenrick and Griskevicius, 2013).

On the other hand, estrogens are a group of sex hormones that promote the development and maintenance of female characteristics (e.g., sexual reproductivity) in the human body. In contrast to testosterone, estrogens increase social behaviour, caring, and empathy, while reducing aggressiveness, risk-taking, and competitiveness (Bos et al., 2012; Riedl and Javor, 2012; Carré and Olmstead, 2015).

Oxytocin and vasopressin hormones, segregated by women, increase trust, approach behaviour, affection, care, attachment, bondage, and fidelity in all human beings (Zak et al., 2005; Kosfeld et al., 2005; Mikolajczak et al., 2010). According to Kosfeld et al. (2005) and Dondaldson and Young (2008), field rats with high levels of oxytocin tend to be monogamous, that is, tend to have high fidelity. Oxytocin increases fidelity towards the spouse and the bondage between the mother and child. Ewes (female sheep) in general tend to behave harshly towards lambs. However, when a ewe has a lamb (i.e., when the segregation of oxytocin increases), they become tender mothers (Insel and Young, 2001). Kosfeld et al.'s (2005) study tested trusting and betrayal behaviours of people in an investment game. While one group received a single dose of intranasal oxytocin, the control group received a placebo. The findings of the research showed that the group members who had intranasal oxytocin remained loyal and did not show betrayal behaviours.

The level of oxytocin hormone can be increased by a) breastfeeding, b) sexual intercourse, c) eating chocolate, ice-cream, and relaxing food, d) being kind to people, e) hugging and kissing, f) having a massage, g) being with friends and being in safe environments, h) doing meditation, i) receiving an acupuncture session, and j) spending time with pets.

Hotel customers from highly masculine cultures tend to be more direct, which results in more complaints to the management and third parties (Crotts and Erdmann, 2002). On the other hand, hotel customers from feminine cultures are less likely to make complaints (Huang et al., 1996). As customers from feminine cultures would have more sympathy for the weak, their attribution of service failures (and the way they make complaints (if any)) may be influenced by their cultural orientation. In other words, they may be expected to be less critical and not make strong complaints. On the other hand, people from masculine cultures may be more likely to make stronger complaints due to their higher level of assertiveness. Yuksel et al. (2006) found that Turkish tourists (moderately feminine and collectivistic culture) may feel sad to voice their dissatisfaction through making a complaint, as they feel that making a complaint may harm the employee in some way. The sympathy for the weak in feminine societies (e.g., a customer's sympathy towards an employee, or a manager's or a fellow employee's sympathy towards another employee) may cause a lack of performance orientation as accepting lower standards may cause inefficiency and effectiveness. The toleration of incompetence appears to be one of the important signs of organisational decline (Lorange and Nelson, 1987; Pretorius and Le Roux, 2011).

Customer loyalty

In line with the assertiveness of people from masculine cultures, Crotts and Erdman's (2000) research on airport and air flight services found that tourists from masculine cultures did not appear to have strong loyalty and showed a much higher rate of defection (switching) behaviour. Likewise, Bathaee (2011) found that masculinity positively impacted variety-seeking. Hence, while tourism and hospitality customers from feminine cultures may tend to be more loyal, customers from masculine cultures may be more likely to switch service providers and brands.

This means that tourism and hospitality managers need to be aware that it is more difficult to please customers from masculine cultures, and additional measures need to be established so that they do not provide negative word of mouth communication, and do not switch to other service providers. Loyalty associated with femininity also influenced tourism and hospitality customers' complaint behaviours. Kim et al. (2014) found that first-time customers were more likely to voice their complaints, share their bad experiences with friends and family, and switch to other providers. On the other hand, highly loyal customers tend to reflect upon positive prior experiences or on the strong bond they have with the service provider (Rust et al., 1999).

Conclusion

This chapter explains the influence of masculinity and femininity dimension of culture, together with the related concepts of assertiveness and egalitarianism, on various aspects of tourism and hospitality marketing management. Masculinity, which is associated with assertiveness, makes both customers and employees tough and goal-oriented. On the other hand, femininity, which is associated with egalitarianism (gender egalitarianism), makes customers and employees more relationship-oriented. As explained in the chapter, these differences influence the value attributions of customers, employees, and managers.

Questions

1. How do masculinity and femininity influence customers' responses to monetary and non-monetary sales promotions?
2. What sort of holiday products, or activities may be preferred by tourists from masculine and feminine cultures?
3. What is the influence of masculinity and femininity on corporate social responsibility? What may be the implications of corporate social responsibility on customers and employees?
4. Which service quality dimensions may be more important for tourism and hospitality managers who are from masculine cultures? Why?
5. Which service quality dimensions may be more important for tourism and hospitality managers who are from feminine cultures? Why?
6. How do masculinity and femininity influence customers' responses to service failures and service recovery attempts?
7. Explain and discuss Socrates's (470–399 bce) quote "Once made equal to man, woman becomes his superior" from the perspective of masculinism, femininity, and gender egalitarianism.

Research questions/ideas to pursue for researchers

As explained in the chapter, customers from feminine cultures would have more sympathy for the weak, they may be less likely to make (strong) complaints. Based on this premise, the responses of tourism and hospitality customers from both masculine and feminine cultures towards the same failure scenarios may be investigated and compared. Additionally, their responses towards sales recovery attempts may also be investigated to see whether they place greater significance on the dimensions of justice (e.g., distributive, procedural, and interactional).

As a second research idea, the influence of Dutch directness on the truthfulness of data collected from the Dutch participants may be tested. The Netherlands (as a low power distance, low masculine and highly egalitarian culture) and a high power-distance, highly masculine, and assertive culture may be compared. Tourism and hospitality customers' responses from these two countries may be compared by using a traditional data collection method (e.g., a survey or an interview) together with neuromarketing tools. The study may show whether the size of the gap in terms of the responses of customers varies in these two countries.

Recommended further reading

Hofstede, G., Hofstede, G. J., and Minkov, M. (2010), Cultures and organizations: Software of the Mind (rev. and expanded 3rd ed.). New York: McGraw-Hill.

Hofstede, G. (2001). Maculinity/femininity. In G. Hofstede (Ed.), *Culture's consequences: Comparing values, behaviors, institutions, and organizations across nations* (2nd ed., pp. 279–350). Thousand Oaks, CA: Sage

Koc, E. (2019). Do women make better in tourism and hospitality? A conceptual review from a customer satisfaction and service quality perspective. *Journal of Quality Assurance in Hospitality and Tourism*, 1–28.

Neuliep, J. W. (2018). *Intercultural communication: A contextual approach* (7th ed.). Thousand Oaks, CA: Sage.

References

Abbasi, A., Mansouri, Z., and Mahmoud Shahi, S. H. (2016). The influence of corporate social responsibility on customers' satisfaction and purchase intention: The mediation effect of customers' satisfaction. *Journal of Business Management*, 8(4), 883–900.

Albers-Miller, N., and Gelb, B. (1996). Business advertising appeals as a mirror of cultural dimensions: A study of eleven countries. *Journal of Advertising*, 25, 57–70.

Alberti, R., and Emmons, M. (2017). *Your perfect right: Assertiveness and equality in your life and Relationships*. San Luis, Obispo, CA: Impact.

Anderson, G. (2019). *Biological influences on criminal behavior*. Boca Raton, FL: CRC Press.

Apicella, C. L., Dreber, A., Campbell, B., Gray, P. B., Hoffman, M., and Little, A. C. (2008). Testosterone and financial risk preferences. *Evol. Hum. Behav.*, 29, 384–390.

Baker, M. (2017). Service failures and recovery: Theories and models. In E. Koc (Ed.), *Service failures and recovery in tourism and hospitality* (pp. 27–41). Wallingford, Oxford: CABI.

Bart, C., and McQueen, G. (2013). Why women make better directors. *International Journal of Business Governance and Ethics*, 8(1), 93–99.

Bartosik-Purgat, M. (2014). Cultural traits of the future managers from generation Y–an example of young Europeans. *Journal of Intercultural Management*, 6(3), 37–55.

Bathaee, A. (2011). Culture affects consumer behavior: Theoretical reflections and an illustrative example with Germany and Iran (No. 02/2011). Wirtschaftswissenschaftliche Diskussionspapiere.

Bem, S. L. (1974). The Measurement of Psychological Androgyny. *Journal of Consulting and Clinical Psychology*, 81, 506–520.

Bhattacharyya, K., and Borhart, A. (2018). National Cultural Values on Service Quality: A Typology for Global Dining Experience in the 21st Century. *Journal of Service Science Research*, 10(1), 1–24.

Bos, P. A., Panksepp, J., Bluthé, R. M., and van Honk, J. (2012). Acute effects of steroid hormones and neuropeptides on human social–emotional behavior: A review of single administration studies. *Frontiers in Neuroendocrinology*, 33(1), 17–35.

Boz, H. (2015). *Turistik Ürün Satın Alma Karar Sürecinde İtkiselliğin Rolü: Psikonörobiyokimyasal Analiz* (Unpublished doctoral thesis). Balıkesir, Turkey: Balikesir University, Institute of Social Sciences.

Boz, H., Arslan, A., and Koc, E. (2017). Neuromarketing aspect of tourısm pricing psychology. *Tourism Management Perspectives*, 23, 119–128.

Breukel, E. (2020). z.d. Dutch Business Culture and Etiquette. http://www.intercultural.nl/Publications-Detail.aspx?GroupID7c9ece9c-8800-47c4–91e4–341b2a57895a=e772c8d0–319f-41a2-a932-adf3baa86dd1andItemID7c9ece9c8800–47c4–91e4–341b2a57895a=6b099954–9fd2–4dbb-8350-bf254601c55f (accessed 10 January 2020).

Brosnan, S.F., and de Waal, F.B.M. (2003). Capuchin monkeys reject unequalpay. *Nature*, 425, 297–299.

Bradberry, T., and Greaves, J. (2005). *The emotional intelligence quickbook*. New York: Simon & Schuster.

Bradberry, T. and Greaves, J. (2009). *Emotional intelligence 2.0*. California: Talent Smart.3

Buss, D. M., Shackelford, T. K., Kirkpatrick, L. A., Choe, J. C., Lim, H. K., Hasegawa, M., ... and Bennett, K. (1999). Jealousy and the nature of beliefs about infidelity: Tests of competing hypotheses about sex differences in the United States, Korea, and Japan. *Personal Relationships*, 6(1), 125–150.

Carlini, J. (2015). *The influence of corporate social responsibility on employees* (Doctoral dissertation). Griffith University.

Carré, J. M., and Olmstead, N. A. (2015). Social neuroendocrinology of human aggression: examining the role of competition-induced testosterone dynamics. *Neuroscience*, 286, 171–186.

Carvalho, I., Costa, C., Lykke, N., Torres, A., and Wahl, A. (2018). Women at the top of tourism organizations: Views from the glass roof. *Journal of Human Resources in Hospitality and Tourism*, 17(4), 397–422.

Chen, F. R., Gao, Y., Glenn, A. L., Niv, S., Portnoy, J., Schug, R., ... and Raine, A. (2016). Biosocial bases of antisocial and criminal behavior. In A. R. Piquero (Ed.), *The handbook of criminological theory* (pp. 355–379). Chichester: Wiley.

Cho, M. (2001). Japanese, US tourists: Hotel selections. *Hospitality Review*, 19(1), 5.

Costa, C., Bakas, F. E., Breda, Z., Durão, M., Carvalho, I., Caçador, S. (2017). Gender, flexibility and the "ideal tourism worker." *Anna. Tour. Res.*, 64, 64–75.

Crotts, J. C., and Erdmann, R. (2000). Does national culture influence consumers' evaluation of travel services? A test of Hofstede's model of cross-cultural differences. *Managing Service Quality: An International Journal*, 10(6), 410–419.

Cultural Atlas (2020) Inderct Communication. https://culturalatlas.sbs.com.au/turkish-culture/1859-communication#1859-communication (accessed 20 January 2020).

Dabbs Jr, J. M., Carr, T. S., Frady, R. L., and Riad, J. K. (1995). Testosterone, crime, and misbehavior among 692 male prison inmates. *Personality and Individual Differences*, 18(5), 627–633.

DeMooij. M. (2000). The future is predictable for intentional marketers: Converging incomes lead to diverging consumer behaviour. *International Marketing Review*, 17(2), 103–113.

Dimitriou, C. (2017). Understanding and dealing with service failures in tourism and hospitality. In E. Koc (Ed.), *Service failures and recovery in tourism and hospitality* (pp. 9–26). Wallingford, Oxford: CABI

Donaldson, Z. R., and Young, L. J. (2008). Oxytocin, vasopressin, and the neurogenetics of sociality. *Science*, 322(5903), 900–904.

DuBrin, A. J. (1991). Sex and gender differences in tactics of influence. *Psychological Reports*, 68, 635–646.

Durante, K. M., Griskevicius, V., Hill, S. E., Perilloux, C., and Li, N. P. (2011). Ovulation, female competition, and product choice: Hormonal influences on consumer behavior. *Journal of Consumer Research*, 37(6), 921–934.

Eagley, A., and Carli, L. (1981). Sex of researchers and sex typed communications as determinants of sex differences on influenceability: A meta-analysis of social influence studies. *Psychological Bulletin*, 90(1), 1–20.

Ellis, B. J., Del Giudice, M., Dishion, T. J., Figueredo, A. J., Gray, P., Griskevicius, V., ... and Wilson, D. S. (2012). The evolutionary basis of risky adolescent behavior: implications for science, policy, and practice. *Developmental Psychology*, 48(3), 598.

Gettler, L. T., McDade, T. W., Feranil, A. B., and Kuzawa, C. W. (2011). Longitudinal evidence that fatherhood decreases testosterone in human males. *Proceedings of the National Academy of Sciences*, 108(39), 16194–16199.

Griskevicius, V., Tybur, J. M., Ackerman, J. M., Delton, A. W., Robertson, T. E., and White, A. E. (2012). The financial consequences of too many men: Sex ratio effects on saving, borrowing, and spending. *Journal of Personality and Social Psychology*, 102(1), 69.

Heatherington, L., Burns, A. B., and Gustafson, T. B. (1998). When another stumbles: Gender and self-presentation to vulnerable others. *Sex Roles*, 38, 889–913.

Higgins, R. L., and Snyder, C. R. (1989). The business of excuses. In R. A. Giacalone and P. Rosenfeld (Eds.), *Impression management in the organization* (pp. 73–89). Hillsdale, NJ: Erlbaum.

Hofstede, G. (1998). *Masculinity and femininity: The taboo dimension of national cultures*. Thousand Oaks, CA: Sage.

Hofstede, G. (2001). Maculinity/femininity. In G. Hofstede (Ed.), *Culture's consequences: Comparing values, behaviors, institutions, and organizations across nations* (2nd ed., pp. 279–350). Thousand Oaks, CA: Sage

Hofstede, G. (2020). Cultural dimensions. https://www.hofstede-insights.com/product/compare-countries/ (accessed 20 January 2020).

Hofstede, G., Hofstede, G.J. and Minkov, M. (2010), Cultures and organizations: Software of the mind (rev. and expanded 3rd ed.). New York: McGraw-Hill.

Hoskin, A. W. (2017). Male sex hormones and criminal behavior: the predictive power of a two-factor model of organizational androgen exposure. *Personality and Individual Differences*, 108, 86–90.

House, R. J., Hanges P. J., Javidan M., Dorfman, P.W., Gupta, V. (2004) Culture, Leadership, and Organizations. The Globe Study of 62 Societies. Thousand Oaks, CA: Sage.

Huang, J. H., Huang, C. T., and Wu, S. (1996), National character and response to unsatisfactory hotel service. *International Journal of Hospitality Management*, 15(3), 229–243.

Independent. (2019). Finland's new prime minister backs four-day working week. Independent Newspaper. https://www.independent.co.uk/news/world/europe/finland-four-day-working-week-hours-prime-minister-sanna-marin-a9272476.html (accessed 12 January 2020).

Insel, T. R., and Young, L. J. (2001). The neurobiology of attachment. *Nature Reviews Neuroscience*, 2(2), 129–136.

Jansen-Verbeke, M. (1996). Cross-cultural differences in the practices of hotel managers: a study of Dutch and Belgian hotel managers. *Tourism Management*, 17(7), 544–548.

Jones, E. E., and Wortman, C. (1973). *Ingratiation: An attributional approach*. Morristown, NJ: General Learning Press.

Joy, L., Carter, N. M., Wagener, H. M., and Narayanan, S. (2007). The Bottom Line: Corporate Performance and Women's Representation on Boards, Catalyst Research Report, 15 October. http://www.catalyst.org/knowledge/bottom-line-corporate-performance-and-womensrepresentation-boards

Kang, K.H., Lee, S., and Yoo, C. (2016). The effect of national culture on corporate social responsibility in the hospitality and tourism industry. *International Journal of Contemporary Hospitality Management*, 28(8), 1728–1758.

Karimi Sarame, Z., Esmaeilpour, R., and Mobasher Amini, R. (2020). Investigating the effect of green wash in corporate social responsibility on purchasing intention for green products: The mediating effects of green satisfaction and green perceived risk. *Journal of Business Management*, 11(4), 850–868.

Kemper, T. D. (1990). *Social structure and testosterone*. London: Rutgers University Press.

Kenrick, D. T., and Griskevicius, V. (2013). *The rational animal: How evolution made us smarter than we think*. New York: Basic Books.

Kim, M. G., Lee, C. H., and Mattila, A. S. (2014). Determinants of customer complaint behavior in a restaurant context: The role of culture, price level, and customer loyalty. *Journal of Hospitality Marketing and Management*, 23(8), 885–906.

Kim, S. H., Kim, M. S., Holland, S., and Han, H. S. (2018). Hospitality employees' citizenship behavior: the moderating role of cultural values. *International Journal of Contemporary Hospitality Management*, 30(2), 662–684.

Koc, E. (2002). The impact of gender in marketing communications: The role of cognitive and affective cues. *Journal of Marketing Communications*, 8(4), 257–275.

Koc, E. (2006). Total quality management and business excellence in services: The implications of all-inclusive pricing system on internal and external customer satisfaction in the Turkish tourism market. *Total Quality Management and Business Excellence*, 17(7), 857–877.

Koc, E. (2010). Services and conflict management: Cultural and European integration perspectives. *International Journal of Intercultural Relations*, 34(1), 88–96.

Koc, E. (2013). Power distance and its implications for upward communication and empowerment: Crisis management and recovery in hospitality services. *The International Journal of Human Resource Management*, 24(19), 3681–3696.

Koc, E. (2016). *Tüketici Davranışı ve Pazarlama Stratejileri: Global ve Yerel Yaklaşım (Vol. 7).* Ankara, Turkey: Baskı, Seçkin Yayınları.

Koc, E. (2019). *Emotional intelligence in tourism and hospitality.* Wallingford, Oxford: CABI.

Koc, E. (2020). Do women make better in tourism and hospitality? a conceptual review from a customer satisfaction and service quality perspective. *Journal of Quality Assurance in Hospitality and Tourism*, 1–28.

Koc, E., and Boz, H. (2014a). Triangulation in tourism research: A bibliometric study of top three tourism journals. *Tourism Management Perspectives*, 12, 9–14.

Koc, E., and Boz, H. (2014b). Psychoneurobiochemistry of tourism marketing. *Tourism Management*, 44, 140–148.

Koc, E., and Boz, H. (2020). Development of hospitality and tourism employees' emotional intelligence through developing their emotion recognition abilities. Journal of Hospitality *Marketing and Management*. Article in Press.

Kogovsek, M., and Kogovsek, M. (2015). Hospitality and tourism gender issues remain unsolved: A call for research. *Quaestus*, 6, 194–203.

Kosfeld, M., Heinrichs, M., Zak, P. J., Fischbacher, U., and Fehr, E. (2005) Oxytocin increases trust in humans. *Nature*, 435, 673–676.

Kwok, S., and Uncles, M. (2005). Sales promotion effectiveness: the impact of consumer differences at an ethnic-group level. *Journal of Product and Brand Management*, 14(3), 170–186.

Lee, S., Quigley, B., Nesler, M., Corbett, A., and Tedeschi, J. (1999). Development of a self-presentation tactics scale. *Personality and Individual Differences*, 26, 701–722.

Lida, A. (2018). Gender inequality in Japan: The status of women, and their promotion in the workplace. *Corvinus Journal of International Affairs*, 3(3), 43–52.

Lorange. P., and Nelson, R. (1987). How to recognize- and avoid- organizational decline. *Sloan Management Review*, 28, 41–48.

Mazur, A., and Booth, A. (1998). Testosterone and dominance in men. *Behavioral and Brain Sciences*, 21, 353–63.

Meyers-Levy, J., and Loken, B. (2015). Revisiting gender differences: What we know and what lies ahead. *Journal of Consumer Psychology*, 25(1), 129–149.

Mikolajczak, M., Gross J. J., Lane A., Corneille O., de Timary P., and Luminet O. (2010) Oxytocin makes people trusting, not gullible. *Psychol. Sci.*, 8, 1072–1074

Minkov, M., and Hofstede, G. (2011). The evolution of Hofstede's doctrine. *Cross-Cultural Management: An International Journal*, 18(1), 10–20.

Mitsis, A., and Foley, P. W. (2009). Do business students' culturally anchored values shape student-driven or teacher-driven learning style preferences?. *Journal of Marketing Education*, 31(3), 240–252.

Mlodinow, L. (2013). *Subliminal: How your unconscious mind rules your behavior.* London: Random House LLC

Moss, G. (2014). Why men like straight lines and women like polka dots: Gender and visual psychology. John Hunt Publishing.

Nelson, M. R., and Paek, H. J. (2005). Cross-cultural differences in sexual advertising content in a transnational women's magazine. *Sex Roles*, 53(5–6), 371–383.

Neuliep, J. W. (2018). *Intercultural communication: A contextual approach* (7th ed.). Thousand Oaks, CA: Sage.

Nikolić, M. (2014). The relationship between globe organizational culture values and the emotional intelligence of employees in Serbian organizations. *Primenjena psihologija*, 7(2), 137–156.

OECD (2015). Income equality. https://data.oecd.org/inequality/income-inequality.htm (accessed 5 January 2020).

Park, S., and Reisinger, Y. (2012). Cultural differences in tourism web communication: A preliminary study. *Tourism Analysis*, 17(6), 761–774.

Pease, A., and Pease, B. (2001) *Why men don't listen and women can't read maps: How were different and what to do about it*. New York: Broadway.

Pizam, A., and Fleischer, A. (2005). The relationship between cultural characteristics and preference for active vs. passive tourist activities. *Journal of Hospitality and Leisure Marketing*, 12(4), 5–25.

Pretorius, M., and Le Roux, I. (2011). Successive failure, repeat entrepreneurship and no learning: A case study. *SA Journal of Human Resource Management*, 9(1), 1–13.

Prewitt-Freilino, J. L., Caswell, A. T., and Laakso, E. K. (2012). The gendering of language: A comparison of gender equality in countries with gendered, natural gender, and genderless languages. *Sex Roles*, 66, 268–281.

Reisinger, Y., and Mavondo, F. (2006). Cultural consequences on traveler risk perception and safety. *Tourism Analysis*, 11(4), 265–284.

Remington, J., and Kitterlin-Lynch, M. (2018). Still pounding on the glass ceiling: A study of female leaders in hospitality, travel, and tourism management. *Journal of Human Resources in Hospitality and Tourism*, 17(1), 22–37.

Riedl, R., and Javor, A. (2012). The biology of trust: Integrating evidence from genetics, endocrinology, and functional brain imaging. *Journal of Neuroscience, Psychology, and Economics*, 5(2), 63.

Rust, R. T., Inman, J. J., Jia, J., and Zahorik, A. (1999). What you don't know about customer-perceived quality: The role of customer expectation distributions. *Marketing Science*, 18(1), 77–92.

Sagarin, B. J. (2005). Reconsidering evolved sex differences in jealousy: Comment on Harris (2003). *Personality and Social Psychology Review*, 9(1), 62–75.

Sedlak, P. (1975). The influence of Corporate Social Responsibility on Employees' Job Satisfaction. *Management Science in Transition Period in Moldova and Poland*, 28, 57.

Shiu, E., and Dawson, J. (2002). Cross-national consumer segmentation of Internet shopping for Britain and Taiwan. *The Service Industries Journal*, 22(1), 147–166.

Snell, W. E., Jr. (2013). The Masculine and Feminine Self-Disclosure Scale (MFSDS). Measurement instrument database for the social sciences. www.midss.ie.

Strutton, D., Pelton, L. E., and Lumpkin, J. R. (1995). Psychological climate in franchising system channels and franchisor–franchisee solidarity. *Journal of Business Research*, 34, 81–91.

Tannen, D. (1994). *Talking from 9 to 5: Women and men at work*. New York: Quill.

van der Horst, H. (2001). *The low sky. Understanding the Dutch*. Schiedam: Scriptum.

Yukl, G. A. (2010). *Leadership in organization* (7th ed.). Upper Saddle River, NJ: Prentice Hall.

Yuksel, A., Kilinc, U.K. and Yuksel, F. (2006). Cross-national analysis of hotel customers' attitudes toward complaining and their complaining behaviors. *Tourism Management*, 27(1), 11–24.

Yurur, S., Koc, E., Taskin, C., and Boz, H. (2020). Factors influencing intercultural sensitivity of hospitality employees. *International Journal of Hospitality and Tourism Administration*, Article in Press.

Zak, P. J., Kurzban, R., and Matzner, W. T. (2005) Oxytocin is associated with human trustworthiness. *Hormones and Behavior*, 48, 522–527.

Zheng, L., and Zheng, Y. (2011). The relationship of masculinity and femininity to the Big Five personality dimensions among a Chinese sample. *Social Behavior and Personality: An International Journal*, 39(4), 445–450.

Chapter 9

The influence of individualism and collectivism on tourism and hospitality

Learning Objectives

After reading this chapter, you should be able to:

- understand the main characteristics of individualism and collectivism as a cultural dimension;
- explain how individualism and collectivism may influence the behaviour of people as customers, employees, and managers in tourism and hospitality;
- understand the main influential factors which determine whether a society is individualistic or collectivistic;
- understand the influence of individualism and collectivism on the design of marketing mix elements;
- explain how individualism and collectivism may influence the emphasis on tourism and hospitality customers place on service quality dimensions;
- understand the influence of individualism and collectivism dimension on service failures and service recovery perceptions of customers.

Introduction

This chapter explains and discusses the influence of individualism and collectivism on tourism and hospitality marketing and management. Research shows that individualism and collectivism is one of the most widely studied dimensions in business and management (Kirkman et al., 2006), consumer services (Sharma et al., 2012), and in tourism and hospitality (Magnini et al., 2013; Gi Park et al., 2014; Koc, 2019).

In basic terms individualism deals with a) the subordination of the collective goals in exchange for individual goals, b) a sense of independence, and c) lack of concern for others (Hui and Triandis, 1986). Later, Triandis (1993) and Triandis et al. (1995) used the following four groups of attributes to explain the main characteristics of individualism and individualists:

1. Individualistic people are loosely linked individuals who view themselves as independent of groups. Their self and identity are defined almost entirely based on individual terms. They tend to have a high level of internal control and there is a congruence between the private self and public self.
2. Individualistic people tend to be mainly motivated by their own preferences, needs, rights, and the contracts they have established with other people.
3. Individualistic people emphasise rational analyses of the advantages and disadvantages of associating with others, rather than the emotional analyses.
4. The personal goals have precedence over their in-group goals. They are emotionally detached from their in-groups. They may be more ready to confront in-group members when they are in disagreement.

Therefore, in basic terms, individualism and collectivism, referred to as individualism and communitarianism by Trompenaars and Hampden-Turner (1998), are about the strength of the ties that people have with others within their community (Hofstede et al., 2010). Individualism can be defined as the extent to which members of a society show strong concern for personal goals, personal identity, and personal freedom over those of the group (Gudykunst and Lee, 2003). On the other hand, collectivism is the extent to which members of a society show stronger concern for group well-being, group identity, group norms, and group accomplishments over those of the self (Gudykunst and Lee, 2003).

Individualism is a characteristic tendency of industrialised and post-industrialised societies. All societies tend to develop similar characteristics during their modernisation process. The characteristics of modern societies outlined by Yang (1988) tend to be rather similar to the characteristics of individualised societies:

- the sense of personal efficacy (anti-fatalism)
- egalitarian attitude towards others
- belief in sexual equality
- independence or self-reliance
- tolerance of, and respect for, others
- empathetic capacity
- high need for information
- secularization in religious belief
- high educational and occupational aspirations
- low social integration with relatives
- openness to innovation and change
- high achievement motivation
- active participation in social organisations
- cognitive and behavioural flexibility
- future organisation
- the propensity to take risks in life
- preference for urban life

As individualism and collectivism influence the way people interact with others, the beliefs, attitudes, and behaviours of tourism and hospitality customers, employees, and managers may be significantly influenced by their individualistic or collectivistic orientation. However, the main characteristics of individualistic and collectivistic cultures need to be explained first.

The concept of individualism and collectivism

According to Hofstede (1980), people in individualistic cultures are independent of one another and take care of themselves or their immediate family. On the other hand, in collectivist cultures, people are strongly integrated and mutually bonded in the ways in which they belong to one or more close in-groups (Hofstede, 1980; Han et al., 2017). Table 9.1 shows the individualism and collectivism (IDV) scores for 72 selected countries in the world. A lower score indicates the lack of individualism (i.e., the existence of collectivism) in a given country, while a higher score indicates a lack of collectivism (i.e., the existence of individualism). According to Table 9.1 countries such as the United States, Australia, United Kingdom, Netherlands, New Zealand, Italy, Belgium, Denmark, Sweden, France, Switzerland, Germany, and Finland appear to be individualistic, while countries such as Guatemala, Ecuador, Venezuela, Indonesia, Pakistan, South Korea, Bangladesh, China, Nigeria, Thailand, Malaysia, and Kenya appear to be collectivistic.

In individualistic cultures, people take less responsibility for others' actions and outcomes, while in a collectivistic culture people take responsibility for another's actions and well-being. In a collectivistic culture, people are expected to be loyal to the group they belong to, in exchange for the protection of her/his interests by the group (Hofstede et al., 2010). Table 9.2 provides a summary of the main characteristics of individualistic and collectivistic societies.

Information zone

The common use of "we" instead of "I" in Turkey

Although the collectivistic orientation may be seen to weaken in Turkey, due to the increasing level of affluence, and metropolitan lifestyle, many collectivistic characteristics still seem to prevail. The common use of "we" form instead of "I" communication is one of these characteristics. For instance, when universities put up announcements for students, the widespread use of "we" can be detected. Although the students may need to be addressed as individuals (for instance, paying fees – each student pays her/his own fees individually – that is, it is not a collective activity), they are still addressed in the plural form (e.g., Dear Students).

Likewise, a university professor in Turkey, when explaining her/his research to a group of scholars or postgraduate students, generally uses the "we" form, although the whole research may have been carried by himself or herself. This is because using the "I" form may be perceived as arrogant and conceited.

Individualistic cultures place a high value on people's time, their need for privacy and freedom. People do not tend to mix work life with private life and expressions of people's own ideas and debates are encouraged. People in individualistic cultures enjoy challenges and expect individual rewards for their hard work. However, in collectivistic cultures, people tend to work more for intrinsic rewards (such as the feeling of belongingness, safety) and emphasise building skills and becoming a master of something.

Table 9.1 Individualism scores selected countries in the world

Rank	*Country*	*Individualism*	*Rank*	*Country*	*Individualism*	*Rank*	*Country*	*Individualism*
1	Guatemala	**6**	25	Tanzania	**27**	49	Spain	**51**
2	Ecuador	**8**	26	Zambia	**27**	50	Israel	**54**
3	Panama	**11**	27	Portugal	**27**	51	Hungary	**55**
4	Venezuela	**12**	28	Romania	**30**	52	Austria	**55**
5	Colombia	**13**	29	Mexico	**30**	53	Czechia	**58**
6	Indonesia	**14**	30	Philippines	**32**	54	Estonia	**60**
7	Pakistan	**14**	31	Croatia	**33**	55	Poland	**60**
8	Costa Rica	**15**	32	Greece	**35**	56	Finland	**63**
9	Peru	**16**	33	Uruguay	**36**	57	South Africa	**65**
10	Taiwan	**17**	34	Turkey	**37**	58	Germany	**67**
11	South Korea	**18**	35	Egypt	**38**	59	Switzerland	**68**
12	El Salvador	**19**	36	Iraq	**38**	60	Norway	**69**
13	Bangladesh	**20**	37	Kuwait	**38**	61	Ireland	**70**
14	China	**20**	38	Lebanon	**38**	62	Latvia	**70**
15	Ghana	**20**	39	Libya	**38**	63	France	**71**
16	Nigeria	**20**	40	Saudi Arabia	**38**	64	Sweden	**71**
17	Sierra Leone	**20**	41	United Arab Emirates	**38**	65	Denmark	**74**
18	Singapore	**20**	42	Brazil	**38**	66	Belgium	**75**
19	Thailand	**20**	43	Russia	**39**	67	Italy	**76**
20	Chile	**23**	44	Jamaica	**39**	68	New Zealand	**79**
21	Hong Kong	**25**	45	Iran	**41**	69	Netherlands	**80**
22	Malaysia	**26**	46	Japan	**46**	70	United Kingdom	**89**
23	Ethiopia	**27**	47	Argentina	**46**	71	Australia	**90**
24	Kenya	**27**	48	India	**48**	72	United States	**91**

Source: Hofstede (2020). Used with permission.

Table 9.2 Summary of the main characteristics of individualistic and collectivistic cultures

	Individualistic Cultures E.g., United States, Australia, United Kingdom, Netherlands, New Zealand, Italy, Belgium, Denmark, Sweden, France, Switzerland, Germany, and Finland	*Collectivist Cultures (Low Individualism) E.g., Guatemala, Ecuador, Venezuela, Indonesia, Pakistan, South Korea, Bangladesh, China, Nigeria, Thailand, Malaysia, and Kenya*
Consciousness	"I" conscious. "I" is more often used.	"We" conscious. "We" is more often used.
Identity	Identity is based on the individual. Right of privacy.	Identity is based on the social system. The focus is on belonging.
Social Framework	Loosely knit social framework.	Tightly knit social framework.
Expression	Speaking one's mind is healthy.	Maintaining harmony and avoiding confrontation is important.
Communication	Low context – explicit communication, direct speech and direct emotional expressions.	High context – implicit, communication, the indirect speech and indirect emotional expressions.
	Non-verbal acts are individualistic.	Non-verbal acts are contextualistic (role-based).
	Controlling, confrontational, and solution-oriented style.	Obliging, avoiding, and affective-oriented style.
Relationships	Relations are built actively. Mutual advantages are the basis of relationships.	Relations are given. Relationships bring in rights and obligations.
Face Saving	Keep self-respect.	Save *face* for in-group.
Interests and Rewards	Focus on individual interests and rewards.	Focus on group interests and rewards.
Task and Relation	The task is more important than a good relation.	No task/business without a good relation.
	Task prevails over the relationship.	The relationship prevails over the task.
Others	Others are classified as individuals.	Others are classified as in-group or out-group.
Opinions	Personal opinions are expected. One vote per person.	Opinions and votes are predetermined by the in-group.
Education	The main objective of education is learning how to do it.	The main objective of education is learning how to learn.
Care-giving	Everyone is expected to take care of herself/himself or her/his immediate family.	People are born into in-groups (families or clans) which protect them in exchange for loyalty.

Table 9.2 continued

	Individualistic Cultures E.g., United States, Australia, United Kingdom, Netherlands, New Zealand, Italy, Belgium, Denmark, Sweden, France, Switzerland, Germany, and Finland	*Collectivist Cultures (Low Individualism) E.g., Guatemala, Ecuador, Venezuela, Indonesia, Pakistan, South Korea, Bangladesh, China, Nigeria, Thailand, Malaysia, and Kenya*
Violation of Norms and Face	Violation of norms leads to a feeling of guilt.	Violation of norms leads to a feeling of shame.
	Loss of self-respect and guilt.	Loss of face and shame.
	The focus is on keeping self-respect.	The focus is on saving *face* for the group.
Work and Private Life	Work and private life are separated.	Work and private life are combined.
Rewards and Promotion	Promotion is based on results and achievements.	Promotion is based on loyalty and seniority.
Orientation	Universalistic – everybody is treated as subject to the same rules.	Particularistic – some people are more equal than others. To get things done in the government and bureaucracy one needs friends, relatives, or relationships.

Source: Hofstede et al. (2010).

CASE STUDY

Survivor games: individual and group oriented behavior

Survivor is an international reality television competition franchise shown in several countries in the world. The programme is derived from the Swedish television series *Expedition Robinson* created by Charlie Parsons, which first premiered in 1997. The reality show places a group of strangers in an isolated location (usually an isolated island), where they must provide food, fire, and shelter for themselves. The contestants compete for rewards, both individually and as a group, and immunity from elimination. The contestants are progressively eliminated from the game as they are voted out by their fellow contestants, until one contestant remains, who receives the title of "Sole Survivor", and the grand prize.

During the course of the competition, as the contestants get both individual and group rewards, they are expected to alternate between individual and group-oriented behaviours. The *Survivor* games and competitions were inspired by the

Robbers Cave experiments carried out by Turkish-American psychologist Muzafer Sherif. Muzafer Sherif's realistic group conflict theory proposed that competition (e.g., based on the scarcity of resources) among members for the group created hostility and reduced the potential of cooperation (Sherif, 1967). He proposed that superordinate goals may be used to reduce intergroup conflict and increase cooperation.

In his experiments, Sherif assigned the boys who participated in the camp into two groups, blue and red. Both groups spent time separately, for example, both groups had separate games and activities and lived in different cabins, had their meals at different tables. When Sherif introduced athletic contests between the groups he saw that competition created conflict and resulted in hostile attitudes towards the members of the other group, such as shows of group pride, negative stereotyping, and even occasionally physical violence (Whitley and Kite, 2010). To reduce conflict and hostility, Sherif arranged the groups to spend more time together without competition. He encouraged them to mix, eat together, and play games with the boys from the other team. However, hostility between the groups remained. One morning Sherif cut off the water supply. The boys had to find the water tank and fix it. As both groups needed the water (superordinate goal) they cooperated and worked together and group hostility was forgotten.

Task

Based on this case study, explain how the *Survivor* TV reality show and Sherif's Robbers Cave Experiments may be useful in establishing team cohesion among tourism and hospitality employees who may have different cultural backgrounds.

According to Triandis (1995), the most influential factors in determining a country's orientation to be individualistic or collectivistic are threefold. These factors are a) the level of complexity, b) the level of affluence, and c) the level of heterogeneity of the society.

Complexity	Compared with the primitive societies of the past (e.g., hunter and gatherer nomads) people now have more groups to identify with. This means that they would be less loyal to any group and would place greater focus on personal, rather than collective goals. For instance, it may be estimated that, not long ago, even during the period of World War I, many societies used to be more collectivistic than they are today. Also, people who lived in smaller communities such as villages tended to be more collectivistic. With the increasing numbers of people living in urban areas, they will tend to lack a strong attachment to groups and may be more likely to be individualistic. For instance, while most people in rural areas in Turkey may view the compulsory military service as a debt to pay for the homeland, in large cities, the proportion of people who share the same view may be expected to be lower.

Affluence	As people become more affluent and accumulate wealth, their interdependence on others will decrease. This results in lower levels of loyalty to groups and a greater focus on personal goals rather than the collective goals. Although various other factors may have some influence, poorer people tend to pay (willingly) a higher proportion of their income as taxes, compared with more affluent people.
Heterogeneity	Societies that are homogeneous or tight (in which members share the same language, religion, cultural norms, and traditions) are more likely to be rigid and intolerant towards people who do not conform to norms and traditions. On the other hand, societies that are diversified or loose (in which people speak different languages, may have different religions and cultural norms and traditions) may be more permissive towards those who do not conform to norms and traditions.

CASE STUDY

Conformity to group

The Asch group conformity experiments were a series of psychological experiments carried out by Solomon Asch during the 1950s. The experiments showed how an individual's opinions were influenced by a group. Asch (1951, 1952) found that people were willing to ignore the fact and the truth and to give an incorrect answer in order to conform to the rest of the group.

In the experiments, a naive student participant was placed in a room with several other actors/confederates. The naive subject was informed that s/he was taking part in a "vision test".

The confederates knew the true aim of the experiment but were introduced to the subject as other participants. Each student viewed a card with a line on it, followed by one with three lines labelled A, B, and C (see Figure 9.1).

One of these lines (Line C) was the same as that on the first card, and the other two lines (Line A and B) were clearly longer or shorter (i.e., a near-100% rate of correct responding was expected).

Each participant in the class was then asked to say aloud which line matched the length of that on the first card. Before the experiment, all actors were given detailed instructions on how they should respond to each trial (card presentation). In the experiments, a significant proportion of the participants (36.8%) conformed to the actors' (incorrect) answers. In other words, almost 40% of the participants ignored reality and conformed to the group.

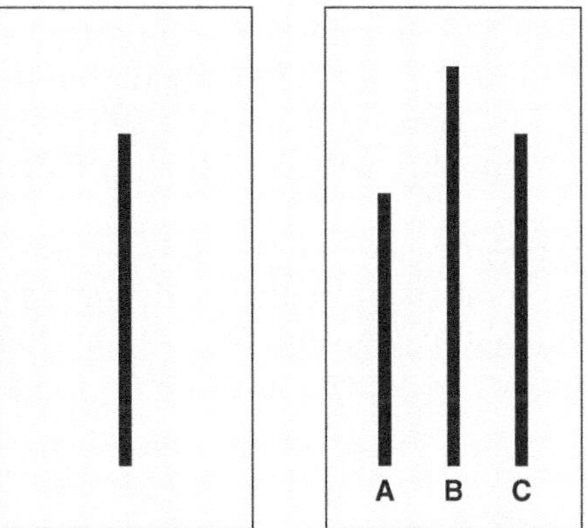

Figure 9.1 Lines used in the Asch's experiments

Activity

Individualism and collectivism scale (cultural orientation scale)

Measure your level of individualism (or collectivism) score by filling in the following questionnaire.

Important Note: Throughout the book, there are a number of self-report scales/tests like the one below. Please save your personal test score records (especially the ones relating to cultural awareness, cultural competence, ethnocentrism, cultural intelligence, etc.) to make comparisons later After studying the whole book you are advised to go back and redo all of these tests once more. By doing this you can compare your scores with the ones you had earlier on. This is expected to enable you to see the changes taken place as a result of the learning experience.

Instructions: Please read the statements below and indicate how much each statement describes you when you interact with people from other cultures by assigning a value, in the blank section on the left of each statement, from 1 to 9 (1 meaning strongly disagree and 9 meaning strongly agree).

Please keep in mind that there is no right or wrong response for each statement. In order to avoid biased responses, you are recommended to record your initial response without elaborating too much on the statements.

Description of the scale

This scale is a 16-item scale designed to measure four dimensions of collectivism and individualism:

- Vertical Collectivism: viewing the self as a part of a collective and being willing to accept hierarchy and inequality within that collective.
- Vertical Individualism: viewing seeing the self as fully autonomous, but recognising that inequality will exist among individuals and accepting this inequality.
- Horizontal Collectivism: viewing the self as part of a collective but perceiving all the members of that collective as equal.
- Horizontal Individualism: viewing the self as fully autonomous, and believing that equality between individuals is the ideal.

	Items	*Value (1 to 9)*
	Horizontal Individualism	
1	I'd rather depend on myself than others.	
2	I rely on myself most of the time; I rarely rely on others.	
3	I often do "my own thing".	
4	My personal identity, independent of others, is very important to me.	
	Vertical individualism	
5	It is important that I do my job better than others.	
6	Winning is everything.	
7	Competition is the law of nature.	
8	When another person does better than I do, I get tense and aroused.	
	Horizontal Collectivism	
9	If a coworker gets a prize, I would feel proud.	
10	The well-being of my coworkers is important to me.	
11	To me, pleasure is spending time with others.	
12	I feel good when I cooperate with others.	
	Vertical Collectivism	
13	Parents and children must stay together as much as possible.	
14	It is my duty to take care of my family, even when I have to sacrifice what I want.	
15	Family members should stick together, no matter what sacrifices are required.	
16	It is important to me that I respect the decisions made by my groups.	

Scoring: Each dimension's items are summed up separately to create a VC, VI, HC, and HI score.

Source: Triandis and Gelfland (1998).

Exercise

In addition to the previous individualism and collectivism scale, there are other relevant scales that may be used. You may visit the website at https://fetzer.org/sites/default/files/images/stories/pdf/selfmeasures/CollectiveOrientation.pdf to test your individualism and collectivism orientation based on the following scales:

- Individualism and Collectivism Scale (INDCOL)
  Singelis, T. M., Triandis, H. C., Bhawuk, D. P. S., and Gelfand, M. J. (1995). Horizontal and vertical dimensions of individualism and collectivism: A theoretical and measurement refinement. *Cross-Cultural Research*, 29, 240–275.
- Communal Orientation Scale (COS)
  Clark, M., Ouellette, R., Powell, M., and Milberg, S. (1987). Recipient's mood, relationship type, and helping. *Journal of Personality and Social Psychology*, 53, 94–103.
- Collective Self-Esteem Scale
  Luhtanen, R., and Crocker, J. (1992). A collective self-esteem scale: Self-evaluation of one's social identity. *Personality and Social Psychology Bulletin*, 18, 302–318.

The implications of individualism and collectivism for tourism and hospitality

Crotts and Erdmann (2000) argued that tourism and hospitality customers, in general, think and behave in parallel with their mental programme shaped by their culture. Litvin and Kar (2003), who studied the influence of individualism and collectivism on tourists' self-image and the congruity of their self-image with the image of the destinations, found that tourists' self-images were shaped by their individualistic or collectivistic orientations. Tourists chose destinations whose images were congruent with their self-image. Additionally, the congruency between tourists' self-image and destination image appeared to have caused an increase in the level of satisfaction they had. Hosany and Martin's (2012) study reached similar conclusions, emphasising the influence of individualism and collectivism dimension on the purchases of destinations and holidays. Based on these studies, it may be put forward that individualistic or collectivistic characteristics (explained in the previous section) of tourists influence their choice of what they purchase (destinations and holidays), and the amount of satisfaction they get from these holidays.

People in collectivistic cultures suppress feelings and emotions that may endanger harmony and hence they may tend to have more restraint-oriented culture characteristics than indulgence-oriented culture characteristics (see Chapter 5). They also tend to avoid giving negative feedback and are more likely to have high power distance culture characteristics (see Chapter 6). People in collectivistic cultures find it difficult to say "No" unless it is intended to be polite, as it may cause a loss of face. In collectivistic cultures, offers may be rejected out of politeness (see the following case study).

CASE STUDY

Peculiar collectivistic characteristics of Turkish culture

One of the most important virtues of traditional Turkish culture is hospitality. Since the Ottoman period there is a social obligation for the host to offer food or drinks to their guests. Following the initial exchange of niceties (such as saying "Hello. How are you?"), shopkeepers asked their customers (who were seen as guests) whether they were hungry and thirsty. The customers would not have been sent away without at least drinking a cup of tea or coffee.* As another sign of collectivistic culture, when the customers have purchased some items from their shops, the shopkeepers would send away customers to other shops (their competitors) so that their competitors can also earn their living and survive.

Most people in Turkey take great pride in hospitality and many genuinely enjoy entertaining guests. In the Turkish culture, being hospitable to guests is believed to bring honour to the host. A failure in hospitality is seen as something to be ashamed of. For hosts, insisting on another round of a drink is not an obligation, but a delight.

Many people (nowadays especially outside large cities and non-touristic places) consider international tourists as guests. If international tourists strike up a conversation with someone in a café or on the street, they can see that they are treated like guests. Hence, it is not uncommon for tourist after striking up a conversation to see (nowadays especially outside large cities and non-touristic places) a restaurant owner refusing to accept payment from them, or someone giving a lift to a tourist even if it may mean changing his direction. This is because after striking up a conversation they are seen as guests, not as tourists.

In Turkey, restaurant and café bills are not usually split up. They are usually paid by one person. When two friends go to a restaurant or a cafe, it is quite common for both friends to insist on paying the bill, even it may mean playing tricks to prevent the payment of the other person. Even the newly met people attempt to pay the restaurant bills of each other, as otherwise, paying her/his bill only may be perceived as rude, insincere, and selfish. However, caution must be taken as insisting to pay for something, when normally the other person is expected to pay, may cause a feeling of humiliation for the other person.

When a host makes an offer (of foods and drinks) s/he is expected to insist and repeat the offer a few times. Guests usually decline the initial food and drink offers of the host politely. Out of politeness and as a sign of sincerity, the host insists on the offer. Then, the guest would show consent and accept the offer or may state her/his food or drink preference. The host repeats the offer until the guest reluctantly accepts. In some cases, the host would still bring out the offered food or drink even if the guest has declined the offer.

In many instances, the offer is usually accepted by the guest after repeated and insistent offers of the host. If the host does not insist, it may be perceived that the offer was not genuine, and it was just made out of politeness. By not insisting a host may also be perceived as being unfriendly or rude and not fulfilling her/his hospitality obligations as a host. Insistence means that the host is sincere about the offer. However, when people are really close and see each other often some of these formalities may be omitted to some extent. Someone from an individualistic and low-context culture observing the above situation may be confused and unable to understand the why there is so much fuss about it.

A final collectivistic feature of Turkish culture is to do with *face*-saving. Up until the 1990s, most Turkish houses used to have rooms used for/with guests only (called guest rooms). These rooms normally would not have been used on regular days, as they were meant to be used to entertain guests. The guest rooms were better furnished and decorated than the other rooms in the house. These rooms were only used on an occasional basis. They were not used when there were no guests present in the house to ensure that they looked clean and tidy all the time.

* Though nowadays this may be used quite as often as a persuasive tool, or a strategy, due to the rising individualism caused by increasing affluence and widespread metropolitan lifestyle. Reciprocity principle of persuasion states that in many social situations people pay back what they receive from others. People (e.g., salespeople) tend to give a little something to get something (perhaps something larger) in return (Cialdini, 2013). According to the reciprocity principle of persuasion, people are usually conditioned to return favours and pay back their debts (Koc, 2016).

The influence of individualism and collectivism on tourism and hospitality marketing and management may be pervasive. The influence of individualism on people (as a marketing mix element) will be explained under the headings of service quality dimensions, service failures and complaint behaviour, service recovery, attribution and justice, and customer loyalty and risk.

Marketing mix elements

Individualism and collectivism orientation appears to have some influence almost on all marketing mix elements (product, price, place, promotion, physical evidence, people and processes). According to Pollay and Gallagher (1990), the five advertising appeals which are related to individualism and collectivism are independence, distinctiveness, family, community, and popularity. While independence, distinctiveness, and family strongly relate to individualism, community and popularity reflect collectivism.

Independence	Self-sufficiency, self-reliance, autonomy, unattached, do it yourself, do your own thing, original, unconventional, singular
Distinctiveness	Rare, unique, unusual, scarce, infrequent, exclusive, tasteful, elegant, subtle, esoteric, hand-crafted
Family	Nurturance within the family, having a home, being at home, having a home, family, privacy, companionship of siblings, kinship, getting married

Community	Relating to the community, state, national publics, national identity, group unity, civic and community organisations, patriotism
Popularity	Commonplace, customary, well-known, conventional, regular, usual, ordinary, normal, standard, typical, universal, general, everyday

Albers-Miller and Gelb (1996) added affiliation appeal to the above collectivism appeals and self-respect to individualism appeals. While affiliation appeal comprises things such as to be accepted, liked by peers, colleagues, and community at large, to be social, to gather with, unite, companionship, to conform to social customs, cooperation, to bond in friendship, self-respect comprises things such as being confident, possessing dignity, self-worth, self-esteem, peace of mind.

Exercise

Based on the advertising appeals developed by Pollay and Gallagher (1990) prepare a marketing mix (7Ps) table (one for a market segment aimed at tourism or hospitality customers from a collectivistic culture and one for a market segment aimed at tourism and hospitality customers from an individualistic culture) and write down notes to be used in the design of each marketing mix element.

CASE STUDY

Teamwork, cooperation, and collectivism in the animal kingdom

It is known that Bonobo monkeys live in peaceful, matriarchal communities where they use complex vocal sounds to communicate with each other and engage collectively in sex in certain social situations. When they get stressed, bonobos tend to hug each other rather than be aggressive. Unlike Bonobo monkeys, chimpanzees tend to be aggressive. Bonobos do not like competition and prefer cooperation and engage in truly altruistic behaviours. They are sensitive towards others and avoid behaviours which may disturb them. They are patient (especially towards younger members of the clan) and show signs of empathy and sympathy towards others, although they may be strangers. They help others who are in difficulty. As explained in Chapter 3, Bonobo monkeys engage in mutual grooming, sharing and affection, petting-soothing and give food gifts or "food-offerings" (de Waal, 1995).

Likewise, wolves, bees, ants, and dolphins are observed to engage in cooperation and prosocial behaviours. For instance, Bottleneck dolphins use learned vocal labels to address each other to cooperate and work as a team (King and Janik, 2013).

Dolphins hunt in teams of three or five (even numbers). When hunting as a team, one dolphin herds the fish towards the others, which line up their bodies to make a wall/barrier. As the fish jump from the water, "the driver" surfaces alongside the barrier dolphins to catch the fish in mid-air. This shows that dolphin teams have a division of labour (each carrying out a different task) and cooperate towards a common goal (Gazda et al., 2005). Also, when a dolphin gives birth, two other female dolphins stay with her (as "mid-wives") and protect the defenseless mother and the baby dolphin from attack by other animals and fish.

In terms of sales promotions and pricing, customers from individualistic cultures with a shorter-term orientation tend to respond positively to heavy pricing discounting, while customers from collectivistic and long-term oriented cultures tend to be the least pleased with price discounting-based of sales promotion activities (McNeill 2006; McNeill et al., 2014).

When marketing tourism and hospitality services to collectivistic customers, marketing communication messages and other marketing mix elements are expected to emphasise the direct and indirect benefits to the community. On the other hand, when marketing to individualistic customers, the individual benefits are expected to be emphasised through marketing communications and other marketing mix elements.

These characteristics do not only apply to promotion (or marketing communications) alone as a marketing mix. As they reflect what people seek when they make purchases, tourism and hospitality managers may use these themes in designing their whole marketing mix elements. For instance, while individualistic cultures tend to prefer individual holidays (product element of the marketing mix), people in collectivist cultures tend to go on package holidays. Stauss and Mang (1999) and Muller et al. (2003) found that customers from individualistic cultures expected more personalised products and services.

Again, while people from countries with a high level of individualism may prefer novel and distinct restaurants, people from countries with a high level of collectivism may be more conservative in their choice of restaurants. As in the case of uncertainty avoidance (see Chapter 7), people from individualistic cultures may be more likely to have neophilia (tendency to like and try new foods) due to their search for distinctiveness, uniqueness, scarcity, exclusivity, elegance, subtleness, rarity, esoteric-ness, and hand-crafted, while people from collectivistic cultures may be more likely to have neophobia (fear of eating new or unfamiliar foods) due to their motive to search for things that are commonplace, customary, well-known, conventional, regular, usual, ordinary, normal, and standard.

In relation to the product element of marketing mix in tourism and hospitality, Reisinger (2009) argues that due to their group orientations collectivistic customers (e.g., Koreans) tend to buy more gifts, give gifts on more occasions and have a higher gift budget than individualistic customers, who buy, give fewer gifts, and have fewer gift-giving occasions, and thus are under less pressure to reciprocate (Park, 1998). Hence, the design of tourism destinations, establishments, and package tours targeting tourists from collectivistic cultures should take the importance of gift-giving and gift-buying tendencies into the account.

Exercise

Visit the websites at https://www.pandotrip.com/top-10-unusual-restaurants-around-the-world-26052/, https://www.bookculinaryvacations.com/news/most-unusual-restaurants-world, and https://www.touchbistro.com/blog/the-100-most-unique-restaurant-concepts-around-the-world/ to see the world's most innovative and novel (and perhaps and usual and bizarre restaurants) in the world.

Based on the advertising appeals explained previously describe the main characteristics of people who may go to these restaurants and their likely motives.

The appeals mentioned earlier may be also used in the design of hotels, restaurants, airline offices, and lounges (as the place element of the marketing mix). Additionally, for instance, the exclusivity may be reflected in the exclusive prices of a tourism and hospitality establishment. For instance, while standard rooms range between 15,000 and 20,000 dollars per night, the Empathy Suite at Palms Casino Resort (Las Vegas) may cost as much as 100,000 dollars per night. Dinner for one person in the world's most expensive restaurant SubliMotion (Spain) may cost over 2,000 dollars. Again a flight ticket with Ethiad Airways (United Arab Emirates) may cost more than a few times the cost of the flight ticket of a standard airline.

Correia et al. (2011) found that tourists from collectivistic cultures were more likely to make their decisions based on brand, prices, and the number of alternatives available, while individualistic customers had their own criteria. Jeong et al.'s (2019) study draws parallels with Correia et al.'s (2011) study. Jeong et al. found that hospitality customers from collectivistic and high-context cultures were much more concerned about the price-quality relationship than the hospitality customers from individualistic and low-context cultures.

Service quality dimensions

Research shows that customers in individualistic and collectivistic cultures have different expectations regarding service quality (Mattila, 1999; Patterson and Smith, 2003; Lorenzoni and Lewis, 2004; Gi Park et al., 2014). Magnini et al. (2013) who researched the influences of collectivism in tourism and hospitality settings (hotels and restaurants) put forward that tourism and hospitality employees from collective cultures may display more organisational citizenship behaviour due to their collective "we" orientation, and their motivation to maintain harmony and avoid confrontation. Organisational citizenship behaviour can be defined as the discretionary behaviour of individual employee behaviour, not directly or explicitly recognised by the formal reward system, but promotes the effective functioning of the organisation (Organ, 1988; Magnini et al., 2013).

In other words, in collectivistic cultures employees and managers may be more devoted to their organisations, and may be more willing to engage in self-sacrifice for the benefit of the organisation. It is known that, as a relatively collectivistic country, in Japan, many people willingly work overtime, without even expecting overtime payment.

However, as explained in Chapters 4 and 7 (as in the case of high-context and high-uncertainty avoidance cultures), the motivation to maintain harmony and tendency to avoid confrontation and conflict may have detrimental effects for the organisation. The problems may not be allowed to come out in the open, and consequently, may never get resolved. As also explained in Chapter 7, as the group members value cohesion and consensus significantly, groupthink may arise, that is, the issues relating to efficiency and effectiveness may be subordinated (Janis and Janis, 1982). This, in turn, may create problems in terms of all service quality dimensions, especially for reliability, assurance, responsiveness, and empathy.

Another downside of collectivism, as pointed out by Magnini et al. (2013) in their research, is that employees in collectivistic cultures tend to have lower levels of comfort with empowerment. Empowerment may have significant implications for tourism and hospitality businesses in terms of reliability and responsiveness dimensions of service quality, and service recovery process (Koc, 2013a; Dalgic et al., 2017; Dimitrou, 2017). Based on Magnini et al's (2013) findings, it may be suggested that managers in tourism and hospitality businesses be more insistent on empowerment and should look for novel ways to make their employees feel comfortable with empowerment. Additionally, as people from an individualistic culture tend to enjoy autonomy (LaRoche et al., 2005), managers are advised to establish systems to ensure the empowerment of employees, which would be expected to increase employee satisfaction and motivation. Moreover, as people from individualistic cultures tend to be more autonomy oriented, tourism and hospitality customers may be expected to be more positive towards customer participation (co-creation and co-production) (Koc et al., 2017b). When customers participate in the service, the involvement of service employees in the service would be expected to decrease.

Furrer et al.'s (2000) study of service encounters and Mattila (1999) and Tsaur et al.'s (2005) studies on tourism and hospitality customers showed that the customers from individualistic cultures, due to their drive and self-responsibility ethic, and their emphasis on competition, self-reliance, personal goals, achievement, and independence, tend to demand that others be efficient, and hence expect a higher quality of service. As individualism implies loose ties, customers from individualistic societies pursue mainly their own interests (not others), and, hence are not willing to accept poor service (Furrer et al., 2000; Sigala and Sakellaridis, 2004).

In contrast, tourism and hospitality customers from a collectivist culture (e.g., China) with a focus on betterment of society, cooperativeness, team efforts, and harmony, concern for others, respect for tradition, stressing of interdependence, in-group obligations, humility, preserving the welfare of others, and adherence to societal norms (Gudykunst, 1998; Kim et al., 2017; Radojevic et al., 2019) may take a different stance when they encounter service failures. Tourism and hospitality customers from collectivistic cultures are more likely to tolerate poor service as they do not want to break the harmony (i.e., the good relationship they may have with the service provider) (Donthu and Yoo, 1998; Sigala and Sakellaridis, 2004; Baker, 2017).

Furrer et al's (2000) research in tourism and hospitality found that customers from individualistic cultures tend to demand responsiveness and reliability, and due to their self-confidence and self-responsibility, they do not expect to be assured and do expect a high level of quality relating to tangibles as service quality dimensions. In terms of websites, individualistic customers have higher expectations of responsiveness, interactivity, design and visual appeal, but tend to have lower expectations about trust than collectivistic customers (Furrer et al., 2000; Sigala and Sakellaridis, 2004). Kong and Jogaratnam's (2007) study on restaurants showed that while South Korean (collectivistic) customers expected higher levels of courtesy, civility, and concern, American (individualistic) customers put more emphasis on customisation and individual recognition.

Tsaur et al.'s (2005) study is supportive of the above. They found that British tourists (with a relatively high level of individualism) tended to depend more on tangible cues in the physical environment to evaluate service quality (technical quality – a more objective, concrete and direct way of evaluation of a service) than highly collectivistic Asian tourists. Reisinger (2009) argues that while tourists from individualistic cultures tend to demand more efficient, prompt, and error-free service, tourists from collectivistic cultures place importance on the sincerity of employees. In other words, while individualistic tourism and hospitality customers tend to pay more attention to outcomes, collectivistic tourism and hospitality customers tend to pay more attention to processes (Kim et al., 2014; Mariani and Predvoditeleva, 2019). This means that tourism and hospitality establishments targeting and serving customers from individualistic cultures need to place more attention on tangibles (as a service quality dimension) and physical evidence (as a marketing mix element).

As in the case of low-context cultures (e.g., Germany, Austria, Switzerland, Australia, Denmark, South Africa, Norway, United States, Canada (English), Finland, Sweden, Israel, United Kingdom, Belgium, Netherlands, and Luxembourg) (see Chapter 4), individualistic tourists tend to maintain a distance between themselves and the service provider, hence, tangibles and technology (e.g., self-service technologies) (Kelly et al., 2017) can be used more often for individualistic customers to reduce the intensity and frequency of interaction with staff (Tsaur et al., 2005). Hence, tourism and hospitality managers from collectivistic cultures may train their staff in terms of maintaining personal distance when they serve customers from individualistic cultures (as well as customers from low-context cultures), and try to look for innovative use of tangibles and technology to reduce the intensity and frequency of interaction between customers and service providers.

Information zone

Territoriality and space

In Chapter 4, territoriality and space were explained in relation to high- and low-context communication. However, the concepts of territoriality and space are also important from the perspectives of individualism and collectivism. People in individualistic cultures tend to value independence and autonomy, and consequently prioritise themselves over the groups they are a member of (Triandis, 1995). Hence, people in individualistic cultures prefer to be apart from the others at a reasonable personal distance (e.g., about 81.5 centimetres in the United States and the United Kingdom). They do not tend to touch and are likely to avoid physical contact in interpersonal relationships (Miyamoto and Schwarz, 2006).

The distance people keep determines whether the other person is a stranger, friend, lover, children or close family members. In collectivistic cultures, personal space tends to be closer (e.g., 60 centimetres in most Latin and Mediterranean countries) and people touch each other more often in interpersonal relationships. Studies (Thayer, 1982; Pearce et al., 2015; Nummenmaa et al., 2016) show that touching between people increases their social bonding. According to Kraus et al. (2010), touching increases cooperation between people, which is another attribute of collectivistic societies, and it shows the strength of bonding between people. According to Kraus et al., by touching, cooperation and bonding between people can be increased.

However, factors such as gender and age may be influential in the level of personal distance people keep. For instance, women and children tend to have a shorter personal distance (Fischer and Evers, 2013). In addition, climate may be another factor influencing personal distance. In contrast with colder climates, people in warmer climates tend to have a closer personal distance. Warmer climate influences emotional intensity (Sorokowski et al., 2013), which results in intense and closer interpersonal contacts, and a closer personal distance. According to Hall and Hall (1990) people from warmer climates, for example, Latin America and the Mediterranean, prefer close distances, whereas those from colder climates, for example, Nordic and North European countries, appear to prefer relatively large physical distances in interpersonal communication. The previous explanations regarding the influence of Covid-19 pandemic on physical distance and touch need to be taken into account.

According to Miyamoto and Schwarz (2006), the two main functions of communication are: a) informational (to convey and exchange information), and b) relation (to form, build and maintain relationships with others). Miyamoto and Schwarz assert that while people from individualistic cultures attach more value to the informational function of communication, people from collectivistic cultures place more emphasis on the relational function of communication.

Moreover, individualistic customers place more importance on the assurance element of service quality as they tend to expect service providers to give them confidence about the service they are receiving (Tsaur et al., 2005). As explained in Chapter 5, restraint cultures (e.g., Bulgaria, Russia, Serbia, Ukraine, China, Poland, Italy, and to an extent Japan and Turkey) may have service orientation problems. When tourism and hospitality businesses serve customers from individualistic cultures (e.g., from the United States, Australia, United Kingdom, Netherlands, New Zealand, Italy, Belgium, Denmark, Sweden, France, Switzerland, Germany, and Finland), they need to make sure that their staff are well trained to meet customers' confidence and assurance needs.

Service failures, attribution, and complaint behaviour

Studies relating to complaint behaviour of tourism and hospitality customers from individualistic and collectivistic cultures show that their complaint behaviours differ. While the customers from individualistic cultures (the United States, Australia, France, Germany, the United Kingdom) tend to voice their complaints and directly complain to the management of tourism and hospitality business, or to third parties in the form of word-of-mouth communications, the customers from collectivistic cultures (e.g., China, Japan, Hong Kong, the Philippines, Taiwan) do not tend to complain directly to the management in order to make the tourism and hospitality business accountable, improve service quality, or redeem their losses (Huang et al.,1996; Liu and McClure, 2001; Patterson et al., 2006; Yuksel et al., 2006; Gi Park et al., 2014) due to their "I" orientation.

These findings are in line with the general characteristics of collectivistic cultures since in an individualistic society everyone is expected to take care of himself or herself. Banerjee and Chai (2019) found that compared with tourism and hospitality customers from collectivistic cultures, customers from individualistic cultures provided more negative online reviews based on the variability of preference associated with individualism and aggregate expectations they formed. Fan et al.'s (2018) study on restaurants compared the consumption intentions of customers from an individualistic culture (American) with a collectivistic culture (Chinese). They found that while American customers relied more on online recommendations (regardless of the source), Chinese customers depended on known sources (Ruiz-Equihua et al., 2019). Wen et al. (2018), who investigated the motives to create eWOM, found that eWOM depended on two positive emotions of pleasure and pride. Individualism, power distance, and indulgence appeared to be the antecedents of pleasure and pride (Wen et al. 2018; Ruiz-Equihua et al., 2019).

On the other hand, collectivistic customers do not tend to make direct complaints to the management of tourism and hospitality businesses. They rather engage in private complaint behaviour, that is, warn their friends and relatives about their unsatisfactory tourism and hospitality experiences, and engage in WOM communication (Huang et al., 1996; Liu and McClure, 2001; Patterson et al., 2006; Yuksel et al., 2006; Ngai et al., 2007; Gi Park et al., 2014). Engaging in the private WOM communications (i.e., warning friends and relatives) is based on the motivation not to allow in-group members to experience negative consequences which are important in a collectivist culture (Ngait et al., 2007; Swanson et al., 2014). Maintaining strong relationships in a collectivistic culture requires "allowing others to escape the humiliation implicit in not knowing, failing to understand, having been mistaken", so that "saving each other's face is extremely important" (Mok and DeFranco, 1999: 107).

These findings are also in line with the general characteristics of collectivist cultures. As they do not like to confront, and do not directly complain to hotel management. Asian hotel guests with a higher uncertainty avoidance and collectivistic orientation are more likely to be more fearful of losing face when making a complaint than non-Asian hotel guests (Becker, 2000; Liu and McClure, 2001; Gi Park et al., 2014). For instance, the Japanese do not want to be confrontational and do not want to "lose face" by making a direct complaint.

In terms of the attribution of service failures, Ngai et al. (2007) found that collectivists (Asians) attributed service failures to individual hotel employees, while individualists (Americans) tended to attribute service failures to hotel management (i.e., they tend to blame the management for the failures). As explained in Chapter 4, Japanese people, as a collectivistic culture, tend to attribute positive outcomes to external factors, and negative outcomes to internal factors due to their flexhumble characteristics (Bergiel et al., 2012).

Yuksel et al. (2006) found that Turkish tourists (moderately collectivistic) may feel sad when they voice their dissatisfaction through a complaint. This may be related to feminine (see Chapter 8) and collectivistic characteristics of Turkish culture. Riggs (2016) also found that businesses in collectivistic cultures had a significant amount of sympathy for employees, and employees could only be fired under very rare conditions. These sorts of work environments may inadvertently foster inefficiency and ineffectiveness.

Customers from collectivistic cultures may feel that making a complaint could harm an employee in some way (Yuksel et al., 2006). Koc's (2013b) study showed that Turkish hospitality customers (collectivistic and feminine), especially the older ones, had a relatively higher sympathy for the employees, though as a country, Turkey's humane orientation score (see Chapter 10), was not particularly high. The feeling of sympathy for the weak in collectivistic cultures influences tourism and hospitality customers' reactions towards employees and their evaluations of service encounters.

As collectivistic people find it disturbing to voice a complaint, they are more likely to ignore unsatisfactory services, engage in negative WOM communication, and/or quit repurchasing (Patterson et al., 2006; Yuksel et al., 2006; Gi Park et al., 2014). Public voice is not valued socially in a collectivistic culture and it is discouraged to maintain harmony (Hoare and Butcher, 2008). Customers from a collectivistic culture are more likely to warn their friends and relatives, as in a collectivistic society strong family and extended family ties exist, and people are expected to look after each other due to the "we" orientation (Ngai et al., 2007). For instance, as a collectivist society in Turkey, although it is illegal, many drivers in traffic warn other drivers (complete strangers) of a speed trap by flashing their headlights.

Service recovery, attribution, and justice

Studies regarding service recovery, attribution, and justice also show marked perceptual differences between customers from individualistic and collectivistic cultures. Research shows that in service recovery situations while customers from individualistic cultures prefer financial gains, customers from collectivistic cultures concentrate on avoiding losses (Markus and Kitayama, 1990; Briley and Wyer, 2002; Gi Park et al., 2014). Hui and Au's (2001) research in the hospitality industry found that the most important part of the service recovery for Chinese (collectivistic) hotel customers was to provide opportunities for customers to communicate their dissatisfaction with the company (especially with someone high in status, such as a manager, due to their high power-distance characteristics) and employees. On the other hand, for Canadian hotel customers (individualistic) the most important part of service recovery was the offering of compensation. Mattila and Patterson's (2004) research is also supportive of this as they found that Americans were more satisfied with compensation than the collectivistic East Asians.

Swanson et al. (2014) put forward that hospitality customers from collectivist cultures (e.g., Chinese) are more likely report the utilisation of some socially based service recovery tactics, while hospitality customers from individualist cultures (e.g., Americans) are more likely to report the utilisation of some financially based service recovery tactics (Hui and Au, 2001; Mattila and Patterson, 2004; Swanson et al., 2014).

These findings draw parallels regarding the power-distance orientations and justice expectations of customers explained in Chapter 6. In other words, in service recovery situations while customers from individualistic cultures (and with low power distance) concentrate on procedural and interactional justice, customers from individualistic cultures (and with high power distance) concentrate on distributive justice. This means that while customers from a lower power-distance culture attach more weighting to distributive justice (i.e., how fair the compensation received was), customers from a high power-distance culture tend to attach more weighting to procedural justice (i.e., how fair the process was), and interactional justice (i.e., how fair the customer was treated) during the service recovery process.

Additionally, Hui and Au (2001) found individualistic Canadian hotel guests tended to perceive a higher level of fairness and showed more favourable post-complaint behaviours than did collectivist Chinese guests. This finding may also relate to indulgence and restraint orientations (see Chapter 5) of these customers to do with remembering past events. Kim (2017) emphasised the importance of remembering and memory in the consumption of tourism and hospitality services.

Koc et al. (2017, 2020) found that in restraint cultures, tourism and hospitality customers may be more likely to remember negative experiences, and hence service recovery paradox (see Chapter 5) may be less likely to occur. On the other hand, in indulgence cultures (e.g., Canada who are also individualistic) people may be more likely to remember positive experiences, and hence service recovery paradox (see Chapter 5) may be more likely to occur.

Customer loyalty and risk

Tourism and hospitality customers' (and employees') individualism or collectivism orientations may have a significant influence on their perceptions of risk and their feeling of loyalty (Han et al., 2017). As explained in Chapter 7, in cultures where there is a high level of uncertainty avoidance, people tend to be risk aversive (Noja et al., 2018), and in countries where there is a low level of uncertainty avoidance, people tend to be happy taking risks regarding the various aspects of their lives. According to Cosgrave (2006) and Ozorio et al. (2010), individualism was negatively correlated with uncertainty avoidance (i.e., individualistic tend to be risk-takers), and positively correlated with per capita gambling turnover in a country or region. In individualistic and capitalist societies, risk-taking is often rationalised, capitalised through legislation, and marketed extensively as a leisure activity.

As explained in Chapter 7, due to the main service characteristics (e.g., intangibility, heterogeneity, and inseparability), tourism and hospitality activities involve some degree of risk. Specifically, as there would be more unknowns (in terms of destinations, transportation, and accommodation), tourism activities may cause higher levels of perception of risk by customers (Koc, 2006). Package holidays offer a structured mode of tourism activity, minimise risk and uncertainty, and provide an environment for collective social interaction (Manrai and Manrai, 2011). Hence, package holidays usually correspond with high-uncertainty avoidance and collectivism. However, as put forward by Han and Heather (2001), from time to time, people from collectivistic societies, who are also from high power-distance cultures, may be competitive. While these people still engage in international package holidays, they may prefer added elements of novelty. These collectivistic tourists may join package tours to take advantage of collectiveness, structure and risk reduction, but also choose international destinations due to their motives of adventure and novelty seeking (Manrai and Manrai, 2011). As opposed to risk aversion, the social integration motive, which includes factors such as courtesy, prudence, trustworthiness, and contentedness, explains a significant proportion of the reasons for participating in package holidays in collective societies (Manrai and Manrai, 2011).

According to Tsai and Levenson (1997), in individualistic cultures there is less emphasis on controlling emotions, emotional experience, and expression (Bathaee, 2011). Owing to a high level of emotional control in collectivistic societies, people may suppress the desire to seek variety. Variety seeking relates to being different and so tends to be considered negative behaviour (Triandis, 1995; Kim and Markus, 1999; Bathaee, 2011). As a moderately collectivistic culture in Turkey, especially in rural areas, the word "different" (*değişik*) is used to express insult. In terms of variety-seeking behaviour, collectivistic customers may feel that they should restrain their actions and impulses, ignore temptations and desires such as having more and different brands or varieties of similar products (Schwartz and Blisky, 1990; Bathaee, 2011). As a moderately collectivistic culture in Turkey, especially in rural areas, the word different (*değişik*) is used to express insult.

According to Han et al. (2017), while independence, self-reliance, and uniqueness in individualistic cultures cause reduced levels of loyalty and increased levels of variety-seeking behaviour, loyalty, harmony, humility, interdependence, controlling emotions and conformity, collectivistic culture characteristics result in increased levels of loyalty and reduced levels of variety-seeking behaviour.

Conclusion

This chapter explores the influence of individualism and collectivism on tourism and hospitality marketing and management. As one of the the most widely researched and most influential cultural dimensions, individualism and collectivism appear to have a significant influence on marketing mix elements, service quality dimensions, service failures, attribution, service recovery, justice, risk, and complaint behaviours. Individualism and collectivism tend to have a strong relationship with other cultural dimensions such as uncertainty avoidance, indulgence and restraint, power distance and high- and low-context cultures. Individualism also influences the physical distance people would like to have with others and the way they think, act, and communicate.

Questions

1. Identify five individualistic and five collectivistic cultures. What sort of similarities and differences are there within each group of countries?
2. What are the key characteristics of collectivistic and individualistic cultures?
3. What are the three main influential factors that determine whether a country is individualistic or collectivistic? Find countries which match these factors and explain the extent to which such factors have been influential.
4. How may individualism and collectivism influence the design of marketing mix elements?
5. How do customers from individualistic and collectivistic customers differ in terms of the emphasis they place on service quality dimensions?
6. How do customers from individualistic and collectivistic customers differ in terms of their perceptions towards various service recovery attempts?

7. What are the main differences between individualistic and collectivistic customers in terms of loyalty, variety-seeking, and brand switching?
8. For want of a nail, the shoe was lost.
   For want of a shoe, the horse was lost.
   For want of a horse, the rider was lost.
   For want of a rider, the message was lost.
   For want of a message, the battle was lost.
   For want of a battle, the kingdom was lost.
   And all for the want of a horseshoe nail.

   The first mention of the above quote was related to King Richard III's death during the Battle of Bosworth in 1485. The story was illustrated in William Shakespeare's historical play *Richard III*, dating back to around 1591. Later, in the twentiety century, the American novelist Richard Baldwin included a short version of the "For want of a nail" proverb in his work titled *Fifty Famous People*, which also referred to King Richard's Battle of Bosworth in August 1485. Explain and discuss this quote from the perspective of the individualism–collectivism paradigm.

Research questions/ideas to pursue for researchers

As was mentioned previously, the reciprocity principle of persuasion is based on the idea that in many social situations people are inclined to pay back their debts and return favours they receive from others (Cialdini, 2013; Koc, 2016). The chapter also discussed how tourists from collectivistic societies tended to buy and give more gifts than individualistic tourists, who felt less pressure to reciprocate (Park, 1998; Reisinger, 2009). Based on these issues, a study may be carried out to measure and compare the extent of influence of reciprocity-based persuasion exercises on tourism or hospitality customers from the perspectives of collectivistic and individualistic cultures.

Recommended further reading

Gi Park, S., Kim, K., and O'Neill, M. (2014). Complaint behavior intentions and expectation of service recovery in individualistic and collectivistic cultures. *International Journal of Culture, Tourism and Hospitality Research*, 8(3), 255–271.

Hofstede, G., Hofstede, G. J., and Minkov, M. (2010). Cultures and organizations: Software of the mind (3rd ed.). New York: McGraw-Hill.

Hsieh, A. T., and Tsai, C. W. (2009). Does national culture really matter? Hotel service perceptions by Taiwan and American tourists. *International Journal of Culture, Tourism and Hospitality Research*, 3(1), 54–69.

Litvin, S. W., and Kar, G. H. (2003). Individualism/collectivism as a moderating factor to the self-image congruity concept. *Journal of Vacation Marketing*, 10(1), 23–42.

Manrai, L. A., and Manrai, A. (2011). Hofstede's cultural dimensions and tourist behaviors: A review and conceptual framework. *Journal of Economics, Finance and Administrative Science*, 16(31), 23.

Sigala, M., and O. Sakellaridis (2004). The impact of users' cultural characteristics on e-service quality: Implications for globalizing tourism and hospitality websites. In A. Frew (Ed.), *Information and Communication Technologies in Tourism* (pp. 106–117). Vienna, Austria: Springer Verlag.

Triandis, H.C. (1995). Individualism and collectivism. New York: Westview.

Trompenaars, A., and Hampden-Turner, C. (1998). *Riding the waves of cultural diversity in global business*. London: Nicholas Brealey Publishing.

References

Albers-Miller, N., and Gelb, B. (1996). Business advertising appeals as a mirror of cultural dimensions: A study of eleven countries. *Journal of Advertising*, 25, 57–70.

Asch, S. E. (1951). Effects of group pressure upon the modification and distortion of judgments. In H. Guetzkow (Ed.), *Groups, leadership, and men* (pp. 177–190). Pittsburgh, PA: Carnegie.

Asch, S. E. (1952). *Social psychology*. Englewood Cliffs, NJ: Prentice Hall.

Baker, M. (2017). Service failures and recovery: Theories and models. In E. Koc (Ed.), *Service failures and recovery in tourism and hospitality* (pp. 27–41). Wallingford, Oxford: CABI.

Banerjee, S., and Chai, L. (2019). Effect of individualism on online user ratings: theory and evidence. *Journal of Global Marketing*, 1–22.

Bathaee, A. (2011). Culture affects consumer behavior: Theoretical reflections and an illustrative example with Germany and Iran (No. 02/2011). Wirtschaftswissenschaftliche Diskussionspapiere.

Becker, C. (2000). Service recovery strategies: The impact of cultural differences. *Journal of Hospitality and Tourism Research*, 24(4), 526–538.

Bergiel, E. B., Bergiel, B. J., and Upson, J. W. (2012). Revisiting Hofstede's dimensions: Examining the cultural convergence of the United States and Japan. *American Journal of Management*, 12(1), 69–79.

Briley, C. A., and Wyer, R. S., Jr (2002). The effect of group membership salience on the avoidance of negative outcomes: Implications for social and consumer decisions. *Journal of Consumer Research*, 29(3), 400–415.

Cialdini, R. B. (2013). *Influence: Science and practice*. New York: Harper Collins.

Correia, A., Kozak, M., and Ferradeira, J. (2011). Impact of culture on tourist decision-making styles. *International Journal of Tourism Research*, 13(5), 433–446.

Cosgrave, J. (2006). Introduction: Gambling, risk and late capitalism. In J. Cosgrave (Ed.), *The sociology of risk and gambling reader* (pp. 1–24). New York: Routledge.

Crotts, J. C., and Erdmann, R. (2000) Does national culture influence consumers' evaluation of travel services? A test of Hofstede's model of cross-cultural differences. *Managing Service Quality*, 10(5), 410–419.

Dalgic, A., Toksoz, D., and Birdir, K. (2017). The role of empowerment, internal communication, waiting time and speed in service recovery. In E. Koc (Ed.). *Service failures and recovery in tourism and hospitality* (pp. 181–196). Wallingford, Oxford: CABI.

De Waal, B. (1995). Motivations for video game play: A study of social, cultural and physiological factors (Doctoral dissertation theses). Simon Fraser University.

Dimitriou, C. (2017). Understanding and dealing with service failures in tourism and hospitality. In E. Koc (Ed.), *Service failures and recovery in tourism and hospitality* (pp. 9–26). Wallingford, Oxford: CABI.

Donthu, N., and Yoo, B. (1998). Cultural influences on service quality expectations. *Journal of Service Research*, 1(2), 178–186.

Fan, A., Shen, H., Wu, L., Mattila, A. S., and Bilgihan, A. (2018). Whom do we trust? Cultural differences in consumer responses to online recommendations. *International Journal of Contemporary Hospitality Management*, 30(3), 1508–1525.

Fischer, A. H., and Evers, C. (2013). The social basis of emotion in men and women. *The SAGE handbook of gender and psychology*, 183–198.

Furrer, O., Liu, B., and Sudharshan, D. (2000). The relationships between culture and service quality perceptions: Basis for cross-cultural market segmentation and resource allocation. *Journal of Service Research*, 2(4), 355–371.

Gazda, S. K., Connor, R. C., Edgar, R. K., and Cox, F. (2005). A division of labour with role specialization in group–hunting bottlenose dolphins (Tursiops truncatus) off Cedar Key, Florida. *Proceedings of the Royal Society B: Biological Sciences*, 272(1559), 135–140.

Gi Park, S., Kim, K., and O'Neill, M. (2014). Complaint behavior intentions and expectation of service recovery in individualistic and collectivistic cultures. *International Journal of Culture, Tourism and Hospitality Research*, 8(3), 255–271.

Gudykunst, W. B. (1998). Applying anxiety\uncertainty management (AUM) theory to intercultural adjustment training. *International Journal of Intercultural Relations*, 22(2), 227–250.

Gudykunst, W. B., and Lee, C. M. (2003). Assessing the validity of self-construal scales: A response to Levine et al. *Human Communication Research*, 29, 253–274.

Hall, E. T., and Hall, M. R. (1990). *Hidden differences*. Garden City, NY: Anchor Books.

Han, B., and Heather, J. (2001). Korean Tourists' Characteristics in Guam. *Journal of Photo-Geographers*, 11(1), 69–83.

Han, H., Kiatkawsin, K., Kim, W., and Lee, S. (2017). Investigating customer loyalty formation for wellness spa: Individualism vs. collectivism. *International Journal of Hospitality Management*, 67, 11–23.

Hoare, R. J., and Butcher, K. (2008). Do Chinese cultural values affect customer satisfaction/loyalty? *International Journal of Contemporary Hospitality Management*, 20(2), 156.

Hofstede, G. (1980). *Culture's consequences: International differences in work-related values*. Beverly Hills, CA: Sage.

Hofstede, G., Hofstede, G. J., and Minkov, M. (2010). Cultures and organizations: Software of the mind (3rd ed.). New York: McGraw-Hill.

Hofstede, G. (2020). Cultural dimensions. https://www.hofstede-insights.com/product/compare-countries/ (accessed 20 January 2020).

Hosany, S., and Martin, D. (2012). Self-image congruence in consumer behavior. *Journal of Business Research*, 65(5), 685–691.

Huang, J. H., Huang, C. T. and Wu, S. (1996). National character and response to unsatisfactory hotel service. *International Journal of Hospitality Management*, 15(3), 229–243.

Hui, C. H., and Triandis, H. C. (1986). Individualism collectivism: A study of cross-cultural researchers. *Journal of Cross-Cultural Psychology*, 17, 225–248.

Hui, M. K., and Au, K. (2001). Justice perceptions of complaint-handling: A cross-cultural comparison between PRC and Canadian customers. *Journal of Business Research*, 52(2), 161–173.

Janis, I. L., and Janis, I. L. (1982). *Groupthink: Psychological studies of policy decisions and fiascoes* (Vol. 349). Boston: Houghton Mifflin.

Jeong, J. Y., Crompton, J. L., and Hyun, S. S. (2019). What makes you select a higher price option? Price–quality heuristics, cultures, and travel group compositions. *International Journal of Tourism Research*, 21(1), 1–10.

Kelly, P., Lawlor, J., and Mulvey, M. (2017). Self-service technologies: Service failures and recovery. In E. Koc (Ed.), *Service failures and recovery in tourism and hospitality: A practical manual* (pp. 100–121). Wallingford, Oxford: CABI.

Kim, J. H. (2017). Memorable service experiences: A service failure and recovery perspective. In E. Koc (Ed.), *Service failures and recovery in tourism and hospitality* (pp. 56–69). Wallingford, Oxford: CABI.

Kim, H., and Markus, H. (1999). Deviance or uniqueness, harmony or conformity? A cultural analysis. *Journal of Personality and Social Psychology*, 77(4), 785–800.

Kim, M., Choi, L., Knutson, B. J., and Borchgrevink, C. P. (2017). Hotel employees' organizational behaviors from cross-national perspectives. *International Journal of Contemporary Hospitality Management*, 29(12), 3082–3100.

Kim, M. G., Lee, C. H. and Mattila, A. S. (2014). Determinants of customer complaint behavior in a restaurant context: The role of culture, price level, and customer loyalty. *Journal of Hospitality Marketing and Management*, 23(8), 885–906.

King, S. L., and Janik, V. M. (2013). Bottlenose dolphins can use learned vocal labels to address each other. *Proceedings of the National Academy of Sciences*, 110(32), 13216–13221.

Kirkman, B. L., Lowe, K. B. and Gibson, C. B. (2006). A quarter century of culture's consequences: A review of empirical research incorporating Hofstede's cultural values framework. *Journal of International Business Studies*, 37(3), 285–320.

Koc, E. (2006). Total quality management and business excellence in services: The implications of all-inclusive pricing system on internal and external customer satisfaction in the Turkish tourism market. *Total Quality Management and Business Excellence*, 17(7), 857–877.

Koc, E. (2013a). Power distance and its implications for upward communication and empowerment: Crisis management and recovery in hospitality services. *The International Journal of Human Resource Management*, 24(19), 3681–3696.

Koc, E. (2013b). Inversionary and liminoidal consumption: Gluttony on holidays and obesity. *Journal of Travel and Tourism Marketing*, 30(8), 825–838.

Koc, E. (2016). *Tüketici Davranışı ve Pazarlama Stratejileri: Global ve Yerel Yaklaşım* (Vol. 7). Ankara, Turkey: Baskı, Seçkin Yayınları.

Koc, E. (2019). Service failures and recovery in hospitality and tourism: A review of literature and recommendations for future research. *Journal of Hospitality Marketing and Management*, 28(5), 513–537.

Koc, E., Ar, A. A., and Aydin, G. (2017a). The potential implications of indulgence and restraint on service encounters in tourism and hospitality. *Ecoforum Journal*, 6(3) 1–6. http://www.ecoforumjournal.ro/index.php/eco/article/view/657

Koc, E., Ulukoy, M., Kilic, R., Yumusak, S., and Bahar, R. (2017b). The influence of customer participation on service failure perceptions. *Total Quality Management and Business Excellence*, 28(3–4), 390–404.

Koc, E. Yilmaz, O., and Boz, H. (2020). Service Recovery Paradox in Restraint Cultures: An Implementation in Tourism Sector. Journal of Empiricial Economics and Social Sciences. Article in Press.

Kong, M., and Jogaratnam, G. (2007). The influence of culture on perceptions of service employee behavior. Managing Service Quality, 17 (3), 275–297.

Kraus, M. W., Huang, C., and Keltner, D. (2010). Tactile communication, cooperation, and performance: An ethological study of the NBA. Emotion, 10(5), 745.

LaRoche, M., Kalamas, M. and Cleveland, M. (2005), "'I' versus 'we': how individualists and collectivists use information sources to formulate their service expectations", International Marketing Review, Vol. 22 No. 3, pp. 279–308.

Litvin, S. W., and Kar, G. H. (2003). Individualism/collectivism as a moderating factor to the self-image congruity concept. Journal of Vacation Marketing, 10(1), 23–42.

Lorenzoni, N. and Lewis, B.R. (2004), "Service recovery in the airline industry: a cross-cultural comparison of the attitudes and behaviors of British and Italian front-line personnel", Managing Service Quality, Vol. 14 No. 1, pp. 11–25.

Liu, R. R., and McClure, P. (2001). Recognizing cross-cultural differences in customer complaint behavior and intentions: An empirical examination. *The Journal of Customer Marketing*, 18(1), 54–75.

Magnini, V. P., Hyun, S., Kim, B., and Uysal, M. (2013). The influences of collectivism in hospitality work settings. International Journal of Contemporary Hospitality Management, 25(6), 844–864.

Manrai, L. A., and Manrai, A. (2011). Hofstede's cultural dimensions and tourist behaviors: A review and conceptual framework. *Journal of Economics, Finance and Administrative Science*, 16(31), 23.

Mariani, M., and Predvoditeleva, M. (2019). How do online reviewers' cultural traits and perceived experience influence hotel online ratings?. International Journal of Contemporary Hospitality Management.

Markus, H. and Kitayama, S. (1990), "Culture and the self: Implications for cognition, emotion, and motivation", Psychological Review, Vol. 98 No. 2, pp. 224–253.

Mattila, A. S. (1999). The role of culture in the service evaluation process. Journal of Service Research, 1 (3), 250–261.

Mattila, S.A. and Patterson, P.G. (2004), "The impact of culture on consumers' perceptions of service recovery efforts", Journal of Retailing, Vol. 80 No. 3, pp. 196–206.

McNeill, L. (2006). The influence of culture on retail sales promotion use in Chinese supermarkets. *Australasian Marketing Journal*, 14(2), 34–46.

McNeill, L. S., Fam, K. S., and Chung, K. (2014). Applying transaction utility theory to sales promotion–the impact of culture on consumer satisfaction. *The International Review of Retail, Distribution and Consumer Research*, 24(2), 166–185.

Miyamoto, Y., and Schwarz, N. (2006). When conveying a message may hurt the relationship: Cultural differences in the difficulty of using an answering machine. Journal of Experimental Social Psychology, 42(4), 540–547.

Mok, C. and DeFranco, A.L. (1999), "Chinese cultural values: their implications for travel and tourism marketing", Journal of Travel and Tourism Marketing, Vol. 8 No. 2, pp. 99–114.

Mueller, R. D., Palmer, A., Mack, R., and McMullan, R. (2003). Service in the restaurant industry: An American and Irish comparison of service failures and recovery strategies. *International Journal of Hospitality Management*, 22, 395–418.

Ngai, E. W., Heung, V. C., Wong, Y. H., and Chan, F. K. (2007). Consumer complaint behaviour of Asians and non-Asians about hotel services: An empirical analysis. *European Journal of Marketing*, 41(11/12), 1375–1391.

Noja, G. G., Petrović, N., and Cristea, M. (2018). Turning points in migrants' labour market integration in Europe and benefit spillovers for Romania and Serbia: the role of socio-psychological credentials. *Zbornik Radova Ekonomski Fakultet u Rijeka*, 36(2), 489–518.

Nummenmaa, L., Tuominen, L., Dunbar, R., Hirvonen, J., Manninen, S., Arponen, E., ... and Sams, M. (2016). Social touch modulates endogenous μ-opioid system activity in humans. *Neuroimage*, 138, 242–247.

Organ, D. (1988). *Organizational citizenship behavior: The good soldier syndrome.*, Lexington, MA: Lexington Books.

Ozorio, B., Lam, D., and Fong, H. N. (2010). The influence of individualism and uncertainty avoidance on per capita gambling turnover. *International Gambling Studies*, 10(3), 221–238.

Park, S. Y. (1998). A comparison of Korean and American gift-giving behaviours. *Psychology and Marketing*, 15(6), 577–593.

Patterson, P. G., and Smith, T. (2003). A cross-cultural study of switching barriers and propensity to stay with service providers. *Journal of Retailing*, 79(2), 107–120.

Patterson, P., Cowley, K., and Prasongsukarn, K. (2006). Service failure recovery: The moderating impact of individual-level cultural value orientation on perceptions of justice. *International Journal of Research in Marketing*, 23(3), 263–277.

Pearce, E., Launay, J., and Dunbar, R. I. (2015). The ice-breaker effect: Singing mediates fast social bonding. *Royal Society Open Science*, 2(10), 150221.

Pollay, R. W., and Gallagher, K. (1990). Advertising and cultural values: Reflections in the distorted mirror. *International Journal of Advertising*, 9(4), 359–372.

Radojevic, T., Stanisic, N., and Stanic, N. (2019). The culture of hospitality: From anecdote to evidence. *Annals of Tourism Research*, 79, 102789.

Reisinger, Y. (2009). Cross-cultural differences in tourist behaviour. In M. Kozak and A. Decrop (Eds), *Handbook of tourist behaviour: Theory and practice* (pp. 237–255). Routledge: New York.

Riggs, A. M. (2016). *Working in the Middle East: An American woman's story*. Santa Barbara, CA: ABC-CLIO.

Ruiz-Equihua, D., Romero, J., and Casaló, L. V. (2019). Better the devil you know? The moderating role of brand familiarity and indulgence vs. restraint cultural dimension on eWOM influence in the hospitality industry. *Journal of Hospitality Marketing and Management*, 1–19.

Schwartz, S., and Bilsky, W. (1989). Toward a theory of the universal content and structure of values: Extensions and cross-cultural replications. *Journal of Personality and Social Psychology*, 58, 878–891.

Sharma, P., Chen. I. S. N., and Luk, S. T. K. (2012). Exploring the role of IND–COL as a moderator in the comprehensive service evaluation model. *Journal of International Consumer Marketing*, 24(1–2), 129–142.

Sherif, M. (1967). *Group conflict and co-operation: Their social psychology*. London: Routledge and Kegan Paul.

Sigala, M., and Sakellaridis, O. (2004). The impact of users' cultural characteristics on e-service quality: implications for globalizing tourism and hospitality websites. In A. Frew (Ed.), *Information and communication technologies in tourism* (pp. 106–117). Vienna, Austria: Springer Verlag.

Sorokowski, P., Sorokowska, A., Onyishi, I. E., and Szarota, P. (2013). Montesquieu hypothesis and football: Players from hot countries are more expressive after scoring a goal. *Polish Psychological Bulletin*, 44, 421–430.

Stauss, B., and Mang, P. (1999). Culture shocks in inter-cultural service encounters. *Journal of Services Marketing*, 13(4/5), 329–346.

Swanson S. R., Huang Y., and Wang B. (2014). Hospitality-based critical incidents: a cross-cultural comparison. *International Journal of Contemporary Hospitality Management*, 26(1), 50–68.

Thayer, S.,. (1982). Social touching. In W. Schiff, and E. Foulke (Eds), *Tactual perception: A sourcebook* (pp. 263–304). New York: Cambridge University Press.

Triandis, H. C. (1993). Collectivism and Individualism as Cultural Syndromes. *Cross-Cultural Research*, 3–4, 155–180.

Triandis, H. C. (1995), *Individualism and collectivism.* San Francisco, CA: West View Press.

Triandis, H. C., and Gelfland, M. J. (1998). Converging measurement of horizontal and vertical individualism and collectivism. *Journal of Personality and Social Psychology*, 74, 118–128.

Triandis, H. C., Chan, D. K.-S., Bhawuk, D. P. S., Iwao, S., and Sinha, J. B. P. (1995). Multimethod probes of allocentrism and idiocentrism. *International Journal of Psychology*, 30, 461–480.

Trompenaars, A., and Hampden-Turner, C. (1998). *Riding the waves of cultural diversity in global business*. London: Nicholas Brealey Publishing.

Tsai, J. L., and Levenson, R. W. (1997). Cultural influences on emotional responding: Chinese American and European American dating couples during interpersonal conflict. *Journal of Cross-Cultural Psychology*, 28, 600–662.

Tsaur, S. H., Lin, C. T., and Wu, C. S. (2005). Cultural differences of service quality and behavioral intention in tourist hotels. *Journal of Hospitality and Leisure Marketing*, 13(1), 41–63.

Wen, J., Hu, Y., and Kim, H. J. (2018). Impact of individual cultural values on hotel guests' positive emotions and positive eWOM intention: Extending the cognitive appraisal framework. *International Journal of Contemporary Hospitality Management*, 30(3), 1769–1787.

Whitley, B. E., and Kite, M. E. (2010). *The psychology of prejudice and discrimination.* Belmont, CA: Wadsworth.

Yang, K.-S. (1988). Will societal modernization eventually eliminate cross-cultural psychological differences? In M. H. Bond (Ed.), *The cross-cultural challenge to social psychology* (pp. 67–85). Newbury Park, CA: Sage.

Yuksel, A., Kilinc, U. K., and Yuksel, F. (2006). Cross-national analysis of hotel customers' attitudes toward complaining and their complaining behaviors. *Tourism Management*, 27(1), 11–24.

Chapter 10

Performance and humane orientation as cultural variables

Learning Objectives

After reading this chapter, you should be able to:

- understand the concepts of performance and humane orientation;
- explain the main characteristics of performance and humane orientation;
- understand the main implications of performance orientation on the attitudes and behaviour of tourism and hospitality customers, employees, and managers;
- understand the main implications of humane orientation on the attitudes and behaviour of tourism and hospitality customers, employees, and managers.

Introduction

This chapter explains performance and humane orientations as two cultural variables and their implications for the management and marketing of tourism and hospitality businesses. The origins of the performance orientation go back to McClelland's (1961) work, *The Achieving Society*, on need achievement. The need for achievement can be defined as a value, or an intrinsic desire to perform well against a standard of excellence. On the other hand, the origins of the humane orientation go back to Kluckhohn and Strodtbeck's (1961) work, *Variations in Value Orientations*, on the "Human Nature is Good versus Human Nature is Evil" dimension. Kluckhohn and Strodtbeck thought that every society had five basic problems to solve:

1. On what aspect of time should we primarily focus – past, present or future?
2. What is the relationship between humanity and its natural environment – mastery, submission, or harmony?

3. How should individuals relate with others – hierarchically (which they called "lineal"), as equals ("collateral"), or according to their individual merit?
4. What is the prime motivation for behaviour – to express one's self ("Being"), to grow ("Being-in-becoming"), or to achieve?
5. What is the nature of human nature – good, bad ("evil") or a mixture?

While the first problem or issue identified by Kluckhohn and Strodtbeck relates to time orientation, the third problem/issue relates to power distance as cultural dimensions explained in this book. Again, while the fourth problem/issue relates partially to individualism, masculinity and performance orientation, the fifth problem/issue relates to humane orientation.

Performance orientation and humane orientations are the least studied values or cultural dimensions. There is a dearth of empirical research findings relating to business and management applications, and research results relating especially to tourism and hospitality marketing and management are almost non-existent. Hence, implications of the characteristics of these dimensions, and the guidelines provided in the chapter, in general, will be based on the interpretations of the characteristics.

The concepts of performance orientation and humane orientation

Performance orientation can be defined as the extent to which a society or an organisation encourages and rewards the members of a group to be goal-directed, competitive, hard-working, improving performance, and excellence. In a society where performance orientation is low, people tend to pay less attention to performance, and more attention to loyalty, belonging, and background (Hofstede and Bond, 1984). Table 10.1 summarises some of the distinct characteristics of cultures with high and low performance orientation.

Exercise

Study the "Average Usual Weekly Hours Worked" table for the OECD countries (prepared by the OECD) available at https://stats.oecd.org/Index.aspx?DataSetCode=AVE_HRS.

Is working long hours a good indicator of performance orientation? If not, explain why? What other factors may be influential?

It can be seen that some of the high and low performance-orientation characteristics resemble the certain characteristics of other cultural dimensions. Table 10.2 shows the potential associations of the characteristics of high and low performance orientations with other cultural dimensions, or perspectives.

Although McClelland (1961) argued that the climate had an important impact on the need for achievement, Javidan's (2004) study found very little support for the climate's influence on performance orientation. Javidan's (2004) study found that while 13% of the variations of performance orientation were explained by climatic differences, 87% of

Table 10.1 Summary of the main characteristics of high and low performance orientation

High Performance-Oriented Cultures E.g., Switzerland, Singapore, New Zealand, South Korea, China, Australia, Netherlands, and Germany	*Low Performance-Oriented Cultures E.g., Greece, Venezuela, Russia, Hungary, Portugal, Argentina and Turkey Greece, Russia, Hungary, Portugal, Argentina, and Turkey*
Value education, training and development	Value societal and family relationships
Emphasise results more than people	Emphasise loyalty and belongingness
Reward performance	Have a high level of respect for the quality of life
Value assertiveness, competitiveness, and materialism	Emphasise seniority and experience
Expect demanding targets	Value harmony with the environment rather than control
Believe that individuals are in control	Have performance appraisal systems that emphasise integrity, loyalty, and cooperative spirit
Have a "can-do" attitude	View feedback and appraisal as judgemental and discomforting
Value and reward individual achievement	View assertiveness as socially unacceptable
Have performance appraisal systems that emphasise achieving results	Regard being motivated by money as unacceptable
View feedback as necessary for improvement	View merit pay as potentially destructive to harmony
Value taking initiative	Value "attending the right school" as an Important success criterion
Value bonuses and financial rewards	Emphasise tradition
Believe that anyone can succeed if he or she tries hard enough	Have a high value for sympathy
Believe that schooling and education are critical for success	Associate competition with defeat and punishment
Value what you do more than who you are	Value who you are more than what you do
Attach little importance to age in promotional decisions	Pay particular attention to age in promotional decisions
Value being direct, explicit, and to the point in communication	Value ambiguity and subtlety in language and communications
Have a monochronic approach to time	Have a polychronic approach to time
Have a sense of urgency	Have a low sense of urgency

Source: House et al. (2004: 244).

Table 10.2 Associations of high and low performance orientations with other cultural dimensions

High Performance-Oriented Cultures E.g., Switzerland, Singapore, New Zealand, South Korea, China, Australia, Netherlands, and Germany	*Potential Association with Other Cultural Dimensions*	*Low Performance-Oriented Cultures E.g., Greece, Venezuela, Russia, Hungary, Portugal, Argentina and Turkey Greece, Russia, Hungary, Portugal, Argentina, and Turkey*	*Potential Association with Other Cultural Dimensions*
Value education, training, and development	Long-term orientation	Value societal and family relationships	Femininity, collectivism
Emphasises results more than people	Individualism, masculinity, low power distance, low-context	Emphasise loyalty and belongingness	Femininity, collectivism
Reward performance	Masculinity, individualism	Have a high level of respect for the quality of life	Femininity, collectivism
Value assertiveness, competitiveness, and materialism	Masculinity, assertiveness, individualism, high power distance	Emphasise seniority and experience	Collectivism, high power distance
Expect demanding targets	Masculinity, individualism, high power distance	Value harmony with the environment rather than control	Femininity, collectivism
Believe that individuals are in control	Long-term orientation, indulgence	Have performance appraisal systems that emphasise integrity, loyalty, and cooperative spirit	Femininity, collectivism, high power distance
Have a "can-do" attitude	Masculinity, individualism	View feedback and appraisal as judgemental and discomforting	Femininity, restraint
Value and reward individual achievement	Individualism, masculinity	View assertiveness as socially unacceptable	Egalitarianism, collectivism, femininity
Have performance appraisal systems that emphasise achieving results	Individualism, masculinity	Regard being motivated by money as unacceptable	Collectivism, femininity
View feedback as necessary for improvement	Assertiveness, individualism	View merit pay as potentially destructive to harmony	Collectivism, egalitarianism

Table 10.2 continued

High Performance-Oriented Cultures E.g., Switzerland, Singapore, New Zealand, South Korea, China, Australia, Netherlands, and Germany	*Potential Association with Other Cultural Dimensions*	*Low Performance-Oriented Cultures E.g., Greece, Venezuela, Russia, Hungary, Portugal, Argentina and Turkey Greece, Russia, Hungary, Portugal, Argentina, and Turkey*	*Potential Association with Other Cultural Dimensions*
Value taking initiative	Low power distance	Value "attending the right school" as an important success criterion	High power distance
Value bonuses and financial rewards	Masculinity, individualism, high power distance	Emphasise tradition	Long-term orientation, past orientation, polychronic
Believe that anyone can succeed if he or she tries hard enough	Assertiveness, masculinity	Have a high value for sympathy	Femininity, collectivism
Believe that schooling and education are critical for success	Assertiveness	Associate competition with defeat and punishment	Femininity, collectivism, restraint
Attach little importance to age in promotional decisions	Low power distance	Pay particular attention to age in promotional decisions	High power distance
Value being direct, explicit, and to the point in communication	Low context, individualism	Value ambiguity and subtlety in language and communications	High context, collectivism
Have a monochronic approach to time	Low-context, present, and future orientations	Have a polychronic approach to time	High-context, past orientation
Have a sense of urgency	Monochronic	Have a low sense of urgency	Polychronic

the differences were attributable to societal differences. However, 68% of the differences in performance orientation were explainable by the geography of a country.

On the other hand, humane orientation is the extent to which a society or an organisation encourages and rewards the members of the group to be fair, altruistic, friendly, generous, caring and kind to others. In a society where humane orientation is high, people tend to play a high value on helping others and being kind; whilst in a country where human orientation is low, people tend to place more emphasis on self-enhancement and gratification, and they are expected to take care of themselves. Table 10.3 summarises some of the distinct characteristics of cultures with high performance and human orientation.

Table 10.3 Summary of the main characteristics of high and low human orientation

High Humane-Oriented Societies *E.g., Zambia, Philippines, Ireland, India, Denmark, China, Japan, and Australia*	*Low Humane-Oriented Societies* *E.g., Germany, Spain, Greece, France, Singapore, Switzerland, Italy, and Brazil*
Others are important (e,g., family, friends, community, strangers	Self-interest is important
Fewer psychological and pathological problems	More psychological and pathological problems
Values of altruism, benevolence, kindness, love, and generosity have high priority	Values of pleasure, comfort, self-enjoyment have high priority
Need for belonging and affiliation motivate people	Power and material possessions motivate people
Personal and family relationships induce protection for individuals	The welfare state guarantees social and economic protection of individuals
Close circle receives material, financial, and social support; concern extends to all people and nature	Lack of support for others; predominance of self-enhancement
Members of the society are responsible for promoting the well-being of others; the state is not actively involved	State provides social and economic support for individuals' well-being
The state supports the private sector and maintains a balance between public and private domains	The state sponsors public provisions and sectors
Public policy makers establish sanctions against child labour practices	Public policy makers consider child labour practices as a somewhat less-important issue
Members of the society are urged to be sensitive to all forms of racial discrimination	Members of society are not sensitive to all forms of racial discrimination
People are expected to promote paternalistic norms and patronage relationships	Formal welfare institutions replace paternalistic norms and patronage relationships
People are expected to provide social support to each other	People are expected to solve personal problems on their own
The children of less-developed societies are expected to give material support to their parents in their old age	The children of more-developed societies are not expected to give material support to their parents in their old age
The children of less-developed societies can participate in the labour force to help out their families	The children of more-developed societies are not expected to participate in labour force to help out their families
Children are expected to be obedient	Children should be autonomous
Parents should closely control their children	Family members are independent

Source: House (2004: 570).

Information zone

Altruism

Warneken and Tomasello's (2006) experiments with 18-month-old human infants and monkeys produced similar results in terms of altruistic behaviours. In the experiments, an adult was shown as having difficulties in achieving a goal. Warneken and Tomasello explain that helping someone solve a problem is an interesting cognitive phenomenon as in order to do so one must understand the goal and the obstacles. In Warneken and Tomasello's experiments, infants helped adults in different situations such as by handing out-of-reach objects to the experimenter, completing the experimenter's piling of books when he failed in his attempt, and opening the door of a cabinet when the experimenter's hands were full. In all the cases, the infants helped the experimenter when he looked to them or verbally explained his problem. The infants helped the experimenter without receiving any benefits, that is, they behaved altruistically. When Warneken and Tomasello conducted similar tests with chimpanzees, chimpanzees reliably retrieved objects for humans, again without receiving any benefits.

As in the case of performance orientation, human orientation characteristics also resemble certain characteristics of other cultural dimensions. It can be seen that some of the high and low performance-orientation characteristics resemble certain characteristics of other cultural dimensions. Table 10.4 provides the potential associations of the characteristics of high and low humane with other cultural dimensions, or perspectives.

As in the case of Javidan's (2004) research on performance orientation, Kabasakal and Bodur (2004) also found a weak relationship between climatic conditions and humane orientations of countries. However, Kabasakal and Bodur (2004) found that humane orientation scores were negatively correlated with gross national products of countries.

Information zone

Performance orientation, assertiveness, emotional intelligence, and NLP

As explained in Chapter 8, self-motivation, as an element of emotional intelligence, can be one of the best predictor of assertiveness values, and performance orientation (Nikolić, 2014). Thus, neurolinguistic programming (NLP), which is used for self-development and achieving objectives in life, can be expected to increase an individual's assertiveness and performance orientation. Bandler and Grinder (1975), the two developers of neurolinguistic programming,as a pseudoscientific approach to communication, personal development, and psychotherapy, claim that there is a connection between neurological processes (neuro-), language (linguistic), and behavioural patterns. NLP has been discredited as a pseudoscience, as there is no

Table 10.4 Associations of high and low humane orientations with other cultural dimensions

High Humane-Oriented Societies E.g., Zambia, Philippines, Ireland, India, Denmark, China, Japan, and Australia	*Potential Association with Other Cultural Dimensions*	*Low Humane-Oriented Societies E.g., Germany, Spain, Greece, France, Singapore, Switzerland, Italy, and Brazil*	*Potential Association with Other Cultural Dimensions*
Others are important (e.g., family, friends, community, and strangers	Collectivism, femininity, egalitarianism, low context	Self-interest is important	Individualism, masculinity, assertiveness, high-context
Fewer psychological and pathological problems	Indulgence	More psychological and pathological problems	Restraint
Values of altruism, benevolence, kindness, love, and generosity have high priority	Collectivism, femininity, egalitarianism	Values of pleasure, comfort, self-enjoyment have high priority	Individualism, masculinity, assertiveness
Need for belonging and affiliation motivate people	Collectivism, femininity, egalitarianism, low power distance, high context	Power and material possessions motivate people	Individualism, masculinity, assertiveness, high power distance, low context
Personal and family relationships induce protection for the individuals	Collectivism, femininity	Welfare state guarantees the social and economic protection of individuals	Individualism, masculinity
Close circle receives material, financial, and social support; concern extends to all people and nature	Collectivism, high in-group collectivism femininity	Lack of support for others; predominance of self-enhancement	Individualism, masculinity
Members of the society are responsible for promoting the well-being of others; the state is not actively involved	Collectivism, high in-group collectivism femininity	State provides social and economic support for individuals' well-being	Individualism, masculinity (also high feminine cultures as in the case of Scandinavia as the state applies measure to ensure the welfare of citizens)
Members of the society are urged to be sensitive to all forms of racial discrimination	Egalitarianism, femininity	Members of the society are not sensitive to all forms of racial discrimination	Assertiveness, masculinity

Table 10.4 continued

High Humane-Oriented Societies E.g., Zambia, Philippines, Ireland, India, Denmark, China, Japan, and Australia	*Potential Association with Other Cultural Dimensions*	*Low Humane-Oriented Societies E.g., Germany, Spain, Greece, France, Singapore, Switzerland, Italy, and Brazil*	*Potential Association with Other Cultural Dimensions*
People are expected to provide social support to each other	Collectivism, femininity	People are expected to solve personal problems on their own	Individualism, masculinity
Children are expected to be obedient	High-power distance, high-risk avoidance	Children should be autonomous	Low-power distance, low-risk avoidance
Parents should closely control their children	High-power distance, high-risk avoidance	Family members are independent	Low-power distance, low-risk avoidance

scientific evidence supporting the claims made by NLP advocates (Sharpley, 1987; Witkowski, 2010; Thyer and Pignotti, 2015). However, the NLP has been adopted by many hypnotherapists and also by several business and behavioural consultancy companies to train people in businesses and government agencies on management, leadership, and personal and organisational development. According to NLP, the inner communication, which is made up of images, sounds, and feelings, developed within oneself, can help people adjust behaviour and achieve goals. Several centuries before Bandler and Grinder (1975), Rumi (1207–1273), an eastern philosopher who lived in Asia Minor (Turkey), emphasised the importance of inner communication in adjusting one's behaviour and achieving personal goals with his famous quote "What you seek is seeking you".

Table 10.5 shows the performance and humane-orientation scores of selected countries researched in the GLOBE project by House et al. (2004). According to Table 10.5, countries such as Switzerland, Singapore, New Zealand, South Korea, China, Australia, Netherlands, and Germany have a high-performance orientation, while countries such as Greece, Venezuela, Russia, Hungary, Portugal, Argentina, and Turkey appear to have a relatively low level of performance orientation. Likewise, while countries such as Zambia, Philippines, Ireland, India, Denmark, China, Japan, and Australia have a high level of humane orientation, countries such as Germany, Spain, Greece, France, Singapore, Switzerland, Italy, and Brazil have a low level of humane orientation.

In the GLOBE Project (House et al., 2004), cultural dimensions were investigated from the perspectives of the values of people (i.e., what they prefer, their ideals), and

Table 10.5 Performance- and humane-orientation scores of selected countries

Performance-Orientation Society (Practices*)					
Rank	*Country*	*Score*	*Rank*	*Country*	*Score*
1	Switzerland	4.94	31	Mexico	4.10
2	Singapore	4.90	32	Germany [f]	4.09
3	Hong Kong	4.80	33	England	4.08
4	New Zealand	4.72	34	Israel	4.08
5	South Africa [a]	4.66	35	Brazil	4.04
6	Iran	4.58	36	Spain	4.01
7	Taiwan	4.56	37	Morocco	3.99
8	South Korea	4.55	38	Kuwait	3.95
9	Canada [b]	4.49	39	Colombia	3.94
10	U.S.	4.49	40	Thailand	3.93
11	Philippines	4.47	41	Nigeria	3.92
12	China	4.45	42	Poland	3.89
13	Austria	4.44	43	Georgia	3.88
14	Indonesia	4.41	44	Turkey	3.83
15	Australia	4.36	45	Finland	3.81
16	Ireland	4.36	46	Guatemala	3.81
17	Malaysia	4.34	47	Sweden	3.72
18	Netherlands	4.32	48	El Salvador	3.72
19	Egypt	4.27	49	Namibia	3.67
20	Switzerland [c]	4.25	50	Slovenia	3.66
21	Germany [d]	4.25	51	Argentina	3.65
22	India	4.25	52	Bolivia	3.61
23	Zimbabwe	4.24	53	Portugal	3.60
24	Denmark	4.22	54	Italy	3.58
25	Japan	4.22	55	Kazakhstan	3.57
26	Ecuador	4.20	56	Qatar	3.45
27	Zambia	4.16	57	Hungary	3.43
28	Costa Rica	4.12	58	Russia	3.39
29	South Africa [e]	4.11	59	Venezuela	3.32
30	France	4.11	60	Greece	3.20

Table 10.5 continued

Humane-Orientation Society (Practices)*

Rank	*Country*	*Score*	*Rank*	*Country*	*Score*
1	Zambia	5.23	31	Kazakhstan	3.99
2	Philippines	5.12	32	Argentina	3.99
3	Ireland	4.96	33	Mexico	3.98
4	Malaysia	4.87	34	Finland	3.96
5	Thailand	4.81	35	Namibia	3.96
6	Egypt	4.73	36	Turkey	3.94
7	Indonesia	4.69	37	Russia	3.94
8	Ecuador	4.65	38	Switzerland[c]	3.93
9	India	4.57	39	Portugal	3.91
10	Kuwait	4.52	40	Hong Kong	3.90
11	Canada [a]	4.49	41	Guatemala	3.89
12	Zimbabwe	4.45	42	Netherlands	3.86
13	Denmark	4.44	43	South Korea	3.81
14	Qatar	4.42	44	Slovenia	3.79
15	Costa Rica	4.39	45	Austria	3.72
16	China	4.36	46	Colombia	3.72
17	South Africa [b]	4.34	47	England	3.72
18	New Zealand	4.32	48	El Salvador	3.71
19	Japan	4.30	49	Brazil	3.66
20	Australia	4.28	50	Italy	3.63
21	Venezuela	4.25	51	Poland	3.61
22	Iran	4.23	52	Switzerland	3.60
23	Morocco	4.19	53	South Africa [d]	3.49
24	Georgia	4.18	54	Singapore	3.49
25	U.S.	4.17	55	Germany [e]	3.40
26	Taiwan	4.11	56	France	3.40
27	Sweden	4.10	57	Hungary	3.35
28	Nigeria	4.10	58	Greece	3.34
29	Israel	4.10	59	Spain	3.32
30	Bolivia	4.05	60	Germany [f]	3.18

Source: House et al. (2004).
* Higher scores indicate greater assertiveness. **Higher scores indicate greater humane orientation.
[a] South Africa (White sample); [b] Canada (English-speaking) [a] Canada (English-speaking); [b] South Africa (Black sample)
[c] Switzerland (French-speaking); [d] Germany (East): Former GDR; [c] Switzerland (French-speaking); [d] South Africa (White sample)
[e] South Africa (White sample) [f] Germany (West): Former FRG [e] Germany (West): Former FRG; [f] Germany (East): Former GDR

the actual practices within the country. A comparison of practice and value tables in the GLOBE Project shows that there are large differences between practice and value scores of countries, that is, the difference between what people state as preferable (valued) and real practices. For instance, while Turkey's performance orientation score (practice) is 3.83, its performance orientation value score is 5.39 (Javidan, 2004).

CASE STUDY

Protection of one's *face* and performance orientation

As a relatively short-term oriented culture, in Turkey, the protection of one's *face* (not to be ashamed of in front of other people) and impression management is important. Protecting one's *face* and image, coupled with status orientation (due to the high level of power distance) results in conspicuous consumption, that is, the purchase of luxury goods and high-priced technology products. Although Turkey has the highest proportion of employees earning minimum wage among the European countries, with over 40% of employees earning wages below or equal to minimum wage (EUROSTAT, 2014), the amount of money spent for importing mobile phones between 2007 and 2017 reached about $24 billion (TUIK, 2019). Many people in Turkey work for low wages but do not refrain from purchasing the latest models of mobile phones, although it may mean paying an amount of money equal to several months of their salaries. Many people may also go for holidays worth several months' of salaries, or eat at luxury restaurants so that they can share their holidays or dining photos from luxury destinations, hotels, and restaurants in social media.

The protection of one's *face* and impression management efforts reflect in issues relating to performance orientation too. In Turkey, many students when they turn up for an exam tend to whinge to their friends and say "Oh I haven't studied at all", although they may have studied really hard. This is done a) because they are from a restraint culture (they tend to pessimistic), and b) for the protection of *face*, that is, if they receive lower marks in the exam, they do not want to be labelled as "stupid" (i.e., worked hard but still got low marks in the exam). This is because being labelled "stupid" is much worse than being labelled "lazy" in the society. On the other hand, in high-performance societies, for example, in Germany, if a student states that s/he has not studied at all for the exam, when s/he turns up for the exam, s/he may be perceived as totally irrational and weird.

Again, while Turkey's human orientation score (practice) is 3.94, its human orientation value score is 5.52 (Kabasakal and Bodur, 2004). In other words, while Turkish citizens view themselves as highly humane and performance oriented, in practice they are below average in both their performance and humane orientations. As stated in the "Research questions/ideas to pursue for researchers" section of this chapter, this difference may be investigated from the perspective of other cultural dimensions. It resembles the difference

Table 10.6 GDP per hour worked in OECD countries

Rank	*Country or Region*	*GDP per hour worked as % of USA (USA = 100)*	*Rank*	*Country or Region*	*GDP per hour worked as % of USA (USA = 100)*
1	Norway	135.1	19	Canada	73.8
2	Luxembourg	128	20	OECD Total	72.9
3	Ireland	111	21	Italy	72.8
4	United States	100	22	Iceland	65.1
5	Belgium	96.4	23	Japan	62.5
6	Netherlands	93.8	24	Slovenia	61.1
7	Denmark	92.9	25	New Zealand	58.9
8	France	92.8	26	Slovak Republic	54.1
9	Germany	90.9	27	Greece	53.7
10	G7 countries	86.0	28	Portugal	53.0
11	Switzerland	85.9	29	Czech Republic	48.3
12	Sweden	85.3	30	Korea	45.0
13	Austria	83.7	31	Turkey	45.0
14	Australia	82.7	32	Poland	43.8
15	Euro area	82.5	33	Estonia	43.4
16	Spain	78.0	34	Hungary	44.1
17	Finland	76.4	35	Russian Federation	37.4
18	United Kingdom	75.7	36	Mexico	29.9

Source: OECD (2020).

between the actual self-concept (who a person is) and the ideal self-concept (who a person wants to be or wants to be seen as) (Koc, 2016). As explained in Chapters 4, 8, and 9, people from the high-context, feminine, and collectivistic cultures may be more likely to be subjective, as opposed to the low-context, individualistic and masculine cultures. A realistic way of understanding performance orientation in a country would be to look at GDP per hour worked (Noja and Cristea, 2018). Table 10.6 shows a list of the GDP per hour worked in selected OECD countries and regions.

Exercise

Study the Global Competitiveness Report (2019) prepared by the World Economic Forum at http://www3.weforum.org/docs/WEF_TheGlobalCompetitivenessReport2019.pdf.

Identify the countries that are highly competitive and countries which are not so competitive. Do you see a link between a country's' levels of competitiveness and their levels of performance orientation?

Likewise, study the Travel and Tourism Competitiveness Report (2019) prepared by the World Economic Forum at https://www.weforum.org/reports/the-travel-tourism-competitiveness-report-2019.

Identify the countries which have highly competitive travel and tourism industries and countries which do not have competitive travel and tourism industries. Do you see a link between a country's' levels of competitiveness and its level of performance orientation? Please note that travel and tourism and competitiveness index in these reports measure competitiveness based on the following dimensions:

- enabling environment (business environment, safety and security, health and hygiene, human resources and labour market, information and communication technology readiness);
- travel and tourism policy and enabling conditions (prioritisation of travel and tourism industry, international openness, price competitiveness, environmental sustainability);
- infrastructure (air transport infrastructure, ground and port infrastructure; tourist service infrastructure);
- natural and cultural resources (natural resources, cultural resources and business travel).

NB: You are recommended that some of the measures such as natural and cultural resources in the Travel and Tourism Competitiveness Index may not be relevant for your performance-orientation analysis. Take out these and other factors which may appear irrelevant to you and make your evaluations accordingly.

The implications of performance orientation and humane orientation for tourism and hospitality

As mentioned in the introduction section, there is a dearth of research on performance and humane orientations in business and management. Hence, some of the following explanations and implications are based on inferences made of the general cultural characteristics of these orientations.

Marketing mix

Diehl et al.'s (2016) research with 924 participants from six countries found that humane orientation in an advertisement (i.e., displaying values of altruism, benevolence, kindness, love, and generosity; emphasising belongingness and affiliation, personal and family relationships, and protection of individuals) increased positive evaluation of the advertisement and perceived degree of social responsibility of the advertiser.

CASE STUDY

Altruism and conscience in primates

Researchers from the Northwestern University, Jules Masserman, Stanley Wechkin, and William Terris trained a group of rhesus monkeys to pull a different chain to dispense a food pellet in response to a blue or red light. In the first three days of the experiment, monkeys pulled chains to get their food. On the fourth day, one of the chains was programmed to administer a mild electric shock to the monkey in the chamber next door, visible through a one-way mirror.

The monkey pulling the chain was able to see that when s/he pulled the chain, the monkey in the next cage received a painful shock. It was observed that the majority of the monkeys (87% of them) refused to pull the chain. They would go hungry rather than hurt the monkey next door (Masserman et al., 1964; Wechkin et al., 1964)

NB. As the above experiments involved cruelty to animals they have been widely criticised.

It was interesting to see that the advertisement produced a positive attitude even in countries in which humane orientation was less highly valued. The higher the perceived degree of humane orientation in an advertisement, the more positive the evaluation of the advertisement, and the more likely participants were to evaluate the advertiser as being socially responsible. The variables of having humane orientation and being socially responsible positively influenced attitudes towards the product and, consequently, their behavioural intentions. This means that emphasising the humane elements not only in marketing communications but also in all other marketing mix elements may increase positive attitudes towards a tourism and hospitality business and its services in high or low humane-oriented societies.

CASE STUDY

Getir

Getir, which means "bring" in Turkish, is an Istanbul (Turkey)-based company that offers ultrafast deliveries (from fast-moving consumer goods (FMCG) products such as a single ice-cream to dog food, and iphone chargers to toothpaste, and all sorts of cooked meals from kebabs and pizzas to hamburgers). Its fast growth attracted $40m funding in 2020 from a group of investors led by the venture capitalist Michael Moritz. Getir planned to launch its operations in London in mid-2020, followed by Sao Paulo, Paris, and Mexico City. Nazim Salur, the entrepreneur who founded Getir, explains the mission of his company by stating that "We're democratising laziness."

In the first week of January 2020, Nazim Salur, as the CEO of Getir, shared the following tweet on Twitter:

> Due to harsh winter conditions of fierce storm and snow let's announce to all businesses which use motorcycle couriers to take a break from work to protect the well-being of motorcycle couriers. Taking a break is not the end of the world. Don't worry your customers would be understanding.

In the days following Mr Nazim Salur's tweet, there was a significant increase in customer orders to Getir.

1. Discuss how Getir's CEO tweet relates to the humane-orientation characteristics explained earlier.
2. Discuss the company's mission from the perspective of indulgence orientation (Chapter 5).

Information zone

Infants can distinguish good and evil

A study by a group of researchers at Yale University showed that even the youngest human beings had a sense of right and wrong, and, moreover, an instinct to prefer good over evil. Experiments carried out by Hamlin et al. (2008, 2010, 2013) with one-year-old infants showed that they preferred puppets who were shown to be good. In addition, when toddlers were asked to take a treat away from one puppet, they took it from the pile of the "naughty" (bad or evil) puppet. Further, some toddlers leaned over and smacked the bad puppet on the head.

Henrich et al.'s (2010) cross-cultural research with 15 diverse populations found that people's propensities to behave kindly to strangers and punish unfairness tended to be strongest in large-scale market economies. This is attributable to the fact that in these societies such norms are essential for the smooth functioning of trade (Bloom, 2013). Perhaps, to some extent contradicting Hamlin et al. (2008, 2010, 2013), Henrich et al. (2010) concluded that much of the morality and goodness that human beings possess is a consequence of the culture in which they were raised, not their innate capacities.

In addition, as in the case of individualistic and masculine customers, when targeting performance-oriented customers, emphasising efficiency in the advertisements of tourism and hospitality businesses may result in the development of positive attitudes towards the business and its services.

Diehl et al.'s (2008) earlier research on performance orientation in relation to advertising showed that higher performance orientation in an advertisement (i.e., cues emphasising a sense of urgency, results, achievement, and control) led to a more positive evaluation of the advertisement in both high and low performance-oriented countries. However, an important finding of Diehl et al.'s research was that in high performance-oriented countries, stronger performance orientation cues were needed by customers for them to be considered as performance oriented, while in low performance-oriented countries weaker cues may have been sufficient for the advertisements to be perceived as performance oriented by the customers. Hence, when targeting customers from high performance-oriented countries, tourism and hospitality management may try finding and communicating stronger performance-oriented cues. Likewise, in other marketing mix elements (such as product, place, promotion, process, physical evidence, and people), an emphasis on a higher level of performance orientation could be made to develop and increase the positive attitudes of customers.

Service quality

Countries with high performance orientation are likely to emphasise results when they evaluate performance (e.g., when a customer evaluates service quality, or when a manager evaluates the performance of a service employee) (House et al., 2004: 245). In addition, as they value initiative (House et al., 2004), they may place greater importance on the quick recovery of service failures just like individualistic, masculine, and low-context cultures. In Chapter 6, the importance of employee empowerment in quick recovery of service failures was explained (Koc, 2013a, 2017; Dimitrou, 2017). Employees from restraint (see Chapter 5) and collectivistic (see Chapter 9) cultures may be uncomfortable with taking initiative and empowerment. Magnini et al.'s (2013) research in hospitality work settings showed that employees in collectivistic cultures tended to have lower levels of comfort with empowerment. This means that tourism and hospitality staff from restraint and collectivistic cultures serving customers from individualistic, masculine and high-performance orientation countries need to be carefully trained in taking initiative, empowerment, and service recovery processes.

Naor et al.'s (2010) research found that in cultures where there is a high level of performance orientation, businesses tended to concentrate more on goal-direct behaviour, and encouraged their employees to work harder for higher levels of efficiency. Likewise, Vecchi and Brennan (2011) in high performance-orientation cultures showed that more efforts and money tended to be spent on preventive mechanisms, which showed the emphasis on result-oriented behaviour at work.

As explained in Chapter 9, customers from collectivistic cultures may be more sympathetic towards service employees (e.g., they would not complain in order not to jeopardise employees' jobs) (Yuksel et al., 2006; Koc, 2013b), while managers may have more empathy for the employees (e.g., they would be fired only under very rare circumstances) (Riggs, 2016). This means that in these societies, together with high humane-oriented and low performance-oriented societies, problems of efficiency and effectiveness can be observed. For instance, as humane-oriented cultures are more relationship oriented and have stronger feelings of empathy and sympathy, efficiency and effectiveness problems may be encountered in these societies. In line with Blake and Mouton's (1964) leadership grid (or management styles), while leaders or managers from a performance-oriented culture would be expected to be more task oriented (concern for results), leaders or managers from a humane-oriented culture would be expected to be more people oriented (concern for people). However, both higher scores in task orientation (9/9) and people orientation (9/9) are required for success in leading and managing teams and organisations.

Organisational behaviour

The characteristics of high performance-orientation societies resemble masculinity (e.g., assertiveness, competitiveness, and materialism), and those of low performance-orientation societies resemble femininity (e.g., loyalty and belongingness) (Koc, 2010). Hence, the comparisons of masculine and feminine cultures and the attributes of two genders in Chapter 8 may be re-read for a better understanding of the implications of high and low performance orientations.

One of the most significant outcomes of humane orientation from the perspective of organisational behaviour is the increased job satisfaction of employees. Vukonjanski et al.'s (2012) research showed that humane orientation resulted in increased satisfaction with all aspects of a job by the employees. It is known that employee job satisfaction (see Chapter 5) is an antecedent of a wide variety of positive outcomes. The positive consequences of employee job satisfaction include an increase in job involvement, organisational commitment, motivation, organisational citizenship behaviour, job performance, and a reduction in withdrawal, counter-productive behaviour, absenteeism and employee turnover (Morrison, 2008; Kaya et al., 2010; Guglielmi et al., 2016). These consequences have significant implications for organisational efficiency, effectiveness, and establishment of competitive advantage for tourism and hospitality businesses. Hence, a humane-oriented approach (as well as concern for results) in a business may result in significantly positive results; organisations may be advised to develop values of humane orientation, as well as performance orientation, as suggested in Blake and Mouton's (1964) leadership grid (or management styles), mentioned earlier.

From organisational communication and employee participation perspectives high performance-orientation cultures resemble low-context cultures as they value taking initiative, competitiveness, and individual achievement; and expect direct and explicit communications. On the other hand, low performance-orientation cultures resemble high-context cultures as they value societal and family relationships more than competitive success, seek harmony with their environment, and may view formal feedback as judgemental and discomfiting (House et al., 2004; Elele and Fields, 2010). In addition, as people in high performance-orientation societies tend to place more emphasis on personal accountability for work performance (House et al., 2004), employees may be more enthusiastic about participating in decisions that affect work-related matters (House et al., 2004; Elele and Fields, 2010). In line with personal accountability, Zhao et al.'s (2012) study found a positive relationship between highperformance orientation and entrepreneurship. In a highly competitive and fast-changing business environment, a tourism and hospitality manager who wishes to establish an intrapreneurial approach process among her/his staff may start by establishing performance-orientation values in the business. The intrapreneurial approach can be defined as the establishment of processes in which "innovative products, services or processes are developed by creating an entrepreneurial culture within an already existing organization" (Fry, 1993: 373).

Conclusion

This chapter explains and discusses the concepts of performance and humane orientation. A study of the literature shows that there is a dearth of research regarding the applications of these orientations on consumer behaviour and organisational behaviour, particularly within the scope of tourism and hospitality businesses. Therefore, where available, limited research was discussed, while in other cases the main characteristics of performance and humane orientations have been interpreted in terms of their associations with other cultural dimensions.

Questions

1. What may be the consequences of attaching little importance to age (seniority) (as a characteristic of high performance orientation) when promoting employees?
2. Explain the relationship between the characteristics of performance and humane orientations with other cultural dimensions (e.g., masculinity, femininity, individualism, and collectivism).
3. What are the main implications of performance and humane orientations for designing marketing communications messages?
4. Study Tables 10.1 and 10.4 and prepare guidelines for each 7P element of the marketing mix when targeting customers from a) high performance-orientation culture, and b) high humane-orientation culture.
5. Is high humane orientation the opposite of high performance orientation? Can they co-exist? Check country scores provided in Tables 10.1 and 10.3 and discuss.
6. Explain and discuss the anonymous quote "Strong people stand up for themselves, but stronger people stand up for others" from the perspective performance and humane orientations.

Research questions/ideas to pursue for researchers

As mentioned previously there may be large differences between practice and value scores of certain countries, that is, the difference between what people state as preferable (valued) and real practices. This means that people are different from what they claim to be. In Chapters 4 (high context/low context cultures), 8 (masculinity/femininity), and 9 (individualism/collectivism), it was explained that high-context cultures, feminine cultures, and collectivistic cultures may be more subjective compared with low-context, individualistic, and masculine cultures. Hence, a study may be carried out to compare different countries' practice and value scores from these perspectives, and other cultural dimensions. In addition, the differences in people's actual and ideal-self concepts may be investigated in terms of their self-efficacy beliefs regarding their knowledge, skills, and abilities. Large distances may mean that research studies in these countries through self-report traditional research methods (e.g., surveys and interviews) may not reflect the actual truth. Hence, modern research tools using psychophysiological or neuromarketing tools (e.g., EEG, eye tracker, GSR, HR, and facial recognition) may be more relevant to use in these countries to obtain more realistic research outcomes.

Recommended further reading

Diehl, S., Terlutter, R., and Mueller, B. (2016). Doing good matters to consumers: The effectiveness of humane-oriented CSR appeals in cross-cultural standardized advertising campaigns. *International Journal of Advertising*, 35(4), 730–757.

Hofstede, G., and M. H. Bond, 1984. Hofstede's culture dimensions: An independent validation using Rokeach's value survey. J. *Cross-Cultural Psychol.*, 15, 417–433.

House, R. J., Hanges, P. J., Javidan, M., Dorfman, P. W., Gupta, V., and GLOBE associates (2004) *Leadership, culture and organizations: The GLOBE study of 62 nations*. Thousand Oaks, CA: Sage.

Javidan, M. (2004). Performance orientation. In R. J. House, P. J. Hanges, M. Javidan, P. W. Dorfman, and V. Gupta (Eds.), *Culture, leadership, and organization: The GLOBE study of 62 societies* (pp. 239–281). Thousand Oaks, CA: Sage.

Kabaskal, H., and Bodur, M. (2004). Humane orientation in societies, organizations and leadership attributes. In R. J. House, P. J. Hanges, M. Javidan, P. W. Dorfman, and V. Gupta (Eds.), *Culture, leadership, and organizations: The GLOBE study of 62 societies* (pp. 564–601). Thousand Oaks, CA: Sage.

Koc, E. (2017). Service failures and recovery in tourism and hospitality: A practical manual. Wallingford, Oxford: CABI.

Schlosser, O. (2006). *Humane orientation: A cross-cultural study in 26 countries* (Diploma Thesis). Department of Psychology, Justus-Liebig-Universitat Gieben, Germany.

References

Bandler, R., and Grinder, J. (1975). *The structure of magic: A book about language and therapy*. Palo Alto: Science and Behavior Books.

Blake, R. R., and Mouton, J. S. (1964). *The managerial grid: Key orientations for achieving production through people*. Houston, TX: Gulf Pub. Co.

Bloom, P. (2013). *Just babies*. New York: Crown.

Diehl, S., Terlutter, R., and Mueller, B. (2008). The influence of culture on responses to the globe dimension of performance orientation in advertising messages: Results from the U.S., Germany, France, Spain, and Thailand. *Advances in Consumer Research*, 35, 269–275.

Diehl, S., Terlutter, R., and Mueller, B. (2016). Doing good matters to consumers: the effectiveness of humane-oriented CSR appeals in cross-cultural standardized advertising campaigns. *International Journal of Advertising*, 35(4), 730–757.

Dimitriou, C. (2017). Understanding and dealing with service failures in tourism and hospitality. In E. Koc (Ed.), *Service failures and recovery in tourism and hospitality* (pp. 9–26). Wallingford, Oxford: CABI.

Elele, J., and Fields, D. (2010). Participative decision making and organizational commitment: Comparing Nigerian and American employees. *Cross Cultural Management: An International Journal*, 17(4), 368–392.

EUROSTAT. (2014). Proportion of Mimimum Wage Earners. https://ec.europa.eu/eurostat/statistics-explained/index.php?title=Minimum_wage_statistics#Proportion_of_minimum_wage_earners (accessed15 January 2020).

Fry, F. L. (1993). *Entrepreneurship: A planning approach*. Minneapolis: West Publishing.

Global Competitiveness Report, The. (2019). World Economic Forum. www3.weforum.org/docs/ WEF_TheGlobalCompetitivenessReport2019.pdf (accessed 25 January 2020).

Guglielmi, D., Avanzi, L., Chiesa, R., Mariani, M. G., Bruni, I., and Depolo, M. (2016). Positive aging in demanding workplaces: the gain cycle between job satisfaction and work engagement. *Frontiers in Psychology*, 7, 1224.

Hamlin, J. K., Mahajan, N., Liberman, Z., and Wynn, K. (2013). Not like me = bad: Infants prefer those who harm dissimilar others. *Psychological Science*, 24(4), 589–594.

Hamlin, J. K., Wynn, K., and Bloom, P. (2008). Social evaluation by preverbal infants. *Pediatric Research*, 63(3), 219.

Hamlin, K. J., Wynn, K., and Bloom, P. (2010). Three-month-olds show a negativity bias in their social evaluations. *Developmental Science*, 13(6), 923–929.

Henrich, J., Ensminger, J., McElreath, R., Barr, A., Barrett, C., Bolyanatz, A., ... and Lesorogol, C. (2010). Markets, religion, community size, and the evolution of fairness and punishment. *Science*, 327(5972), 1480–1484.

Hofstede, G., and Bond, M. H. (1984). Hofstede's culture dimensions: An independent validation using Rokeach's value survey. J. *Cross-Cultural Psychol.*, 15, 417–433.

House, R. J., Hanges, P. J., Javidan, M., Dorfman, P. W., Gupta, V. and GLOBE associates. (2004). *Leadership, culture and organizations: The GLOBE Study of 62 nations*. Thousand Oaks, CA: Sage.

Javidan, M. (2004). Performance orientation. In R. J. House, P. J. Hanges, M. Javidan, P. W. Dorfman, and V. Gupta (Eds.), *Culture, leadership, and organization: The GLOBE study of 62 societies* (pp. 239–281). Thousand Oaks, CA: Sage.

Kabaskal, H., and Bodur, M. (2004). Humane orientation in societies, organizations and leadership attributes. In R. J. House, P. J. Hanges, M. Javidan, P. W. Dorfman, and V. Gupta (Eds.), *Culture, leadership, and organizations: The GLOBE study of 62 societies* (pp. 564–601). Thousand Oaks, CA: Sage.

Kaya, N., Koc, E., and Topcu, D. (2010). An exploratory analysis of the influence of human resource management activities and organizational climate on job satisfaction in Turkish banks. *The International Journal of Human Resource Management*, 21(11), 2031–2051.

Kluckhohn, F. R., and Strodtbeck, F. L. (1961). *Variations in value orientations*. Evanston, IL: Row, Peterson.

Koc, E. (2010). Services and conflict management: Cultural and European integration perspectives. *International Journal of Intercultural Relations*, 34(1), 88–96.

Koc, E. (2013a). Power distance and its implications for upward communication and empowerment: Crisis management and recovery in hospitality services. *The International Journal of Human Resource Management*, 24(19), 3681–3696.

Koc, E. (2013b). Inversionary and liminoidal consumption: Gluttony on holidays and obesity. *Journal of Travel and Tourism Marketing*, 30(8), 825–838.

Koc, E. (2016). *Tüketici Davranışı ve Pazarlama Stratejileri: Global ve Yerel Yaklaşım* (Vol. 7). Ankara, Turkey: Baskı, Seçkin Yayınları.

Koc, E. (2017). *Service failures and recovery in tourism and hospitality: A practical manual.* Wallingford, Oxford: CABI.

Magnini, V. P., Hyun, S., Kim, B., and Uysal, M. (2013). The influences of collectivism in hospitality work settings. *International Journal of Contemporary Hospitality Management*, 25(6), 844–864.

Masserman, Jules H., Wechkin, S., and Terris, W. (1964). "Altruistic" behavior in rhesus monkeys. *American Journal of Psychiatry*, 121, 584–585.

McClelland, D. (1961). *The achieving society*. New York: Free Press.

Morrison, R. (2008). Negative relationships in the workplace: Associations with organizational commitment, cohesion, job satisfaction and intention turnover. *Journal of Management and Organization*, 14, 330–344.

Naor, M., Linderman, K., and Schroeder, R. (2010) The globalization of operations in Eastern and Western countries: Unpacking the relationship between national and organizational culture and its impact on manufacturing performance. *J. Oper. Management*, 28(3), 194–205.

Nikolić, M. (2014). The relationship between globe organizational culture values and the emotional intelligence of employees in Serbian organizations. *Primenjena psihologija*, 7(2), 137–156.

Noja, G. G., and Cristea, M. (2018). Working conditions and flexicurity measures as key drivers of economic growth: Empirical evidence for Europe. *Ekonomický časopis (Journal of Economics)*, 66(7), 719–749.

OECD (2020). Labour productivity levels – GDP per hour worked. https://stats.oecd.org/Index.aspx?DatasetCode=LEVEL (accessed 20 January 2020).

Riggs, A. M. (2016). *Working in the Middle East: An American woman's story*. Santa Barbara, CA: ABC-CLIO.

Sharpley, C. F. (1987). Research findings on neurolinguistic programming: Nonsupportive data or an untestable theory? *Journal of Counseling Psychology*. 34(1): 103–107.

Thyer, B. A., and Pignotti, M. G. (2015). *Science and pseudoscience in social work practice*. Berlin: Springer.

TUIK. (2019). Turkish Statistical Institute – Foreing Trade Statistics. http://tuik.gov.tr/PreTablo.do?alt_id=1046.

Travel and Tourism Competitiveness Report (2019). World economic forum. https://www.weforum.org/reports/the-travel-tourism-competitiveness-report-2019 (accessed 25. January 2020).

Vecchi, A., and Brennan, L. (2011) Quality management: A cross-cultural perspective based on the GLOBE framework. *Internat. J. Oper. Production Management*, 31(5), 527–553.

Vukonjanski, J., Nikolić, M., Hadžić, O., Terek, E., and Nedeljković, M. (2012). Relationship between GLOBE organizational culture dimensions, job satisfaction and leader-member exchange in Serbian organizations. *Journal for East European Management Studies*, 333–368.

Warneken, F., and Tomasello, M. (2006). Altruistic helping in human infants and young chimpanzees. *Science*, 311, 1301–1303.

Wechkin, S., Masserman, J. H., and Terris, W. (1964). Shock to a conspecific as an aversive stimulus. *Psychonomic Science*, 1, 47–48.

Witkowski, T. (2010). Thirty-five years of research on neuro-linguistic programming. NLP research data base. state of the art or pseudoscientific decoration? *Polish Psychological Bulletin*, 41(2), 58–66.

Yuksel, A., Kilinc, U. K. and Yuksel, F. (2006). Cross-national analysis of hotel customers' attitudes toward complaining and their complaining behaviors. *Tourism Management*, 27(1), 11–24.

Zhao, X., Li, H., and Rauch, A. (2012). Cross-country differences in entrepreneurial activity: The role of cultural practice and national wealth. *Frontiers of Business Research in China*, 6(4), 447–474.

Chapter 11

Time orientation as a cultural variable

Learning Objectives

After reading this chapter, you should be able to:

- explain the main characteristics of cultures that are long- and short-term oriented;
- understand how time orientation influences the attitudes and behaviours of people in relation to their social and work lives;
- explain how time orientation relates to marketing and consumer behaviour (e.g., the design or marketing mix elements, responses to service failures);
- explain how time orientation relates to organisational behaviour and management aspects of tourism and hospitality operations;
- understand the implications of monochronic and polychronic time orientation for tourism and hospitality marketing and management.

Introduction

This chapter explains the long-term (time) orientation as a cultural dimension developed by Geert Hofstede in 1991, as the fifth dimension, and its implications for tourism and hospitality marketing and management. The long-term orientation dimension is originally based on the responses to the Chinese Value Survey (see the following Information Zone) carried out with people from 23 societies in the world by Bond (1988). The survey was later replicated and extended by Hofstede and Minkov (2010) based on the World Values Survey (WVS) (1995–2004) data.

The long-term dimension is about the emphasising of pragmatic virtues oriented towards future rewards, perseverance, thrift, and adapting to changing circumstances. Table 11.1 shows the future orientation scores of selected countries researched in the GLOBE project by House et al. (2004).

Table 11.1 Future orientation scores of selected countries

*Future Orientation: Society Practices**

Rank	*Country*	*Score*	*Rank*	*Country*	*Score*
1	Singapore	5.07	31	El Salvador	3.80
2	Switzerland	4.73	32	Qatar	3.78
3	South Africa[a]	4.64	33	Zimbabwe	3.77
4	Netherlands	4.61	34	China	3.75
5	Malaysia	4.58	35	Turkey	3.74
6	Austria	4.46	36	Ecuador	3.74
7	Denmark	4.44	37	Portugal	3.71
8	Canada[b]	4.44	38	Iran	3.70
9	Sweden	4.39	39	Zambia	3.62
10	Japan	4.29	40	Bolivia	3.61
11	England	4.28	41	Costa Rica	3.60
12	Switzerland[c]	4.27	42	Slovenia	3.59
13	Germany[d]	4.27	43	Kazakhstan	3.57
14	Finland	4.24	44	Spain	3.51
15	India	4.19	45	Namibia	3.49
16	Philippines	4.15	46	France	3.48
17	The U.S.	4.15	47	New Zealand	3.47
18	South Africa[e]	4.13	48	Thailand	3.43
19	Nigeria	4.09	49	Georgia	3.41
20	Australia	4.09	50	Greece	3.40
21	Hong Kong	4.03	51	Venezuela	3.35
22	Ireland	3.98	52	Colombia	3.27
23	South Korea	3.97	53	Kuwait	3.26
24	Taiwan	3.96	54	Morocco	3.26
25	Germany[f]	3.95	55	Italy	3.25
26	Mexico	3.87	56	Guatemala	3.24
27	Egypt	3.86	57	Hungary	3.21
28	Indonesia	3.86	58	Poland	3.11
29	Israel	3.85	59	Argentina	3.08
30	Brazil	3.81	60	Russia	2.88

Source: House et al. (2004).
* Higher scores indicate greater future orientation.
[a] South Africa (Black sample); [b] Canada (English-speaking); [c] Switzerland (French-speaking); [d] Germany (West): Former FRG; [e] South Africa (White sample); [f] Germany (East): Former GDR

As opposed to long-term orientation, short-term orientation in a society emphasises the virtues related to past and present, such as national pride, respect for tradition, preservation of *face* (a relatively strong feeling of shame), and fulfilling social obligations. The quote "When I want to understand what is happening today or try to decide what will happen tomorrow, I look back" by the Persian poet Omar Khayyam (1048–1131) explains the focus on the past in a short-term oriented society.

Information zone

Chinese value survey

The Chinese Value Survey (Chinese Culture Connection, 1987) measures the following items:

1	Filial piety (obedience to parents, respect for parents, honoring of ancestors, financial support of parents)	**21**	Sincerity
2	Industriousness (working hard)	**22**	Keeping oneself disinterested and pure
3	Tolerance for others	**23**	Thrift
4	Harmony with others	**24**	Persistence (perseverance)
5	Humbleness	**25**	Patience
6	Loyalty to superiors	**26**	Repayment of both the good or the evil that another person has caused you
7	Observation of rites and social rituals	**27**	A sense of cultural superiority
8	Reciprocation of greetings, favours, and gifts	**28**	Adaptability
9	Kindness (forgiveness, compassion)	**29**	Prudence (carefulness)
10	Knowledge (education)	**30**	Trustworthiness
11	Solidarity with others	**31**	Having a sense of shame
12	Moderation, following the middle way	**32**	Courtesy
13	Self-cultivation	**33**	Contentedness with one's position in life
14	Ordering relationships by status and observing this order	**34**	Being conservative
15	Sense of righteousness	**35**	Protecting your "face"
16	Benevolent authority	**36**	A close, intimate friend
17	Non-competitiveness	**37**	Chastity in women
18	Personal steadiness and stability	**38**	Having few desires
19	Resistance to corruption	**39**	Respect for tradition
20	Patriotism	**40**	Wealth

Source: Chinese Culture Connection (1987).

Activity

Long-term orientation scale

Measure your level of long-term orientation score by filling in the following questionnaire.

Important Note: Throughout the book, there are a number of self-report scales/tests like the one below. Please save your personal test score records (especially the ones relating to cultural awareness, cultural competence, ethnocentrism, cultural intelligence, etc.) to make comparisons later After studying the whole book you are advised to go back and redo all of these tests once more. By doing this you can compare your scores with the ones you had earlier on. This is expected to enable you to see the changes taken place as a result of the learning experience.

Instructions

Please read the following statements and indicate how much each statement describes you when you interact with people from other cultures by assigning a value, in the blank section on the left of each statement, from 1 to 5 as follows:

(5) strongly agree (4) agree (3) neutral (2) disagree (1) strongly disagree

Please keep in mind that there is no right or wrong response for each statement. In order to avoid biased responses, you are recommended to record your initial response without elaborating too much on the statements.

	Items	*Value (1 to 5)*
1	Respect for tradition is important to me	
2	I plan for the long term	
3	Family heritage is important to me	
4	I value a strong link to my past.	
5	I work hard for success in the future	
6	I don't mind giving up today's fun for success in the future	
7	Traditional values are important to me	
8	Persistence is important to me	
TOTAL		

Scoring: Calculate your total score. If your total score is 32 or more you are a more long-term oriented individual. If your total score is 16 and below you are more short-term oriented.

Source: Bearden et al. (2006).

The concept of time orientation

Table 11.2 shows the long-term orientation (LTO) scores for 72 selected countries in the world. A lower score indicates a short-term, and a high score indicates long-term orientation in a country. According to Table 11.2, countries such as Nigeria, Colombia, Venezuela, Argentina, Australia, Mexico, Ireland, United States, and Portugal appear to be short-term oriented cultures, while countries such as South Korea, Taiwan, Japan,

Table 11.2 Long-term orientation scores for countries in the world

Rank	*Country*	*LTO Score Value*	*Rank*	*Country*	*LTO Score*	*Rank*	*Country*	*LTO Score*
1	Ghana	**4**	25	New Zealand	**33**	49	Vietnam	**57**
2	Egypt	**7**	26	Tanzania	**34**	50	Hungary	**58**
3	Nigeria	**13**	27	South Africa	**34**	51	Croatia	**58**
4	Colombia	**13**	28	Norway	**35**	52	Austria	**60**
5	Lebanon	**14**	29	Denmark	**35**	53	Hong Kong	**61**
6	Iran	**14**	30	Canada	**36**	54	Italy	**61**
7	Jordan	**16**	31	Saudi Arabia	**36**	55	Indonesia	**62**
8	Venezuela	**16**	32	Poland	**38**	56	France	**63**
9	El Salvador	**20**	33	Finland	**38**	57	Luxembourg	**64**
10	Argentina	**20**	34	Israel	**38**	58	Netherlands	**67**
11	Australia	**21**	35	Malaysia	**41**	59	Bulgaria	**69**
12	Libya	**23**	36	Brazil	**44**	60	Latvia	**69**
13	Mexico	**24**	37	Greece	**45**	61	Czechia	**70**
14	Ireland	**24**	38	Turkey	**46**	62	Singapore	**72**
15	Iraq	**25**	39	Malta	**47**	63	Slovakia	**77**
16	Peru	**25**	40	Bangladesh	**47**	64	Russia	**81**
17	Uruguay	**26**	41	Spain	**48**	65	Belgium	**82**
18	United States	**26**	42	Slovenia	**49**	66	Estonia	**82**
19	Philippines	**27**	43	Pakistan	**50**	67	Lithuania	**82**
20	Iceland	**28**	44	India	**51**	68	Germany	**83**
21	Portugal	**28**	45	United Kingdom	**51**	69	China	**87**
22	Zambia	**30**	46	Romania	**52**	70	Japan	**88**
23	Chile	**31**	47	Serbia	**52**	71	Taiwan	**93**
24	Thailand	**32**	48	Sweden	**53**	72	South Korea	**100**

Source: Hofstede (2020). Used with permission.

China, Germany, Belgium, Russia, Netherlands, Bulgaria, Luxembourg, France, and Italy appear to be long-term oriented cultures.

The typical features of a long-term oriented society are acceptance of change for slow, long-term results, thrift (saving for tomorrow), and persistence. In these societies, people tend to value long-term commitments and have respect for tradition. They are more likely to reciprocate greetings, favours, and gifts. Long-term orientation is measured based on thrift, ordering relationships by status and observing this order, persistence/perseverance, and having a sense of shame (Hofstede and Minkov, 2010).

CASE STUDY

Prudence, thrift, future orientation, and gambling in monkeys

The researcher Katia Karg and her colleagues from the Max Planck Institute for Evolutionary Anthropology in Leipzig, Germany found that chimpanzees could keep secrets in certain circumstances (Karg et al., 2015). Karg et al. observed that junior chimpanzees avoided eating hidden food when the dominant chimpanzees were around, as the dominant would take the food away from them. The chimps were good at actively hiding bananas given to them by the researchers by moving them under cover, something human infants could do by around 2.5 years.

Karg et al. put forward that, based on their experience through a cognitive process, chimps engaged in deception strategies. "Chimpanzees were able to understand others' intentions, and they adjusted their behaviours according to these intentions by flexibly manipulating what they made visible to others. This helped individual chimps prosper in their social groups, as junior males could do well to conceal their attempts to mate from the dominant males, who would punish them."

In another research, Pelé et al. (2014), who carried out experiments with three different groups of monkeys (Brown capuchin monkeys, long-tailed macaques, and orang-utans), found that these animals were capable of taking into account the chances of loss and gain when gambling one food item for another. Throughout the study, all three groups of monkeys gambled actively for probable future gains. Some individual monkeys continued betting despite having experienced an accumulation of negative outcomes in a given session. The results of the study showed that decisions made by subjects were mostly in accordance with first-order stochastic dominance, and exhibited risk aversion for capuchins and orangutans and risk-seeking for macaques with regard to second-order stochastic dominance (Pelé et al., 2014).

Long-term orientation often results in strong work ethics, expecting short term efforts to be rewarded (financial and non-financial rewards) in the long term. When people deal with issues and problems in the short term, they deal with them with patience, tolerance, and perseverance as they are oriented towards future goals. As they have a long-term vision, problems may not be solved quickly, and the change may be made slowly (Williams and Zinkin, 2008; Hofstede and Minkov, 2010). In a long-term oriented culture, there would not be one absolute truth, good and evil can be judged according to circumstances and occasions (Hofstede and Hofstede, 2005).

On the other hand, in short-term oriented societies, people are very concerned with personal steadiness and stability, protecting one's *face*, respect for tradition, and reciprocation of greetings, favours, and gifts. People tend to spend in today and expect quick results, and are concerned with one absolute truth as they would have a universal perception of what is good or evil, and right and wrong. Short-term orientation is measured based on personal steadiness and stability, protecting your face, respect for tradition, and reciprocation of greetings, favours, and gifts (Hofstede and Minkov, 2010). The general characteristics of long- and short-term oriented cultures are summarised in Table 11.3.

Table 11.3 Summary of the main characteristics of long- and short-term oriented cultures

Short-Term Oriented Cultures *E.g., Nigeria, Colombia, Venezuela, Argentina, Australia, Mexico, Ireland, United States and Portugal*	*Long-Term Oriented Cultures* *E.g., South Korea, Taiwan, Japan, China, Germany, Belgium, Russia, Netherlands, Bulgaria, Luxembourg, France, and Italy*
Emphasis is on quick results	Emphasis is on persistence
Status is not a major issue in relationships	Relationships are based on status and hierarchy
Personal steadfastness and stability are considered to be important	Personal adaptability is considered to be important
Protection of one's face is important	Face considerations may be common but seen as a weakness
Leisure time is important	Leisure time is not too important
Tend to spend more	Tend to be saving oriented; thrift is important
People emphasise quick results	People emphasise long-term quick results
There are universal guidelines about what is good or evil; loyalty varies according to needs; priority is given to abstract rationality	Good or evil depends on the circumstances and the occasion; people invest in long-term relationships and networks; priority is given to common sense
Most important events in life that occurred in the past or take place now; past and present tell people how people should live; people tend to learn what is needed currently	Most important events in life will occur in the future; the future shows how people will live; people tend to learn and prepare for vague future events
People are proud of their country	People are ready to learn from other countries
Tend to attribute success, and especially the failure to luck	Failure is attributed to a lack of effort
Disagreement may hurt	Disagreement does not hurt
Instant gratification	Delaying of gratification

Source: Hofstede et al. (2010).

It may be seen that the above cultural characteristics appear to overlap with other cultural dimensions explained and discussed throughout the book. According to Trompenaars and Hampden-Turner (2011), short-term orientation is often associated with individualistic cultures, while long-term orientation is often associated with collectivistic cultures. In addition, low-level importance is given to leisure in long-term oriented cultures, and the delay of gratification overlaps with restraint culture characteristics; high level of importance given to leisure in short-term oriented cultures, and instant gratification orientation overlaps with indulgent culture characteristics (Koc, 2019). In addition, the fact that characteristics of relationships are based on status and hierarchy in long-term oriented cultures overlaps with the high power-distance culture characteristics.

Information zone

Delaying gratification and making achievements in life

Professor Walter Mischel, from Columbia University's Department of Psychology, carried out a series of research with children (4 to 6 years old) on delaying gratification, self-control, and resisting temptation. The experiment or test was later called the Marshmallow Test or experiment.

In the test, a marshmallow was placed on the table in front of each child. The children were told that they could eat the marshmallow anytime they wanted. However, they were also told that if they waited a while (15–20 minutes), they were going to be given two marshmallows to eat. The children varied widely in terms of their patience, that is, how long they were able to wait before the ringing of the bell.

Longitudinal studies of the tested children showed that the children who had been able to hold out longer for the bigger reward (i.e., was able to delay gratification for future gains) were more likely to have higher SAT scores, to function better socially, and manage temptation and stress better in the later parts of their lives. In addition, in their adulthood, they were less likely to show extreme aggression, less likely to over-react if they became anxious about social rejection, and less likely to become obese. Mischel (2015) argues that delaying gratification, self-control (controlling of impulses), and resisting temptation is a master aptitude of emotional intelligence (Rivera, 2019; Wilson-Wünsch and Decosta; 2019) and the inability to delay gratification (having a short-term orientation) can have serious potential negative effects on people.

Source: Mischel (2015).

Time orientation and tourism and hospitality marketing and management

Based on the characteristics explained previously, it can be seen that long- or short-term orientation may have significant implications for tourism and hospitality. The implications of long- and short-term orientation are explained as follows.

Organisational behaviour

Time orientation may influence employees', managers', and entrepreneurs' attitudes and behaviours, work ethics, and social responsibility. Employees and managers from short-term oriented cultures tend to have short-term career plans (Miles and Sledge, 2009; Noja et al., 2018). This may be a major hindrance, as service quality, customer satisfaction, and establishment of competitive advantage require long-term efforts from tourism and hospitality employees and managers (Koc, 2017; Kim, 2017).

From an entrepreneurial perspective, Hwang and Lee's (2012) research showed that long-term orientation had a positive influence on the market orientation of businesses. Time orientation also influences entrepreneurial activity. Hong et al. (2018) found that long-term orientation and creativity had a strong influence on the entrepreneurial intentions of people. Long-term orientation also corroborates with stronger work ethics and a higher level of dedication for social responsibility (Williams and Zinkin, 2008).

As shown in Table 11.3, people from short-oriented cultures tend to attribute success, and especially failure, to luck. Likewise, as explained in Chapters 4 and 12, context orientation influences attributions people make and their level of locus of control. As the internal locus of control (e.g., attribution of failures internally) is an important characteristic of entrepreneurs (Hisao et al., 2016) and leaders (Turnipseed, 2017), it may be proposed that there would be fewer people in short-oriented cultures with entrepreneurial and leadership traits.

The short-term perspective of managers from short-term oriented cultures may cause managers to resort to monetary sales promotions (and discounts) too often to cope with the perishability nature of tourism and hospitality businesses. This, in turn, may hinder the establishment of a strong brand image for the business in the long run (Koc, 2006).

Implications of temporality for tourism and hospitality

Although temporality (whether a culture is monochronic or ploychronic) relates to a culture's high- or low-context orientation (Chapter 4), as it relates to people's perception of time, it is also explained within this chapter. High- and low-context orientations influence the way people view time. In general, high-context cultures typically have a polychronic perception of time, while people from low-context cultures have a monochronic perception of time. People from monochronic cultures perceive time as tangible and prefer carrying out tasks one at a time. On the other hand, polychronic individuals may perceive time as fluid (Hall, 2000).

Monochronic people make and adhere to strict deadlines, value punctuality, and concentrate on the single task they have at hand. Time orientation also supports the technical quality orientations of low-context tourists (Mattila, 1999) as explained previously. Tourists from low-context cultures place greater emphasis on the technical quality aspects of a service such as efficiency and time savings. Chapter 6 showed that customers' waiting time was one of the important service quality issues on which tourism and hospitality establishments need to concentrate. Customers from low-context cultures may see longer waiting times as more of a service problem, and they may tend to evaluate unpunctual service recovery attempts negatively. As a result, they may pay more significant attention to procedural justice, which is to do with the timely solutions of service failures (Koc, 2015, 2017).

On the other hand, polychronic people do not put much emphasis on punctuality and view deadlines as something to aim for but not to meet at all costs. They work with multiple tasks and switch back and forth. However, this does not necessarily mean that people from polychronic cultures are better at multitasking. People in monochronic cultures tend to attend to schedule and deal with one task or event at a time. They consider time as an important (like a tangible phenomenon), and are, in general, more oriented towards planning and scheduling of tasks and events to ensure efficiency and effectiveness. In contrast, people from polychronic cultures tend to be the opposite and believe that things will happen when the time comes.

Valette-Florence (1994) identified three temporal orientations as *past*, *present*, and *future*. As mentioned previously, people with a past orientation tend to consider that the past and roots are important, and hence they believe that more resources need to be allocated to teaching history and building museums, and tangible and intangible elements of tradition and culture (Legohérel et al., 2009).

People with present orientation tend to focus on the here and now. Although, it may not be always enjoyable, the present needs to be accepted for what is: the true reality they live in (Valette-Florence, 1994; Legohérel et al., 2009). Finally, people with the temporal orientation towards the future, easily and precisely plan and have a vision of their future as they believe that the future will be better and bigger. They tend to be project oriented, appreciate the achievements in science, and prepare for the long term.

In terms of time orientation, the present time and fast pace of life may be related to polychronicity and clock time as people in these cultures focus on quick turnarounds and fast results (Arman and Adair, 2012). Fisher and Hartel (2003) put forward that Hispanics (e.g., Spanish, Mexican, Cuban) and people from Anglo culture (e.g., English, Anglo-Americans) differ in terms of their time orientation. In general, Hispanics (polychronic culture) feel that they are on time even if they attend a task 15–20 minutes late (Marín et al., 1987). People from Hispanic cultures are present oriented, consider the present as being more important than the future (Okun et al., 1999), engage in relatively less planning for the future, have relatively more relaxed and spontaneous lifestyle, and are less likely to delay gratification (Marín and Marín, 1991). These explanations may have important implications for employees from a polychronic culture in terms of reliability and responsiveness as service quality dimensions, as well as procedural justice in service recovery attempts.

On the other hand, people from Anglo culture (monochronic) prefer to focus on one task at a time and often complete what they have started before starting something new (Okun et al., 1999). In addition, people from Anglo cultures, as they consider the "bottom line" to be more important, tend to place greater significance on outcomes or products of work, rather than work activities or processes (Stone-Romero and Stone, 1998).

According to Hall (2000), monochronic and polychronic orientations of societies influence how people act, focus, pay attention time, etc. Table 11.4 provides some of the characteristics of monochronic (sequential) and polychronic cultures (synchronised) cultures.

Low context cultures are present and future oriented, while high-context cultures tend to have a deep respect for the past, that is, past oriented. This results in low-context cultures preferring change over tradition, while high-context cultures prefer tradition over change. Low-context cultures tend to more explicit, written, and formal planning

Table 11.4 Monochronic and polychronic cultures

Subject	*Monochronic Tendency*	*Polychronic Tendency*
Actions	Do one thing at a time	Do many things at the same time
Focus	Concentrate on the job at hand	Get easily distracted
Attention to time	Concentrate on when things must be achieved	Concentrate on what will be achieved
Priorities	Place the job/task as the first priority	Place the relationship as the first priority
Respect for property	May seldom borrow and lend things	May borrow and lend things often and easily
Timeliness	Emphasise promptness; tend to be punctual; plan ahead methodically, and tend to stick to plans	Base promptness on relationship factors; tend to be unpunctual; plan a grand outline (e.g., a vision) and tend to change plans
Communication	Communication tends to be focused, and to the point; writes memoranda, and uses written records	Communication may be not so focused; dislikes writing, and keeping written records; prefers flexibility and commitment

Adapted from Hall (2000).

horizons, while high-context cultures tend to have more implicit, oral, and informal planning horizons. When making decisions, people in low-context cultures go through a logical, linear (sequential, step by step), and rule-oriented decision process, whilst high-context people go through an intuitive and relational decision process.

Also, in low-context cultures, everything is treated as if it had its own time, and time is highly organised. The final product (achieving the end goal) is more important than the process. In contrast, in high-context cultures, time is flexible, is viewed as a process that belongs to others and nature. In high-context cultures time is open and flexible, that is, time does not tend to be easily scheduled, and the process is more important than the final product.

As explained in Chapter 6, and stated previously, customers' waiting time is one of the most important factors when customers evaluate the service quality of a tourism and hospitality establishment. In high-context cultures, due to problems in scheduling time, heterogeneity, that is, a lack of standardisation and formation of well-defined procedures, may occur. This, in turn, may cause problems relating to the *Standards Gap* (Gap 2) and *Delivery Gap* (Gap 3), as explained in Chapter 1. Having been exposed to these gaps, customers may assign lower values to reliability dimension items when they evaluate the service quality of a tourism and hospitality business.

However, in low-context cultures, as time is viewed as a commodity to be spent or saved, and, events and tasks are scheduled and programmed, processes, service quality systems, and the marketing mix elements may be designed and implemented in a more efficient and effective manner. One other aspect of temporality is that, in contrast to low-context cultures, in high-context cultures change may take place slowly, which may result in an inability to respond to changes in consumer and employment markets, leading to problems relating to establishing and maintaining a competitive advantage in the market.

Marketing mix elements

From the consumption perspective, one of the most apparent consequences of time orientation is that customers with long-term orientation are less likely to make purchases impulsively, without making careful purchasing plans, evaluating alternatives, or making judgements about the future (Kwak et al., 2004). Correia et al. (2011) found that tourists from long-term oriented societies were more likely to make their purchase decisions based on brand image, and use a number of information sources. Gu and Ryan (2008) and Au et al.'s (2010) research showed that long-term oriented Chinese tourists placed importance on price and value relationships and had expectations (e.g., in terms of surroundings of the hotel) in relation to the price they paid. Park et al. (2013) showed that customers from long-term oriented cultures were less impulsive, were more likely to be able to delay their gratification, tended to be more frugal, and were more unlikely to become unable to pay their credit card bills.

Time orientation may influence people's attitudes towards advertising, as a marketing communications element. According to Rojas-Méndez et al.'s (2005) findings, people with high past orientation are more likely to avoid advertising. On the other hand, people with present time orientation tend to have a more positive attitude towards advertising and are less likely to skip advertising as they are more hedonistic and seek immediate gratification. Finally, the attitudes of future-oriented people towards advertising are similar to present-oriented people, but for a different reason. Future-oriented people concentrate on future benefits, which may accrue from learning through viewing or reading advertisements.

Kaynak et al. (2013) compared the attitudes of customers from Georgia (a country in the Caucasus) (more past-oriented) with customers from Macau (in Asia) (more future-oriented) towards advertising. Georgians appeared to be more suspicious of advertising and took strong action to avoid advertisements. On the other hand, customers from Macau had more positive attitudes towards advertising as they saw more value in advertising in terms of information and educational value. Based on the above explanations, tourism and hospitality managers can be recommended to resort to means other than advertising to reach customers from past-oriented customers. Additionally, advertisements aimed at present and future-oriented customers may also be distinguished. It would make more sense to have more entertaining content in advertisements aimed at present-oriented customers, while the advertisements aimed at customers who are future oriented could have a stronger emphasis on the informational and educational content.

In terms of the themes to be used in advertising (as a promotional element in the marketing mix) and product design, Parker (2003) suggests that when targeting customers from long-term oriented cultures the main themes should be health and nutrition (see the following Exercise). Cheong et al.'s (2010) research also support Parker's (2003) recommendation, as they found that, in general, nutrition and health were more relevant for Chinese (long-term oriented) (Hsu and Huang, 2016) customers than American (short-term oriented) customers. Therefore, the tourism and hospitality products can be designed in a way to emphasise aspects of health and nutrition, and these themes can be used in marketing communications to attract and please customers from long-term oriented cultures.

Exercise

According to Parker (2003), the two main advertising appeals which are related to long-term orientation cultures are health and nutrition.

Appeal	*Description*
Health	Health benefits, safety, and security, for example, "good for you", "good for your health", "good for your body"
Nutrition	Nutrient content of the food and drinks, for example, "all the nutrition your body needs"

Task

Each of these appeals may have important implications for the design of marketing mix elements. Prepare a marketing mix (7Ps) table and write down notes to be used in the design of each marketing mix element.

Valaei et al. (2016) found that long-term values had an influence on advertisement themes in China. For instance, the advertising themes such as a) careful management of money (thrift), b) going on resolutely in spite of opposition (persistence), c) personal steadiness and stability, d) long-term planning, e) giving up today's fun for success in the future, and f) working hard for success in the future appeared to be effective on long-term oriented Chinese customers.

In terms of the product element of the marketing mix, Lu et al. (2016) found that past-oriented tourists were more likely to travel with the intention of sensation seeking (hedonistic, indulgent) (e.g., a beach resort visit or a cruise vacation) (Miao et al., 2011), while future-oriented tourists were more likely to travel with the intention of self-fulfilment and knowledge enhancement. Cotte and Ratneshwar (2001) showed that past-oriented women enjoyed activities linked with childhood memories, present-oriented women were more likely to engage in hedonic pursuits, and the future-oriented women preferred personal development activities.

Future-oriented people, in general, are more able than others to foresee and articulate future goals and to direct action in the attainment of future goals (Lu et al., 2016). They make decisions based on cost-benefit analysis of the anticipated outcomes of future events. These customers display a strong interest in knowledge seeking (Bergadaa, 1990), and tend to prefer personal development activities (Cotte and Ratneshwar, 2001). In general, senior tourists with future orientation prefer holidays for personal development and learning new things (Li and Chai, 2012; Lu et al., 2016). They tend to be aware that travel promotes healthy aging, helps older people avoid certain illnesses, and maintains their physical and mental health (Ahn and Janke, 2011; Lu et al., 2016).

It should also be noted that due to long-term commitments in their relationships, customers from long-term oriented cultures are more likely to buy, give, and reciprocate gifts. Hence, the design of tourism and hospitality products targeted at long-term oriented customers, as a marketing mix element, should take gift-buying and gift-giving into consideration. In addition to giving gifts to customers, tourism and hospitality establishments may be recommended to have a variety of suitable souvenirs and gifts available to the customers to purchase. As mentioned previously, to some extent, long-term oriented values overlap with collectivistic values. As explained in Chapter 9, collectivistic customers tend to buy more gifts, give gifts on more occasions and have a higher gift budget than individualistic customers, who buy and give fewer gifts and have fewer gift-giving occasions, since due to less pressure they feel less need to reciprocate (Park, 1998; Reisinger, 2009). In addition, as long-term oriented customers may be more likely to reciprocate gifts and favours, just like the collectivistic customers (see Chapter 9), they may be more influenced by sales tactics based on the reciprocity principle. As mentioned in Chapter 9, according to the reciprocity principle of persuasion, people are usually conditioned to return favours and pay back their debts (Cialdini, 2013; Koc, 2016).

In terms of the distribution element of the marketing mix in tourism and hospitality, Gil-Saura et al. (2011) found that long-term orientation had a positive influence on customer commitment towards suppliers. Hwang and Lee (2012) also found that long-term orientation had an influence on commitment and dependence on suppliers.

Buyers in long-term oriented cultures had long-term goals in their relationships with the suppliers. Hwang et al. (2013) argue that in long-term oriented cultures buyers depend and trust their suppliers as they tend to believe their suppliers would consider how their decisions and actions would affect them. However, Hsu and Huang (2016) showed that with the recent exposure to dishonest service providers and travel agencies, Chinese customers' (long-term oriented) trust in travel agencies has declined.

Finally, as long-term oriented tourism and hospitality customers take a longer view of time and make their plans and schedules (i.e., they do not tend to be last-minute customers), presale activities with dynamic pricing (yield management pricing) (Boz et al., 2017) may be more effective on them. As short-term oriented customers focus more on the near future and do not have a tendency to plan for the more distant future (Zhang et al., 2020), presale activities with dynamic pricing (yield management pricing) may not be suitable for them. They may be more likely to find this pricing system unfair, as they would be unable to benefit from low prices due to a lack of planning for the future.

Service quality, service failures, service recovery, complaints, and loyalty

Long-term oriented cultures tend to develop long-term relationships with service providers and view relationships as important (Furrer et al., 2000). Okumus (2020) put forward that customers from long-term oriented cultures may have lower expectations of service quality than customers from short-term oriented cultures. In line with the findings of Furrer et al. (2000), Swanson et al (2011) found that long-term oriented cultures place a greater value on reliability, responsiveness, and empathy. However, Donthu and Yoo (1988) found that tourism and hospitality customers may find responsiveness relatively less important among the service quality dimensions. Kanousi (2005) found that long-term oriented customers tended to have higher expectations of tangibles, for example, tidy and clean appearance of service personnel.

When tourism and hospitality customers from long-term oriented cultures encounter service failures (Ro and Olson, 2019), they are more likely to accept poor service, especially in the short run. They may have a tendency to believe that every service experience may not be perfect, and may be willing to give the service provider time, or another chance, to improve (Donthu and Yoo, 1998). As such they may be less likely to engage in negative WOM communication. Liu et al. (2001) argue that customers with a long-term orientation are less likely to engage in negative WOM communication, which may lead to confrontation (Koc, 2010). On the other hand, Swanson et al. (2011) found that long-term orientation did not decrease WOM, but restricted its width and social networking.

Other studies show that tourism and hospitality customers from long-term oriented cultures (e.g., South Korea) tend to be less likely to provide negative feedback regarding their service experience compared with customers from short-term oriented cultures (e.g., Argentina) (Stamolampros et al., 2019). This is due to the fact that they do not wish to jeopardise their long-term relationship with the service provider (Furrer et al., 2000; Ryu and Moon 2009). Long-term oriented customers value loyalty with the service provider (Bartikowski et al., 2011; Li et al. 2011), and in general, this attitude is reflected in their service ratings.

On the other hand, as short-term oriented tourism and hospitality customers have higher expectations from service providers and are more likely to be critical (Mazheri et al., 2011). This may be due to the fact that service failures would prevent them from achieving immediate-need gratification. Short-term oriented customers prioritise immediate benefits and efficiency and care less about loyalty.

In terms of service recovery attempts, Kanousi's (2005) research showed that long-term oriented customers tended to expect detailed information during the service recovery attempts, and were more likely to place greater importance on procedural and interactional justice during the service recovery process.

With regard to the loyalty aspect of tourism and hospitality services, Park et al.'s (2013) research on restaurants showed that short-term oriented customers, in line with their short-term goals and inability to delay gratification, strongly favoured immediate rewards (e.g., cash). In addition, they found that a monetary reward's positive influence on loyalty was greater when provided to customers with a low short-term orientation than when provided to customers with a high long-term orientation. Customers with long-term orientation placed greater value on non-monetary and accumulative rewards, compared with immediate rewards, for example, cash payments. Customer reward programmes can also be considered as a sales promotion tool providing additional benefits to customers in return for their purchases (Uncles et al., 2003). Hence, Park et al.'s (2013) findings can be interpreted from the perspective of sales promotions as well.

Conclusion

This chapter explains the concept of long- and short-term orientation and the influence of these cultural orientations on organisational behaviour and marketing management. Specifically, short-termism has a number of negative implications for tourism and hospitality employees, managers, and entrepreneurs as short-termism corroborate with short-term career plans for employees, tendency to resort to monetary sales promotions, and low level of intention to become an entrepreneur. In addition, time orientation has implications for consumer behaviour and services marketing (e.g., the design and implementation of the marketing mix), and management (e.g., service quality, service failures, service recovery, complaints, and loyalty) perspectives.

Questions

1. Are the characteristics of instant gratification, placing more importance on leisure time, and tendency to spend more associated with long- or short-term orientation? What are social and work-life (especially in tourism and hospitality) implications of these characteristics?
2. What are the specific implications of long-term orientation for the product and marketing communications (e.g., advertising) as the two marketing mix elements of tourism and hospitality businesses?
3. Explain the monochronic and polychronic perceptions of time. How may these perceptions relate to tourism and hospitality service encounters? What sort of potential problems may arise due to the differences in perceptions of time?
4. Explain the characteristics of people with a temporal orientation towards the past, present, and future.
5. How does time orientation influence holiday intentions and holiday preferences of tourists?
6. How does time orientation influence service quality perceptions and responses of tourism and hospitality customers?
7. Explain and discuss the Mother Teresa's (1910–1997) quote of "Yesterday is gone. Tomorrow has not yet come. We have only today. Let us begin" from the perspective of cultural time orientations.

Research questions/ideas to pursue for researchers

As mentioned previously, people from short-term oriented cultures are proud of their country, while people from long-term oriented cultures may be more prepared to learn from other countries or cultures. Based on this premise, two countries (one long-term oriented and the other one short-term oriented) may be selected to compare tourism and hospitality employees' levels of ethnocentrism, cultural competence, cultural intelligence, and intercultural sensitivity. Based on the results of the study, recommendations can be made to managers in terms of the recruitment of personnel and training.

Recommended further reading

Bearden, W. O., Money, R. B., and Nevins, J. L. (2006). A measure of long-term orientation: Development and validation. *Journal of the Academy of Marketing Science*, 34(3), 456–467.

Hofstede, G. (2001). *Culture's consequences: Comparing values, behaviors, institutions and organizations across nations*. Thousand Oaks, CA: Sage.

Hofstede, G., and Minkov, M. (2010). Long-versus short-term orientation: new perspectives. *Asia Pacific Business Review*, 16(4), 493–504.

Swanson, S. R., Frankel, R., Sagan, M., and Johansen, D. L. (2011). Private and public voice: exploring cultural influence. *Managing Service Quality: An International Journal*, 21(3), 216–239.

Trompenaars, F., and Woolliams, P. (2002). A new framework for managing change across cultures. *Journal of Change Management*, 3(4), 361–375.

References

Ahn, Y. J., and Janke, M. C. (2011). Motivations and benefits of the travel experiences of older adults. *Educational Gerontology*, 37(8), 653–673.

Arman, G., and Adair, C. K. (2012). Cross-cultural differences in perception of time: Implications for multinational teams. *European Journal of Work and Organizational Psychology*, 21(5), 657–680.

Au, N., Law, R., and Buhalis, D. (2010). The impact of culture on eComplaints: Evidence from Chinese consumers in hospitality organisations. Information and communication technologies in tourism, 2010, 285–296.

Bartikowski, B., Walsh, G., and Beatty, S. E. (2011). Culture and age as moderators in the corporate reputation and loyalty relationship. *Journal of Business Research*, 64(9), 966–972.

Bearden, W. O., Money, R. B., and Nevins, J. L. (2006). A measure of long-term orientation: Development and validation. *Journal of the Academy of Marketing Science*, 34(3), 456–467.

Bergadaa, M. (1990). The role of time in the action of the consumer. *Journal of Consumer Research*, 17(3), 289–302.

Bond, M. H. (1988). Finding universal dimensions of individual variation in multicultural studies of values: The Rokeach and Chinese value surveys. *Journal of Personality and Social Psychology*, 55(6), 1009.

Boz, H., Arslan, A., and Koc, E. (2017). Neuromarketing aspect of tourism pricing psychology. *Tourism Management Perspectives*, 23, 119–128.

Cheong, Y., Kim, K., and Zheng, L. (2010). Advertising appeals as a reflection of culture: a cross-cultural analysis of food advertising appeals in China and the US. *Asian Journal of Communication*, 20(1), 1–16.

Chinese Culture Connection, (1987). Chinese values and the search for culture-free dimensions of culture. *Journal of Cross-cultural Psychology*, 18(2), 143–164.

Cialdini, R. B. (2013). *Influence: Science and practice*. New York: Harper Collins.

Correia, A., Kozak, M., and Ferradeira, J. (2011). Impact of culture on tourist decision-making styles. *International Journal of Tourism Research*, 13(5), 433–446.

Cotte, J., and Ratneshwar, S. (2001). Timestyle and leisure decisions. *Journal of Leisure Research*, 33(4), 396–409.

Donthu, N., and Yoo, B. (1998). Cultural influences on service quality expectations. *Journal of Service Research*, 1(2), 178–186.

Fisher, G., and Hartel, C. (2003). Cross-cultural effectiveness of Western expatriate-Thai client interactions: lessons learned for IHRM research and theory. *Cross Cultural Management*, 16(1), 1–21.

Furrer, O., Shaw-Ching Liu, B., and Sudharshan, D. (2000). The relationships between culture and service quality perceptions basis for cross-cultural market segmentation and resource allocation. *Journal of Service Research*, 2(4), 355–371.

Gil-Saura, I., Ruiz-Molina, M.-E., and Arteaga-Moreno, F. (2011). Value, supplier dependence and long-term orientation: outcomes for B2B commerce in the travel industry. *Industrial Management and Data Systems*, 111(5), 791–808.

Gu, G., and Ryan, C. (2008). Chinese Clientele at Chinese Hotels – preferences and Satisfaction. *International Journal of Hospitality Management*, 27, 337–345.

Hall, E. T. (2000). Monochronic and polychronic time. *Intercultural Communication: A Reader*, 9, 280–286.

Hofstede, G. (2020). Cultural dimensions. https://www.hofstede-insights.com/product/compare-countries/ (accessed 20 January 2020).

Hofstede, G., and Minkov, M. (2010). Long-versus short-term orientation: New perspectives. *Asia Pacific Business Review*, 16(4), 493–504.

Hofstede, G., and Hofstede, G. J. (2005). *Cultures and organizations: Software of the mind* (2nd ed.). New York: McGraw-Hill.

Hong, J., Yang, N., and Hou, B. (2018). The effects of long-term orientation on entrepreneurial intention: A mediation model of creativity. *Creativity and Innovation*, 2018, 455.

House, R. J., Hanges, P. J., Javidan, M., Dorfman, P. W., and Gupta, V. (2004). *Culture, leadership and organizations: The GLOBE study of 62 societies*. Thousand Oaks: Sage.

Hsiao, C., Lee, Y. H., and Chen, H. H. (2016). The effects of internal locus of control on entrepreneurship: The mediating mechanisms of social capital and human capital. *The International Journal of Human Resource Management*, 27(11), 1158–1172.

Hsu, C. H., and Huang, S. S. (2016). Reconfiguring Chinese cultural values and their tourism implications. *Tourism Management*, 54, 230–242.

Hwang, Y., and Lee, K.C. (2012). Investigating the moderating role of uncertainty avoidance cultural values on multidimensional online trust. *Information and Management*, 49(3–4), 171–176.

Hwang, J., Chung, J. E., and Jin, B. (2013). Culture matters: The role of long-term orientation and market orientation in buyer-supplier relationships in a Confucian culture. *Asia Pacific Journal of Marketing and Logistics*, 25(5), 721–744.

Kanousi, A. (2005). An empirical investigation of the role of culture on service recovery expectations. *Managing Service Quality: An International Journal*, 15(1), 57–69.

Karg, K., Schmelz, M., Call, J., and Tomasello, M. (2015). The goggles experiment: can chimpanzees use self-experience to infer what a competitor can see?. *Animal Behaviour*, 105, 211–221.

Kaynak, E., Kara, A., Chow, C. S. F., and Riza Apil, A. (2013). Pattern of similarities/differences in time orientation and advertising attitudes: A cross-cultural comparison of Georgian and Macau consumers. *Asia Pacific Journal of Marketing and Logistics*, 25(4), 631–654.

Kim, J. H. (2017). Memorable service experiences: A service failure and recovery perspective. In E. Koc (Ed.), *Service failures and recovery in tourism and hospitality: A practical manual* (pp. 56–69). Wallingford, Oxford: CABI.

Koc, E. (2006). Total quality management and business excellence in services: The implications of all-inclusive pricing system on internal and external customer satisfaction in the Turkish tourism market. *Total Quality Management and Business Excellence*, 17(7), 857–877.

Koc, E. (2010). Services and conflict management: Cultural and European integration perspectives. *International Journal of Intercultural Relations*, 34(1), 88–96.

Koc, E. (2015). *Hizmet Pazarlaması ve Yönetimi*, 1. Ankara: Baskı, Seçkin Yayıncılık.

Koc, E. (2016). *Tüketici Davranışı ve Pazarlama Stratejileri: Global ve Yerel Yaklaşım* (Vol. 7). Ankara, Turkey: Baskı, Seçkin Yayınları.

Koc, E. (2017). *Service failures and recovery in tourism and hospitality: A practical manual.* Wallingford, Oxford: CABI.

Koc, E. (2019). *Emotional intelligence in tourism and hospitality*. CABI: Wallingford, Oxford: CABI.

Kwak, H., Zinkhan, G. M., and Roushanzamir, E.P.L. (2004). Compulsive comorbidity and its psychological antecedents: a cross cultural comparison between the US and South Korea. *Journal of Consumer Marketing*, 21(6), 418–434.

Legohérel, P., Daucé, B., Hsu, C. H., and Ranchhold, A. (2009). Culture, time orientation, and exploratory buying behavior. *Journal of International Consumer Marketing*, 21(2), 93–107.

Li, M., and Cai, L. A. (2012). The effects of personal values on travel motivation and behavioral intention. *Journal of Travel Research*, 51(4), 473–487.

Li, X. R., Lai, C., Harrill, R., Kline, S., and Wang, L. (2011). When East meets West: An exploratory study on Chinese outbound tourists' travel expectations. *Tourism Management*, 32(4), 741–749.

Liu, B. S., Furrer, O., and Sudharshan, D. (2001). The relationship between culture and behavioral intentions toward services. *Journal of Service Research*, 4(2), 118–129.

Lu, J., Hung, K., Wang, L., Schuett, M. A., and Hu, L. (2016). Do perceptions of time affect outbound-travel motivations and intention? An investigation among Chinese seniors. *Tourism Management*, 53, 1–12.

Marín, G., and Marín, B. V. (1991). *Research with Hispanic populations*. Newbury Park, CA: Sage.

Marín, G., Sabogal, F., Marín, B. V., Otero-Sabogal, R., and Perez-Stable, E. J. (1987). Development of a short acculturation scale for Hispanics. *Hispanic Journal of Behavioral Sciences*, 9, 183–205.

Mattila, A. S. (1999). The role of culture and purchase motivation in service encounter evaluations. *Journal of Services Marketing*, 13(4/5), 376–389.

Mazaheri, E., Richard, M.-O., and Laroche, M. (2011). Online consumer behavior: comparing Canadian and Chinese website visitors. *Journal of Business Research*, 64(9), 958–965.

Miao, L., Lehto, X., and Wei, W. (2011). The hedonic experience of travel-related consumption. International CHRIE conference-referred track, paper 7. http:// scholarworks.umass.edu/ refereed/ICHRIE_2011/Saturday/7.

Miles, A. K., and Sledge, S. (2009). Satisfaction, service, and culture: cross-cultural reflections from the hotel industry. *Tourism Culture and Communication*, 9(3), 165–179.

Mischel, W. (2015). *The marshmallow test: Why self-control is the engine of success.* New York: Little, Brown.

Noja, G., Cristea, S., Yüksel, A., Pânzaru, C., and Drăcea, R. (2018). Migrants' role in enhancing the economic development of host countries: Empirical evidence from Europe. *Sustainability*, 10(3), 894.

Okun, B. F., Fried, J., and Okun, M. L. (1999). *Understanding diversity: A learning as practice primer*. Pacific Grove, CA: Brooks/Cole.

Park, S. B., Chung, N., and Woo, S. C. (2013). Do reward programs build loyalty to restaurants? The moderating effect of long-term orientation on the timing and types of rewards. *Managing Service Quality: An International Journal*, 23(3), 225–244.

Park, S.Y. (1998). A comparison of Korean and American gift-giving behaviours. *Psychology and Marketing*, 15(6), 577–593.

Parker, B. J. (2003). Food for health: The use of nutrient content, health, and structure/function claims in food advertisement. *Journal of Advertising*, 32(3), 4755.

Pelé, M., Broihanne, M. H., Thierry, B., Call, J., and Dufour, V. (2014). To bet or not to bet? Decision-making under risk in non-human primates. *Journal of Risk and Uncertainty*, 49(2), 141–166.

Reisinger, Y. (2009). Cross-cultural differences in tourist behaviour. In M. Kozak and A. Decrop (Eds), *Handbook of Tourist Behaviour: Theory and Practice* (pp. 237–255). New York: Routledge.

Rivera, D. J. (2019). Emotional intelligence and its relationship with personality, gender, age and culture in tourism and hospitality. In E. Koc (Ed.), *Emotional intelligence in tourism and hospitality* (pp. 75–94). Wallingford, Oxford: CABI.

Ro, H., and Olson, D. E. (2019). Service failures, recovery and emotional intelligence. In E. Koc (Ed.), *Emotional intelligence in tourism and hospitality* (pp. 121–133). Wallingford, Oxford: CABI.

Rojas-Méndez, J. I., Davies, G., Omer, O., Chetthamrongchai, P. and Madra, C. (2002). "A time attitude scale for cross-cultural research. *Journal of Global Marketing*, 15(3/4), 117–147.

Ryu, S., and Moon, C. W. (2009). Long-term orientation as a determinant of relationship quality between channel members. *The International Business and Economics Research Journal*, 8(11), 1–9.

Stamolampros, P., Korfiatis, N., Kourouthanassis, P., and Symitsi, E. (2019). Flying to quality: Cultural influences on online reviews. *Journal of Travel Research*, 58(3), 496–511.

Stone, D. L., and Stone-Romero, E. F. (1998). A multiple stakeholder model of privacy in organizations. In M. Schminke (Ed.), *Managerial ethics: Morally managing people and processes* (pp. 35–59). Mahwah, NJ: Lawrence Erlbaum.

Swanson, S. R., Frankel, R., Sagan, M., and Johansen, D. L. (2011). Private and public voice: exploring cultural influence. *Managing Service Quality: An International Journal*, 21(3), 216–239.

Trompenaars, F., and Hampden Turner, C. (2011). *Riding the waves of culture: Understanding diversity in global business*. London: Nicholas Brealey International.

Turnipseed, D. (2017). Locus of control and psychological empowerment. Individual variances and substitutes for leadership. *Academy of Management Proceedings*, 1, 13162.

Uncles, M. D., Dowling, G. R., and Hammond, K. (2003). Customer loyalty and customer loyalty programs. *Journal of Consumer Marketing*, 20(4), 294–316.

Valaei, N., Rezaei, S., Ismail, W. K. W., and Oh, Y. M. (2016). The effect of culture on attitude towards online advertising and online brands: applying Hofstede's cultural factors to internet marketing. *International Journal of Internet Marketing and Advertising*, 10(4), 270–301.

Valette-Florence, P. (1994). Introduction à l'analyse des chaînages cognitifs. *Recherche et Applications en Marketing* (French Edition), 9(1), 93–117.

Williams, G., and Zinkin, J. (2008). The effect of culture on consumers' willingness to punish irresponsible corporate behaviour: Applying Hofstede's typology to the punishment aspect of corporate social responsibility. *Business Ethics: A European Review*, 17(2), 210–226.

Williams, G., and Zinkin, J. (2008). The effect of culture on consumers' willingness to punish irresponsible corporate behaviour: applying Hofstede's typology to the punishment aspect of corporate social responsibility. *Business Ethics: A European Review*, 17(2), 210–226.

Wilson-Wünsch, B. R. and Decosta, N. P. L. (2019). Development of personal expertise in tourism and hospitality professions: cognitive knowledge, personality and learning style. In E. Koc (Ed.), *Emotional intelligence in tourism and hospitality* (pp. 62–74). Wallingford, Oxford: CABI.

Zhang, P., Gerdes Jr, J. H., and Meng, F. (2020). The impact of national culture on hotel guest evaluation: A big data approach. *International Journal of Tourism Research*.

Chapter 12

A review of Trompenaars and Hampden-Turner's cultural dimensions

Learning Objectives

After reading this chapter, you should be able to:

- understand the main characteristics of universalistic and particularistic societies;
- explain the potential implications of universalism and particularism for tourism and hospitality;
- understand the main characteristics of neutral and affective societies;
- explain the potential implications of the characteristics of affective and neutral societies from a tourism and hospitality perspective;
- understand the relationship between Trompenaars and Hampden-Turner's dimensions and other dimensions explained in other chapters of this book.

Introduction

A Dutch organizational theorist and management consultant Fons Trompenaars and British professor of management Charles Hampden-Turner formed a consultancy business in 1989 called the Centre for International Business Studies. In 1998 they published a book titled *Riding the Waves of Culture: Understanding Diversity in Global Business*. In their book, Trompenaars and Hampden Turner (1998) developed a framework for cross-cultural communication applied to general business and management. The framework categorises societies according to the following:

1. Universalism vs particularism. (What is more important for people in society, the rules or the relationships?)

2. Individualism vs collectivism (communitarianism). (Do people in the society function in a group or as individuals?)
3. Neutral vs emotional. (Do people in the society display or hide their emotions?)
4. Specific vs diffuse. (How separate do people keep their private and working lives?)
5. Achievement vs ascription. (Do people have to prove themselves to receive status or is it given to them?)
6. Sequential vs synchronic. (Do people do things one at a time or several things at the same time?)
7. Internal vs external control. (Do people believe that they can control the environment or do they believe that they are controlled by the environment?)

Although there are several research studies mentioning Trompenaar and Hapmden-Turner's cultural framework, or dimensions, there is a dearth of publications specifically investigating these dimensions, especially in tourism and hospitality, due to a lack of valid and measurable criteria to apply. Hence, this chapter explains Trompenaars and Hampden-Turner's (1998) framework, in relation to the association of their dimensions with other dimensions explained throughout the book. Additionally, as most of the dimensions of Trompenaars and Hampden-Turner's overlap significantly with other dimensions, it would be useful to refer to the other relevant chapters in the book, especially in terms of their implications for tourism and hospitality.

Characteristics of societies according to Trompenaars and Hampden-Turner's framework

Trompenaars and Hampden-Turner (1998) put forward that culture describes what products and services mean for the people in a society, how people in a society solve problems, and how they interact with each other in an organisation. Trompenaars and Hampden-Turner's main message is that there is no such thing as an optimal or ideal culture, as all cultures operate within their own system. However, with the increasing globalisation of the markets (as in tourism and hospitality), there has been a growing need to understand the implications of these cultural categorisations for the effective marketing and management of businesses. The seven categorisations of societies (mentioned previously) of Trompenaaras and Hampden-Turner's are explained below.

Universalism versus particularism

As mentioned in Chapter 9, individualistic cultures (such as United States, Australia, United Kingdom, Netherlands, New Zealand, Italy, Belgium, Denmark, Sweden, France, Switzerland, Germany, and Finland) were universalistic, while collectivistic cultures (such as Guatemala, Ecuador, Venezuela, Indonesia, Pakistan, South Korea, Bangladesh, China, Nigeria, Thailand, Malaysia, and Kenya) were particularistic. According to Trompenaars and Hampden-Turner (1998), Western cultures (e.g., Western Europe, the United States, and Canada) are universalistic, that is, everybody is treated as subject to the same rules, while in particularistic cultures (e.g., Southern Europe, Asia, South America, and Russia) people are not treated as subject to the same rules. In these countries, some people are treated as if they are more equal than others.

Table 12.1 Characteristics of universalistic and particularistic societies

Universalistic	*Particularistic*
Focus is more on rules than relationships	Focus is more on relationships than rules
Legal contracts are readily drawn up	Legal contracts are readily modified
A trustworthy person is the one who honours their word and/or contracts	A trustworthy person is the one who honours changing mutualities
There is one truth or reality, that which has been agreed to	There are several perspectives on reality relative to each participant involved
A deal is a deal	Relationships evolve

Source: Trompenaars and Hampden-Turner (1998).

In universalistic cultures, people place a high level of importance on laws, rules, values, and obligations. People from universalistic cultures try to be objective and deal fairly with people based on the rules that are considered to be more important than relationships. On the other hand, people in particularistic cultures tend to be more subjective and believe that each circumstance and each relationship determines the rules that will be applied. People's responses to situations may change depending on the nature of the event they have encountered and the people involved. Table 12.1 provides a summary of the universalistic and particularistic cultures.

In universalistic cultures, people's attitudes and behaviours towards in-group and out-group differ (see Chapter 4) minimally as in individualistic, low-context and performance-oriented cultures. In universalistic cultures when somebody does something illegal, it would be quite normal for the friends of this person to testify against her/him if they have witnessed an illegal act, for example, hitting a pedestrian on the road as a result of over speeding. In universalistic societies, people would believe that that person deserves punishment because of her/his illegal and wrong behaviour, no matter who s/he is.

However, in particularistic cultures, people's attitudes and behaviours towards in-group and out-group differ significantly, that is, there may be a quite large difference as in some collectivistic, high-context and low-performance (or in humane-oriented) cultures (Koc, 2010). The friends of the person who has acted illegally may refrain from testifying against her/him. Particularism comprises a wide variety of interpersonal relationships and transactions as well as personal-state transactions in the form of clientelism, bribery, corruption, patronage, nepotism, and other favouritisms (Rothstein and Torsello, 2014).

Particularism would be detected not only in relation to the government but also in individuals' social dealings and interactions within the society. Hence, rather than merit, status, and relationships or connections, people tend to have more influence in transactions. For instance, groupthink (see Chapters 7 and 9) would be more likely to take place in businesses in particularistic societies. Table 12.2 lists recommendations based on the characteristics of universalistic and particularistic societies.

Figure 12.1 shows a continuum of universalistic and particularistic societies.

Table 12.2 Recommendations for interacting with people from universalistic and particularistic cultures

Recommendations for Interacting with People from Universalistic Cultures	*Recommendations for Interacting with People from Particularistic Cultures*
Be prepared for "rational" and "professional" arguments and presentations.	Be prepared for personal "meandering" or "irrelevancies" that may not seem to be leading anywhere.
Carefully prepare the legal ground – when needed with the help of a lawyer.	Consider the personal implications of legal issues.
Strive for consistency and uniform procedures and provide clear instructions, processes, and procedures.	Build informal networks and create private understandings. Give people autonomy to make their own decisions and respect people's needs when you make decisions.
Signal changes openly and publicly. Use an objective process to make decisions yourself, and explain your decisions if others are involved.	Pull levers privately and individually. Take time to build relationships and get to know people so that you can better understand their needs. Be flexible in the way you make decisions and underline the important rules and policies that need to be followed.
Strive for fairness by making sure that you treat all cases in the same standardised manner. Keep promises and be consistent.	Strive for fairness by treating all cases on their special circumstances and merits.

Source: adapted from Trompenaars and Hampden-Turner (1998).

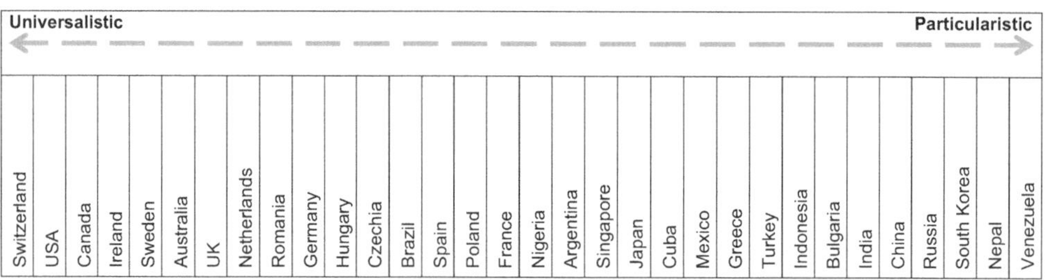

Figure 12.1 Universalistic and particularistic cultures continuum
Source: adapted from Trompenaars and Hampden-Turner (1998).

It should be noted that particularism should not be confused with networking, people's attempts to develop and maintain relationships with others who have the potential to assist them in their works or careers (Forret and Dougherty, 2004). As such, networking is advocated even in universalistic societies such as the United States, Germany, and the United Kingdom. Many international MBA (Master of Business Administration) programmes compete on the basis of networking opportunities they provide for their students. Although networking may also involve preferential treatment, it should not normally involve illegal or unlawful acts or wrong behaviours.

Individualism vs communitarianism (collectivism)

As explained in Chapter 9, individualism and collectivism refer to whether individuals in a particular society put themselves as a person first in a group, or whether they put the importance of the group first. In individualistic cultures, people do not tend to feel responsible for the actions and outcomes of others, while in collectivistic cultures people take responsibility for others' actions and well-being, and are expected to be loyal to the group they belong to in exchange for the protection of their interests by the group. Table 12.3 summarises the characteristics of individualistic and communitarian (collectivistic) cultures.

As explained in Chapter 9, individualistic cultures are more concerned with people's time and their need for privacy and freedom. In addition, in individualistic societies, people do not tend to mix their private and work lives and tend to enjoy challenges and expect individual rewards for their hard work. Table 12.4 lists recommendations based on the characteristics of individualistic and communitarian (collectivistic) societies.

Han et al.'s (2017) study showed that the independent and self-reliant nature of people from individualistic cultures resulted in a low level of loyalty and a high level of variety-seeking behaviour of customers. However, the interdependent, harmonious, and controlling emotions nature of people from collectivistic cultures increased levels of loyalty and reduced levels of variety-seeking behaviour.

In another study, Filimonau et al. (2018), who investigated tourists' attitudes towards environmental issues from the perspective of Trompenaars and Hampden-Turner's (1998)

Table 12.3 Characteristics of individualistic and communitarian (collectivistic) societies

Individualistic	*Communitarian (Collectivistic)*
The "I" form is more frequently used in communication.	The "we" form is more frequently used in communication.
Decisions are made on the spot by representatives.	Decisions are referred back by delegates to the organisation.
People ideally try achieving things on their own and take personal responsibility.	People ideally try achieving things collectively requiring joint responsibility.
Vacations tend to be taken in pairs, or alone.	Vacations tend to be taken in organised groups, or with the extended family.
Job turnover and mobility may be high.	Job turnover and mobility may be low.

Source: Trompenaars and Hampden-Turner (1998).

Table 12.4 Recommendations for interacting with people from universalistic and particularistic cultures

Recommendations for Interacting with People from Individualistic Cultures	*Recommendations for Interacting with People from Communitarian (Collectivistic) Cultures*
Take the initiative and make decisions quickly. People may not have to refer many issues to their superiors. The aim is to make a quick deal. Provide an environment in which individuals can take individual initiatives. Make sure that you link individual needs to organisational or group needs. Introduce individual incentives.	Show respect and patience for the time taken to consent and consult. The aim is to build long-lasting relationships. Make sure that people have superordinate goals for all to meet.
Conducting business alone means that this particular individual is respected by his company and has its esteem.	Conducting business when surrounded by helpers means that this individual has a high status in his company.
Praise and reward individual performance, and give people autonomy to make their own decisions and to use their initiative.	Praise and reward group performance. Praising of individuals publically may be inappropriate.
Allow people to be creative and to learn from their mistakes.	Allow people to involve others in decision making.

Source: adapted from Trompenaars and Hampden-Turner (1998).

dimensions, found that individualism demonstrated by the majority of Polish tourists were positively and significantly related to anti-environmental attitudes. Filimonau et al.'s (2018) study draws parallels with Kang et al.'s (2016) study (see Chapter 8), which found that masculinity had a negative and significant influence on positive corporate social responsibility at a business firm level. As mentioned previously, high individualism corresponds with a high level of masculinity. Filimonau et al. (2018) found that individualism was negatively and significantly related to personal environmental interest. Communitarianism (collectivism) was well correlated with tourists' positive environmental attitudes. These tourists were more willing to modify their individual tourist behaviour to make it more environmentally responsible. Filimonau et al. also found that long-term orientation dimension was negatively and significantly associated with anti-environmental attitudes, and positively related to tourist perceptions of the environmental impacts of tourism.

Based on the above, it may be suggested that when designing marketing mix elements for tourists from communitarian (collectivistic) and long-term oriented cultures (or individual tourists with these orientations), concentrating on environmental issues may prove to be useful in eliciting more positive responses in the form or purchase, repurchase, brand loyalty, and positive WOM communication. For instance, in terms of the product element of the marketing mix, when designing tourism products/services/holidays or activities, greater emphasis can be placed on environmental issues. Likewise,

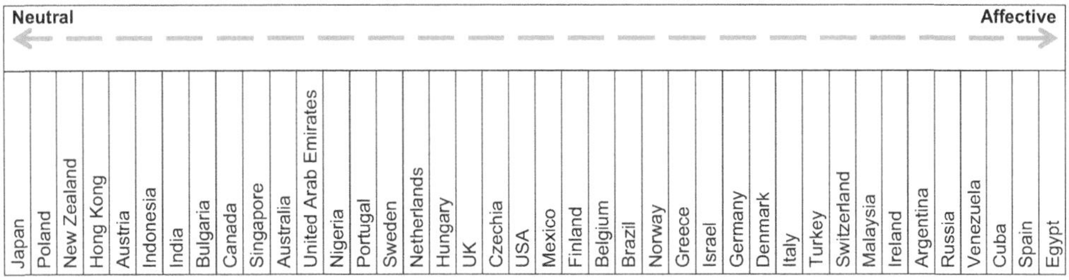

Neutral ⟵ ⟶ Affective

Japan	Poland	New Zealand	Hong Kong	Austria	Indonesia	India	Bulgaria	Canada	Singapore	Australia	United Arab Emirates	Nigeria	Portugal	Sweden	Netherlands	Hungary	UK	Czechia	USA	Mexico	Finland	Belgium	Brazil	Norway	Greece	Israel	Germany	Denmark	Italy	Turkey	Switzerland	Malaysia	Ireland	Argentina	Russia	Venezuela	Cuba	Spain	Egypt

Figure 12.2 Neutral and affective cultures continuum

Source: adapted from Trompenaars and Hampden-Turner (1998).

marketing communications messages (e.g., advertisements) cues may be used to reflect the environmental sensitivity and leave a minimum environmental footprint.

As Chapter 9 is solely allocated to the dimension of individualism and collectivism, readers are referred to Chapter 9 for detailed explanations and the characteristics of individualistic and collectivistic cultures, and the list of countries in each group.

Neutrality versus affective neutrality

The neutrality versus affect dimension was first introduced by Parsons (1951) and further validated by Hampden-Turner and Trompenaars (1993). People in affective societies tend to make decisions based on their emotions, while people from neutral societies base their decisions on information and facts. Affective cultures tend to use more body language and gestures (as individuals from high-context cultures) (see Chapter 4) and raise their voice to reflect their emotions. Interrupting someone in communication is more acceptable in affective cultures. For example, while in Latin America, Italy, and Turkey people may use a lot of gestures and increase the volume of their voices when communicating, in the UK using gestures frequently can be considered quite inappropriate. Figure 12.2 shows the affective neutral continuum of countries.

Trompenaars and Hampden-Turner (1998) describe three ways of communication in societies:

- In Anglo-Saxon cultures (as in high-context cultures), silence in a conversation may be perceived as rather uncomfortable, almost frightening. When people converse they tend to let each other speak, but as soon as the first speaker finishes her/his sentence, the second person would wish to join immediately.
- In Latin cultures, people usually do not tend to wait until the other person finishes her/his speaking. It is quite common to interrupt each other as soon as one understands what the other person wants to say.
- In Oriental cultures it is customary to have a short silence after each sentence, to make sure that the speaker has been able to say everything s/he wished to say.

Exercise

A search of the word "gestures" in the Cultural Atlas webpages (https://culturalatlas.sbs.com.au/) shows the following differences across nations.

Country	*Gestures – Explanation**	*Country*	*Gestures – Explanation**
Austria	Hand gestures are used conservatively in conversation. People tend to express themselves more through words than gestures and body language.	**Italy**	Italians are naturally more expressive in their tone of voice, facial expressions, and body language, often motioning with their hands to emphasise their point. This can sometimes seem theatrical.
Brazil	Brazilians are often verbose in their physical expressions, particularly with gestures	**Mexico**	Mexicans tend to use many hand and arm gestures throughout the conversation.
Germany	As Germans are direct communicators and can interpret gestures literally, even when they are made as a token of politeness. For example, if a German asks if you want food and you respond "no" to avoid appearing greedy, they may accept your first answer and not ask again. This can put some foreigners in difficult positions when their refusal or protest of an offer is taken at face value.	**Netherlands**	Dutch people rely heavily on words and generally make less use of body language to emphasise a point in communication. Some hand gestures may be used during the conversation.
Great Britain	Gestures are usually quite reserved, polite and less demonstrative.	**Portugal**	Portuguese may be animated in their physical expressions and gestures. Usually, such gestures are used to help emphasise their point.

Country	*Gestures – Explanation**	*Country*	*Gestures – Explanation**
Greece	Expect many hand gestures to be used during communication. Greeks tend to be very expressive in their body language.	**Romania**	Like Italians, Romanians are naturally more expressive in their tone of voice, facial expressions, and body language, often motioning with their hands to emphasise their point.
Ireland	The Irish tend to have a warm and friendly disposition, but generally, refrain themselves from showing a great deal of physical affection in public. Men are usually less comfortable touching one another than women, but a friendly slap on the back and other gestures are still common.	**Singapore**	Singaporeans are generally less accustomed to a receiving lot of physical affection from strangers and tend to reserve touching (such as back-slapping, hugging and holding hands) for close friends. Public displays of affection amongst couples are not always appreciated. However, Singaporeans are generally used to accidental touching (i.e., on public transport) due to how crowded the country is.
Japan	It is rare to see big bursts of laughter with corresponding gestures. When communicating bad news, a Japanese person may smile and laugh to diffuse the uncomfortable situation. People may also cover their mouths when they giggle.	**South Korea**	South Koreans generally speak quite firmly and use fewer gestures and facial expressions.

Tasks

1. Look at the table and distinguish affective and neutral cultures.
2. Determine five countries whose gestures and body languages you wish to study. Then by using https://culturalatlas.sbs.com.au/ what sorts of gestures people use to get across messages in a variety of communication contexts.

Source: Explanations have been extracted from Culture Atlas – https://culturalatlas.sbs.com.au/.

Based on these explanations, it may be put forward that tourism and hospitality customers from an affective society are more likely to prefer marketing communications messages with emotional cues. On the other hand, emotional cues may not have such a positive influence on tourism and hospitality customers from a neutral society. However, tourism and hospitality customers from both affective and neutral countries may influence their response to marketing communications messages. Koc's (2002) study showed that while male tourists preferred to process limited marketing communications messages of holidays with rational/neutral (cognitive) content, females preferred to process the extensive amount of marketing communications messages which contained both emotional/affective and cognitive cues.

Specific versus diffuse

As in the case of affective and neutrality dimension explained previously, specify and diffuseness dimensions also relate to high- and low-context dimensions of culture explained in Chapter 4. In a diffuse culture, people understand and prefer indirect communication and use contextual cues (e.g., mimics, body language) (as in the case of high-context cultures). On the other hand, specific cultures are more direct and use clear and descriptive words (as in the case of low-context cultures).

When interacting with people from specific cultures (low-context) a) be direct and to the point, b) focus on people's objectives before focusing on strengthening relationships, c) provide clear instructions, processes, and procedures; and d) allow people to keep their work and home lives separately. On the other hand, when interacting with people from diffuse cultures (high-context) a) focus on building a good relationship before focusing on business objectives, b) find out and learning about the other person, c) be prepared to discuss business on social occasions, and have personal discussions at work, and d) try to avoid turning down invitations to social functions as much as possible.

Hornikx and le Pai's (2017) study found that customers from diffuse (high-context) cultures perceived visual metaphors as less complex than customers who were from specific (low-context) cultures. In addition, customers from a diffuse/high-context culture preferred visual metaphors more than did specific/low-context customers. Moreover, customers from diffuse cultures are expected to place more importance on contextual cues in making their service quality evaluations. Based on the findings of Mattila (1999) and other researchers explained in Chapter 4, it may also be put forward that tourism and hospitality customers from diffuse cultures are more likely to provide significantly lower ratings to the service encounter and overall service quality as they tend to have higher service expectations.

For other characteristics of specific and diffuse cultures and country scores of specificity, the detailed explanations of the characteristics of this dimension, and its implications for tourism and hospitality readers are referred to Chapter 4.

Achievement versus ascription

Achievement orientation implies that a person's worth in society is evaluated and judged by her/his record of achievements. For instance, in the United States status is assigned to people based on their performance and merit. People believe that what an individual becomes in life depends on what s/he does and her/his worth. They value, recognise, and reward performance no matter who the person is. In these societies people use titles only when it is relevant.

On the other hand, ascription orientation means that status in the society depends on characteristics such as an individual's birth, age, family background, where s/he comes from, kinship, sex, etc. For instance, in Japan and China respect, power, title, and position are important and used frequently. People are expected to pay respect to people in authority, for example, senior members of an organisation (Trompenaars and Hampden-Turneer, 1998). Challenging people in authority is extremely difficult, and when it is to be done, a higher level of respect needs to be shown. Trompenars and Hampden-Turner present a case study from Turkey, an ascription-oriented country. The case study presents the difficulties experienced by an expatriate female director (aged 34) in the 1990s. The newly appointed female director had a successful internationally proven track of record. However, she was unable to establish authority over her staff because a) most of the managers under the director were male and they were not used to being supervised by a female director, and b) the director was younger than most of the managers. As can be seen in this case, in ascription societies gender and age may be important factors influencing the status of a manager. According to Turkish Higher Education Council (2020) statistics, while 45% of academicians in Turkey are women, only 34% of the professors and 7.5% of university rectors are women. In ascription societies, egalitarianism and gender egalitarianism tend to be rather low (Koc, 2010). It was explained in Chapter 8 that gender discrimination or segregation (both vertically and horizontally) was a major problem in the tourism and hospitality sector overall in the world (Koc, 2020).

While achievement orientation can be associated with assertiveness, high-performance orientation (Chapter 10), low-context (Chapter 4), individualism (Chapter 9), and low-power distance (Chapter 6) characteristics, ascription orientation can be associated with low-performance orientation, high-context, collectivism, and high-power distance characteristics (Koc, 2013). Figure 12.3 shows the affective neutral continuum of countries. For other characteristics of achievement and ascription cultures, and also for their implications for tourism and hospitality marketing and management, Chapters 4, 6, 9, and 10 may be referred to.

Sequential time versus synchronous time

The sequential time versus synchronous time dimension relates to how people in a society perceive time (as explained in Chapter 11). In sequential time cultures (i.e., monochronic

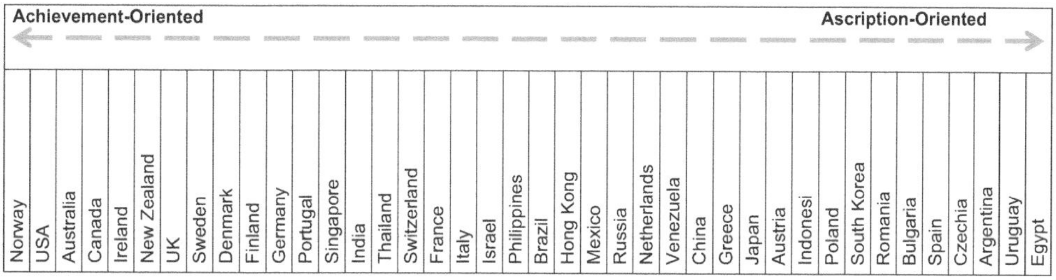

Achievement-Oriented ←→ Ascription-Oriented

Norway | USA | Australia | Canada | Ireland | New Zealand | UK | Sweden | Denmark | Finland | Germany | Portugal | Singapore | India | Thailand | Switzerland | France | Italy | Israel | Philippines | Brazil | Hong Kong | Mexico | Russia | Netherlands | Venezuela | China | Greece | Japan | Austria | Indonesi | Poland | South Korea | Romania | Bulgaria | Spain | Czechia | Argentina | Uruguay | Egypt

Figure 12.3 Achievement-oriented and ascription-oriented cultures continuum

Source: Adapted from Trompenaars and Hampden-Turner (1998).

cultures such as Western Europe, Canada, and the United States) people like events to happen in order and place a high value on being punctual as they believe that "time is money". Preparing plans and schedules are important and people expect everyone to adhere to plans, schedules, and deadlines. In sequential cultures tasks are completed one by one.

However, in synchronous time cultures (i.e., polychronic cultures such as Southern Europe, South America, and Asia) people view the past, present, and future as interwoven periods. They may often work on several projects at the same time and consider plans and commitments as flexible. People in polyhronic cultures are more likely to arrive at a meeting late because on their way they met a friend, or interrupt a telephone call to welcome a guest. For other characteristics of sequential time versus synchronous time dimensions of cultures, and also for their implications for tourism and hospitality marketing and management, Chapter 11 may be referred to.

Internal versus external control

Internal control, internal direction, or internal locus of control is related to the extent to which people believe that they can control nature or their environment to achieve goals. In internal control cultures, people believe that they can control the environment and believe that the outcomes (e.g., success or failure) depend on their efforts, knowledge, and abilities. In general, as leaders (McCullough et al., 1994; De Hoogh and Den Hartog, 2009) and entrepreneurs (Chatterjee and Das, 2015; Hsiao, 2016) tend to have a high level of internal locus of control, the numbers of potential leaders and entrepreneurs in a country may be influenced by internal or external directions (internal and external locus of control) in a society. Table 12.5 provides a

Table 12.5 Characteristics of individualistic and communitarian (collectivistic) societies

Societies with Internal Control	*Societies with External Control*
I/we can control the environment.	I/we cannot control the environment.
Tend to develop skills and take control of their learning.	People are dependent on others for developing skills. They may find it difficult to take control of their learning.
	People expect, and are more dependent on encouragement.
Employees can take initiative more easily and may be more comfortable with employee empowerment.	Employees may have a lack of initiative. They may need continuous guidance and direction.
People prefer to work against clear objectives that they have agreed with.	
They tend to be open about conflict and disagreement.	They may be uncomfortable with confrontation and conflict. They may prefer the conflicts to be solved quickly and quietly.
People can engage in constructive conflict.	

Source: adapted from Trompenaars and Hampden-Turner (1998).

summary of the characteristics of societies with internal and external control/direction (Trompenaars and Hampden-Turner, 1998).

In external control (external locus of control) cultures, people believe that nature or the environment controls them. For instance, although a significant proportion of Turkey is susceptible to earthquakes, a very small proportion of people insured their houses for earthquakes, as they believed that they could not control earthquakes and "whatever will happen will happen" (Aydin and Koc, 2016). People in external control societies tend to believe that they must work with the environment to achieve their goals. In these cultures, people attribute the outcomes (especially the negative outcomes) to outside factors.

CASE STUDY

External control and external attribution in Turkey

Turkish people tend to be externally directed and attribute outcomes, especially the negative ones, to outside factors (Koc, 2016). The inability to control an external attribution is strongly embedded in Turkish culture. In general, many students attribute their low marks to teachers or professors who *do not like them*. When a student receives a high mark in the exam, s/he tends to state that s/he has received it. However, when the same student receives a low mark (e.g., 20 out of 100 marks) in the exam, s/he tends to state that the teacher/the lecturer has given her/him 20. Employees tend to attribute their low salaries or not being able to get a promotion to nasty superiors. Likewise, government officials and politicians tend to attribute the problems of the country to other countries that are not on friendly terms with Turkey.

The overall cultural factors and mistakes rooted in upbringing may be influential in Turkish people's external attribution of negative outcomes. For instance, in Turkey when an infant falls and hits her/his head on the table or a chair, the mother, or whoever is looking after the infant, spanks the table or the chair, and says things like "you naughty table/chair you have hurt my son/ daughter" so as to soothe the infant. These type of irrational behaviours may cause children to begin to think that "I am normal, but things like furniture (other things/external things) are trying to hurt me". Hence, when they go to school, they blame teachers/lecturers, and when they start working they blame their superiors. Eventually, many negative things may be associated even with the country they live in. They may end up saying things like "if I were to live in a different country (e.g., the United States, or Germany) I would have been a lot more successful and happier".

In addition, especially in traditional and rural families, parents and other people do not tend to engage in communication in a logical, objective and rational communication manner. For instance, when a two-year-old girl visits her uncle with her parents, the uncle, so as to tease the child, may engage in irrational conversation with her and may say things like "You have a nice skirt on. Can I borrow it? I think it would look good on me?" The idea of wearing a skirt of a two-year-old girl, by someone who is a male and someone who is much bigger in size is insensible. In another situation when a child's mother leaves the room and goes to the kitchen or the lavatory, the child may start crying due to the absence of the mother in the room. In these situations, people in the room may attempt to distract the child to stop her/him cry and say insensible things like "Have you just seen the bird that has flown? Have you seen the bird?" Although, these sorts of attempts may distract the child and stop her/him cry in the short-run, in the long-run the child's cognitive abilities, ability to reason rationally and objectively may be severely affected. This is perhaps why in Turkey there is a high level of uncertainty avoidance (risk perception) and the trust for another fellow citizen is quite low.

In external attribution countries, people may have a lack of initiative, inertia to get into action, and a low-level of self-efficacy beliefs. Moreover, tourism and hospitality employees and managers from an external direction society may be more likely to attribute inefficiencies (e.g., service failures) (Loo and Boo, 2017) to outside factors. Likewise, customers from an external direction society may blame the management of the tourism and hospitality business for their own mistakes. Hence, to some extent, their attribution of the causes of the problem, for example, a service failure, and their justice evaluations may be subjective and biased. Also, customer participation may be difficult to implement in these cultures. Koc et al.'s (2017) research showed that customer participation reduced the severity of the responses of tourism and hospitality customers to service failures. However, customers with a high external locus of control may be more likely to attribute causes externally (Loo and Boo, 2017). When externally oriented customers engage in customer participation (cognitive/mental, physical or emotional participation) in the service, if they encounter service problems, they may be less likely to reduce the severity of their negative responses as much as the customers who are internally oriented.

Exercise

Study the following table based on the information provided in the other relevant chapters.

Country	*Universalism (U) – Particularism (P)*	*Individualism I) – Communitarianism/ Collectivism (C)*	*Neutral (N) – Affective (A)*	*Specific (S) – Diffuse (D)*	*Achievement (AC) – Ascription (AS)*
China	High (P)	(C)	(A)	Extreme (D)	(AS)
France	Middle	(C)	Low (A)	(S)	Middle
Germany	High (U)	(C)	Middle	Middle	(AC)
Japan	Middle	High (C)	Extreme (N)	Low (D)	Low (AS)
Mexico	Low (P)	(I)	Extreme (A)	Low (D)	(AC)

Country	*Universalism (U) – Particularism (P)*	*Individualism I) – Communit-arianism/ Collectivism (C)*	*Neutral (N) – Affective (A)*	*Specific (S) – Diffuse (D)*	*Achievement (AC) – Ascription (AS)*
Russia	Very High (P)	(I)	(A)	(D)	(AS)
Spain	Middle	Low (I)	(A)	(D)	Low (AS)
USA	Very High (U)	Very High (I)	Low (A)	High (S)	Extreme (AXC)

Tasks

1. Develop guidelines to be used in designing marketing mix elements aimed at tourism and hospitality customers from the above countries.
2. Develop guidelines for the effective management of tourism and hospitality employees from these countries.

Conclusion

This chapter explains Trompenaars and Hampden-Turner's (1998) cultural variables of universalism versus particularism, individualism versus communitarianism, neutrality versus emotional, specificity versus diffuseness, achievement versus ascription, sequential versus synchronic, and internal versus external control. These dimensions appear to overlap with other dimensions explained throughout the book. The explanations in the chapter show that Trompenaars and Hampden-Turner's dimensions can influence communication and interactions in multicultural tourism and hospitality environments. However, as there is a dearth of pertinent research on these dimensions, readers are recommended to look at the relevant research findings matching the dimensions explained in this chapter.

Questions

1. Explain the characteristics of universalistic and particularistic countries. How do a tourism and hospitality manager's universalistic or particularistic orientation influence organisational behaviour and human resource management practices in the business?
2. Explain the characteristics of achievement and ascription dimensions and their relationships with other dimensions.
3. Explain the potential implications of the internal and external direction (locus) of control for the marketing and management of tourism and hospitality businesses.

4. What are the main differences in communication between specific and diffuse societies? What are the implications of this dimension for the design of marketing mix elements and managing people in tourism and hospitality businesses?
5. What do affectivity and neutrality mean? What sorts of communicational problems arise when customers, staff, and managers have different orientations?

Research questions/ideas to pursue for researchers

As explained in this chapter, customer participation in tourism and hospitality services reduces the severity of responses to service failures. However, customers from external direction societies may still attribute the causes of failures to service employees and to the management of the service business. Based on this premise, tourism and hospitality customers' responses to service failures, their attributions, and justice evaluations may be compared in internal-external direction countries from the perspective of customer participation. The study may have important practical implications for the managers in tourism and hospitality.

Recommended further reading

Hall, E. T. (2000). Monochronic and polychronic time. *Intercultural communication: A reader*, 9, 280–286.

Hofstede, G. (2010). *Cultures and organizations: Software of the mind* (3rd ed.). New York: McGraw-Hill.

House, R. J., Hanges, P. J., Javidan, M., Dorfman, P. W., and Gupta, V. (2004). *Culture, leadership and organizations: The GLOBE study of 62 societies.* Thousand Oaks, CA: Sage.

Moldovan, O. (2012). Organizational culture under the microscope: Empirical analysis of a romanian local authority. *Managerial Challenges of the Contemporary Society*, (4), 34–39.

Trompenaars, A., and Hampden-Turner, C. (1998). *Riding the waves of cultural diversity in global business.* London: Nicholas Brealey Publishing.

References

Aydın, G., and Koc, E. (2016). Social marketing analysis of attitude toward compulsory earthquake insurance in Turkey. *Management and Economics: Celal Bayar University Journal of the Faculty of Economics and Administrative Sciences*, 23(2), 389–407.

Chatterjee, N., and Das, N. (2015). Key psychological factors as predictors of entrepreneurial success: A conceptual framework. *Academy of Entrepreneurship Journal*, 21(1), 102.

De Hoogh, A. H., and Den Hartog, D. N. (2009). Neuroticism and locus of control as moderators of the relationships of charismatic and autocratic leadership with burnout. *Journal of Applied Psychology*, 94(4), 1058.

Filimonau, V., Matute, J., Mika, M., and Faracik, R. (2018). National culture as a driver of pro-environmental attitudes and behavioural intentions in tourism. *Journal of Sustainable Tourism*, 26(10), 1804–1825.

Forret, M. L., and Dougherty, T. W. (2004), Networking behaviours and career outcomes: differences for men and women? *Journal of Organizational Behaviour*, 25(3), 419–437.

Hampden-Turner, C. and Trompenaars, F. (1993), *Seven cultures of capitalism: Value systems for creating wealth in the United States, Britain, Japan, Germany, France, Sweden and Netherlands*. New York: Doubleday.

Han, H., Kiatkawsin, K., Kim, W., and Lee, S. (2017). Investigating customer loyalty formation for wellness spa: Individualism vs. collectivism. International *Journal of Hospitality Management*, 67, 11–23.

Hornikx, J., and le Pair, R. (2017). The influence of high-/low-context culture on perceived Ad complexity and liking. *Journal of Global Marketing*, 30(4), 228–237.

Hsiao, C., Lee, Y. H., and Chen, H. H. (2016). The effects of internal locus of control on entrepreneurship: the mediating mechanisms of social capital and human capital. *The International Journal of Human Resource Management*, 27(11), 1158–1172.

Kang, K.H., Lee, S., and Yoo, C. (2016) The effect of national culture on corporate social responsibility in the hospitality and tourism industry. *International Journal of Contemporary Hospitality Management*, 28(8): 1728–1758.

Koc, E. (2002). The impact of gender in marketing communications: The role of cognitive and affective cues. *Journal of Marketing Communications*, 8(4), 257–275.

Koc, E. (2010). Services and conflict management: Cultural and European integration perspectives. *International Journal of Intercultural Relations*, 34(1), 88–96.

Koc, E. (2013). Power distance and its implications for upward communication and empowerment: Crisis management and recovery in hospitality services. *The International Journal of Human Resource Management*, 24(19), 3681–3696.

Koc, E. (2016). *Tüketici Davranışı ve Pazarlama Stratejileri: Global ve Yerel Yaklaşım* (Vol. 7). Ankara, Turkey: Baskı, Seçkin Yayınları.

Koc, E. (2020). Do women make better in tourism and hospitality? A conceptual review from a customer satisfaction and service quality perspective. *Journal of Quality Assurance in Hospitality and Tourism*, 1 28.

Koc, E., Ulukoy, M., Kilic, R., Yumusak, S., and Bahar, R. (2017). The influence of customer participation on service failure perceptions. *Total Quality Management and Business Excellence*, 28(3–4), 390–404.

Loo, P. T., and Boo, H. C. (2017). Customer attribution in service failures and recovery. In E. Koc (Ed.), *Service failures and recovery in tourism and hospitality* (pp. 70–82). Wallingford, Oxford: CABI.

Mattila, A. S. (1999). The role of culture and purchase motivation in service encounter evaluations. *Journal of Services Marketing*, 13(4/5), 376–389.

McCullough, M., Ashbridge, D., and Pegg, R. (1994). The effect of self-esteem, family structure, locus of control, and career goals on adolescent leadership behavior. *Adolescence*, 29(115), 605–612.

Parsons, Talcott (1951). *The social system*. Glencoe, IL: Free Press.

Rothstein, B., and Torsello, D. (2014). Bribery in preindustrial societies: understanding the universalism-particularism puzzle. *Journal of Anthropological Research*, 70(2), 263–284.

Trompenaars, A., and Hampden-Turner, C. (1998). Riding the waves of cultural diversity in global business. London: Nicholas Brealey Publishing.

Turkish Higher Education Council (2020). Yükseköğretim Bilgi Yönetim Sistemi, https://istatistik.yok.gov.tr/ (accessed 30 January 2019).

Chapter 13

Conclusions

Learning Objectives

After reading this chapter, you should be able to:

- explain culture's overall influence on various aspects of tourism and hospitality customers, employees and managers;
- integrate the knowledge relating to consumer behaviour, marketing, organisational behaviour and human resource management;
- explain how culture influences the design and implementation of marketing mix elements.

Introduction

Tourism and hospitality are probably the most relevant fields to study in conjunction with cross-cultural theories and dimensions, due to the intense and continuous interactions between customers, employees, and managers, (see Figures 1.1, 1.2, and 1.3 in Chapter 1) together with highly international and global nature of tourism and hospitality activities.

This final chapter of the book provides an overview and a summary of the dyadic influences of culture on tourism and hospitality. Chapter 1 provided an introduction to fundamental aspects and characteristics, and the context of tourism and hospitality services and how culture may relate to these aspects and characteristics. Chapter 2 explained the culture and the related concepts and presented a brief overview of cultural theories and dimensions explained throughout the book. Chapter 3 explained the intercultural competences, their role and importance in tourism and hospitality service encounters, and how to develop them. Chapter 4 explained the characteristics of high- and low-context cultures and how these characteristics influence communication and relationships between customers, employees, managers, and their activities. Chapter 5 explained the indulgence-restraint paradigm, the latest dimension developed by (Hofstede and Minkov, 2010). Indulgence and restraint dimensions, although highly related to tourism and hospitality, have been largely overlooked by researchers. The chapter explained the implications of indulgence and restraint on marketing and management of tourism and hospitality. Chapter 6 explained power distance and how high and low power-distance orientation influenced communication, relationships, and the systems people established. Chapter 7 explored uncertainty avoidance, as probably the most extensively researched cross-cultural dimension. As tourism and hospitality experiences involve many unknowns and uncertainties, uncertainty avoidance has important implications for the design and implementation of all marketing mix elements, as well as organisational behaviour and human resource management.

Masculinity and femininity dimension was explained and discussed in Chapter 8. It covered how masculinity and femininity influenced customers', employees' and managers' preferences, expectations, attitudes, and behaviour in tourism and hospitality settings. Chapter 9 focused on the individualism and collectivism dimension, a dimension which was put forward by earlier cross-culture scholars such as Parsons (1952), Kluckhohn and Strodtbeck (1961), Stewart (1971), Hofstede (1980), Trompenaars and Hampden-Turner (1998), Maznevski (1994), and Trianidis (1995).

Chapter 10 explained performance orientation, humane orientation, and related concepts such as assertiveness and egalitarianism based on the GLOBE framework (House et al., 2004). Chapter 11 explained and discussed time orientation and discussed the likely implications of long- and short-term, past, present, and future orientations on tourism and hospitality marketing and management. The penultimate chapter, Chapter 12, presented the cross-cultural dimensions proposed by Trompenaars and Hampden-Turner (1998), and explained the potential implications of them for tourism and hospitality.

Exercise

Assume the role of a management and training consultant commissioned to train the employees and managers of an international tourism and hospitality chain owning 20 resort hotels and 30 luxury restaurants throughout the world. You are expected to prepare and make a presentation to the company management so that you win the project to train their employees. You are particularly asked to address how you will train and develop their employees and managers in terms of intercultural sensitivity, intercultural competence, and intercultural intelligence abilities. By taking Figures 1.1, 1.2, and 1.3 from Chapter 1 into account and by using specific examples from the book, prepare a presentation to convince the top management of the company.

The need for and the benefits of the dyadic perspective

As explained in Chapter 1 this book has a dyadic perspective in that it explains cross-cultural aspects of tourism and the implications of culture, based on the following fields:

1. *Customer/Marketing perspective:* marketing, consumer behaviour, services marketing and management, and international marketing.
2. *Service provider/management perspective:* organisational behaviour, human resource management, international management, and management.

Service businesses of today need to be proactive and have an "anticipate and lead" orientation, as opposed to "make and sell" and "sense and respond" orientations which reflect outmoded or reactive orientation in leading businesses. Moreover, there is an increasing need to study and practice marketing and human resource management functions in a more combined and interlinked manner in all service businesses in general, and in tourism and hospitality businesses in particular. The dyadic cross-cultural influences on customers, employees, and managers provided in Chapter 1 emphasised the importance of *people* as the marketing mix in the marketing of services, such as tourism and hospitality. Tourism and hospitality services quite often require constant and intense interactions between customers and service personnel, they are usually referred to as *people business* (Kim et al., 2010; Dolnicar et al., 2011; Koc, 2013b).

CASE STUDY

Service Failure

The following dialogue took place in a 4-star hotel in Antalya, Turkey, between a German couple and the front desk officer. The German couple came to the hotel for their summer vacation and after settling in their room they felt the need to speak to hotel management due to a problem in their room. Read the dialogue and the problems identified in the right-hand column.

Person	*The Dialogue*	*The Problem*
Front-Desk Officer	Hello. How can I help you?	
German Tourist	Hello. We have settled into our room but there is a problem with our room.	
Officer	(Silence)	The front desk officer waited for the guests to explain the problem. He would be expected to show empathy and ask the cause of the problem in the room.
Tourist	There is an awful smell in our room.	
Officer	Which room is it, please?	Still no sign of empathy/sympathy. No apology has been made yet.
Tourist	Room 1312	
Officer	Room 1312? Yes. We have received complaints about that room. It really smells a bit.	Still no apology, no sign of empathy and sympathy. The things said by the front desk officer are aimless. Moreover, they convey signs of a lack of responsiveness and reliability.

Person	*The Dialogue*	*The Problem*
		No explanation has been made to explain why the service failure occurred.
Tourist	If you already know that the room smells. why have you given it to us in the first place?	No satisfactory reply has been provided.
Officer	I am sorry. We have been unable to solve the problem.	Still no effective apology. There are still signs of lack of responsiveness and reliability in the front desk officer's speech.
Tourist	We would like to change our room. Could you please find another room for us?	The solution is offered by the guest, not by the front desk officer.
Officer	Let me see. Room 1425 seems to be available. But the room is available for only two nights. After that, it is booked for someone else. After that, we can give you room 1437 in which you can stay for the remaining part of your holidays, that is, five days.	The solution is not an immediate solution, which puts a burden on the guests as they have to change their rooms twice.
Tourist	Well. All right then. We would like to take those rooms.	
Officer	20 Euros multiplied by seven. That makes 140 Euros.	
Tourist	Additional payment required? What? Why?	
Officer	Your present room, Room 1312, is a room with a mountain view. The rooms 1425 and 1437 have a sea view. The rooms with a sea view cost 20 Euros more per night.	The problem has not been solved. The approach of the front desk officer is in contradiction with the core values of Total Quality Management namely with "Make it right for the customer at any cost".
Tourist	I don't want to pay anything extra. Why should I anyway? I don't want a room with a sea view. All I want is a room with no awful smell.	

Task

Analyse the case study and relate the front-desk officer's and the overall service provider's approach with cultural dimensions explained in the book. For instance, asking an additional amount for replacing rooms shows a short-term orientation of the service provider.

Marketing and consumer behaviour perspective

Chapters 4 to 13 provided potential and actual implications of cultural dimensions regarding consumer behaviour and marketing management as follows.

Marketing mix

Table 13.1 provides some examples showing the implications of cross-cultural dimensions on the design and implementation of marketing mix elements.

In addition to the marketing mix elements, a wide range of other services marketing and consumer behaviour implications were also provided throughout the chapters. These implications included topics such as customer satisfaction, customers' repurchase and WOM intentions, customer complaints, customer switching behaviour, customer loyalty, variety-seeking behaviour, service quality and service quality dimensions, service failures, attribution, service recovery, justice evaluations, service recovery paradox, customer involvement and participation, and service orientation.

Organisational behaviour, HRM, and management perspective

In relation to a wide variety of organisational behaviour, HRM, and management topics and concepts, the influence and implications of cross-cultural dimensions were discussed throughout the book. The organisational behaviour, HRM, and management topics and concepts discussed included staff training, employee empowerment, accountability, organisational communication, subordinate-superior communication and relationships, organisational citizenship behaviour, organisational commitment, leadership, bureaucracy, entrepreneurship, intrapreneurship, ethnocentrism, motivation, performance orientation, change management, teamwork, groupthink, emotional labour, emotional contagion, organisational structure and systems, organisational culture, ethics, legitimacy, nepotism, recruitment, promotion, employee job satisfaction, employee turnover, absenteeism, stress, burnout syndrome, skill development, and organisational training and development.

For instance, Koc's (2013b) study on subordinate superior communication and service recovery found that hospitality employees in the UK (low power distance), had a more direct approach to communication with their superiors, and were able to respond to the same service failure scenarios more quickly and directly than the hospitality employees in Turkey (high power distance). The study pointed out the importance of subordinate–superior relationships and empowerment in service recovery situations. In a similar vein, Magnini et al.'s (2013) research founded that employees in collectivistic cultures tended to have lower levels of comfort with empowerment.

Case study exercise

Re-read the Euro Disney (Paris) case study provided in Chapter 2. Carry out an internet search to find out more and to understand the Euro Disney project, in terms of the context, and the cultural mistakes. List down at least 15 cultural mistakes made by the company at the time. Based on the knowledge you have developed throughout this book, explain why these mistakes were made and what should have been done to avoid them.

Table 13.1 The influence of cultural dimensions on marketing mix

Marketing Mix Elements	*Examples*
Product	Becker (2000) showed that customers from high-context cultures have more sensory involvement in eating, entertaining, and socialising.
	Correia et al. (2011) found power distance as the most influential cultural dimension influencing tourists' holiday product and destination choice decisions. Customers from high-power distance cultures heavily depend on the quality and brand image of the business when making their holiday decisions.
	Past-oriented tourists were more likely to travel with the intention of sensation seeking (hedonistic, indulgent) (e.g., such as a beach resort visit or a cruise vacation), while future-oriented tourists were more likely to travel with the intention of self-fulfilment and knowledge enhancement (Miao et al., 2011; Lu et al., 2016).
Price	Jeong et al. (2019) demonstrated that hospitality customers from collectivistic and high-context cultures were much more interested in the price-quality relationship than the hospitality customers from individualistic and low-context cultures.
	Mattila and Choi's (2006) research showed that presentation of information on a hotel's pricing policy had a positive effect on Korean customers' (high uncertainty avoidance) satisfaction levels, while American customers (low level of risk avoidance) were relatively unaffected by such information.
	Correia et al. (2011) put forward that tourists from collectivistic countries were more likely to make their decisions based on brand, prices, and the number of alternatives, while individualistic customers had their own criteria.
	Sabiote-Ortiz et al. (2016) discovered that the pricing level which tourism and hospitality establishments determine for a service had a direct influence on the perceived risk perceptions of tourists from high-uncertainty cultures.
Place	Money and Crotts (2003) found that tourism and hospitality customers from Japan (collectivistic and high-uncertainty avoidance) were more likely to seek information from channel members such as travel agencies.
	Hsu and Huang (2016) found that with the recent exposure to dishonest service providers and travel agencies, Chinese customers (long-term oriented) tended to have a lower level of trust for travel agencies
	Tourism and hospitality customers from high-uncertainty avoidance cultures are more likely to avoid online purchasing than customers from a low-uncertainty avoidance culture (Lim et al., 2004; Sabiote-Ortiz et al., 2016).
	In general, for customers from high uncertainty avoidance cultures, the perceived risk of using the online medium for making purchases is greater than the traditional channel (Suki and Suki, 2007).

Table 13.1 continued

Marketing Mix Elements	*Examples*
Promotion	Correia et al. (2011) found that tourists from long-term oriented societies were more likely to make their purchase decisions based on brand image, and use a number of information sources. Cheong et al. (2010) found that the advertising appeals of *ornamental*, *status*, and *dear* were more frequently found in Chinese food advertisements (a relatively high power-distance culture) compared with the United States (a relatively more power-distance culture). Swaminathan (2012) showed that the appeals of ornamental, vain, dear, and status were positively correlated while the appeals of cheap, humility, nurturance, and plain were negatively correlated. Rojas-Méndez et al.'s (2002) study showed that people with high past orientation are more likely to avoid advertising; people with present time orientation have a more positive attitude towards advertising and are less likely to skip advertising as they are more hedonistic and seek immediate gratification; future-oriented people's attitude towards advertising is similar to present-oriented people, but for a different reason. Future-oriented people concentrate on future benefits, which may accrue from learning through viewing or reading advertisements.
People	Tsang and Ap (2007) and Manrai and Manrai (2011) found that high power distance would increase the social position between the customer and service provider, resulting in an increase in quality expectations of tourists and their likelihood of providing negative evaluations. Also, a high level of power distance increases reliance on relational services quality attributes such as empathy (including courtesy), and responsiveness. Tourism and hospitality customers from a high power-distance culture (e.g., Japan) tend to view a service employee's attempts to initiate communication negatively as they view themselves superior to the service employees (Lee, 2015).
Physical Evidence	Gu and Ryan (2008) and Au et al.'s (2010) research showed that long-term oriented Chinese tourists placed importance on price and value relationships and had expectations (e.g., in terms of surroundings of the hotel) in comparison with the price they paid. Compared with customers from low power-distance cultures, customers from a high power-distance culture tend to prefer destinations, hotels, restaurants, and services that enhance their credibility of belonging to a superior social class, higher prestige, and wealth (Crotts and Erdmann 2000; Weiermair 2000; Nath et al., 2016).
Process	Hospitality customers from a low power-distance culture (e.g., the United States) tend to ignore formalities in their interactions with the service employees as they see themselves equal with them. Hence, communication initiated by service employees is not perceived as negatively. On the other hand, tourism and hospitality customers from a high-power distance culture (e.g., Japan) are more likely to view a service employee's attempts to initiate communication negatively as they see themselves superior compared with the service employees (Lee, 2015).

Table 13.2 The influence of cultural dimensions on other services marketing and consumer behaviour related issues

Consumer Behaviour and Services Marketing and Management Concepts and Theories	
Service Quality	Lee et al.'s (2015) study of American (low-context) and Japanese (high-context) restaurant customers demonstrated that American customers' perception of service effectiveness, emotional response and intention to revisit increased with more frequent check-backs. American customers felt that they received more prompt and responsive service when the service employee (the waiter) checked back on them often. Lee et al.'s (2015) study found that frequent check-backs increased low- context customers' (from Europe and the US) positive emotional response and their intention to revisit.
Service Failures, Service Recovery	Koc, Ar and Aydin (2017) and Koc, Yilmaz and Boz (2020) found that in restraint cultures tourism and hospitality customers may be more likely to remember negative experiences, and hence service recovery paradox may be less likely to take place.
Service Recovery Paradox	Customers from individualistic cultures tend to prefer financial gains, while customers from collectivistic cultures tend to concentrate on avoiding losses in service recovery situations (Gi Park et al., 2014). Mattila and Patterson (2004) demonstrated that Americans (individualistic) were more satisfied with compensation (distributive justice) than East Asians (collectivistic) were.
Service Orientation	Intercultural sensitivity relates significantly to all services marketing mix elements, service quality dimensions and service orientations of tourism and hospitality employees (Yurur et al., 2020).
Variety – seeking behaviour	Due to a high level of emotional control in collectivistic societies, people may suppress the desire to seek variety. Variety seeking, which relates to being different, tend to be assumed as negative behaviour (Triandis, 1995; Kim and Markus, 1999; Bathae, 2011).
Complaint Behaviour	Customers from collectivistic cultures may feel that making a complaint may harm the employee in some way and hence, they may refrain from making complaints (Yuksel et al., 2006; Koc, 2013a). Swanson et al. (2011) found that power distance was negatively associated with the customer complaining directly to the service provider. Customers from a larger power distance culture are more likely to perceive unsatisfactory goods and services as a fact of life and are less likely to complain when encountered with service failures (Au et al., 2010).
Customer Involvement and Customer Participation	Customers from an indulgence culture tend to place more value on leisure and fun, and hence their level of involvement in the purchase (pre-purchase, purchase, and post-purchase), use and consumption stages of tourism and hospitality products and services may be high (Koc, 2017). Money and Crotts (2003) found that as a restraint culture people in Japan tended to leave travel arrangements to professionals rather than to themselves, that is, they were not highly involved with their holidays.

How to use cross-cultural dimensions and conclusions

There have been criticisms of cultural studies, primarily based on the fact that culture is not a static phenomenon and it changes over time (McSweeney 2002a, 2002b; Guiso et al., 2006; Ailon, 2008). Hofstede (Hofstede, 2002, 2009; Minkov and Hofstede, 2011) argued that culture is fairly stable over time and that the dimensions were based on centuries-old roots. Hofstede and Minkov's (2010) study of the country scores over the period of 1970 and 2010 showed that although the absolute scores of countries can change over time, the relative country positions and the difference between the countries remained the same over the studied period.

As stated previously, it should be noted that people's attitudes and behaviour may change over time. For instance, although people from collectivistic cultures traditionally tended to make their travel and holiday arrangements through travel agencies and intermediaries, their attitudes and behaviours may alter when they experience negative outcomes. For instance, as mentioned earlier, Hsu and Huang (2016) showed that in China (a collectivistic society) with the recent exposure to dishonest service providers and travel agencies, Chinese customers' (long-term oriented) tended to have a lower level of trust for travel agencies.

Information zone

People and habits* do *change

Shia Saide LaBeouf, an American actor, performance artist, and filmmaker, is attributed with the following:

> In 1998 we were told not to get in a car with strangers. In 2008, we were told not to meet people from the internet alone. In 2019 you use Uber ... order yourself a stranger from the internet to get in the car alone.

Moreover, as countries have different cultural characteristics, the implications should not be interpreted based on one cultural dimension or characteristic. For instance, collectivistic features of a country (e.g., Turkey's) may cause people in the society to place greater importance on cooperation and harmony. However, at the same time, if the power distance is high in this country (e.g., Turkey again), people in the society may wish to purchase products and services (e.g., tourism and hospitality services) to enhance social status and prestige.

Such differences may be seen on an individual basis as well. While the social needs of individuals may cause them to be similar to others (e.g., friends), they may also be different from them due to their prestige and status needs. Therefore, another recommendation can be made here regarding the use of cultural characteristics and dimensions. Other factors, such as people's age, income, personality (see Chapters 7 and 8), also need to be taken into account as they may shape and alter their perceptions, attitudes, and behaviour. A final word of caution can be made by quoting Alexander Dumas "All generalisations are dangerous, including this one."

Activity

Study the following quotes by Rumi (an eastern philosopher who lived in Asia Minor (Turkey) between 1207 and 1273) in relation to cultural orientations. Discuss which specific characteristic of a particular dimension each quote may relate to.

- **Individualism-Collectivism:** "Don't be satisfied with stories, how things have gone with others. Unfold your own myth"; "Set your life on fire. Seek those who fan your flames"; "Open your hands if you want to be held"; "You are not a drop in the ocean. You are the entire ocean, in a drop"; "I want to sing like the birds sing, not worrying about who hears or what they think"; "The whole universe is contained within a single human being"; "You are not one you are a thousand. Just light your lantern"; "Do not feel lonely, the entire universe is inside you"; "Achieve some perfection yourself, so that you may not fall into sorrow by seeing the perfection in others"; "Be a lamp, or a lifeboat, or a ladder. Help someone's soul heal. Walk out of your house like a shepherd."
- **High and Low Context:** "Raise your words, not voice. It is rain that grows flowers, not thunder"; "Words are a pretext. It is the inner bond that draws one person to another, not words"; "There is a voice that doesn't use words, listen"; "Keep silent, because the world of silence is a vast fullness"; "In silence there is eloquence. Stop weaving and see how the pattern improves"; When I am silent, I fall into the place where everything is music"; "My words are like a ship, and the sea is their meaning. Come to me and I will take you to the depths of spirit. I will meet you there."
- **Indulgence-Restraint:** "Be full of sorrow, that you may become hill of joy; weep, that you may break into laughter"; "Either give me more wine or leave me alone These pains you feel are messengers. Listen to them"; "Lovers have heartaches that can't be cured by drugs or sleep, or games, but only by seeing their beloved"; "Beauty surrounds us, but usually we need to be walking in a garden to know it"; "Let the lover be disgraceful, crazy, absentminded. Someone sober will worry about events going badly. Let the lover be"; "Death has nothing to do with going away. The sun sets. The moon sets. But they are not gone."
- **Power Distance:** "Anything which is more than our necessity is poison. It may be power, wealth, hunger, ego, greed, laziness, love, ambition, hate or anything."
- **Uncertainty Avoidance:** "Gamble everything for love, if you're a true human being. If not, leave this gathering"; "Forget safety. Live where

you fear to live. Destroy your reputation. Be notorious"; "Trust means you're ready to risk what you currently have."

- **Indulgence – Restraint-Performance Orientation:** "We carry inside us the wonders we seek outside us."
- **Indulgence – Restraint, Individualism-Collectivism:** "Come, come, whoever you are. Wanderer, worshiper, lover of leaving. Ours is not a caravan of despair."
- **Humane Orientation, Masculinity-Femininity, Individualism-Collectivism:** "Let us carve gems out of our stony hearts and let them light our path to love"; "Love is the whole thing. We are only pieces."
- **Achievement-Performance Orientation:** "What you seek is seeking you"; "Two there are who are never satisfied: the lover of the world and the lover of knowledge"; "As you start to walk out on the way, the way appears"; "There is a fountain inside you. Don't walk around with an empty bucket"; "You wander from room to room hunting for the diamond necklace. That is already around your neck"; "Moonlight floods the whole sky from horizon to horizon; how much it can fill your room depends on the windows"; "Why do you stay in prison when the door is so wide open?"; "You were born with wings. Why prefer to crawl through life?"; "The garden of the world has no limit except in your mind"; "Whether one moves slowly or with speed, the one who is a seeker will be a finder"; "Why should I stay at the bottom of a well when a strong rope is in my hand?"; "I know you're tired but come, this is the way."
- **Humane-Affective Orientation:** "Be drunk with love, for love is all that exists"; "Whoever has heart's doors wide open, could see the sun itself in every atom"; "Gratitude is the wine for the soul. Go on. Get drunk"; "Let's only say what our hearts desire"; "Whenever we can manage to love without expectations, calculations, negotiations, we are indeed in heaven."
- **Time Orientation:** "When you lose all sense of self, the bonds of a thousand chains will vanish"; "Everything about yesterday has gone with yesterday. Today, it is needed to say new things"; "Whenever they rebuild an old building, they must first of all destroy the old one"; "Yesterday I was clever, so I wanted to change the world. Today I am wise, so I am changing myself"; "I died as a mineral and became a plant, I died as a plant and rose to animal, I died as an animal and I was Man. Why should I fear? When was I less by dying?"
- **Assertiveness:** "If you are irritated by every rub, how will your mirror be polished?"; "Anyone who genuinely and consistently with both hands looks for something, will find it."
- **Affective-Neutral Affective Orientation:** "Wisdom tells us we are not worthy; love tells us we are. My life flows between the two"; "Only from the heart can you touch the sky."

Exercise

To get to know yourself better re-do the following tests in the book you did earlier on. For the ones marked with an asterisk (*), compare your present scores with your earlier scores to see whether there have been any changes.

Test	*Developed by*	*Relevant Chapter*
Social Anxiety and Avoidance Test	Liebowitz et al. (1985)	1
GENE (Generalized Ethnocentrism) Scale	Neuliep and McCroskey (1997)	1
Intercultural Willingness to Communicate Test*	Kassing (1997)	3
Cultural Intelligence Test*	Ang et al. (2007)	3
Intercultural Sensitivity Scale*	Chen and Starosta (2000)	3
Cross-Cultural Awareness Test*	Goodman (1994)	3
Intercultural Communication Competence Scale*	Arasaratnam (2009)	3
Intercultural Communication Apprehension Test*	Neuliep and McCroskey (1997)	3
Low- and High-Context Communication Scale	Gudykunst et al. (1996).	4
Service Orientation Scale (SERV* OR)*	Lytle et al. (1998)	5
Self-Assessment Power Distance Scale	Hofstede and Minkov (2010)	6
Control Scale: Customers' Willingness to Have Control	Koc and Boz (2017)	7
Control Scale: Service Business' Ability or Willingness to Offer Control to its Customer	Koc and Boz (2017)	7
The Masculine and Feminine Self-Disclosure Scale (MFSDS)	Snell (2013)	8
Individualism and Collectivism Scale (Cultural Orientation Scale)	Triandis and Gelfland (1998).	9

Questions

1. Why is studying cross-cultural aspects of tourism and hospitality important? Discuss.
2. Explain the need for a dyadic perspective for the study of the cross-cultural aspects of tourism and hospitality.

3. Do culture and cultural orientations of nations change over time? Discuss.
4. How correct is it to make inferences based on cultural dimensions or characteristics? Discuss.
5. Explain and discuss the Alexander Dumas's (1802–1870) quote of "All generalisations are dangerous, including this one" from the perspective of the study of cultures.

Research questions/ideas to pursue for researchers

A research study may be carried out to explore the relationship between the intercultural competence, intercultural intelligence and intercultural sensitivity scores of a) entrepreneurs, b) managers, and c) employees and organisational performance in tourism and hospitality businesses serving international customers. Organisational performance can be measured based on marketing related indicators (such as customer satisfaction, customer loyalty), human resource management related indicators (such as employee job satisfaction, absenteeism, turnover, organisational commitment, motivation , individual performance), or financial indicators (such as profitability, return on investment).

Recommended further reading

Hofstede, G. Hofstede, G. J., and Minkov, M. (2010). Cultures and organizations: Software of the mind (3rd ed.). New York: McGraw-Hill.

Koc, E. (2013). Power distance and its implications for upward communication and empowerment: Crisis management and recovery in hospitality services. *The International Journal of Human Resource Management*, 24(19), 3681–3696.

Yurur, S., Koc, E., Taskin, C., and Boz, H. (2020). Factors influencing intercultural sensitivity of hospitality employees. *International Journal of Hospitality and Tourism Administration*, 1–19.

References

Ailon, G. (2008). Mirror, mirror on the wall: Culture's Consequences in a value test of its own design. *The Academy of Management Review*, 33(4), 885–904.

Ang, S., Van Dyne, L., Koh, C., Ng, K. Y., Templer, K. J., Tay, C., and Chandrasekar, N. A. (2007). Cultural intelligence: Its measurement and effects on cultural judgment and decision making, cultural adaptation and task performance. *Management and Organization Review*, 3(3), 335–371.

Arasaratnam, L. A. (2009). The Development of a New Instrument of Intercultural Communication Competence. *Journal of Intercultural Communication*, 20.

Au, N., Law, R., and Buhalis, D. (2010). The impact of culture on e-complaints: Evidence from the Chinese consumers in hospitality organizations. In U. Gretzel, R. Law, and

M. Fuchs (Eds.), *Information and communication technologies in tourism 2010* (pp. 285–296). Vienna, Switzerland: Springer-Verlag.

Becker, C. (2000). Service recovery strategies: The impact of cultural differences. *Journal of Hospitality and Tourism Research*, 24(4), 526–538.

Chen, G. M., and Starosta, W. J. (2000). The development and validation of the intercultural communication sensitivity scale. *Human Communication*, 3, 1–15.

Cheong, Y., Kim, K., and Zheng, L. (2010). Advertising appeals as a reflection of culture: a cross-cultural analysis of food advertising appeals in China and the US. *Asian Journal of Communication*, 20(1), 1–16.

Correia, A., Kozak, M., and Ferradeira, J. (2011). Impact of culture on tourist decision-making styles. *International Journal of Tourism Research*, 13(5), 433–446.

Crotts, J. C., and Erdmann, R. (2000). Does national culture influence consumers' evaluation of travel services? A test of Hofstede's model of cross-cultural differences. *Managing Service Quality*, 10(6), 410–419.

Dolnicar, S., Grabler, K., Grün, B., and Kulnig, A. (2011). Key drivers of airline loyalty. *Tourism Management*, 32(5), 1020–1026.

Goodman, N. R. (1994). Cross-cultural training for the global executive. In R. W. Brislin and T. Yoshida (Eds.), *Improving Intercultural Interaction: Models for Cross-Cultural Training Programs* (pp. 34–54). Thousand Oaks, CA: Sage.

Gu, G., and Ryan, C. (2008). Chinese Clientele at Chinese Hotels – preferences and Satisfaction. *International Journal of Hospitality Management*, 27, 337–345.

Gudykunst, W. B., Matsumoto, Y., Ting-Toomey, S., Nishida, T., Kim, K., and Heyman, S. (1996). The influence of cultural individualism-collectivism, self construals, and individual values on communication styles across cultures. *Human Communication Research*, 22(4), 510–543.

Guiso, L., Paola, S., and Zingales, L. (2006). Does culture affect economic outcomes? *Journal of Economic Perspectives*, 20(2), 23–48.

Hofstede, G. (1980). *Culture's consequences: International differences in work-related values*. Beverly Hills: Sage.

Hofstede, G. (2002). Dimensions do not exist: A reply to Brendan McSweeney. *Human Relations*, 55(11), 1355–1361.

Hofstede, G. (2009). Who is the fairest of them all? Galit Ailon's mirror. *Academy of Management Review*, 34(3), 570–571.

Hofstede, G. J., and Minkov, M. (2010). *Cultures and organizations: Software of the mind* (3rd rev. ed.). New York: McGrawHill.

House R. J., Hanges, P. J., Javidan, M., Dorfman, P. W., and Gupta, V. (2004) Culture, *leadership, and organizations: The GLOBE study of 62 societies*. Thousand Oaks, CA: Sage.

Hsu, C. H., and Huang, S. S. (2016). Reconfiguring Chinese cultural values and their tourism implications. *Tourism Management*, 54, 230–242.

Jeong, J. Y., Crompton, J. L., and Hyun, S. S. (2019). What makes you select a higher price option? Price–quality heuristics, cultures, and travel group compositions. *International Journal of Tourism Research*, 21(1), 1–10.

Kassing, J. W. (1997). Development of the Intercultural Willingness to Communicate Scale. *Communication Research Reports*, 14, 399–407.

Kim, M. G., Wang, C., and Mattila, A. S. (2010). The relationship between consumer complaining behavior and service recovery: an integrative review. *International Journal of Contemporary Hospitality Management*, 22(7), 975–991.

Kluckhohn, F. R., and Strodtbeck, F.L. (1961). *Variations in value orientations*. New York: Harper and Row.

Koc, E. (2013b). Power distance and its implications for upward communication and empowerment: Crisis management and recovery in hospitality services. *The International Journal of Human Resource Management*, 24(19), 3681–3696.

Koc, E. and Boz, H. (2017). Development of Scales to Measure Customers' Willingness to Have Control and the Control Offered by Service Businesses. *Ecoforum*, 6(3), 27–35.

Lee, H. E. (2015). Does a server's attentiveness matter? Understanding intercultural service encounters in restaurants. *International Journal of Hospitality Management*, 50, 134–144.

Liebowitz, M. R., Gorman, J. M., Fryer, A. J., and Klein, D. F. (1985). Social phobia: Review of a neglected anxiety disorder. *Archives of General Psychiatry*, 42, 729–736.

Lim, K. H., Leung, K., Sia, C. L., and Lee, M. K. O. (2004). Is e-commerce boundary-less? Effects of individualism-collectivism and uncertainty avoidance on internet shopping. *Journal of International Business Studies*, 35(6), 545–559.

Lu, J., Hung, K., Wang, L., Schuett, M. A., and Hu, L. (2016). Do perceptions of time affect outbound-travel motivations and intention? An investigation among Chinese seniors. *Tourism Management*, 53, 1–12.

Lytle, R. S., Hom, P. W., and Mokwa, M. P. (1998). SERV* OR: A managerial measure of organizational service-orientation. *Journal of Retailing*, 74(4), 455–489.

Magnini, V. P., Hyun, S., Kim, B., and Uysal, M. (2013). The influences of collectivism in hospitality work settings. *International Journal of Contemporary Hospitality Management*, 25(6), 844–864.

Manrai, L. A., and Manrai, A. (2011). Hofstede's cultural dimensions and tourist behaviors: A review and conceptual framework. *Journal of Economics, Finance and Administrative Science*, 16(31), 23.

Mattila, A. S., and Choi, S. (2006). A cross-cultural comparison of perceived fairness and satisfaction in the context of hotel room pricing. *International Journal of Hospitality Management*, 25(1), 146–153.

Maznevski, M. L. (1994). *Synergy and performance in multi-cultural teams* (Unpublished doctoral dissertation). University of Western Ontario, London, Canada.

McSweeney, B. (2002a). Hofstede's model of national cultural differences and their consequences: a triumph of faith – a failure of analysis. *Human Relations*, 55(1): 89–117.

McSweeney, B. (2002b). The essentials of scholarship: A reply to Hofstede. *Human Relations*, 55(11), 1363–1372.

Miao, L., Lehto, X., and Wei, W. (2011). The hedonic experience of travel-related consumption. In International CHRIE conference-referred track. Paper 7 http:// scholarworks.umass.edu/refereed/ICHRIE_2011/Saturday/7.

Minkov, M., and Hofstede, G. (2011). The evolution of Hofstede's doctrine. *Cross Cultural Management: An International Journal*, 18(1), 10–20.

Money, R. B., and Crotts, J. C. (2003). The effect of uncertainty avoidance on information search, planning, and purchases of international travel vacations. *Tourism Management*, 24(2), 191–202.

Nath, P., Devlin, J., and Reid, V. (2016). Expectation formation in case of newer hotels: The role of advertising, price, and culture. *Journal of Travel Research*, 55(2), 261–275.

Neuliep, J. W., and McCroskey, J. C. (1997). The development of a U.S. and Generalized Ethnocentrism Scale. *Communication Research Reports*, 14, 385– 398.

Parsons, T. (1952). *The social system*. London: Tavistock Publications; Glencoe: The Free Press.

Rojas-Méndez, J. I., Davies, G., Omer, O., Chetthamrongchai, P., and Madra, C. (2002). A time attitude scale for cross-cultural research. *Journal of Global Marketing*, 15 (3/4), 117–147.
Sabiote-Ortiz, C. M., Frías-Jamilena, D. M., and Castañeda-García, J. A. (2016). Overall perceived value of a tourism service delivered via different media: A cross-cultural perspective. *Journal of Travel Research*, 55(1), 34–51.
Snell, W. E., Jr. (2013). The Masculine and Feminine Self-Disclosure Scale (MFSDS). Measurement instrument database for the Social Science. www.midss.ie.
Stewart, R. A. (1971). Cross-cultural personality research and basic cultural dimensions through factor analysis. *Personality*, 2, 45–72.
Suki, N., and Suki, N. (2007). Online buying innovativeness: Effects of perceived value, perceived risk and perceived enjoyment. *International Journal of Business and Society*, 8(2), 81–93.
Swaminathan, F. (2012). The Uncommon Sense of Advertising–Understanding Contemporary Advertising Appeals in Press of Top Advertisers in India. *Proceedings of the LCBR European Marketing Conference.*
Trandis, H. C. (1995). *Individualism and collectivism*. Boulder, CO: Westview Press.
Triandis, H. C., and Gelfland, M. J. (1998). Converging measurement of horizontal and vertical individualism and collectivism. *Journal of Personality and Social Psychology*, 74, 118–128.
Trompenaars, F., and Hampden-Turner, C. (1998). *Riding the waves of cultural diversity in global business*. London: Nicholas Brealey Publishing.
Tsang, N. K., and Ap, J. (2007). Tourists' perceptions of relational quality service attributes: a cross-cultural study. *Journal of Travel Research*, 45, 355–363.
Weiermair, K. (2000), Tourists' perceptions towards and satisfaction with service quality in the cross-cultural service encounter: Implications for hospitality and tourism management. *Managing Service Quality*, 10(6), 397–409.

Index

Perishability 4, 8, 9, 10, 20, 175, 302